Curr

HOW TO TEACH READING

HOW TO TEACH READING

WAYNE OTTO The University of Wisconsin—Madison
ROBERT RUDE Rhode Island College
DIXIE LEE SPIEGEL The University of North Carolina—Chapel Hill

ADDISON-WESLEY PUBLISHING COMPANY

Reading, Massachusetts • Menlo Park, California
London • Amsterdam • Don Mills, Ontario • Sydney

This book is in the
Addison-Wesley Series in Education

Photograph credits

page 103: Owen Franken/Stock, Boston
page 145: Frank Siteman/Stock, Boston
page 189: Mervin Davis
page 257: Zane B. Williams
All other photographs by Marshall Henrichs.

Library of Congress Cataloging in Publication Data

Otto, Wayne.
   How to teach reading.

   (Addision-Wesley series in education)
   Includes bibliographies and index.
     1. Reading. I. Rude, Robert, 1942-   joint author.
II. Spiegel, Dixie Lee, 1942-   joint author.
III. Title.
LB1050.083   372.4'1   78-67949
ISBN 0-201-05518-X

ISBN 0-201-05518-X
ABCDEFGHIJ-HA-79

Preface

The best teachers of reading have at least one thing in common. They *think* about reading.

That isn't to say that the best teachers all have the same thoughts, however. Many of the best teachers probably have no particular knowledge or preferences regarding theories of the reading process or the pedagogy of reading. And they most certainly do not agree on the specific methods, materials, and procedures for teaching reading. What sets them apart is their inclination to think about their role in teaching children to read and, in so doing, to develop a personal approach to teaching reading that combines what they know about the reading process, about themselves as teachers, about the teaching of reading, and about the children they teach.

Our main purpose in *How to Teach Reading* is to help both the prospective and the practicing teacher of reading think about reading as a basis for developing a personal approach to teaching. The book is organized to provide perspective for viewing the teaching of reading, substance for coming to grips with the content of reading instruction, and alternative approaches for dealing with the realities of day-to-day teaching. Each of the three main themes of *How to Teach Reading* is developed in two or more chapters.

The first theme, a *framework* for viewing the teaching of reading, is developed in Chapters 2 and 3. The second theme, a *foundation* for teaching reading, is developed in Chapters 4 through 8. The chapters deal, respectively, with the management of instruction, the concept of readiness, and the content of instruction in decoding, comprehension, and study skills. *Specific approaches* to teaching reading, the third theme, are described in Chapters 9, 10, and 11. The chapters deal with procedures for using basal readers effectively, the language-experience approach, and an approach to individualizing the instruction of reading.

Two additional topics are discussed in Chapters 12, "Evaluating for a Purpose," and Chapter 13, "Organizing and Managing Instruction." Chapter 12 is designed to help the teacher think through what the teaching of reading is all about in order to assess the impact of the teaching. And the purpose of Chapter 13 is to help the teacher bring together information from all of the preceding chapters in organizing a classroom for teaching reading.

How to Teach Reading is a basic elementary reading-methods text. We have included the things one needs to know in order to teach reading. We have also included an invitation to become actively involved in thinking about the teaching of reading and in developing a personal approach. Although the information is intended primarily for teachers in training, it should also be useful to teachers in the field.

January 1979

W.O.
R.R.
D.L.S.

Contents

Combine principles derived from psycholinguistic study with the attention to specifics and to systematic development derived from skill-development routines, temper them with an empathic concern for natural learning, and the sum will be much more than its parts.

Part I
Reading:
More than
Its Parts

Chapter 1
Introduction

Once upon a time, in a place not far from where you are right now, there lived a beautiful but befuddled young teacher. She had always wanted to be a teacher, so being a teacher made her happy. Yet she was troubled. She worried and wondered about teaching reading.

She was befuddled.

Then one day she decided she could bear it no more. She would find the TRUTH about reading. She would go to a far-off land to see the guru who KNEW! So she sold her MG-Midget and set out to see the guru.

The journey was long and difficult. The route was unmarked, as few had ever been there before. She was beset by false prophets, who said that *they* knew the truth. But she was not convinced. Her step was strong and her direction was true. And finally she came face to face with the guru.

"Wise one," she said, "I must know the TRUTH about reading. Tell me, and I will give my life to telling others."

Meek and humble man that he was, the guru was taken aback. Others had come and others had queried. Yet none had asked a question so profound! The truth he knew, for he had spent a lifetime reading. But how could he say all that he had learned? He paused, he puzzled, and then he spoke.

"Reading," he said, "*IS* a complex process."

The guru returned to his meditation.

And the beautiful young teacher, now reassured and no longer befuddled, happily returned to teaching reading.

Moral: Once you acknowledge that reading is a complex process, you may be able to concentrate on teaching it as well as you can.

The guru was right: Reading *is* a complex process! But there is no need to be befuddled. We can acknowledge, even appreciate, the complexity of the process without being overwhelmed by it. What is needed is perspective, common sense, and confidence that reading can be *taught*, even though the reading process is not fully understood by anyone.

This book is designed to help you develop all three: perspective, common sense, and confidence. A sentence from Chapter 2 sums up the approach: *Combine principles derived from psycholinguistic study with the attention to specifics and to systematic development derived from skill-development routines, temper them with an empathic concern for natural learning, and the sum will be much more than its parts.* Our purpose is to help you gain perspective for viewing the teaching of reading, to help you develop an approach to teaching reading that appeals to your own common sense, and to show you how—in spite of all its complexity—reading can be taught effectively and with confidence. All of our suggestions are guided by some basic beliefs we have about how reading ought to be taught.

We believe that the effective *teaching* of reading amounts to teaching the essential subskills of reading. The reading process is so complex that to try to tackle it all at one time—for *teaching* purposes—is almost certain to lead only to frustration and confusion. This is why *we* talk about skills, objectives, and skills-management systems. The complex process of reading can be taught most effectively when it is approached in a systematic, orderly way.

But we also believe that reading—what goes on when a child interacts with a book—is much more than a sum of the parts we identify for *teaching* reading. Good teachers, then, must not only teach skills, but also see to it that these skills are put properly back together again.

One of the present authors wrote about the apparent paradox. The focus of the passage that follows is on reading comprehension, but the passage reflects Otto's (1977, pp. 214–215) attempt to deal with the problem:

> I would like to acknowledge an apparent problem that turns out to be a non-problem if we view it in perspective. . . . How do we strike a balance between an *approach* that focuses on the subskills of comprehension and a process that clearly requires the simultaneous application of a vast array of skills? The question can be a difficult one, because it tends to push us toward taking either a holistic or a subskills position. The answer, in my opinion, is that we must acknowledge the need to concern ourselves not only with the teaching of subskills but also with the development of the process. We really do not need to make a choice between conflicting realities, because a conflict exists only if we make one.
>
> I see no conflict in directing the development of children's comprehension through questions and activities while at the same time teaching comprehension by focusing on the mastery of specific subskills. To me, the approaches are a perfect complement. On the one hand we stimulate thinking and stress application; on the other hand, we stress the sharpening of specifics in order to enhance overall performance. What we need most is to develop our procedures so as to be assured that the activities for sharpening skills and opportunities for applying them are always in concert.*

To put it another way, we believe that *reading* is a holistic process—more than a mere aggregation of parts—but we also believe that reading can most successfully be *taught*—and, more important, *learned*—by focusing on subskills. The approach we advocate is presented in detail in Chapter 2, and the rest of the book is our elaboration of that approach.

The book has four main themes, each developed in two or more chapters:

HOW TO USE THE BOOK

1. A framework for teaching reading (Chapters 2–4);
2. Helping children develop reading strategies: what children need to know (Chapters 5–8);
3. Helping children develop reading strategies: what teachers need to know (Chapters 9–11);
4. The wholeschool reading program: organizing and evaluating (Chapters 12–13).

*Wayne Otto, "Design for Developing Comprehension Skills," in John T. Guthrie, ed., *Cognition, Curriculum and Comprehension*, Newark, Delaware: International Reading Association, 1977, pp. 193–232.

Each theme is interwoven with the discussion throughout the book. That is, there is no abrupt shifting of focus as one moves from chapter to chapter, from theme to theme. The teaching of reading must, ultimately, be perceived as a unitary process by the learner. The main task of the successful teacher of reading is to strike the balances that make it possible for this to be so. The overlap is there in the book to help you strike the balances, but the focus of each chapter is there to give assurance that the substance is explicitly and adequately covered. Chapter 4, for example, deals explicitly with skills-management systems, but applications of the ideas presented are suggested throughout the book.

You will continue to learn more about reading as long as you continue to read. And you will learn more about *teaching* reading from each child you teach. Our intent in *How to Teach Reading* is to give you what you need in order to get started.

Each chapter has the following elements:

- *Objectives.* Each chapter begins with a list of specific objectives. You can use them to get an overview of the content before you read the chapter. Then, because the objectives focus on the important facts and concepts covered, the objectives can guide your attention as you read the chapter.

- *Review questions.* The review questions given at the end of each chapter are closely tied to the chapter objectives. You can use the questions to check whether you got the facts and concepts identified in the objectives. Responding to the review questions will also encourage you to tie together all of the facts and concepts in the chapter and to look for applications that are consistent with your own style.

- *Overview.* A brief authors' overview of the chapters follows the chapter objectives. In each instance the overview supplements the specific objectives by previewing the content of the chapter. In many instances the overview describes the particular orientation of the chapter or underscores important points to be made.

- *Application.* Within each chapter there are sections that call for application of the facts and concepts presented. In the chapter on objectives, for example, we ask you, first, to identify the several kinds of objectives that are discussed, and then to write some objectives of your own. In the chapter on comprehension we suggest activities for teaching the specifics of comprehending in line with the discussion of the nature of reading comprehension. In the first instance we ask you to make the application; in the second we suggest a number of applications for you. In either case we invite you to apply what is presented.

- *Summary.* The exposition of each chapter ends with a summary. Usually this is an explicit section headed "Summary," but in some instances the summary is a final section that pulls together suggestions for applying the ideas in the chapter. In either case there is a summary of the facts and concepts presented in the chapter.

- *References.* Finally, all of the references cited in the chapter are listed. In many instances when we cite a reference, we give only a very brief glimpse of what is included in the source. You will find that by tracking down and studying complete references, you will be able to pursue interests and to develop better understandings of points that are important to you.

Here is a brief overview of each of the chapters as it contributes to the four main themes of the book.

Taken together, Chapters 2, 3, and 4 (Part II) give the basis—the framework—for the approach to teaching reading that we develop in this book. Our position throughout the book is that to be an effective teacher, one must be able to focus instruction. That is, the teacher who *first* decides what the purpose of any given instructional effort is and *then* pursues that purpose is more likely to succeed than one who merely does what the teacher's manual suggests.

"Thinking About Reading," Chapter 2, amounts to examining different models and conceptions of reading and finally arriving at one's own notion of what reading—or, more explicitly, the *teaching* of reading—is all about. Chapter 2 presents a range of theories and models of reading, then compares two different conceptions of the teaching of reading, and finally suggests a commonsense approach. The chapter gives you a start toward building a personal framework for teaching reading. Chapter 3, "Focusing Instruction: Objectives," deals with the nature and function of instructional objectives. It provides you with vehicles for pinning down and making specific your conception of the reading process and your personal approach to teaching reading.

Chapter 4, "Getting Ready to Teach," deals mainly with the very practical matter of finding ways to focus instruction—to determine what students do and do not know about reading and to help them get what they need by way of instruction. Basal-reader series generally do a good job of covering the entire range of skills and abilities children need to read effectively. But they are inefficient, because the inclination is to teach *everything* to *everyone* whether they need it or not. Skills-management systems make it possible to focus on what individual learners really need. Skills-management systems are what Chapter 4 is mainly about. Positive and negative aspects of skills-management systems are discussed, and a number of alternative systems are presented.

People who *teach* reading need to know certain things in order to be able to teach effectively. They need to know how to teach. But they must also think carefully about *what* to teach—what children need to know in order to read successfully. The chapters in Part III (Chapters 5, 6, 7, and 8) deal mainly with the substance of reading—what children need to know. Part IV deals mainly with the kinds of things teachers need to know in order to *teach* reading.

The title of Chapter 4, "Getting Ready to Teach," is self-explanatory; Chapter 5, "The Nature of Readiness," deals with the matter of being assured that children are *ready* to respond to any given sequence of teaching. A major

WHAT THE CHAPTERS ARE ABOUT A Framework for Teaching Reading

Helping Children Develop Reading Strategies: What Children Need to Know

point made in the chapter is that "readiness" depends very much on the nature of the instruction that is proposed. That is, whether a child is ready for instruction—be it beginning reading instruction or more advanced developmental teaching—is heavily dependent on the type and form of instruction to be offered.

Chapters 6 ("The First Step: Decoding"), 7 ("Understanding What You Decode: Comprehension"), and 8 ("Learning How to Learn: Study Skills") zero in on the actual *content* of teaching reading. In each chapter we give you an orientation to approaching an important aspect of the overall act of reading—decoding, comprehension, study skills—and then we make specific suggestions as to how to get on with the teaching. Taken together these three chapters deal with the essential substance of teaching reading. The chapters that follow have more to do with *how* to get the job done.

Helping Children Develop Reading Strategies: What Teachers Need to Know

Many "different" approaches to teaching reading have been described, and many different terms have been used to describe them. But we do not attempt to give you a survey of the full range. Given the purpose of this book, such a survey would take us far away from the important considerations of how to teach reading. Instead, we characterize what we believe are the three most commonly used and, indeed, the most useful approaches to teaching reading. Chapters 9, "Making the Most of the Basal Reader," 10, "Expanding Horizons: The Language-Experience Approach," and 11, "Individualized Instruction" (Part IV) present three alternatives that you can match to your beliefs, inclinations, and personal style.

The Wholeschool Reading Program: Organizing and Evaluating

The topics of the two final chapters (Part V)—*evaluation* and *managing instruction*—are important considerations for not only individual teachers, but also the success of the entire school's reading program.

The main point of Chapter 12, "Evaluating for a Purpose," is that one's operational definition of reading is best demonstrated by what one looks for as the end result of reading instruction. Fancy definitions and high-sounding goals are nice to have, but only the things that teachers are willing to be accountable for are likely to get serious attention. The chapter includes a discussion of the *purpose* for evaluation, the *content* of evaluation, and *approaches* to evaluation. The goal of the chapter is to help you think through exactly what the teaching of reading is all about so that you can assess how you are doing and what the outcomes are.

Finally, Chapter 13, "Organizing and Managing Instruction," is designed to help you organize your classroom for teaching reading. Seven alternative plans for organizing reading groups are compared and contrasted, guidelines for making effective use of various instructional materials are suggested, and the principles of reinforcement and transfer are discussed. The chapter ought to help you pull together the information from the chapters that precede it and help you to plan your own, personal approach to teaching reading.

Perspective, common sense, and confidence. Keep each of those in mind as you study the book, and you will be on your way to understanding how to teach reading.

Part II
A Framework
for Teaching
Reading

Before you can begin teaching reading to a group of children, you have to know what each student still needs to learn about reading. Before you can identify your students' individual reading needs, you have to be able to think about what it is you want *any* reader to be able to do. And before you can identify tasks an accomplished reader should be able to do, you have to do some serious thinking about the nature of reading and the reading process itself.

Part II (Chapters 2–4) introduces three main themes of this book. First, reading is a very complex process. Second, despite the complexity of this process, instructional objectives can help teachers focus reading instruction in such a way that it becomes less awesome and more manageable. Third, teachers must have a systematic way of identifying the needs of their students in order to focus instruction for individual students. Altogether, these three themes form a framework for teaching reading that can be summarized as follows: At present, we don't know all about reading that we want to, but we do know enough to be able to design effective instruction for students as individuals. Objective-based instruction can help students develop the skills needed to become mature, fluent readers.

Chapter 2
Thinking About
Reading

OBJECTIVES FOR THE CHAPTER

After reading this chapter, you will be able to:

1. Discuss the implications of the concept of cognitive confusion for teaching—and thinking about—reading.
2. List some important benefits teachers can derive by becoming knowledgeable about theoretical conceptions of reading.
3. Contrast *macro* versus *micro*, *developmental* versus *descriptive*, and *molecular* versus *holistic* approaches to theory building.
4. Identify the strengths and limitations of approaching the teaching of reading as a skill-development process.
5. Identify the strengths and limitations of approaching the teaching of reading as a psycholinguistic process.
6. Choose or formulate a conception of the reading process and discuss the implications for reading instruction.

People "think about" reading from different perspectives and for different reasons. Children probably do some of their most productive thinking about reading as they learn the meanings of the special words that adults use to talk about reading. Educational psychologists, linguists, research workers, and reading specialists think about reading as they attempt to direct a line of research or explain certain behaviors or devise an instructional approach. Teachers need to think about reading in order to establish a basis for helping their pupils learn to read efficiently and effectively. Yet many teachers probably are influenced more by what they were told about how to teach reading than by their personal views of the reading process.

The specific objectives for this chapter all have to do with thinking about reading. The discussion moves from a consideration of a child's view of reading to theorists' views of the reading process. But the focus throughout is on the *teacher* and on the *teaching* of reading. The purpose is to help you to start thinking about reading so that ultimately you will be able to develop a personal approach to teaching reading.

A CHILD'S VIEW OF READING

Children confronted with the task of learning to read are, according to Downing (1975), more often than not in a state of cognitive confusion. The nature of the confusion is nicely demonstrated in a passage from Downing's paper:

> I'm going to sove some mivvirs. See these mivvirs. Their names are ooth and op. They say "hgugh!" Who knows a yasp with the tauf "hgugh" in it?
>
> What is this nonsense? It is the same kind of nonsense that young beginners hear when they are learning to read. They do not know the technical jargon teachers use to describe speech and writing. "Sove" is as good a nonsense word to them as "write." So also is "mivvirs" for "letters," "ooth" for "sea," "op" for "aitch," "yasp" for "word," "tauf" for "sound," and "hgugh" is the final sound of the Scottish "lock." The child must puzzle out the meanings of these tech-

In learning to read, a child must overcome cognitive confusion.

nical terms. He does so by a series of hunches until he arrives at more or less the same concepts as his teacher has of these linguistic units.*

All children pass through this initial stage of cognitive confusion as they learn to read. In fact, there is considerable evidence that all skill development—whether learning to play tennis, fly an airplane, send Morse code, or read—is characterized by an initial phase of cognitive confusion (Fitts and Posner, 1967). This concept of cognitive confusion is an important one for teachers, for the fact is that children's thinking about reading is prescribed by their general linguistic concepts and their specific vocabulary development.

*John Downing, "Thinking About Reading." Paper presented at the twentieth annual meeting of the International Reading Association, New York City, May 1975.

To get beyond the initial cognitive phase, the child must first learn the vocabulary for talking and thinking about the skill and then discover and attend to the important elements of the skill. In Downing's terms, the child must acquire the *reading instruction register*—the special language used to talk about reading and its relation to speech. Behind the register lie the concepts of language used in thinking about reading and in learning how to read.

School beginners have neither the linguistic concepts nor the register (Reid, 1966; Downing, 1970; Meltzer and Herse, 1969). Furthermore, the time available for acquiring the register is usually limited to the earliest stage of instruction—typically, first grade. Downing argues that the concepts and the register can best be learned through the language-experience approach. Thus when a child dictates a message, she or he sees speech converted into writing and is in a position to discover linguistic concepts. This discovery process through the language-experience approach is dealt with in Chapter 10. The development of a reading instruction register can be one of many positive outcomes associated with the language-experience approach.

A teacher needs to think about reading in order to come to grips with the important aspects of the reading process and to develop a personal style for teaching reading. But to become an empathic teacher—one who can identify with the thoughts, feelings, and attitudes of others—a teacher must also consider how children think about reading. One of your main tasks as a reading teacher, then, is to come to an understanding of each pupil's view of the reading process. Without such an understanding, you can never be assured that so far as your pupils are concerned, you are doing anything but soving mivvers and yasps.

THEORISTS' VIEWS OF READING

As a group, the theorists' views of the reading process may be somewhat like the six blind men's views of the elephant in John Godfrey Saxe's poem "The Blind Men and the Elephant":

> It was six men of Hindustan
> to learning much inclined,
> who went to see the elephant,
> (though all of them were blind);
> that each by observation
> might satisfy his mind.

The first man touched the elephant's side and concluded that elephants are very much like walls. The others touched tusk, trunk, knee, ear, and tail, respectively, and concluded that elephants are like spears, snakes, trees, fans, and ropes, respectively.

> And so these men of Hindustan
> disputed loud and long,
> each of his own opinion
> exceeding stiff and strong,
> though each was partly in the right,
> and all were in the wrong!

And so do theorists approach the reading process with their own views and inclinations, only to come away with rather different impressions of what it is really like.

But don't be disappointed by the analogy. An objective observer who was willing to consider each blind man's description probably would have been able to put together a reasonable facsimile of an elephant. If you become an objective observer of theorists' views of the reading process, you can come away with a reasonable understanding of the reading process and, more important, how to go about teaching it.

A good theory offers the capacity for "summarizing the past, elucidating the present, and predicting the future" (Samuels, 1977). In other words, theoretical models and conceptions of reading can greatly enrich your capacity for thinking about reading. As Williams (1974, p. 553) put it:

> Teachers are practitioners, and any good practitioner seeks to develop solid foundation in theory. A theory will not, of course, provide simple, straightforward answers to a teacher's questions about how to handle a particular child in a particular instructional situation or in a particular management crisis. But the knowledgeable teacher can draw upon what theory and research tell him, and he can use his general understanding to help provide a basis for developing and evaluating instructional programs in general and for making rapid and effective decisions as to how to handle specific, individual problems as they arise.*

A theoretical base gives practitioners guidelines for making decisions on a day-to-day basis. Without such a base, such decisions are likely to be opportunistic at best or, at worst, blatantly inconsistent and confusing. According to Smith (1971, p. vii):

> The current instructional methods are probably not much inferior to the methods we shall develop as we learn more about learning to read. So many instructional methods have been tried, and so many succeed (in some instances at least), that further permutations in the game of instructional roulette are unlikely to produce any great gain, either by chance or design. What will make a difference is an understanding of the reading process.†

Methods for teaching reading, instructional materials, and how-to-do-it books offer guidelines that can be useful, but such guidelines do not provide the specificity and reality of individual applications. Theory and theory development offer a basis for beginning to understand the reading process, which in turn offers a basis for beginning to deal with individual problems as they arise.

In more specific terms, there are at least five good reasons why teachers ought to be active participants in the scholarship and theory development related to reading. The reasons overlap to some extent.

*Joanna P. Williams, "New Theories of Reading: What Do They Tell Us?" *Teachers College Record* 75 (1974): 553. Reprinted by permission of *Teachers College Record*.

†From *Understanding Reading: A Psycholinguistic Analysis of Reading and Learning to Read* by Frank Smith. Copyright © 1971 by Holt, Rinehart and Winston. Reprinted by permission of Holt, Rinehart and Winston.

1. Theory development brings order and system to existing knowledge. A good theory summarizes many specific facts with a few generalizations. The benefit is that then one can work with manageable principles rather than a confusing array of specific findings.

2. Theory brings order and system to pedagogy (teaching). A good theory can help practitioners to understand, or at least to explain, behaviors, processes, and current happenings in the classroom. Teaching may remain more nearly an art than a science, but a theory that offers system and order can ensure reasonable stability in instructional decision making. This is Williams's point in the quotation on p. 15.

3. Theory offers a basis for consistent teaching practices. Despite the recent strides in scholarship and theory development related to reading, there is probably less agreement than ever about how the reading act occurs and how it is learned. The teacher who chooses a reasonably comprehensive theory and then stays with it can spare a pupil the confusion caused by inconsistent and often conflicting practices. Of course, one theory may be more useful than another when it comes to dealing with a given child, so we do not advocate total allegiance to any one theory. The point is simply that consistency can be ensured for a given child if the procedures and materials used in teaching that child to read are consistent with a given theory. We shall return to this point later in the chapter.

4. Theory offers a forward look. Perhaps the most exciting thing about a good theory is that it uses existing knowledge to make predictions about the future. Theory is not static. It is a basis for moving forward as new hypotheses are generated and new knowledge is gained.

5. Teachers are in a good position to become partners with scholars and research specialists in developing theory. Whereas the first four points stressed what teachers can get from theory, this one focuses on the contribution teachers can make to theory. As practitioners, teachers are in a unique position to ensure a tough-minded, reality-oriented approach to theory building. But in order to play the game, teachers must first learn the rules. That can be done by working toward an understanding of existing theories.

Kinds of Theories   Aside from the specifics of any given theory, the novice who begins to study theoretical conceptions of reading is likely to be overwhelmed—if not by the terminology, then most certainly by the apparent shortcomings, overlaps, and inconsistencies among theories. Theories, like almost everything else, are shaped by the perceptions, biases, understandings, and inclinations of the people who build them. A few definitions can help you understand the basic terminology.

Writers talk about *theories, models,* and even *theoretical models.* Sometimes the terms are used almost interchangeably; at other times they seem to mean different things. Samuels (1977) observes that as the terms are most commonly used, *theory* often means a set of broad generalizations that can serve as bases for formulating hypotheses, whereas *model* generally refers to a more precise and probably less comprehensive statement that leads more readily to hypothesis testing. Nevertheless, usage tends to blur any difference between the terms, and they typically are cross-referenced in the index of a book. You can safely assume that for most purposes, the terms have approximately the same meaning.

The main fact to keep in mind is that theories are built for different purposes, so they deal with different segments and different aspects of the reading process. Don't expect theories to be interchangeable in terms of their comprehensiveness or basic assumptions.

Theories are of several types. For example, there are *macrotheories* and *microtheories*. A macrotheory attempts to deal with the entire reading act in all of its complexity.* A microtheory, on the other hand, is designed to describe one small segment of the reading act, such as what goes on when a child attends to visual letter clues while reading.

There are also *developmental* theories and *descriptive* theories. A developmental theory is an attempt to explain the reading act in terms of how the process of reading is learned; a descriptive theory is an attempt to describe the actions of a mature reader engaged in reading. This distinction is an important one, because what one does as a mature reader is very different from what one does as a beginning and as a developing reader. For example, a mature reader has great familiarity with letter forms and sequences, much experience with context cues, and a wealth of background experiences and is therefore able to respond to minimal cues, such as the overall shape or the initial consonant, in decoding the words in a passage. But the beginning reader must attend to virtually every letter in order to decode each word in a passage. A developmental theory is most useful in the developmental teaching of reading because it deals with the steps or stages involved in becoming a mature reader.†

Finally, there are *molecular* and *holistic* approaches to theory building. A molecular approach might involve attempts to break the reading act into explicit behaviors (specific *skills,* in the terminology of reading teachers) and to show how these behaviors are combined in successful reading. A holistic approach, by contrast, would put much less emphasis on explicit behaviors and much more on the complex interrelationships among the component parts of the reading act. In fact, a holistic theorist would tend to view breaking the reading act into components as unnatural and would instead stress the unitary nature of language.‡

*The substrata-factor theory of reading described by Holmes (1953; Holmes and Singer, 1961) is an example of a full-blown macrotheory. Another theory that tends toward the macrotheory end of the scale is the one described by LaBerge and Samuels (1974).

†"The Nature of the Reading Process" by John Carroll (1970) and "Reading: A Psycholinguistic Guessing Game" by Kenneth Goodman (1967; also 1976) are good examples of a developmental approach to theory, although both do contain descriptive elements too. The theories described by Holmes (1953) and by LaBerge and Samuels (1974) are examples of descriptive theories.

‡Carroll's approach tends to be molecular; Goodman's (1967; 1976) tends to be holistic. In other chapters of this book the *Wisconsin Design for Reading Skill Development* and the language-experience approach to teaching reading are discussed. The implicit theory behind the *Design* is molecular; specific skills of reading are identified, tested, and developed. The theory base for the language-experience approach is holistic; the relationship among reading, writing, speaking, and listening form the theoretical core.

Again, keep in mind that different people approach reading from different perspectives and for different purposes. So we have theories that are macro or micro, developmental or descriptive, molecular or holistic—to mention only some of the possible classifications. As a teacher, you will be looking for the theories that have the clearest implications for practice in your classroom with your students.

Five Disciplines In order to provide some direction for your own explorations, we shall offer only a summary of research and theory drawn from five disciplines.* The summary that follows is based on Kling's (1971) discussion of reading as an interdisciplinary matrix. He suggests that five major disciplines—psychology, psycholinguistics, information processing, sociolinguistics, and biobehavioral sciences—are either involved or capable of becoming involved in producing research and theory related to reading. These five categories can give you a framework for taking an objective look at the various types of theories.

Psychology This discipline has a longer tradition of scholarship than do the other four, and considerable work has been done. Kling suggests that five areas have emerged within psychology as it relates to reading.

PERCEPTUAL/CONCEPTUAL The work in this area centers on the visual-perception theories from psychology, so the focus tends to be on the initial acts of decoding (e.g., how children distinguish between the letters *d* and *b*†). Thus the resultant theories are more useful in explaining early reading behaviors than in explaining the more mature reading processes, like comprehension.

BEHAVIORISTIC In the tradition of Pavlov (classical conditioning) and Skinner (operant conditioning), work in this area attempts to explain language acquisition and the reading process in terms of *stimulus* and *response*. At the simplest level, then, the act of reading amounts to associating a printed word (stimulus) with a spoken word (response). There is a great deal of appeal in the straightforward, uncluttered look of a stimulus-response theory,‡ but unfortunately such theories are inadequate when it comes to explaining the higher-order reading behaviors such as inferring meaning or making critical judgments.

NATIVISTIC The basic premise in this area is that language is biologically based and is the manifestation of cognitive roots that are unique to the human species.§ Nativists look for features that are common to all known languages—*language universals*—to support their notion that language in humans develops "naturally"

*Excellent reviews of specific theories of reading have been prepared by Singer (1969), Davis (1971), Williams (1973), and Singer and Ruddell (1976). All of them are worth careful study.

†An article by Gibson (1970) catches the flavor of some of the work in the area.

‡Staats and Staats (1962) and Carroll (1970) have taken a behavioristic approach to explain certain reading behaviors.

§McNeill (1966; 1970) is the most widely cited spokesperson for the nativist position. See Lenneberg (1967) if you decide to dig in.

along with biological maturation. The nativist position with regard to reading is that basically a child is equipped with every skill needed to learn to read; she or he must only discover the particular rules that apply.

Work in the cognitive tradition* relates the reading process to the development of learning and thinking processes of the child. Bloom (1971) and Samuels (1971) have written papers describing the impact of cognitive psychology in reading education. Those papers show how the traditional behavioristic approaches are undergoing modification in line with the cognitive approach (Williams, 1971), which deals more with the child's ability to *interact* with the components and content of reading than with the child's automatic reaction to stimuli.

COGNITIVE

The psychometric approach involves the use of the techniques of measurement and testing to identify specific skills that make up the reading act.† To oversimplify, the approach involves selecting several discrete reading skills, developing items to test each skill, combining those items into a single composite test, administering the test to a group of readers, and then attempting to discover the distinct skill factors that are present in readers' responses to the test items.

PSYCHOMETRIC

The major developments in psycholinguistics have come during the past 25 years.‡ Contributions to the understanding of the reading process center in three areas—graphophonology, syntax, and semantics. Graphophonic information helps to clarify the links between written (symbols) and spoken (sounds) language. This is particularly useful because one of the first tasks of most beginning readers is to transform written symbols (printed words) into spoken sounds (words already in the new reader's spoken vocabulary). Syntactic information helps to clarify the rules for constructing grammatical sentences in the language and, for reading, for extracting information from those grammatical structures. Semantic information clarifies the strategies whereby mature readers derive meaning.

Psycholinguistics

Still at a relatively early stage of development, the information-processing area promises more than it has yet delivered.§ The area draws on concepts from cybernetics, systems analysis, and general communication theory. Athey (1971, pp. 6–47) characterizes the area as follows: "Basically, information processing is the quantification of information into 'bits.' Each bit of information reduces the state of uncertainty of the subject or program."

Information Processing

*Piaget, 1970; Bruner, Goodnow, and Austin, 1966; Gagné, 1966.
†The approach is described by Davis (1971) and by Bormuth (1970).
‡Major spokesmen for this tradition are N. Chomsky and Halle (1968), Goodman (1968, 1969), and Ruddell (1970).
§Papers by Hansen (1971) and by Venezky and Calfee (1970) provide some insights into the area at an early stage of development. LaBerge and Samuels (1974) have described a model of information processing in reading whereby visual information is transformed until it is comprehended.

Sociolinguistics Also at a very early stage of development is sociolinguistics, an area too often ignored by theory builders. Sociolinguistics can help to identify important individual differences among children. "These include," according to Kling (1971, pp. 2–3), "differences in dialect, differences among ethnic groups in information-processing skills, differences in cognitive style, and differences arising from affective factors." As this area is developed, there should be significant contributions to a better understanding of the reading process and, particularly, of the process of *teaching* reading to learners who are unique individuals.* Too many of the existing theories treat the process of reading as if it were stable and unchanging for all who experience it.

Biobehavioral Sciences Study of the neurological and physiological bases of psychological behavior promises, ultimately, to help increase insight into certain aspects of the reading process. Work in the area has already shed light on how people learn and remember.† Future work ought to either support or refute the extreme behavioristic or nativistic positions taken by some theorists.

In Sum According to Samuels (1977, p. 15): "There are few intellectual devices so useful as a good theory which permits us to understand events and processes across time boundaries." And Kling (1971, pp. 2–4) has said: "There seems to be a tendency toward reconciling the differences between the models proposed to explain the nature of reading . . . differences will tend to disappear as changes occur in terminology and level of knowledge in the underlying disciplines, in the type of measurement and analysis employed, and in the methodology used." But however one puts it, the fact is that a thoughtful excursion into theory will probably result in a better understanding of the reading process.

APPLICATION: YOUR OWN VIEW OF READING The more you think about reading—the more you try to develop an empathic understanding of what a child experiences when he or she tackles the reading task—the better you will become at dealing with problems and making proper decisions as you teach. Developing a personal view of reading—particularly of the *teaching* of reading—is a lifelong process. Your view will change as you gain new experiences, as new research results and more definitive theories become available, and even as you encounter an ever-changing array of children who come to the reading task with different backgrounds, attitudes, and motives.

Nevertheless, in order to think through the details of how you intend to approach the task of teaching reading, you need to make some tentative decisions about the reading process and how it should be taught. To help you with that, we offer three ways of viewing the teaching of reading. Two of them— teaching reading as a *skill-development process* and teaching reading as a *psycholinguistic process*—are often presented as alternatives in discussions in the

*Entwisle (1971, 1977) has pointed out implications of sociolinguistics for reading theory and the teaching of reading.
†The work of Geyer (1971), Pribraum (1969), and Lorenz (1969) is in the biobehavioral tradition.

literature and in methods courses on the teaching of reading. That is, the approaches are often presented as if they were completely incompatible, and teachers are urged to choose one and to reject the other. We see strengths and limitations—as well as similarities—in both approaches, and we suggest that certain aspects of each approach be combined in a third view: teaching reading as a *commonsense process*. You may or may not agree with that position. More likely, you may agree with some but not all of the points. Use the discussion to clarify and organize your own personal beliefs and inclinations about teaching reading. You can—and should—modify later as you read more and have new experiences. *But start now.*

Teaching Reading as a Skill-Development Process

The inclination to view the teaching of reading as a skill-development process is firmly rooted in the behaviorist tradition of psychology. In its purest form, skill development is a matter of associating *stimulus* and *response,* e.g., *printed word* and *spoken word* or, ultimately, *printed word* and *meaning of the word.* There is a good deal of appeal in such a straightforward model (see Carroll, 1970), and you will recognize it as the basis for many exercises and activities that appear in the materials for teaching reading. Of course, that simple model breaks down very quickly when it comes to dealing with more complex aspects of the reading process, such as drawing inferences or dealing with relationships. There have been many attempts to extend and augment the model, but our purpose here is not to describe or judge those attempts. The point is that teaching reading as a skill-development process stems from the behaviorist tradition, and there are acknowledged limitations in that approach.

The teaching of reading as a skill-development process got a great deal of impetus from the theories of Edward L. Thorndike, a prolific and influential psychologist of the first third of the 1900s. Thorndike would probably disavow many of the overzealous applications of his ideas. He was always an advocate of the reader's active participation in the reading process; his classic article "Reading as Reasoning" (1917) makes that clear. Nevertheless, it was Thorndike's work that led to look-and-say reading—exposure of a printed word along with the correct oral response, limitation of vocabulary in basal readers to the most frequently occurring words (based on word-frequency counts originally conducted by Thorndike), round-robin reading (beginning readers sit in a circle and read orally when called on by the teacher), and teaching correct responses to word parts. Taken to its extreme, each of these practices tends to treat children as passive pawns in the learning process. On the other hand, each of these practices involves the development of certain skills, which taken together comprise the act of reading—or, at least, certain aspects of it. Good or bad, the fact is that Thorndike's work set the stage for the development of lists of reading skills designed to guide the teaching/learning process.

The most comprehensive list of skills is probably the one offered by Gray (1960) and subsequently amplified and updated by Robinson (1966). Gray presented his list under four headings:

1. Word perception, which includes pronunciation and meaning;
2. Comprehension, which includes a "clear grasp of what is read";
3. Reaction to and evaluation of ideas the author presents;
4. Assimilation of what is read, through fusion of old ideas and information obtained through reading.

Although Gray freely acknowledges that these aspects, each encompassing a number of specific skills, operate simultaneously and that reading must be considered a "unitary act," the effect of the list is to break the complex process of reading into many component parts, or skills.

Reading experts have put together many other lists of skills, although most of them are simply variations of Gray's classic list. Some get more specific and include many more skills; others cut back on the number of skills by listing only the ones that are judged essential. The one thing that all lists of reading skills have in common is that they represent attempts to break the complex act of reading into its component parts. And, implicitly, once these component parts, or skills, have been identified, they become the focus of reading instruction. Reduced to the simplest terms, reading is taken apart to identify teachable bits, which once learned are then put back together again by the successful reader.

Critics of the skill-development approach say that it doesn't work that way, and we shall return to the criticism presently. Advocates of the skill-development approach are convinced that the most efficient way to *teach* reading is to teach the component skills (see Otto, Chester, McNeil, and Myers, 1974).

Advantages Like almost everything else, the skill-development approach has both positive and negative aspects. The most appealing thing about the skill-development approach is that it breaks a bewilderingly complex task into specific, manageable—and presumably *teachable*—skills. With skills the process of diagnosis is greatly simplified: One need only to find out which skills are and which are not in a learner's repertoire. And then instruction can focus on the as yet undeveloped skill(s) that come next in the sequence. Instruction can be highly individualized because the teacher can keep a continuously updated profile of each pupil's skill development and permit each one to proceed at a pace that is most appropriate.

In more general terms the skills in a well-conceived list are said to be *objective, sequential,* and *generalizable.* These are the main points, or assumptions, in the argument in favor of skills. Skills are *objective* in the sense that they are not tied to any given set of materials and procedures. The teacher is free to use whatever materials and procedures are judged to be most appropriate for a given individual in a given situation. Nor are skills tied to any age or grade level. The time to teach *skill x* is after the prerequisite skills have been attained and before the skills that build on *skill x* are introduced. Skills, then, have an implicit *sequence* that goes beyond age or grade level. The sequence is derived from analysis of the reading task itself, so to follow the sequence is to build logically and always on a firm foundation. And skills are *generalizable* in that they can be applied in all content areas. Thus the learner who develops all of the essential reading skills is able to apply them, and to read successfully, in all content areas.

There are critics, however, who disagree with virtually every positive thing we have said about skills and the skill-development approach to teaching reading. Such criticism generally centers on one of two positions.

First, some critics insist that reading is a highly integrated, unitary act. Therefore, they argue, any attempt to break the reading process into components, or subskills, is an unnatural act that denies the very nature of language itself. Take it apart, they say, and like Humpty Dumpty, all the king's horses and all the king's men will never be able to put it together again. Unfortunately, these critics can offer no more definitive evidence to support their position than the skill-development people can offer to support theirs, so the point remains moot. There is no question, though, that if skills are taught in isolation and without application, they are almost certain to remain forever nothing more than disconnected bits and pieces. Spache and Spache (1969, p. 6) summed it up: "The concept of reading as a skill development process is a very limited interpretation of what is really a very complex process. Overacceptance of this concept is widespread and often leads to stereotyped drill with isolated reading behavior or skills."

The first position amounts to a complete rejection of the very idea of subskills in reading. The second amounts to criticisms of the details of the skill-development approach, where the critics question the validity of specific skills and the sequential arrangement of skills in given lists. The critics question the use of instructional objectives, which are commonly used as backup to give substance to lists of skills. They find fault with the record-keeping and management systems that have been devised to keep track of individuals' skill development. And they question the notion of *mastery* and how mastery is measured in the implementation of skill-development approaches. Taken together, these and other criticisms of the artifacts that go with the teaching of subskills raise serious questions about the skill-development approach. They point up the fact that the approach can bog down and become ineffectual for any of a variety of reasons.

Even the most enthusiastic supporters of teaching subskills will admit that a narrowly conceived or badly implemented skill-development approach may do more harm than good. They will also admit that the subskills that are absolutely essential for success in reading are yet to be identified and ordered in an optimum sequence. Nevertheless, they argue that in order to teach reading in a systematic way, one must first identify and then see to the development of important subskills. And until the definitive, research-based list of reading skills becomes available, they are reasonably comfortable with intuitive lists based on experience and task analysis. They say, in effect, that subskills and the related artifacts are the price one pays for an approach to reading instruction that is orderly, systematic, and reasonably objective; and the price is fair.

Some critics would say that the price is too high because once subskills of reading are identified, the skills, not the overall process, become all important. Others—the critics who insist that language is a unitary process and so is not amenable to subdivision—would say simply that there is no price to be paid because there is no product to be bought.

Teaching Reading as a Psycholinguistic Process

Conceptions of the teaching of reading as a psycholinguistic process are not necessarily at odds with the teaching of reading as a skill-development process. There are, indeed, psycholinguists who stress the development of certain skills as an important part of teaching reading. The difference between the two approaches that we wish to stress is more subtle, more a matter of orientation than of substance. The skill-development approach stresses focus, system, and order in teaching the subskills of reading. The psycholinguistic approach stresses the application of what is known about the nature of language in the teaching of reading.

Understand, too, that up to this point we have been using the term "psycholinguistics" in its broadest sense to refer to the work of language scientists who are "interested in exploring the psychological reality of linguistic descriptions" (Ruddell, 1970, p. 239). You will remember from our discussion of theorists' views that there are at least three distinct traditions within the psycholinguistic disciplines that focus on *graphophonology*, *syntax (structural linguistics)*, and *semantics*. The work in each tradition has a somewhat different focus and consequently somewhat different implications for the teaching of reading are stressed.

Graphophonology is concerned with the analysis of the sounds of spoken and written language. Phonologists are inclined to view the act of reading as a translation of the sounds for which letters stand: first into sounds, then into words, and finally into sentences. Although this may sound like traditional phonics warmed over, phonologists say that their approach is very different because it is based on careful analysis of the phonemic patterns of beginning readers' spoken language and of the content of beginning instruction. To oversimplify, then, phonologists advocate the systematic development of sound-symbol relationships consistent with the language development of beginning readers. The derivation of meaning, at least at the early stage, tends to be subordinate to the translation of written symbols to sound.*

The *syntactic tradition*—the structural linguists' position—is reasonably represented by Smith (1971, Chapter 1), who distinguishes between *learning to read* and *reading fluently*. The distinction acknowledges the beginning reader's preoccupation with *word identification* as contrasted to the more mature reader's commitment to *reading for comprehension*. Smith argues that there are two ways of reading for comprehension: *mediated comprehension*, which

---

*Bloomfield and Barnhart (1961) and Fries (1963) provide good examples of phonologists' positions regarding the teaching of reading.

requires the prior identification of individual words, and *immediate comprehension,* which can be accomplished by going directly from visual features to meaning. Immediate comprehension depends on not only immediate word identification, but also the knowledge the reader has built up during his or her reading experience of the patterns of words and letters. Although the processes by which immediate comprehension is accomplished are not specified—nor, for that matter, are they fully understood—the model clearly emphasizes the derivation of meaning through the process of reading. The phonologists' preoccupation with sound-symbol relationships is put aside, and reading is conceived as a process of getting meaning from written language.

In emphasizing meaning in their models of the reading process, the structural linguists are committed to investigation of the structure of language, the basic grammatical concepts. Their work is designed to clarify the essential aspects of language that contribute to the communication of ideas, such as word order or the position of words in sentences, word functions, word groups that modify or amplify simple expressions, and the signals of intonation, such as pitch, stress, and pause.

The *semantic tradition* deals mainly with readers' use of context clues to derive meaning from printed words. Goodman (1967; reprinted 1976) argues that readers use their knowledge of word meanings and grammatical concepts to reduce the probable alternatives of what follows next in a printed passage. Reading, then, is what Goodman calls a "psycholinguistic guessing game" that involves an interaction between thought and language. "Efficient reading does not result from precise perception and identification of all elements, but from skill in selecting the fewest, the most productive cues necessary to produce guesses which are right the first time. The ability to anticipate that which has not been seen, of course, is vital to reading . . ." (Goodman, 1976, p. 498).

Reading-process models based on the semantic tradition emphasize the derivation of meaning as the most important outcome from the reading process. Despite some disagreement as to whether the distinction is a real one (Athey, 1971), the main difference between the two sets of models appears to be that the semantic models attempt to go beyond the literal meaning of language to the deeper meanings that involve the personal interaction of the reader with the material being read. Athey (1971, pp. 6–46) put it this way: "Extracting meaning from the printed page is the essence of reading, but even the fluent reader sometimes fails to grasp what he is reading if his attention is elsewhere, even though he has decoded all the words. He has perused the material, recognized it as grammatical and meaningful, but in some way has failed to assimilate it into his deep structure."* Whether or not the distinction is valid, the fact is that the semantic models stress the reader's need for experience not only with the language in print, but also in everyday life. By emphasizing the need to consider the interaction of the reader and the reading task, the semantic models represent a significant step in the right direction.

*Irene Athey, "Language Models and Reading," in F. B. Davis, ed., *Literature in Research in Reading with Emphasis on Models,* New Brunswick, N.J.: Graduate School of Education, Rutgers University. Available from IRIS Corporation, P.O. Box 372, East Brunswick, N.J. 08816.

Advantages   Whether the specific focus is on phonological, syntactical, or semantic analysis, the psycholinguistic approach—or, as we have seen, *approaches*—represents significant attempts to apply what is known about language to the teaching of reading. Although many basic facts are yet to be discovered and much integration of existing facts remains to be done, the promise of the psycholinguistic approach is amply demonstrated. Graphophonic analyses have already had considerable impact on the revision and sequential arrangements of traditional phonics skills. Further analyses will continue to clarify the nature of an optimal program for teaching children to transform print into sound.

The main contribution of structural and semantic analyses has been the introduction of the concepts of *surface* and *deep structure*. Smith (1971, p. 29) sums up the difference: "The surface level refers to the physical manifestation of language as it impinges on the ear or eye, and the deep level refers to meaning or semantic interpretation." The details of how the two levels ought to be characterized and how (and if) they are interrelated are still disputed by psycholinguists. But the concern for the effective transformation of message to meaning will, with reasonable application, continue to be manifested in more effective reading instruction.

Lundsteen (1976, p. 63) summarized the advantages very succinctly: "Awareness of reading traps in materials and the illumination received from developmental linguistic study create greater patience and understanding in teachers, who then demand appropriate material, a positive attitude toward seeking meaning, and a tolerance of oral reading error (or miscues) that indicates children's willingness to risk, and to predict while using their language backgrounds."*

Disadvantages   The disadvantages are not so much a matter of substance as of style. That is, there is little inclination to quarrel with the guiding principles that linguistic science offers to reading instruction. But the manner in which these principles are offered is occasionally condescending. The psycholinguists' "discovery," for example, that reading is a part of the language process and is strongly dependent on the reader's spoken vocabulary hardly comes as news to any reasonably thoughtful and/or experienced reading teacher. Reading educators have been talking about that relationship for decades. Yet the relationship continues to be pointed out to reading teachers—usually with minor variations in detail and major additions of technical jargon—as if, somehow, they had managed to remain totally ignorant of the totally obvious.

In the final analysis psycholinguists as a group have been disinclined to enter into a collaborative relationship with the practitioners who are responsible for teaching reading. With such a relationship, the phonologists might be less inclined to devise approaches to reading that amount to nothing more than schemes for decoding words. The structural linguists might acknowledge that

*Sara W. Lundsteen, *Children Learn to Communicate: Language Arts Through Creative Problem-Solving,* © 1976, p. 63. Reprinted by permission of Prentice-Hall, Inc.

although deep meaning tends to reside in groups of words, word-by-word processing usually precedes any grasp of total meaning. The semanticists might acknowledge that before readers can tackle semantic meaning, they must first come to grips with not only surface structure, but also literal meaning. In short, there might be more inclination to deal realistically with the facts and with the implications for *teaching* reading.

Perspective

The major flaw in viewing the teaching of reading as a skill-development process is that the approach tends to become too pat. That is, reading tends to be viewed as a list of skills, and teaching reading tends to be a matter of teaching the skills on the list. The major flaw in viewing the teaching of reading as a psycholinguistic process is, as we see it, at the other end of the scale. Whereas the skill-development approaches tend to be too pat, too structured, the psycholinguistic approaches that have been suggested so far tend to be too loose, too unstructured, or even haphazard. (Some of the elaborate routines for teaching symbol-sound relationships must, of course, be excepted, but those approaches do not address a reasonably broad conception of reading.) Goodman's miscue analysis, for example, tells us virtually nothing about how to get a child to a point where she or he can indulge in the luxury of miscuing. Nor does it tell us much of anything about *what to do* once we find a legitimate error. Likewise, the structural linguists tell us very little about *how to* develop the understanding of word order, word function, and other structures that they say is important in getting to deep structure. And again, at a more popular level, the advocates of a language-experience approach offer very little that would help to systematize the important learning that is implicit in the approach.

Perhaps the perspective can be summarized in two brief—and certainly oversimplified—statements. The psycholinguistic approaches offer principles but very little backup. The skill-development approaches offer backup but very few principles.

Teaching Reading as a Commonsense Process

The controversies among theoretical positions or among stylized approaches to teaching reading are not necessarily the conflicts that are important to classroom teachers. In fact, many of the apparent paradoxes and polarities would appear to be open to what we would call *commonsense* clarification or resolution. Yet common sense is not always held in high regard. Goodman (1976, p. 497), for example, deprecates common sense as follows:

> As scientific understanding develops in any field of study, preexisting, naive, commonsense notions must give way. . . . They interfere with the application of modern scientific concepts of language and thought to research in reading. They confuse the attempts at application of such concepts to solution of problems involved in the teaching and learning of reading. The very fact that such naive beliefs are based on common sense explains their persistent and recurrent nature. To the casual and unsophisticated observer they appear to explain, even predict, a set of phenomena in reading.

Common sense then, is dismissed as old-fashioned, uninformed, and unsophisticated. Hardly the kind of wisdom one would apply—if Goodman's indictment is sound—to solve problems or to set directions.

But of course Goodman is not advocating nonsense by questioning what he calls the commonsense notions that dominate thinking about reading. His underlying points are that superficial analyses are not adequate to provide a basis for understanding the reading process and that unquestioning acceptance of traditional practices cannot lead to improvements in the teaching of reading. Our point, then, is that common sense would tell us that. In other words, where Goodman sees common sense as passive and delimiting, we see common sense as open and dynamic. The difference is important. People with the passive view looked at the horizon for millennia, and common sense told them that the world was flat. Others looked with a dynamic view, and their common sense told them to see for themselves. Common sense often offers an array of plausible alternatives—dynamic common sense takes the next step of either choosing among them or striking some reasonable balance among them.

Teaching reading as a commonsense process is largely a matter of striking balances among reasonable alternatives. Consider, then, some alternatives and a reasonable balance.

Alternatives We have already described a skill-development approach and a psycholinguistic approach. The two approaches present some alternatives, and they also present some opportunities for striking balances. More about balances later. First we want to discuss one more approach.

The approach is exemplified by Herbert Kohl (1973, p. xi): "There is no reading problem. There are problem teachers and problem schools. Most people who fail to learn how to read in our society are victims of a fiercely competitive system of training that requires failure. If talking and walking were taught in most schools we might end up with as many mutes and cripples as we now have non-readers."* What Kohl advocates is *natural* learning, and his central point is that anyone who can read his book can teach someone else to read.

In addition to knowing how to read, Kohl suggests, the teacher of reading ought to subscribe to three basic beliefs. First, teaching is more a matter of guiding and assisting another person than of pouring knowledge into him or her. Second, one who teaches must learn how to respond appropriately. To borrow Kohl's example, a person who asks for help with a word may want to learn how to sound out complicated words in general or simply to know the meaning of the word in order to make sense of what is being read. The teacher must sense whether a lesson or a quick answer is the appropriate response. Third, learning is a noncompetitive phenomenon. Any other view must measure success in terms of failure.

Of course, there is much more to Kohl's approach than the few overview statements we can offer here. Read the whole book; it makes good sense. What

*From Herbert Kohl, *Reading, How To.* Copyright © 1973 by Herbert Kohl. Reprinted by permission of the publishers, E. P. Dutton.

should be clear is that Kohl's approach stresses neither the methodology of teaching reading nor the content that should be taught. Kohl is talking about an attitude toward learners and learning, about a belief system for teachers of reading, and about sharing the joy of one who is learning to read.

We have already said that in general, psycholinguistic approaches tend to offer principles but to lack backup details, whereas skill-development approaches tend to offer detail but to lack integrating principles. Both approaches tend to lack or to soft-pedal any consideration of the kind of natural learning that is central to Kohl's approach. Common sense suggests that by striking some balances among the three approaches, one might begin to develop the best approach of all. Combine principles derived from psycholinguistic study with the attention to specifics and to systematic development derived from skill-development routines, temper them with an empathic concern for natural learning, and the sum will be much more than its parts.

Speaking from his vantage point, Kohl (1973, p. 181) said something very similar: "The adult (teacher) is not merely there to create an environment and step out of the way, letting the kids 'do their own thing.' He or she must care about the students learning certain skills and have ideas about how young people can go about acquiring them." The implicit invitation is to combine the *substance* of psycholinguistic study, the *system* of skill development, and the *instincts* of one who is willing and able to share the ability to read. Common sense suggests that the invitation is a good one.

1. What do you see as the main implication for teachers of beginning reading of Downing's idea of "cognitive confusion"? List at least ten words that would be likely sources of confusion for beginning readers. Choose three words from your list and decide how you would present each of them to a young child in a way that would make the meaning clear. If possible, try it out with a child.

2. The text gives five reasons why teachers ought to be active participants in the scholarship and theory development related to reading. Which of them seem(s) most persuasive to you? Why?

3. Which is more likely to be useful to teachers of reading: a *developmental* theory or a *descriptive* theory? Explain your preference.

4. In your personal view, what are the most important *strengths* of a skill-centered approach to teaching reading? What are the most significant weaknesses? How could you emphasize the strengths and minimize the weaknesses as *you* teach reading?

5. In your personal view, what are the most important *strengths* of teaching reading as a psycholinguistic process? What are the most pressing limitations? How could you emphasize the strengths and minimize the weaknesses as *you* teach reading?

6. One of your objectives for this chapter is to choose or to formulate a conception of the reading process. Now that you have read the chapter, perhaps you can begin to see how you might draw from a number of sources

to strengthen your approach to teaching. Of course, the job of formulating your own personal approach is one you will pursue throughout your life as a teacher. Meanwhile, which of the theories (or *models* or *conceptions*) appeal(s) most to you at this time? Can you say why? Pick some of the references related to your choice (listed in the footnotes to the text) and study them. See whether your opinions change as you read more about your choice.

REFERENCES   Athey, Irene J. "Language Models and Reading," in Frederick B. Davis, ed., *The Literature of Research in Reading with Emphasis on Models* (New Brunswick, N.J.: Rutgers University Graduate School of Education, 1971), pp. 6–3 to 6–99.

Bloom, Richard D. "Learning to Read: An Operant Perspective," in Frederick B. Davis, ed., *The Literature of Research in Reading with Emphasis on Models* (New Brunswick, N.J.: Rutgers University Graduate School of Education, 1971), pp. 7–3 to 7–20.

Bloomfield, Leonard, and C. L. Barnhart. *Let's Read* (Detroit: Wayne State University Press, 1961).

Bormuth, John. *On the Theory of Achievement Test Items* (Chicago: University of Chicago Press, 1970).

Bruner, Jerome S., J. J. Goodnow, and Mary Austin. *Studies in Cognitive Growth* (New York: Wiley, 1966).

Carroll, John B. "The Nature of the Reading Process," in Harry Singer and Robert B. Ruddell, eds., *Theoretical Models of the Reading Process* (Newark, Delaware: International Reading Association, 1970), pp. 292–303.

Chomsky, Noam, and M. Halle. *The Sound Pattern of English* (New York: Harper & Row, 1968).

Davis, Frederick B. "Psychometric Research on Comprehension in Reading," in Frederick B. Davis, ed., *The Literature of Research in Reading with Emphasis on Models* (New Brunswick, N.J.: Rutgers University Graduate School of Education, 1971), pp. 8–3 to 8–60.

Davis, Frederick B., ed. *The Literature of Research in Reading with Emphasis on Models* (New Brunswick, N.J.: Rutgers University Graduate School of Education, 1971).

Downing, John. "Children's Concepts of Language in Learning to Read," *Educational Research* **12** (1970): 106–112.

———. "Thinking about Reading." (Paper presented at the twentieth annual meeting of the International Reading Association, New York City, May 1975.)

Entwisle, Doris R. "Implications of Language Socialization for Reading Models and for Learning to Read," in Frederick B. Davis, ed., *The Literature of Research in Reading with Emphasis on Models* (New Brunswick, N.J.: Rutgers University Graduate School of Education, 1971), pp. 6–101 to 6–158.

———. "A Sociologist Looks at Reading" in Wayne Otto, Charles Peters, and Nathaniel Peters, eds., *Reading Problems: A Multidisciplinary Perspective* (Reading, Mass.: Addison-Wesley, 1977).

Fitts, Paul M., and Michael I. Posner. *Human Performance* (Belmont, Calif.: Brooks-Cole, 1967).

Fries, Charles C. *Linguistics and Reading* (New York: Holt, Rinehart and Winston, 1963).

Gagné, Robert M. *The Conditions of Learning*, 2d ed. (New York: Holt, Rinehart and Winston, 1966).

Geyer, John J. "Comprehensive and Partial Models Related to the Reading Process," in Frederick B. Davis, ed., *The Literature of Research in Reading with Emphasis on Models* (New Brunswick, N.J.: Rutgers University Graduate School of Education, 1971), pp. 5–1 to 5–51.

Gibson, Eleanor J. "The Ontology of Reading," *American Psychologist* **25** (1970): 136–143.

Goodman, Kenneth S. "Reading: A Psycholinguistic Guessing Game," *Journal of the Reading Specialist* **4** (1967): 126–135.

———. *The Psycholinguistic Nature of the Reading Process* (Detroit: Wayne State University Press, 1968).

———. "Analysis of Oral Reading Miscues: Applied Psycholinguistics," *Reading Research Quarterly* **5** (1969): 9–30.

———. "Reading: A Psycholinguistic Guessing Game," in Harry Singer and Robert B. Ruddell, eds., *Theoretical Models of the Reading Process* (Newark, Delaware: International Reading Association, 1976), pp. 497–508.

Gray, William, S. "The Major Aspects of Reading," in Helen M. Robinson, ed., *Sequential Development of Reading Abilities*, Supplementary Educational Monographs, No. 90 (Chicago: University of Chicago Press, 1960), pp. 8–24.

Hansen, Duncan N. "Information-Processing Models for Reading-Skill Acquisition," in Frederick B. Davis, ed., *The Literature of Research in Reading with Emphasis on Models* (New Brunswick, N.J.: Rutgers University Graduate School of Education, 1971), pp. 7–45 to 7–71.

Holmes, Jack A. *The Substrata-Factor Theory of Reading* (Berkeley: California Book, 1953). (Out of print)

Holmes, Jack A., and Harry Singer. *Substrata-Factor Differences Underlying Reading Ability in Known Groups*, Final Report covering Contracts 538, SAE-8176, and 538A, SAE-8660 (Washington, D.C.: U.S. Office of Education, 1961).

Kling, Martin. "Quest for Synthesis," in Frederick B. Davis, ed., *The Literature of Research in Reading with Emphasis on Models* (New Brunswick, N.J.: Rutgers University Graduate School of Education, 1971), pp. 2–1 to 2–18.

Kohl, Herbert. *Reading, How To* (New York: Bantam, 1973).

LaBerge, David, and S. Jay Samuels. "Toward a Theory of Automatic Information Processing in Reading," *Cognitive Psychology* **6** (1974): 293–323.

Lenneberg, E. H. *Biological Foundations of Language* (New York: Wiley, 1967).

Lorenz, Konrad. "Innate Bases of Learning," in K. H. Pribraum, ed., *On the Biology of Learning* (New York: Harcourt, Brace and World, 1969), pp. 13–93.

Lundsteen, Sara W. *Children Learn to Communicate* (Englewood Cliffs, N.J.: Prentice-Hall, 1976).

McNeill, David. "Developmental Psycholinguistics," in Frank Smith and George A. Miller, eds., *The Genesis of Language* (Cambridge, Mass.: M.I.T. Press, 1966).

———. "The Development of Language," in P. H. Mussen, ed., *Carmichael's Manual of Child Psychology*, 3rd ed., Vol. 1 (New York: Wiley, 1970).

Meltzer, Nancy S., and Robert Herse. "The Boundaries of Written Words as Seen by First Graders," *Journal of Reading Behavior* 1 (1969): 3–14.

Otto, Wayne, Robert Chester, John McNeil, and Shirley Myers. *Focused Reading Instruction* (Reading, Mass.: Addison-Wesley, 1974).

Piaget, Jean. "Piaget's Theory," in P. H. Mussen, ed., *Carmichael's Manual of Child Psychology*, 3rd ed., Vol. 1 (New York: Wiley, 1970), pp. 703–732.

Pribraum, K. H., ed. *On the Biology of Learning* (New York: Harcourt, Brace and World, 1969).

Reid, J. F., "Learning to Think about Reading," *Educational Research* 9 (1966): 56–62.

Robinson, Helen M. "The Major Aspects of Reading," in H. Alan Robinson, ed., *Reading: Seventy-Five Years of Progress*, Supplementary Educational Monographs, No. 96 (Chicago: University of Chicago Press, 1966), pp. 22–32.

Ruddell, Robert B. "Psycholinguistic Implications for a Systems of Communication Model," in Harry Singer and Robert B. Ruddell, eds., *Theoretical Models and Processes of Reading* (Newark, Delaware: International Reading Association, 1970), pp. 239–258.

Samuels, S. Jay. "Success and Failure in Learning to Read: A Critique of the Research," in Frederick B. Davis, ed., *The Literature of Research in Reading with Emphasis on Models* (New Brunswick, N.J.: Rutgers University Graduate School of Education, 1971), pp. 7–73 to 7–114.

_____. "An Introduction to Theoretical Models of Reading," in Wayne Otto, Charles Peters, and Nathaniel Peters, eds., *Reading Problems: A Multidisciplinary Perspective* (Reading, Mass.: Addison-Wesley, 1977).

Singer, Harry. "Theoretical Models of Reading," *Journal of Communication* 19 (1969): 134–156.

Singer, Harry, and Robert B. Ruddell, eds. *Theoretical Models and Processes of Reading*, 2d ed. (Newark, Delaware: International Reading Association, 1976).

Smith, Frank. *Understanding Reading* (New York: Holt, Rinehart and Winston, 1971).

Spache, George D., and Evelyn B. Spache. *Reading in the Elementary School*, 2d ed. (Boston: Allyn and Bacon, 1969).

Staats, Arthur W., and Carolyn K. Staats. "A Comparison of the Development of Speech and Reading Behavior with Implications for Research," *Child Development* 33 (1962): 831–846.

Thorndike, Edward L. "Reading as Reasoning," *Journal of Educational Psychology* 8 (1917): 323–332. (Reprinted in *Reading Research Quarterly* 6 (1971): 425–434.)

Venezky, Richard L. and Robert L. Calfee. "The Reading Competency Model," in Harry Singer and Robert B. Ruddell, eds., *Theoretical Models and Processes of Reading* (Newark, Delaware: International Reading Association, 1970), pp. 273–291.

Williams, Joanna P. "Learning to Read: Six Papers in Search of a Model," in Frederick B. Davis, ed., *The Literature of Research in Reading with Emphasis on Models* (New Brunswick, N.J.: Rutgers University Graduate School of Education, 1971), pp. 4–1 to 4–5.

_____. "Learning to Read: A Review of Theories and Models," *Reading Research Quarterly* 8 (1973): 121–146.

_____. "New Theories of Reading: What Do They Tell Us?" *Teachers College Record* 75 (1974): 553–561.

Chapter 3
Focusing
Instruction:
Objectives

After reading this chapter, you will be able to:

1. Describe the benefits and limitations of using instructional objectives.
2. Construct three levels of objectives—broad, instructional, specific—to be used in planning reading instruction.
3. List the salient features of a prescriptive, or closed, objective.
4. List the salient features of a descriptive, or open, objective.
5. Identify differences among descriptive, prescriptive, and behavioral objectives.

Your specific objectives for this chapter have to do with the nature and functions of instructional objectives. We view instructional objectives as potentially very useful, but other writers have expressed other opinions about them. Some writers are inclined to see only the negative side of objectives (for example, MacDonald and Wolfson, 1970), and others point out both strengths and limitations (Niles, 1972, and Zahoric, 1976). By becoming familiar with various positions, you will be able to view objectives with some perspective. Once you see what instructional objectives are and what they can—and cannot—do for you, you will begin to see how you can use them to teach reading effectively.

OBJECTIVES IN PERSPECTIVE

Objectives can shackle spontaneity and creativity if they are treated as absolutes and applied with a heavy hand. But they can be beneficial if you use them to provide direction. Perspective makes the difference.

Objectives Pro and Con

If you search the literature for the pros and cons of instructional objectives, you are likely to be struck by the extreme positions of the proponents and critics. Consider, for example, a brief quotation from James Popham, one of the most outspoken advocates of objectives in education (1970, p. 116): "I believe that those who discourage educators from precisely explicating their instructional objectives are often permitting, if not promoting, the same kind of unclear thinking that has led in part to the generally abysmal quality of instruction in this country."

Such an attack is certain to evoke a counterattack from the other side. A response by Apple (1972, p. 10) is sufficient to illustrate:

> . . . the set of assumptions mirrored in [Popham's] statement . . . , [are the] assumptions that provide the ideological foundation for systems management in education. These assumptions are concerned with the tacit advocacy of a view negating the importance of intellectual conflict, a rather limited perspective on scientific endeavor, an inability to deal with ambiguity, and finally an outmoded separation of moral and technical questions. The increasing use of systems terminology in education rests on this set of beliefs which when examined is often unrealistic, and socially and politically conservative.

Or, consider the case against behavioral objectives presented by MacDonald and Wolfson (1970, p. 119): ". . . we would point to the exclusively utilitarian view of education inherent in the behavioral objectives model. We reject this view. Instead, we believe that education can be an exciting happening that leads to aesthetic and functional outcomes. We believe that education can remain related to the pupil's personal meaning as well as to the society in which he lives."*

Given positions like these, one could only conclude that the controversy is beyond conciliation. And so the choice would appear to be to either objectify all of education or abandon objectives entirely. But the fact is that the controversies of the curriculum theorists are often far removed from the conflicts of the classroom.

The conflict that confronts a reading teacher in the classroom boils down to a very simple question: Can I *use* objectives without being *abused by* objectives? We suggest that the answer to that is neither a stark yes nor no, but something more like sometimes or maybe. Two points will help to clarify what must look like an unacceptably ambiguous answer.

First, objectives can be very useful in teaching reading skills whether or not one believes that everything to be taught ought to be described in terms of objectives. That is, one can state objectives for some aspects of teaching reading without feeling compelled to state an objective for every teaching act.

Second, objectives can be very useful in teaching reading skills as long as the application of skills, not simply the mastery of objectives, is the goal of instruction. That is, one can use objectives to break the teaching of reading into manageable bits, but those bits must be reassembled if they are to contribute to overall reading performance.

To put it another way, then, objectives can be useful for teaching reading as long as they are kept in perspective. Niles (1972, p. 110) made the same point in a different way: "The thrust toward curriculum in terms of behavioral objectives has taken many teachers unaware and left them apprehensive. What will it do for the children and for them as teachers in the years immediately ahead? No one knows for sure, but if teachers build on its strengths and are fully aware of its dangers, reading programs should be stronger in (the future) than they are today." Think of objectives as tools that are available for teaching reading. If you learn to use the right ones at the right times, they will serve you well. But if you try to apply them to tasks for which they are not suited, you will find that you have only complicated the job of teaching reading.

Levels of Objectives

We can conveniently think of objectives at three levels that range from broad program objectives to the very specific objectives that one might follow in writing instructional materials (Krathwohl, 1965). The usefulness of objectives *in the classroom* is determined, in part, by the level of application for which they are stated. Teachers in the classroom usually find midlevel objectives—

*James MacDonald and Bernice Wolfson, "A Case Against Behavioral Objectives," *Elementary School Journal* **71** (1970): 119. Reprinted by permission of the University of Chicago Press.

somewhere between the very broad and the very specific—most usable. Consider some examples from each level.

Broad Objectives Written at the most abstract level, these are the broad, general statements that specify goals for an entire school unit (e.g., elementary school or middle school), guide program development, and/or identify courses and areas to be covered. A broad objective for an elementary school might be something as vague as this:

- The students will understand and practice the principles of good citizenship.

Such an objective sets a worthwhile goal, but it gives very few clues as to how one would decide whether or not it had been attained. An example of a more useful broad objective, one that could serve as a guide to program development in reading, is:

- The student, upon completion of all of the word-attack objectives, will be able to independently attack phonically and/or structurally regular words and to recognize on sight all of the words on the prescribed sight-word list.

Such a statement amounts to a *terminal* objective in that it sets a goal or describes an outcome that comes at the end of a learning sequence.

Midlevel Objectives Objectives at this level are stated in more concrete terms than are the broad objectives that set goals and describe desired *terminal* outcomes. Duffy and Sherman (1972) offer what they call *performance* objectives. Their objectives are good examples of objectives written at the midlevel of specificity. Consider two of them:

- Given a word he has learned previously, the learner substitutes the blends *bl, cl, fl, pl, gl,* or *sl* in the initial position and pronounces the new word. (p. 153)

- Given any content word found in reading materials used by the learner, he indicates his understanding of the conceptual meaning of the word by (1) giving a synonym for the concept, (2) using it in an appropriate context, (3) defining it in his own words, or (4) performing a physical operation indicative of the meaning. (p. 218)

The first example, which deals with a specific decoding skill, could be a step along the way toward the goal described in our example of a broad objective. The focus of the second example is on understanding, not decoding, but the level of specificity is quite similar. The objective is a step toward another important goal in reading, understanding what one reads. Both examples permit the teacher flexibility in choosing activities and materials for individual students as they work toward the objective.

At the specific level, objectives are so explicit that they prescribe all of the steps required to attain even a midlevel objective. Objectives at the specific level can serve as a basis for programed instruction. Thus whereas a single midlevel objective would deal with the entire range of letter names in the alphabet—the learner is able to indicate the correct symbols (letters) when the letter names are pronounced by the teacher—a specific objective would be written for each letter-name combination. Examples of specific objectives related to the midlevel example are:

- Given a visual presentation of the letter *a*, the learner names the letter.
- Given a visual presentation of the letter *b*, the learner names the letter. (And so on through the alphabet.)

Whereas midlevel objectives tend to be significant steps along the way toward broad objectives, specific objectives prescribe all of the steps along the way toward midlevel objectives.

Objectives written at each of the three levels can serve useful purposes, but by now you can probably see why midlevel objectives are likely to be the most useful for daily application in the classroom. A teacher we know put it like this: "Broad objectives give me goals to shoot for, but they don't give me much guidance on a day-to-day basis. Specific objectives give me more guidance than I can stand! Who can keep track of that many objectives? Midlevel objectives help me to establish attainable, observable goals without prescribing everything I say or do."

Midlevel objectives, then, serve as milestones or checkpoints along the way toward important terminal objectives, like the one given in the example above. Yet midlevel objectives permit teachers considerable flexibility in choosing activities and materials as they work toward their midlevel milestones. This flexibility is what makes objectives compatible with an individualized/personalized approach to teaching reading. Objectives at the midlevel are in perspective for the classroom, for they offer direction and guidance without usurping the teacher's role in devising instruction that is appropriate for each student. Midlevel objectives are also called *instructional* objectives, for they give goals for day-to-day teaching.

Many proponents of objectives in education insist that objectives must be stated in *behavioral* terms if they are to be effective in facilitating instructional planning and communication. Although the major advocates of *behavioral* objectives—e.g., Tyler (1950), Popham and Baker (1970), Mager (1962), and Gagné (1972)—may use different terms in discussing objectives or stress different elements, all support the need for clarity and precision in stating objectives (Zahorik, 1976). In general, there is agreement that a well-stated behavioral objective: (1) describes the *actual behavior* required to demonstrate competence with, or mastery of, the objective; (2) identifies the *relevant conditions* under which the behavior is to be performed and/or the *results* of the behavior which will be evaluated to determine mastery; and (3) prescribes the *standard* that will be used to assess the success of the performance. The decoding objective that follows qualifies as a behavioral objective:

- Given a maximum one-second exposure per word (the *relevant conditions*), the learner recognizes (the *actual behavior*) at least 80 percent (the *standard*) of the words on a high-frequency sight-word list.

Such precisely stated objectives are defended on the basis of efficiency and effectiveness. The rationale is very straightforward: *If* teachers decide exactly what they want their pupils to learn and exactly how to decide when they have learned it, *then* pupils can be given opportunities to learn with the least expenditure of time and effort.

Yet certain desirable outcomes of schooling cannot be prescribed explicitly or assessed objectively (e.g., Kapfer, 1968). Even Popham (1969), usually an enthusiastic advocate of behavioral objectives, admits to being a bit perplexed by the fact that schools have an obligation to provide certain activities for which outcomes are unable to be prescribed or assessed. Although many arguments and reservations continue to be put forth, most teachers have probably reached a practical conclusion: Behavioral objectives may be appropriate for some applications, but not for others.

In reading instruction behavioral objectives can be appropriate for teaching such things as word-decoding skills, study skills, and even literal-comprehension skills. Yet we have found that fully developed behavioral objectives tend to be needlessly restrictive for general classroom use. And, in our judgment, behavioral objectives are not appropriate for dealing with the interpretive and creative aspects of reading. On the basis of these observations and beliefs, we prefer to talk about *prescriptive* and *descriptive* objectives (Otto, Chester, McNeil, and Meyers, 1974; Otto and Chester, 1976).

Prescriptive Objectives

For some purposes, objectives for reading instruction can appropriately be *prescriptive*. That is, the objective can describe quite precisely what the desired behavior is. Two examples of objectives that *prescribe* performance are:

- The learner identifies the main idea of a paragraph with no topic sentence.
- The learner uses a dictionary to check the meanings of words as needed.

But these are not proper behavioral objectives, according to most specifications, because they neither set a *standard* for assessing successful performance nor make explicit the *conditions* under which the behavior is to be performed. However, both objectives can be transformed into full-blown *behavioral* objectives. The first transformation is easy:

- Given paragraphs with no topic sentences (*relevant conditions*), the learner identifies (the *actual behavior*) the main idea in four out of five attempts (the *standard*).

But the second transformation requires a bit more contriving:

- Given material with words outside his or her meaning vocabulary (*relevant conditions*), the learner uses the dictionary (the *actual behavior*) to check the meaning of all unknown words (the *standard*).

Note that in each instance the transformation required that a very straightforward prescription of expected behavior be modified to the point where the behavior could be evoked and examined only in rather rigidly contrived situations. The controlled (and, therefore, often contrived) situation is essential when *evaluation* is the purpose. But such control is too restrictive for ordinary instructional purposes.

What we call *prescriptive objectives*, then, are like specific behavioral objectives in that they identify, or prescribe, actual behaviors. But they are different in that they do not go to the point of identifying standards, relevant conditions, or other elements that might tend to restrict their application. Like objectives that are written at a midlevel of specificity, objectives that prescribe outcomes without suggesting conditions strike a balance that permits them to be useful in the classroom. (See Zahorik, 1976, for a more extended discussion of the limitations of full-blown behavioral objectives.)

There are important areas in reading instruction for which outcomes cannot— or should not—be prescribed. Take, for example, a common goal of reading instruction: *predicting the outcome of a story*. If we really mean it when we ask a child to predict an outcome, we must be prepared to consider not only the child's prediction, but also the reasons for which it was made. There can be no *prescriptive* objective, because no "right" response or behavior can be prescribed beforehand. Some critics of objectives appear to base their case almost entirely on this point. They reject all objectives because prescriptive, or behavioral, objectives are inadequate to deal with certain important goals or outcomes of schooling.

Rather than reject all objectives because we find them dysfunctional in certain instances, we have found it useful to broaden our conception of instructional objectives to include *descriptive* as well as *prescriptive* objectives. That is, the behaviors associated with certain goals of reading instruction can be prescribed in advance. But there are other goals for which it is quite realistic simply to *describe* a task that pupils are to engage in and then to examine outcomes as they emerge. These are some *descriptive* objectives:

- The learner predicts the outcomes of stories.
- The learner uses drama to transform the content of literature to different modes, moods, or points of view.
- The learner tells stories based on characters or themes in literature.
- The learner notes character traits and motives.

Note that in each instance there is no "correct" answer or behavior like there is a "correct" response when a child is asked to pronounce a word or find

Descriptive Objectives

a fact. Prescriptive objectives call for "correct" responses. Descriptive objectives do not; they simply set the stage for a response.

Application   Classic behavioral objectives are designed to reduce ambiguity and confusion by identifying not only behavioral outcomes, but also standards for judging and conditions for evoking the behaviors. Such precision makes for effective evaluation, but at the same time it tends to complicate a teacher's life in the classroom. Although getting learners to look up unknown words in the dictionary is a worthwhile instructional objective, requiring students to perform up to a predetermined standard with explicitly described materials would be cumbersome in day-to-day teaching and not very useful in terms of transfer to other situations. Prescriptive objectives, which focus mainly on outcomes, are adequate to provide direction and guidance. And, because one cannot characterize all outcomes in advance, descriptive objectives are a worthwhile complement to prescriptive objectives.

Prescriptive objectives will probably be most useful in your day-to-day teaching of basic decoding skills, study skills, and literal-comprehension skills. Desired outcomes can be characterized in advance, and the objectives can provide direction and guidance for instruction.

You may find that classic behavioral objectives are useful for formal evaluation of the outcomes associated with your prescriptive objectives. Consider, for example, this prescriptive objective:

- The learner determines whether given statements represent fact or opinion.

There you have a predetermined outcome (behavior) and a worthwhile instructional goal: to get learners to determine whether statements encountered in their reading are facts or opinions. The objective is adequate to guide instructional planning and to direct specific lessons. But for purposes of assessing pupils' competence with the objective, you may want to prescribe the conditions under which the behavior is to be performed and to set a standard of minimal performance. Simply transform the prescriptive objective into a specific behavioral objective:

- Given materials at an appropriate level of difficulty that contain statements of fact and expressions of opinion, the learner indicates with 80 percent accuracy whether given statements represent fact or opinion.

What you have then is a basis for making a formal assessment of a learner's performance with a given objective.

Of course, the transformation can go either way: Rewrite a specific behavioral objective as a prescriptive objective in order to make it more usable in your regular teaching, or rewrite a prescriptive objective as a specific behavioral objective in order to get a basis for formal evaluation. Remember that objectives should always suit *your* purpose, never the other way around.

Descriptive objectives will be useful in that they permit you to systematize your goals without being forced to characterize all of the outcomes in advance. Although it seems perfectly reasonable to specify in advance the outcome that is expected from instruction on substituting initial consonant sounds in known words, such is not the case when interpretive or creative acts are the desired outcomes. Prescriptive objectives are appropriate to guide the development of convergent reading-related behaviors, such as getting the main idea or making proper use of long and short vowel sounds. Descriptive objectives are needed to guide the development of divergent reading-related behaviors that involve interpretations, appreciations, and creative acts, such as identifying with a character in a story or developing an interest in reading.

Like almost anything else, instructional objectives offer certain benefits if they are used sensibly, but they also have certain limitations. These are some of the benefits and limitations that are most often pointed out by the proponents and the critics.

Benefits and Limitations of Objectives

1. *Objectives set clear purposes for both teachers and learners.* By stating or identifying realistic objectives, teachers clarify their own goals and set goals for their pupils.

2. *Midlevel objectives break broad content or curriculum areas into manageable bits.*

3. *The sequence of reading instruction can be worked out in terms of objectives.* Nobody is entirely certain which reading skills are absolutely essential or whether there is an optimum sequence for teaching them. But good teachers are reasonably confident about certain skills and how they should be sequenced. Once skills have been identified and described in terms of descriptive and prescriptive objectives, they can be arranged in instructional sequences that make sense.

4. *Objectives facilitate evaluation.* We have shown how prescriptive objectives identify goals and how specific behavioral objectives set standards for performance.

5. *Objectives provide a basis for organizing and selecting instructional materials and procedures.*

Benefits

1. *The process of schooling amounts to more than mastering content.* Of course it does. Objectives can help to systematize and focus instruction in certain areas, but the entire process of schooling is more broadly based.

2. *Individuals have idiosyncratic ways of organizing content.* Some children learn to read with no formal instruction at all, and others learn to respond to cues different from the ones that were taught. But these are not adequate reasons to abandon *all* children to their own devices. Most children need some guidance in developing their reading abilities, and instructional objectives can help focus that guidance.

Limitations

3. *Objectives may cause an overemphasis on skills—at the expense of generalizations, interpretations, and applications.* This is the most potent limitation of all. Objectives must be kept in perspective, and the skills that are acquired must be applied. Isolated skills that are mastered but not applied are of no utility at all. Teachers must make careful provisions for helping children integrate and use learned skills when reading a variety of materials.

4. *Certain content areas do not lend themselves to the identification of objectives.* Probably so. But we are concerned with reading instruction, and a combination of prescriptive and descriptive objectives seems quite adequate to cover the important outcomes of learning to read. Even growth in the affective areas of reading (developing an interest in and valuing reading) can be guided through the use of descriptive objectives, used intelligently.

5. *Objectives may be stated with little regard for the realities of the classroom.* True—which is why we have suggested midlevel prescriptive and descriptive objectives and why you will need to choose objectives that are useful to *you*. Simply accepting *in toto* a published list of "reading objectives" that do not match either the reading program used or the classroom organization is foolish. Your reading program and organizational plan should reflect your best ideas about what reading is and how children learn. Your objectives should also reflect these beliefs.

6. *Unanticipated outcomes may be as important as intended results.* True again—and anyone who would continue to teach the *schwa* because that was the objective for the day when a fire breaks out in the hall closet ought to be banished to the dark side of Sesame Street. A good teacher is a flexible teacher, one who can "seize the moment" to teach an idea or a skill at the very time the need arises, even though it means completely scrapping the planned lesson.

Application Most of our comments regarding application are given with the listing of benefits and limitations. Perspective—or perhaps just plain common sense—is what makes objectives usable by and useful to teachers of reading.

Some critics of objectives suggest that the reading teacher who tries to decide what the teaching of reading is all about will lose sight of the forest for all the trees. Perhaps so. One does need to step back occasionally in order to keep everything in perspective. But think of it this way. The reading teacher who identifies objectives may find that reading is much more than just another complex, and unteachable, process.

APPLICATION: INSTRUCTIONAL OBJECTIVES Whether you work with objectives stated by somebody else or state your own, you will need to make certain that your objectives serve your purposes. This section will help you see how objectives can be shaped and, in turn, be used to shape reading instruction. The exercises below will give you a chance to apply some of the ideas we have discussed and to think about how you might use objectives.

- Each of the following statements identifies an aspect or outcome of reading instruction. For each statement, decide whether (1) an appropriate outcome can be identified at the instructional level (midlevel), and (2) the outcome would best be handled as a *descriptive* or as a *prescriptive* objective. The statements are taken from varied sources, so they are not parallel in form.

  1. To use words responsibly.
  2. To become acquainted with the best literature available.
  3. To participate in a variety of independent reading activities.
  4. To develop the skill of using three basic principles in dividing words into syllables.
  5. The student makes a diagram to demonstrate understanding that English is descended from an old German dialect.
  6. The child practices the technique of scanning to find a specific fact and skimming to determine the general theme.
  7. The child notes character traits.
  8. Given a known word illustrating the silent *e* vowel principle, the learner pronounces other words illustrating the principle.
  9. The child identifies a statement of a main idea of a paragraph with no topic sentence.

There are no right or wrong answers, but here are some things to consider when you think about your own judgments. The first two items deal with broad outcomes that are probably beyond the scope of useful instructional, or midlevel, objectives. Item 3 seems to involve an appropriate *midlevel* outcome that could be pursued with a *descriptive* objective. Items 4 and 5 could be pursued with *midlevel, prescriptive* objectives. Items 6 and 7 are both probably appropriate at the *instructional* level, but both seem to call for *descriptive* objectives that provide opportunities to perform without prescribing a particular performance. Items 8 and 9 are stated as *prescriptive* objectives that are appropriate to guide day-to-day instruction.

- A useful *prescriptive* objective specifies the desired observable behavior. Identify the observable behavior that is prescribed in each of the statements that follow.

  1. Given five pictures representing events in a story that was read, the learner arranges the pictures in sequential order.
  2. Given the words *hat, hate, flak, fake, sack, mail, ran, rain, chase, chance,* the learner circles the words with a short *a* sound.
  3. The learner demonstrates interest in the book *Where the Wild Things Are* by voluntarily participating at least once in a small-group discussion.
  4. After three hours of instruction, the learner correctly pronounces 19 out of 20 basic sight words after each one is presented for not more than one second.

The observable behavior is clearly prescribed in each statement. Item 3, however, presents a problem in that although a specific behavior—voluntarily participating at least once—is prescribed, the nature of that participation, or behavior, is not. So, is the statement a worthwhile *prescriptive* objective, or is it a *descriptive* objective? One could argue for either choice, but that kind of argument is seldom very productive. The fact is that item 3 is probably a sensible instructional objective. A teacher can deal with it as descriptive or prescriptive, depending on personal preference and style. Note the time limit for instruction on item 4. Could you impose a time limit in an objective and still claim to be individualizing instruction?

- A useful *descriptive* objective describes a task or activity that pupils are to engage in without prescribing a specific outcome in advance. Each of the following is meant to be a descriptive objective. In each instance, think about why—or whether—the objective should be handled as *descriptive* rather than *prescriptive*.

  1. The learner determines whether a given book contains needed information.
  2. The learner adjusts rate in view of his or her purpose for reading.
  3. The learner identifies with literary characters' emotional reactions.
  4. The learner gives oral and/or musical interpretations of literature.
  5. The learner writes stories or plays that relate some aspect of literature to personal experiences or contemporary situations.

  Our reason for making these *descriptive* objectives is that the desired outcomes cannot be specified in advance. In each instance the learner's response will be determined by his or her experiences, motives, and inclinations.

- A specific behavioral objective is probably most useful for purposes of evaluation when the situation is standardized (*relevant conditions* are prescribed), and an absolute criterion is set for judging the adequacy of performance. Remember, though, that in the discussion we said that somewhat less definitive *prescriptive* objectives are probably most usable for day-to-day reading instruction. The following are fully stated behavioral objectives. As you examine each one, (1) identify the *relevant condition* and the *performance criterion*, and (2) decide whether it amounts to a worthwhile *instructional objective*.

  1. Given written instructions on how to make a simple airplane out of folded paper, the student makes one that flies, without help, exactly according to instructions.
  2. After reading a newspaper article, the student is able to identify in writing at least four of these five: *who, what, when, where,* and *why.*
  3. The student will select at least one library book and either appear to read it during the library period or check it out for possible later reading when given 20 minutes of free time in the library.

Item 1 demonstrates the fact that even a fully developed behavioral objective *may* deal with a trivial act. Of course, the objective actually amounts to a demonstration of a child's ability to follow written instructions. Item 2 meets the minimum criteria for a behavioral objective, but responsibility for judging the quality of the response is left to the teacher. Can you accept that, or would you be inclined to reject the objective as it is stated? The third item is adequately stated, and it deals with an important behavior. Unfortunately, it deals with the behavior in a very superficial way. The *real* instructional objective is not merely to get students to "look at" or to "check out" books, but to *read* books. Do you think that the objective is useful as it is stated? How would you deal with the *real* objective: to get students to *read* books?

- Prescriptive objectives can readily be transformed into specific behavioral objectives for purposes of formal evaluation. We gave some examples in the discussion. Now see if you can transform the *prescriptive* objectives in the list that follows. You may decide that one or two of them ought to be *descriptive* objectives; think about why transforming them into specific behavioral objectives would be inappropriate or undesirable.

    1. The learner selects the word or phrase that is identical to a stimulus word or phrase.
    2. The learner responds to written directions that have been explained by the teacher.
    3. The learner identifies the root word in inflected words.
    4. The learner identifies possessive nouns and pronouns used in context.
    5. The learner independently uses library facilities appropriate to his or her purpose.
    6. The learner is able to recognize sequential relationships among two or three ideas.

  We decided that items 2 and 5 would best be handled by descriptive objectives. Do you agree? Note that in transforming item 1, you must decide whether presentation is to be *visual* or *oral*.

- Now try to write some objectives of your own. Rewrite each of the following, first as a *prescriptive* objective and then as a *specific behavioral* objective.

    1. To make up headlines for newspaper articles read.
    2. To locate needed books in the library by using the card catalog.
    3. To find the main idea and supporting details.
    4. To determine the meaning of unfamiliar words in context.
    5. To use guide words in encyclopedias and dictionaries.
    6. To interpret bar graphs.

  Review the discussion of *prescriptive* and *specific behavioral* objectives. Then decide whether your statements are adequate.

Planning an Objective-Based Lesson

Objectives can help you to focus instruction. Once you identify an objective, you can decide which of your students need additional work related to the objective and then proceed to plan instruction that moves each of the students identified toward the objective. The focusing, then, comes in two steps. First, you identify the students who need additional work related to the objective. Second, you locate instructional materials and activities that are appropriate for the particular students who were identified. Once you become comfortable with your own instructional objectives, you may not need to make detailed lesson plans in order to focus instruction. Teachers differ greatly in their need for formal, detailed planning. But suitable routines are established only through well-directed experience and practice.

The outline that follows can help you to plan objective-based lessons. Use the outline to help you think and work through the process of focusing instruction with objectives. As you gain experience with objective-based teaching, you may be able to proceed more informally with your planning. But first learn the routines by going through all of the steps. Ultimately, you may plan a lesson without going through the written exercise.

Outline for an Objective-Based Lesson

Purpose: _____

Reading level of lesson: _____

1. Instructional objective
   - Identify a prescriptive or descriptive objective
   - State the objective at a midlevel of specificity

2. Focus of the lesson
   - Choose a specific focus for the lesson in view of the time available for instruction

3. Preparation
   - Show how this lesson relates to the instructional objective
   - Describe your procedure for identifying the pupils for this lesson
   - Describe your pupils' prior preparation for this lesson

4. Materials
   - List appropriate textbooks, workbooks, visual aids, teacher-made materials, etc., for teaching the lesson; specify title, author, and source of commercial materials.

5. Procedures
   - Show how you will introduce the lesson and motivate the learners
   - Describe each step in the teaching sequence

6. Evaluation
   - How will you assess your pupils' progress toward the objective?

7. Follow-up
   - Based on your analysis of the lesson, plan additional learning activities as needed

An example of an objective-based lesson that was planned according to the outline follows. Note that the objective for the example is *prescriptive*, so the evaluation is very specific: Each student is to demonstrate competence by placing the picture cards in the appropriate boxes. If the objective were *descriptive*, there would be no definitive evaluation. An appropriate evaluation would be simply a description of the student's actual behaviors.

Purpose: Skill development—beginning consonant sounds

Reading level of lesson: First

1. Instructional objective
   - Given real or nonsense words supplied by the teacher, the learner identifies the letter that stands for the initial sound.

2. Focus of the lesson
   - The sound of *m, s,* and hard *c*

3. Preparation
   - This 20-minute lesson focuses on three consonant sounds and the letter symbols that represent them.
   - Prior assessment showed that the students identified for the lesson were unable to associate the consonant sounds and the symbols that represent them.
   - Prior to this lesson, the students had demonstrated ability to discriminate among the consonant sounds.

4. Materials
   - *The Noisy Book* by Margaret Wise. Published by Brown, Harper & Row
   - Pictures of at least twelve common objects, four for each of the three sounds in the lesson
   - Three boxes, labeled *m, s,* and *c*

5. Procedures
   - Introduction/Motivation: Read from *The Noisy Book* and use the story to motivate a discussion of why sounds are important.
   - Teaching sequence
     — Introduce pictures of objects with names that begin with the three consonant sounds, e.g., *mitten, sock, coat.*
     — Pronounce the object names and stress the beginning sound of each.

— Have the children sort the pictures into three groups, each with a common initial sound.

— Introduce the three boxes labeled with the letters *m, s,* and *c.*

— Associate the letter symbols with the initial sounds of the appropriate object names.

— Scramble the cards and have the children identify the initial sound and place each card in the proper box.

6. Evaluation

   • Each student should correctly place at least three of four cards in each box.

7. Follow-up

   • Children who are unsuccessful with the evaluation exercise will be taken through the teaching sequence again. Additional cards will be added if necessary to give children sufficient practice to learn the skill.

   • Children who are successful with the evaluation exercise will independently find and bring in at least three pictures for each sound in the lesson. They will be reminded to get permission *before* they cut out any pictures.

SUMMARY: FOCUSING INSTRUCTION

Objectives can help you to focus instruction. Think of the approach in terms of *what, who,* and *how.* When you state or choose objectives, you must decide *what* reading instruction is all about. Then, given objectives, you can proceed to focus instruction. First, you decide *who* is likely to benefit from instruction related to a given objective. Then you determine *how* to proceed with the instruction.

In this chapter we have tried to acquaint you with the notion of instructional objectives without attempting to dictate any specific objectives. The purpose of the chapter is to *acquaint* you with objectives and how they can be used in teaching reading, not to suggest a specific set of objectives. You will find that an objective-based approach is compatible with many different styles and orientations to teaching reading. Objectives, then, are *the basis* for focusing instruction—whatever the actual instructional approach may be. In the chapters that follow, we deal more specifically with the *what, who,* and *how* of the approach.

REVIEW QUESTIONS

1. What are the major benefits you could expect to derive from using instructional objectives to guide your teaching of reading? Of the five salient benefits pointed out in the text, which one(s) appeal most to you?

2. Look again at the six major limitations of instructional objectives. Which one(s) do you think would be most likely to cause difficulties for you? Can you think of ways to keep the limitations from offsetting the positive effects of using instructional objectives?

3. If you think of objectives at the three levels of specificity described in the text, which level is most appealing to you for use in the day-to-day teaching of reading? Why? As a teacher, would you ever consider stating objectives at the specific level? If so, for what purposes?

4. How does a prescriptive objective differ from a classic behavioral objective? Do you think that the distinction is a useful one? Can you transform a behavioral objective into a prescriptive objective?

5. List three goals that you, as a reading teacher, would expect your students to attain. How can you decide whether one would most appropriately be stated as a *descriptive* or a *prescriptive* objective?

REFERENCES

Apple, Michael W. "The Adequacy of Systems Management Procedures in Education," *Journal of Educational Research* **66** (1972): 10–18.

Duffy, Gerald G., and George B. Sherman. *Systematic Reading Instruction* (New York: Harper & Row, 1972).

Gagné, Robert M. "Behavioral Objectives? Yes," *Educational Leadership* **29** (1972): 394–396.

Kapfer, Philip G. "Behavioral Objectives in the Cognitive and Affective Domains," *Educational Technology* **8** (1968): 11–13.

Krathwohl, D. R. "Stating Objectives Appropriate for Program, for Curriculum, and for Instructional Materials Development," *Journal of Teacher Education* **16** (1965): 83–92.

MacDonald, James B., and Bernice J. Wolfson. "A Case against Behavioral Objectives," *Elementary School Journal* **71** (1970): 119–127.

Mager, Robert F. *Preparing Objectives for Programmed Instruction* (Palo Alto, Calif.: Fearon, 1962).

Niles, Olive S. "Behavioral Objectives and the Teaching of Reading," *Journal of Reading* **16** (1972): 104–110.

Otto, Wayne, and Robert Chester. *Objective-Based Reading* (Reading, Mass.: Addison-Wesley, 1976).

Otto, Wayne, Robert Chester, John McNeil, and Shirley Myers. *Focused Reading Instruction* (Reading, Mass.: Addison-Wesley, 1974).

Popham, W. James. "Epilogue," in W. J. Popham, E. W. Eisner, H. J. Sullivan, and L. L. Tyler, eds., *Instructional Objectives,* American Educational Research Association Monograph Series on Curriculum Evaluation (Chicago: Rand McNally, 1969), pp. 32–64.

_____. "Probing the Validity of Arguments against Behavioral Goals," in R. J. Kibler *et al.,* eds., *Behavioral Objectives and Instruction* (Boston: Allyn and Bacon, 1970).

Popham, W. James, and Eva I. Baker. *Systematic Instruction* (Englewood Cliffs, N. J.: Prentice-Hall, 1970).

Tyler, Ralph W. *Basic Principles of Curriculum and Instruction* (Chicago: University of Chicago Press, 1950).

Zahoric, John A. "The Virtue of Vagueness in Instructional Objectives," *Elementary School Journal* **76** (1976): 411–419.

Chapter 4
Getting Ready
to Teach

OBJECTIVES FOR THE CHAPTER

After reading this chapter, you will be able to:

1. Describe what is meant by objective-based reading instruction.
2. Describe the basic features of a skills-management system.
3. State the values and limitations of using a skills-management system.
4. Explain the similarities and differences in selected skills-management systems.
5. Choose a skills-management system using the questions supplied in this chapter as a guide.

A good teacher of reading is aware of what his or her students already know and what they are now ready to learn. With this information at hand, the teacher can provide truly focused instruction. Without this information, the teacher may give some children instruction in skills they already have mastered, and other children may be asked to perform new tasks for which they do not have the necessary underlying competencies. Without this information, a teacher is not ready to teach.

In this chapter we suggest that skills-management systems can be used to provide the organizational framework necessary for focusing instruction. The theoretical bases for objective-based instruction and skills-management systems are presented, and the strengths and limitations of such instruction are discussed. The general procedures for implementing objective-based instruction are outlined, and several specific skills-management systems are described in detail. To help you draw the various theoretical and practical considerations of the chapter together, we end with some guidelines for selecting a skills-management system for your own classroom.

Teaching young children to read is an awesome task, even for the most experienced educator. Too often teachers fail to provide the specific, individualized instruction that would be most effective. Objective-based instruction can help teachers get ready to teach *individuals*, not just entire classes.

SKILLS-MANAGEMENT SYSTEMS IN PERSPECTIVE

The key to an effective reading program is a knowledgeable, organized, and perceptive teacher, as educators have long known. However, the actual teaching competence of elementary school teachers has not improved during the past decade (Durkin, 1974). When we examine the reasons for this situation, it is easy to understand why so little progress has been made in improving everyday classroom reading instruction.

First, most preservice teachers have received only minimal training in the teaching of reading. Today, most states still require only one reading-methods course in their teacher-training programs; some lack even this minimum criterion. With this meager training, it is no wonder that many beginning teachers are unprepared and anxious when it comes to teaching reading.

A second reason for inadequate teacher competence is related to the relatively limited opportunities available to undergraduate students for working with elementary school children. Many professors of reading do schedule a practicum component in their courses, realizing that the more contact preservice teachers have with students, the more opportunity these undergraduates will have for integrating theory and practice. However, it is difficult to schedule sufficient contact hours between college and elementary school students to give prospective teachers enough supervised experiences for practicing what the professors have preached.

A third reason why elementary school reading instruction hasn't changed much in the past ten years is related to the schools themselves. Most elementary school teachers are called on to be not just teachers of reading, but also good teachers of mathematics, science, social studies, and a number of other subjects. Even if beginning teachers received an outstanding undergraduate education, in only a few months they would be expected to be highly proficient in all of these areas. It is difficult to be a "superteacher" in all these subject-matter areas.

Professionals in the field of reading have specified their criteria for identifying effective teachers of reading (Harris, 1969; Powell, 1972). Generally, these criteria include: (1) being a good diagnostician; (2) knowing and caring for each individual in the class; (3) providing appropriate feedback to the pupils; (4) being highly enthusiastic about the material being taught; and (5) being knowledgeable about the subject matter. Few people would deny that anyone who demonstrated these characteristics would indeed be a superior teacher. A recent trend that should assist all teachers in moving closer to meeting these "criteria of excellence" is the movement toward objective-based instruction in the field of reading. Objective-based instruction, by identifying the specific needs of individual students, can help teachers focus their instruction for increased effectiveness.

Traditionally, the sequence and pace of instruction have been held constant for all students in a classroom (Coulson and Cogswell, 1965). This has resulted in a familiar phenomenon: The brighter children quickly learn what is presented (if they did not *already* know it) and soon become bored; the slower students have difficulty maintaining the pace, and fall further and further behind. Only the "average" children are both challenged and happy. Highly capable students often become disenchanted with school and may develop into behavior problems. Their less capable peers, on the other hand, face continual frustration on an almost hourly basis, day after day, 180 days per year. In the end, many of these less fortunate students are needlessly retained in the same grade the following year.

Objective-based instruction, on the other hand, can do much to correct this situation. This type of reading instruction is focused to meet the skill-development needs of each child. Ideally, all teachers would use this type of diagnostic instruction. To help teachers handle the vast array of learning abilities—and in many cases, disabilities—within the classroom, criterion-referenced diagnostic tests have been developed and are included as part of commercially available objective-based reading programs. Typically these programs are referred to as skills-management systems.

CHARACTERISTICS OF SKILLS-MANAGE-MENT SYSTEMS

Skills-management systems can provide classroom teachers with the basic materials they need to diagnose and manage reading instruction, regardless of the age or ability of their students. The major advantage of these systems is that they permit teachers to assess quickly and accurately the reading-skill development of individuals through the use of tests that have been constructed to measure performance related to previously specified behavioral objectives. To help you understand how skills-management systems can provide much needed assistance to classroom teachers, a more detailed examination of their components is in order.

Skills

Skills-management systems usually cover the areas of reading readiness, decoding, comprehension, and vocabulary, and some programs also deal with additional areas, such as creative reading and study skills. Although most skills-management systems include literally hundreds of reading skills, the number varies considerably from program to program (Rude, 1974; Stallard, 1977). The number of skills in any one program largely reflects the author's perception of what abilities children need to learn to read.

Essential Skills

Our position is that focused skill instruction will help most students learn to read more quickly and with less frustration than instruction that does not teach specific reading skills. But which skills should be taught? There is little consensus regarding what these skills are or the order in which they should be presented. The task may seem insurmountable. Consider, for example, the following skill areas that have been included in various skill-based programs (Stallard, 1977):

1. Comprehension
2. Creative reading
3. Interpretive or critical reading
4. Oral reading
5. Reading readiness
6. Secondary or content-area reading
7. Self-directed or independent reading
8. Vocabulary development
9. Word attack
10. Bilingual reading

Obviously, if each of these ten areas represents a *broad* category of reading, the identification of independent subskills and their organization into hierarchies within each category is indeed a formidable task. Johnson and Pearson (1975), Stennett *et al.* (1975), Thompson and Dziuban (1973), and Samuels (1976) have all cautioned that the present state of the art does not permit us to simplistically delineate a series of reading skills and then arrange them in a hard-and-fast hierarchy. Samuels (1976, pp. 173–174) says it well:

Despite the fact that learning hierarchies have a logical appeal, that we have known about them for at least three-quarters of a century, and that commercial reading series, with their scope and sequence charts, order the reading tasks as if we did know the nature of the learning hierarchy in reading, the sad truth is that the task is so complex that a validated reading hierarchy does not exist.

This is of little consolation to classroom teachers, however, who are faced with the tremendous task of teaching children to read. While experimentalists and theoreticians strive to resolve the "essential skills dilemma," we offer the following suggestions to classroom teachers.

1. Teach only those skills that are reading-related. Select skills that most resemble the reading task itself. For example, teach visual-discrimination skills that require students to discriminate among letters rather than geometric shapes. Don't include skills that require large-muscle activities, such as walking balance beams and catching balls. Such skills are not highly related to reading, and they have no demonstrated payoff for improving reading ability.

2. Be realistic in selecting an order for teaching the chosen skills. By their very nature, lists of specific reading skills are ordered. However, one should keep in mind that relatively little is known about skill hierarchies. So don't become overly concerned about such matters as whether you should teach consonants or vowels as a first step in decoding. Obviously, most children will need both if they are to become fluent decoders. Although some beginning readers may be able to grasp the "abstractness" of short vowels quickly and to discriminate among their sounds, others may have difficulty. If you find this, shift gears and adjust instruction accordingly. Don't be locked into *one* instructional sequence if it fails to work with *your* students.

On the other hand, skipping blithely from one sequence to another can cause great confusion and even fatal gaps in skill development. Many programs for skill development assume competence in skills introduced earlier in the sequence. Later skills are taught as though the earlier skills were necessary prerequisites. Therefore, if the students do not have these skills, the skills introduced later may be made more difficult to learn.

No one sequence has been validated. Choose one that makes sense to you, and modify the sequence *carefully* if it doesn't work for you.

3. Once you have identified what you consider to be essential reading skills, don't continually add more skills to the list. If you identify too many skills, you may not be able to provide instruction in all of the skill areas. What you will have is a massive, unwieldy skills list. When it comes to identifying essential skills, longer lists are not necessarily better lists.

Skill Mastery

The inherent assumption underlying skills-management systems is that students need to learn, or master, the identified skills. In most skills-management systems, mastery is determined by performance on a paper-and-pencil test. Usually, a score of 80 percent or higher is considered to be the mastery criterion, although individual systems may use other criterion levels. The mastery of these skills supposedly indicates that the child has the necessary tools to perform tasks such as decoding an unknown word, comprehending sequential events, or locating a book by using the card catalog.

One must keep in mind, however, that students must be able to *apply* the skills they learn. Being able to pass a test is not a demonstration of real learning. Real learning is demonstrated when previously taught reading skills are applied when *reading*. Unfortunately, application is often overlooked when skills are taught. We will discuss the specifics of application in more detail in Chapter 13, "Organizing and Managing Reading Instruction."

Objectives   Once a teacher has identified what he or she considers to be essential reading skills (or has chosen a skills-management system that already has an identified skills list), the next step is to translate these skills into meaningful *reading*-related objectives. It is important that these objectives accurately reflect skills that have been demonstrated to be highly related to the learning-to-read process. The objectives should be clearly stated so that all who read them have a clear understanding of the expected student behaviors.

The characteristics of useful objectives were discussed in Chapter 3. If you feel that you will not have the time and/or expertise to write your own objectives, we have three other options to suggest for selecting your objectives. First, a number of organizations have collected literally thousands of behavioral objectives from educators throughout the country. One such source is the *Instructional Objectives Exchange,* or *IOX* as it is commonly called (1972). Teachers who are interested in revising their reading program might first order the collection of behavioral objectives entitled *Decoding Skills K–12, Structural Analysis K–12,* and *Comprehension Skills K–12.* After examining these objectives, teachers could adopt those that best reflect a comprehensive reading program for their particular grade or level.

A second course would be to examine recent curriculum guides from other communities or from state departments of instruction. These guides are usually available at little cost and provide the reader with insights into what other school districts have done with their respective curricula.

A third option is to examine an already existing commercial reading program that utilizes explicitly stated objectives. Generally, all skills-management systems include behavioral objectives, as do an increasing number of the newer basal-reader programs on the market.

Regardless of the method by which objectives are chosen, the objectives should match the instructional program used and the teacher's concept of reading. Lists of objectives that have been prepared by someone other than the classroom teacher should never be adopted in their entirety without careful scrutiny. These lists can be used as starting points and should be modified to fit the special needs of a particular reading program.

Assessment   The heart of any diagnostic approach to the teaching of reading is the testing program. Previously, the grouping of children for reading instruction has too

Skill development can be measured through criterion-referenced assessment.

often been done largely on the basis of standardized, norm-referenced reading test scores. Although tests of this type permit teachers to make *general* distinctions among students and allow students to be placed in reading groups, they do not permit analysis of *specific* skills or test the same skills that particular programs are designed to teach (Coulson and Cogswell, 1965). In short, they *do* provide some indication of overall reading ability, but they *do not* provide detailed information about the *specific* skill development of a child. To get specific skill-development information, teachers need to use criterion-referenced tests.

Criterion-referenced assessment has frequently been referred to as "mastery testing" or "domain-referenced achievement testing" (Proger and Mann, 1973). Criterion-referenced tests are written to allow educators to measure some particular instructional objective and to help determine whether a child has acquired a particular skill—in this case, a reading skill. Although much has been written about norm-referenced testing versus criterion-referenced testing, the basic difference lies not so much in the tests themselves as in how the test results are interpreted. It is not at all unrealistic to have a criterion-referenced test referenced to a normative group and a norm-referenced test referenced to some criterion (Carver, 1974). Criterion-referenced tests, however, measure skill growth *within* individuals, whereas norm-referenced tests measure growth *among* individuals.

Another basic difference between these two types of measures is the way in which performance is reported. Scores from criterion-referenced tests are usually reported as either raw scores or percentage correct. Norm-referenced test results, on the other hand, are usually reported as percentile rankings, standard scores, or grade-level equivalents.

In elementary school classrooms both types of tests have their place. Criterion-referenced tests allow the teacher to see how well students are meeting program objectives. Norm-referenced tests allow the teacher to compare the overall reading ability of his or her students with other students in the school, school system, state, or nation. (See Chapter 12 for a fuller discussion of evaluation and testing, including a further comparison of criterion-referenced and norm-referenced tests.)

Do not expect to be able to assess all reading skills solely through the use of paper-and-pencil tests. You will always need to exercise professional judgment in order to determine whether a reading skill has really been learned. Observation or other informal procedures that involve subjective judgment are legitimate adjuncts to more formal testing procedures. Ultimately, of course, the real demonstration of children's skill acquisition is their ability to use the skill when reading various kinds of printed material, as noted during frequent observations of reading performance.

Management

A pressing problem for most classroom teachers is that of supplying appropriate instruction, based on need, to all students. Skills-management systems can help even the most experienced teachers in this area, since record-keeping systems are an integral part of these programs. Thus at a moment's glance, a teacher can determine students' specific skill needs.

Types of Record-Keeping Systems

A variety of systems can be used to monitor the reading-skill development of students. In general, each system includes the list of skills in the respective program and a notation system to indicate whether each skill has been mastered. The mastery criterion varies among programs, but usually is considered to be 60 to 100 percent of the items correct on one of the criterion-referenced tests for each skill.

One approach to record keeping is to maintain separate record sheets—usually in a file folder—for each student. One advantage of this recording system is that it can be passed along from one teacher to another. Teachers can also use this record sheet to help point out a student's skill-development progress at parent conferences. A disadvantage of this system, however, is that it is cumbersome to form skill groups from information in each child's folder. Teachers need to look at each folder before they can determine where the skill weaknesses of their students lie. The process of leafing through folder after folder is time-consuming and does not readily lend itself to the formation of ad hoc (temporary) groups.

A second technique to help manage record keeping in skills-management systems is to use a wall chart. One axis of the chart usually lists students' names; the other axis lists the skills taught in the program. As students demonstrate mastery of a skill, the cell marking the intersection of the student's name and a skill is coded in some fashion, e.g., a check mark, the date, the test score. The advantage of the wall chart is that whole-class skill profiles are easily seen, and as a result shifting students into ad hoc skill groups is relatively easy. Some teachers are reluctant to use wall charts, however, since each student's progress can be seen by all members of the class. Whether such a public record is appropriate or not will, of course, depend on how it is viewed by the students. If this technique threatens anyone, the wall chart–type record can be reduced in scale and stored in the teacher's desk.

A third technique for record keeping, and one that has found widespread acceptance, is that of using a key-sort filing system. In this system a card represents each student in the classroom. The skills in the program are written around the periphery of the card next to corresponding holes (see Fig. 4.1). Once the student has mastered a skill, the appropriate hole (representing the skill) is clipped open with a special notcher. When ready to group students for skill instruction, the teacher simply places all of the cards in a stack and runs a skewer through the hole representing the skill of interest. Once the skewer is lifted, cards with that notched hole will fall from the skewer, and unnotched cards will remain on it. Cards on the skewer represent students who have not yet learned the chosen skill.

The advantages of this new system are that it is easy to group students for instruction, only the teacher and the child are aware of the student's skill growth, and the card can be handy when explaining a student's progress to a parent during teacher-parent conferences. The disadvantage of this system is that cards need to be continually updated through the notching process and therefore require constant attention by the teacher. This, however, is true of any type of record-keeping system.

A final technique that can assist in grouping students for skill instruction is to have skill-record information stored in a computer bank. Teachers in schools having computer terminals can query the computer to help them form skill groups. In virtually seconds a total class profile can be printed or ad hoc groups can be identified. The advantages of this system are that records are readily available to all concerned, performance criteria can easily be adapted to show *progress* as well as *mastery*, and the progress of an entire school can easily be monitored by the school reading specialist or principal. The disadvantages in this system are the high cost to run the computer and the need to train individuals to operate the terminal.

WISCONSIN DESIGN FOR READING SKILL DEVELOPMENT

© 1972-The Board of Regents of the University of Wisconsin System   V36037X   LITTON ABS

LEVEL A:

- 1 Rhyming words
- 2 Rhyming phrases
- 3 Shapes
- 4 Letters, numbers
- 5 i — Colors
- 6 Words, phrases
- 7 Initial consonants
- All A skills

WORD ATTACK

NOTE: Skills marked **i** are assessed by a performance test or teacher observation.

LEVEL C:

- 1 i — Sight vocabulary
- 2 Consonant variants
- 3 Consonant blends
- 4 Long vowels
- 5 Vowel + r, a + l, a + w
- 6 Diphthongs
- 7 Long & short oo
- 8 Middle vowel
- 9 Two vowels separated
- 10 Two vowels together
- 11 Final vowel
- 12 Consonant digraphs
- 13 Base words
- 14 Plurals
- 15 Homonyms
- 16 Synonyms, antonyms
- 17 i — Independent application
- 18 Multiple meanings
- All C skills

WISCONSIN DESIGN FOR READING SKILL DEVELOPMENT

PUPIL NAME _____   DATE _____

UNIT ____ GRADE ____ SPECIAL CODE _____   LEVEL _____

SKILL	RS	M	%C

LEVEL D:

- 1 i — Sight vocabulary
- 2 Consonant blends
- 3 Silent letters
- 4 Syllabication
- 5 Accent
- 6 Unaccented schwa
- 7 Possessives
- All D skills

LEVEL B:

- 1 i — Sight vocabulary
- 2 i — Left-right sequence
- 3 Beginning consonants
- 4 Ending consonants
- 5 Consonant blends
- 6 Rhyming elements
- 7 Short vowels
- 8 Consonant digraphs
- 9 Compound words
- 10 Contractions
- 11 Base words
- 12 Plurals
- 13 Possessives
- All B skills

DATE	NO. OF SKILLS	GROWTH

Fig. 4.1. A key-sort filing system for record keeping. (Wisconsin Design Word Attack Profile Card. Reprinted by permission of National Computer Systems.)

As we have just pointed out, the record-keeping systems used in skills-management systems vary widely. Unless student records are kept up to date, however, regardless of which system is used, instruction cannot be attuned to skill needs. If you choose to use a skills-management system, you should be aware that keeping records current is a time-consuming job. When combined with the tasks of administering and scoring tests, grouping students, and providing focused instruction, it may seem overwhelming at times. Fortunately, most management problems associated with record keeping are clerical in nature and can be handled by parent aides or volunteers if these resources are available. The use of paraprofessionals frees the teacher to do more creative and teaching-oriented work. Accurate, up-to-date records enable teachers to provide students with the type of skill instruction they need. It is imperative, then, that records reflect the actual skill development of the students.

The Need for Current Records

The instructional practices followed when implementing a skills-management system do not differ significantly from conventional reading instruction. The major difference between objective-based instruction and conventional instruction is that in the former, instruction is attuned to the diagnosed skill weaknesses of the students, whereas in conventional basal-reader programs most instruction is based on the sequential organization of the packaged program, not on diagnosed skill needs.

Instruction

Objective-based instruction is founded on the concept of mastery learning. This simply means that once students' needs have been identified, instruction is focused on these areas until the students master the skills. This type of instruction usually requires the formation of short-term groups to expedite the teaching of skills. In a typical elementary school classroom in which a skills-management system is being used, the teacher may have two, three, or even more skill groups in operation at any one time. As you might expect, teaching this many skill groups during any one period requires a high degree of managerial talent, because while the teacher is working directly with one group, other children must be profitably engaged in more self-directed activities.

To assist teachers in coping with these numerous groups, many skills-management systems have accompanying compendia of instructional materials that have been keyed by publisher, book, and page number. These materials, in addition to things such as ditto masters, transparency masters, and teacher "idea booklets," can be used to provide practice with the skills explicated in the program.

Teachers face the continual problem of not having enough time to teach the material they know students need. The fact is that a skills-management system, because it takes time to maintain, will bring increased pressure to bear on available time.

Time Constraints

A considerable amount of time is necessary for testing students and recording the results before the teacher can ever begin to think about instruction. We feel that this time is well spent, however, especially when you consider that all children will be receiving instruction according to their diagnosed needs. In fact, in one sense the teacher will be gaining time, because there is no compulsion to teach every skill to every student.

The additional time needed for testing has another beneficial side effect. As each skill is mastered and recorded on the pupil progress card or wall chart, the students can see tangible evidence of progress. Usually students will try harder and enjoy reading more when they can see that they are making progress. We feel that the extra time needed to achieve this type of student attitude is a small price to pay for such a benefit.

Application of Skills   When students receive instruction in skill groups, extensive opportunities need to be provided for the students to apply the skill in reading situations. Although we will spend considerable time talking about this in Chapter 13, it is important to note here that a skills-management system is of no value if the students fail to apply the skills when they need them in story settings.

One way to promote application of skills is to develop lessons in such a way that students are led from highly structured, teacher-directed lessons to more independent, self-directed activities. Suppose, for example, that an ad hoc skill group was formed in order to teach the short vowel sounds in the consonant-vowel-consonant pattern. A block of time would be allocated to teach this skill. During the first two or three days of instruction, most of the activities could center on exercises in which the students learned to recognize and differentiate among the five short vowel sounds and their letters and on activities in which the students used the consonant-vowel-consonant pattern to predict a short vowel sound. Such activities would require the teacher to work closely with the students on all of their activities. All of the instruction would be teacher-led. Once the students were able to discriminate among the vowel sounds and to recognize the consonant-vowel-consonant pattern, however, these skills might be reinforced through the use of chalkboard activities or worksheets. Such activities are less teacher-centered than the exercises done in the first phase of instruction, and the children would complete much of the work independently.

The third and final phase of instruction would be to assign students to read words, phrases, sentences, and paragraphs that required them to apply the learned skills (that is, recognize short vowel words in the consonant-vowel-consonant pattern) in a reading situation. This third phase is too often ignored, but it is vital if students are to be able to *use* their skills. The more that instruction resembles actual reading, the easier it will be for children to apply the skills taught when reading independently.

SOME SPECIFIC SKILLS-MANAGEMENT SYSTEMS   Of the many skills-management systems available, we will describe three commercially prepared ones. Our purpose is not to see "which is best," since such comparisons are relatively meaningless. One of these programs, for example, might be highly appropriate for implementation in one school district but not in another. Our intent is simply to point out that although there is a high degree of similarity among skills-management systems, some characteristics are unique to each program.

The *Design*, as it is commonly called, consists of six distinct program elements: word attack, comprehension, study skills, self-directed reading, interpretive reading, and creative reading (Otto and Askov, 1973). Each element is made up of a series of subskills arranged in a loose hierarchy identified as Levels A–G. Approximately 300 skills are included in the entire *Design*, and an instructional objective has been written for each skill.

Assessing reading skills with the *Design* is done in one of two ways— either formally, with paper-and-pencil tests, or informally, by teacher observation and performance tests. The paper-and-pencil tests (see Fig. 4.2) are easily scored with the scoring keys provided in the appropriate test administrator's manuals. Between 12 and 25 test items are used to assess each skill. Whenever students achieve a score of 80 percent or higher on a test, they are considered to have mastered the respective skill. Alternative forms of the tests are available, thereby permitting one form to be used as a pretest and another as a posttest.

Record keeping in the *Design* is accomplished with *Pupil Profile Cards*. Separate cards are used for the word-attack, comprehension, and study-skill elements (see Fig. 4.1). Student skill development in the remaining elements— self-directed, interpretive, and creative reading—is recorded on one card. As students demonstrate mastery of the respective skills, a special notcher is used to open the hole next to the identified skills. Thus when teachers are ready to group their students for skill instruction, they simply set the cards on their edge, pick the skill they want to teach, run a skewer through the appropriate hole, and lift the cards. Cards having the hole notched open fall from the skewer; those that are not notched (representing students needing skill instruction) remain on the skewer. Students needing instruction are then placed in skill groups for between two and three weeks.

Teachers are assisted in their instructional efforts by the *Teacher's Resource File*, a compendium of published materials that have been keyed to the identified skills in the program by publisher, book or workbook, and page number (see Fig. 4.3). By consulting the file, teachers can prescribe materials that will focus specifically on the skill being taught. Also included in the *Teacher's Resource File* are teaching ideas that have been found useful in teaching the skills.

The *Fountain Valley Teacher Support System in Reading* (1971) is somewhat different from the *Wisconsin Design*. Over 350 specific reading skills have been identified by the developers of the *Fountain Valley System*. Word-analysis skills, vocabulary development, comprehension skills, and study skills have been included in this program.

One major difference between this program and the *Design* is the manner by which reading skills are assessed. The *Fountain Valley System* includes a total of 77 one-page, self-scoring tests. Testing directions for students are supplied on cassette tape recordings. This eliminates the need for test administrator's manuals for teachers. There are generally three test items to measure each of the skills in the program. The prerecorded tapes present the test direc-

NAME _____ DATE _____

Wisconsin Tests of Reading Skill Development © 1972—The Board of Regents of the University of Wisconsin System

Raw Score	1	2	3	4	5	6	7	8	9	10	11	12	13	14	15	16	17	18	19	20
% Correct	5	10	15	20	25	30	35	40	45	50	55	60	65	70	75	80	85	90	95	100

Test 3—Beginning Consonant Sounds

Example
① d
② m
③ t
④ b

Example
○ yes
○ no

1. ① b
   ② p
   ③ d
   ④ v

6. ① n
   ② z
   ③ r
   ④ m

11. ○ yes
    ○ no

16. ○ yes
    ○ no

2. ① b
   ② n
   ③ m
   ④ p

7. ① h
   ② x
   ③ v
   ④ z

12. ○ yes
    ○ no

17. ○ yes
    ○ no

3. ① d
   ② l
   ③ h
   ④ t

8. ① f
   ② v
   ③ t
   ④ b

13. ○ yes
    ○ no

18. ○ yes
    ○ no

4. ① m
   ② n
   ③ r
   ④ t

9. ① r
   ② l
   ③ t
   ④ y

14. ○ yes
    ○ no

19. ○ yes
    ○ no

5. ① t
   ② f
   ③ c
   ④ g

10. ① t
    ② k
    ③ p
    ④ d

15. ○ yes
    ○ no

20. ○ yes
    ○ no

Fig. 4.2.   Sample paper-and-pencil test for assessing a reading skill. (Wisconsin Design Word Attack Test—Level B, Test 3. Reprinted by permission of National Computer Systems.)

Word Attack—Level C
▬▬▬ Skill 2: Consonants and Their Variant Sounds ▬▬▬
Objective

Given words containing variant sounds of *c, s,* and *g* (e.g., *cake-city, sit-trees, go-giant*), the child indicates whether the underlined letters in given pairs of words have the same or different sounds.

Printed Materials

Allyn and Bacon, *Arrivals and Departures,* teacher's ed. (1968), pp. 60-61, 174, 192, 330.

Allyn and Bacon, *Believe and Make-Believe,* teacher's ed. (1968), p. 59.

Allyn and Bacon, *Fields and Fences,* teacher's ed. (1968), p. 298.

Allyn and Bacon, *Finding the Way,* teacher's ed. (1968), pp. 100, 102-103, 234.

Allyn and Bacon, *Letters and Syllables,* teacher's ed. (1971), pp. 31-36, T12.

Allyn and Bacon, *Magic Windows,* teacher's ed. (1968), pp. 119, 270, 281.

Allyn and Bacon, *Open Gates,* teacher's ed. (1969), pp. 116, 138-139.

Allyn and Bacon, *Our School,* teacher's ed. (1968), p. 129.

Allyn and Bacon, *Story Caravan,* teacher's ed. (1968), pp. 80, 149.

Allyn and Bacon, *Syllables and Words,* teacher's ed. (1971), pp. T7, T9, 12, 85-88.

Allyn and Bacon, *Town and Country,* teacher's ed. (1968), pp. 52-54, 175-176, 236, 271, 282.

American Book, *And So You Go! Be On the Go! Can You?,* Workbook, teacher's ed. (1968), pp. 35, 71-72.

American Book, *Can You?,* teacher's ed. (1968), p. 52a.

American Book, *Days and Ways,* teacher's ed. (1968), pp. 27a, 27b, 36a, 48b, 71a, 87a, 143a, 151a, 176, 181, 188.

American Book, *Days and Ways,* Workbook, teacher's ed. (1968), pp. 9, 19, 37, 44.

American Book, *Each and All,* teacher's ed. (1968), pp. 62a, 62b, 174, 220.

American Book, *Far and Away,* teacher's ed. (1968), pp. 57a, 57b, 73, 213, 222, 229.

American Book, *Far and Away,* Workbook, teacher's ed. (1968), p. 74.

American Book, *Gold and Silver,* teacher's ed. (1968), pp. 112, 133, 157.

American Book, *Gold and Silver,* Workbook, teacher's ed. (1968), p. 68.

American Book, *High and Wide,* teacher's ed. (1968), pp. 50, 67, 164, 164b, 235.

American Book, *Ideas and Images,* teacher's ed. (1968), pp. 172, 268.

American Book, *Kings and Things,* teacher's ed. (1971), p. 25.

American Book, *Launchings and Landings,* teacher's ed. (1968), p. 71b.

American Book, *Pattern Resources: Phonics Kit A* (1970), nos. 31, 65, 66.

American Book, *Pattern Resources: Phonics Kit C* (1970), nos. 177, 179, 183, 185.

American Education Publications, *Phonics and Word Power,* Program 1: Book B (1965), pp. 19-20.

American Education Publications, *Phonics and Word Power,* Program 2: Book C (1964), p. 6.

American Education Publications, *Phonics and Word Power,* Program 3: Book A (1964), pp. 6, 7.

American Education Publications, *Reading Success Series,* Scores 1-6, teacher's guide (1969), pp. 23, 24.

Benefic, *Reading Laboratory* (1966), Kit 405, card 6.

Continental Press, *Adventures in Wordland E* (1960), pp. 26-27.

Continental Press, *Phonics and Word-Analysis Skills,* Grade 3: Part 1 (1968), p. 14.

Continental Press, *Phonics and Word-Analysis Skills,* Grade 4: Part 1 (1968), p. 2.

Continental Press, *Phonics and Word-Analysis Skills,* Grade 4: Part 2 (1968), p. 2.

Continental Press, *Phonics and Word-Analysis Skills,* Grade 5: Part 2 (1969), p. 6.

Economy, *Keys to Independence in Reading,* Grade 4, teacher's manual (1964), pp. 49, 121.

Economy, *Phonetic Keys to Reading,* Grade 1, teacher's manual (1967), pp. 50-51, 70, 109.

Economy, *Phonetic Keys to Reading,* Grade 2, teacher's manual (1967), pp. 24-25, 27-28, 29, 66-72, 75, 130-133.

Economy, *Phonetic Keys to Reading,* Grade 3, teacher's manual (1967), pp. 67, 69, 105-106, 119.

Ginn, *All Sorts of Things,* teacher's ed. (1969), pp. 62, 64, 75, 77, 81-82, 186, 209, 210-211, 226, 314-315, 324.

Fig. 4.3. Sample *Wisconsin Design* compendium of published materials. (Wisconsin Design Word Attack Teacher's Resource File. Reprinted by permission of National Computer Systems.)

tions to the student. After the test is completed, the top sheet of the self-scoring test paper is removed to reveal the student's correct responses.

The student's skill-development record is maintained on the *Continuous Pupil Progress Profile in Reading* folder (see Fig. 4.4). Just as with the *Design's Profile Card*, the *Progress Profile* becomes a part of the student's school records. Check marks are used to denote a student's skill-development mastery.

Instruction in this program is facilitated by the teacher's *Teaching Alternatives Supplement*, a listing of commercial language arts programs whose skills have been cross-referenced to the *Fountain Valley* skills. Teachers wishing to teach specific skills, therefore, need only consult the *Supplement* in order to determine which materials would be most appropriate for the chosen lesson.

Prescriptive Reading Inventory

The *Prescriptive Reading Inventory (PRI)*, published by McGraw-Hill (1972), is designed for use in grades 1–6. Seven cognitive skill categories have been included in the program:

1. Recognition of sound and symbol;
2. Visual discrimination;
3. Phonic analysis;
4. Structural analysis;
5. Translation;
6. Literal, interpretive, and critical comprehension;
7. Study skills.

Ninety discrete skills are identified, and objectives have been written to correspond with each skill. The skills, according to the publisher, are those which occurred most frequently in five basal-reading programs that were examined.

Student skill development is assessed in the *PRI* with four machine-scorable test booklets. The levels are color-coded by grade level: Level A (grades 1.5–2.5); Level B (grades 2.0–3.5); Level C (grades 3.0–4.5); Level D (grades 4.0–6.5). After being administered, the tests are machine-scored, and test results are stored in a computer bank.

Grouping students for skill instruction is facilitated by computer-printed student (see Fig. 4.5) and class profiles (see Fig. 4.6). These profiles are mailed to the schools once the tests have been scored.

To help the teacher provide appropriate instruction, *Program Reference Guides* may be purchased separately from the publisher. These guides list commercially available textbooks and materials that have been keyed to the specific program objectives. The guides classify materials into two categories: those which students can work on independently and those requiring teacher supervision.

Continuous Pupil PROGRESS PROFILE in READING

DIRECTIONS TO THE TEACHER: These profiles are to be used as a continuous record of the pupil's progress in reading. There is a separate profile for each skill area: Phonetic Analysis, Structural Analysis, Vocabulary Development, Comprehension and Study Skills. In recording the results of each test, make sure you are using the correct skill profile. Each one indicates the objectives on individual tests.

Count the number of incorrect responses for each behavioral objective. Based on the scoring instructions, write the date of the test beside the skill in the "Proceed" or "Reteach" column. At the beginning of the Phonetic Analysis profile is a list of letters representing perceptual-type problems. If a skill number followed by one of these letters is circled, write the letter next to the date of the test beside the skill, and place a check (✓) under "A" for auditory or "V" for visual in the reteach column. See teacher's manual for complete directions.

WORD ANALYSIS / Phonetic Analysis

	Reteach A	V	Proceed			Reteach	Proceed	
a. audio-visual reversals			1-21. long vowel 'e'					
b. m-n-h substitutions			1-22. long vowel 'i'					
c. r-l substitutions			1-23. long vowel 'o'					
d. f-th substitutions			1-24. long vowel 'u'					
e. b-d-p reversals			1-25. regular vowel combination 'ee'					
f. th-wh substitutions			1-26. regular vowel combination 'ay'					
g. s-f substitutions			1-27. 'y' as a vowel					
h. sh-ch substitutions			1-28. irregular vowel combination 'ow'					RED PART 4
i. s-th substitutions			1-29. irregular vowel combination 'ōw'					
p-1. initial consonant 'b'			1-30. irregular vowel combination 'ew'					
p-2. initial consonant 'c'			1-31. murmur diphthong 'ar'					
p-3. initial consonant 'd'			1-32. murmur diphthong 'er'					
p-4. initial consonant 'f'			1-33. murmur diphthong 'ir'					
p-5. initial consonant 'g'			1-34. murmur diphthong 'ur'					
p-6. initial consonant 'h'			1-35. initial consonant 'k'					
p-7. initial consonant 'j'			1-36. initial blend 'sp'					
p-8. initial consonant 'l'			1-37. initial blend 'st'					
p-9. initial consonant 'm'			1-38. initial blend 'sl'					RED PART 5
p-10. initial consonant 'n'			1-39. initial blend 'sm'					
p-11. initial consonant 'p'			1-40. initial blend 'sw'					
p-12. initial consonant 'r'			1-41. initial blend 'spr'					
p-13. initial consonant 's'			1-42. initial blend 'fl'					
p-14. initial consonant 't'			1-43. initial blend 'bl'					
p-15. initial consonant 'w'			1-44. initial blend 'cl'					
p-16. initial consonant 'y'			1-45. initial blend 'tr'					
p-17. initial digraph 'sh'			1-46. initial blend 'gr'					
p-18. initial digraph 'wh'			1-47. initial blend 'cr'					RED PART 6
1-1. final consonant 'd'			1-48. initial blend 'fr'					
1-2. final consonant 'k'			1-49. phonetic part 'qu'					
1-3. final consonant 'l'			1-50. initial digraph 'ch'					
1-4. final consonant 'm'			1-51. initial digraph 'kn'					
1-5. final consonant 'n'			1-52. initial digraph 'th' (voiced)					
1-6. final consonant 'p'			1-53. initial digraph 'th' (unvoiced)					
1-7. final consonant 'r'			2-1. initial consonant 'z'					
1-8. final consonant 't'			2-2. initial consonant 'v'					
1-9. final consonant 'x'			2-3. hard 'g'					
1-10. final phonetic part 'st'			2-4. soft 'g'					ORANGE PART 1
1-11. final phonetic part 'ng'			2-5. regular vowel combination 'ai'					
1-12. final phonetic part 'ch'			2-6. regular vowel combination 'ea'					
1-13. final phonetic part 'ck'			2-7. regular vowel combination 'oa'					
1-14. final phonetic part 'll'			2-8. initial digraph 'ch' (k)					
1-15. short vowel 'a'			2-9. irregular vowel combination 'aw'					
1-16. short vowel 'e'			2-10. phonetic part 'sch'					
1-17. short vowel 'i'			2-11. initial digraph 'gu'					
1-18. short vowel 'o'			2-12. final consonant 's'					ORANGE PART 2
1-19. short vowel 'u'			2-13. final blend 'nk'					
1-20. long vowel 'a'			2-14. final blend 'nd'					

Left margin groupings: RED PART 1, RED PART 2, RED PART 3

STOCK NO. 401001

Fig. 4.4. Sample *Fountain Valley* **skill-development record. (Excerpted from the** *Fountain Valley Teacher Support System in Reading,* **Copyright 1971; Richard L. Zweig Associates, Inc., 20800 Beach Blvd., Huntington Beach, California 92648. Reprinted by permission of the publisher.)**

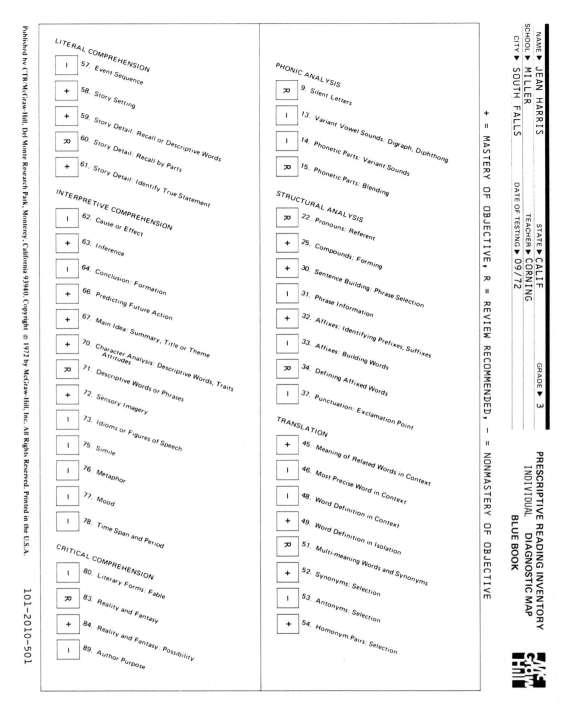

Fig. 4.5. *PRI* student profile. (Reprinted with permission of the publisher, CTB/ McGraw-Hill, Del Monte Research Park, Monterey, CA 93940. Copyright © 1974 by McGraw-Hill, Inc. All rights reserved. Printed in the U.S.A.)

```
TEACHER   CORNING        31    GRADE           3
SCHOOL    MILLER          3    PROCESS NUMBER  2010-101
CITY      SOUTH FALLS     1    DATE OF TESTING 09/72
STATE     CA                   RUN DATE        10/03/72
```

PRESCRIPTIVE READING INVENTORY

CLASS GROUPING REPORT

BLUE BOOK (C)

NAMES	PHONIC ANALYSIS	STRUC ANALYSIS	TRANS-LATION	LITERAL COMP	INTERP COMP I	INTERP COMP II	CRITICAL COMP
BRISCOE, NANCY			*		*	*	*
BROWNE, FRANKLIN	*	*				*	*
CALABRESE, TONY	*	*		*			
DAVIDSON, MAL	*	*	*			*	*
DAVIS, ERNESTINE			*	*		*	*
ELDER, LYNN	*	*			*		
FELICIANO, MIGUEL	*		*	*		*	*
HARRIS, JEAN	*	*				*	*
MINOR, MORRIS	*	*		*		*	*
WOOD, JENNIFER			*		*	*	
TOTAL IN GROUP	7	6	5	4	3	8	7

NOTE - IF A COLUMN IS EMPTY, NO STUDENT NEEDS INSTRUCTION IN THAT CATEGORY

NO. STUDENTS FOR OBJECTIVE

PHONIC ANALYSIS
     9 SILENT LETTERS...........................4
    13 VARIANT VOWEL SOUNDS-DIGRAPH,DIPHTHONG....7
    14 PHONETIC PARTS-VARIANT SOUNDS.............7
    15 PHONETIC PARTS-BLENDING...................5
STRUCTURAL ANALYSIS
    22 PRONOUNS-REFERENT.........................4
    25 COMPOUNDS-FORMING.........................1
    30 SENTENCE BUILDING-PHRASE SELECTION........3
    31 PHRASE INFORMATION........................6
    32 AFFIXES-IDENTIFYING PREFIXES,SUFFIXES.....4
    33 AFFIXES-BUILDING WORDS....................6
    34 DEFINING AFFIXED WORDS....................5
    37 PUNCTUATION-EXCLAMATION POINT.............6
TRANSLATION
    45 MEANING OF RELATED WORDS IN CONTEXT.......2
    46 MOST PRECISE WORD IN CONTEXT..............5
    48 WORD DEFINITION IN CONTEXT................5
    49 WORD DEFINITION IN ISOLATION..............3
    51 MULTI-MEANING WORDS AND SYNONYMS..........4
    52 SYNONYMS-SELECTION........................3
    53 ANTONYMS-SELECTION........................5

NO. STUDENTS FOR OBJECTIVE

LITERAL COMPREHENSION
    57 EVENT SEQUENCE............................3
    58 STORY SETTING.............................4
    59 STORY DETAIL-RECALL OR DESCR. WORDS.......4
    61 STORY DETAIL-IDENTIFY TRUE STATEMENTS.....2
INTERPRETIVE COMPREHENSION I
    62 CAUSE OR EFFECT...........................2
    63 INFERENCE.................................2
    64 CONCLUSION-FORMATION......................3
    66 PREDICTING FUTURE ACTION..................2
    70 CHARACTER ANALYSIS-DESCR.WORDS,TRAITS.....3
INTERPRETIVE COMPREHENSION II
    71 DESCRIPTIVE WORDS AND PHRASES.............4
    72 SENSORY IMAGERY...........................3
    73 IDIOMS OR FIGURES OF SPEECH...............8
    75 SIMILE....................................7
    76 METAPHOR..................................8
    77 MOOD......................................5
    78 TIME SPAN AND PERIOD......................6
CRITICAL COMPREHENSION
    80 LITERARY FORMS-FABLE......................4
    83 REALITY AND FANTASY.......................5
    84 REALITY AND FANTASY-POSSIBILITY...........6
    89 AUTHOR PURPOSE............................7

Fig. 4.6. *PRI* class profile. (Reprinted with permission of the publisher, CTB/McGraw-Hill, Del Monte Research Park, Monterey, CA 93940. Copyright © 1974 by McGraw-Hill, Inc. All rights reserved. Printed in the U.S.A.)

APPLICATION: SELECTING A SKILLS- MANAGEMENT SYSTEM

By this point you should be well acquainted with skills-management systems and the advantages of using them. We have also tried to alert you to the short-comings of these systems. To help you select a skills-management system for your classroom, we have prepared a list of questions to guide you as you review some of these commercially available programs. These questions have been broken down into four major categories that parallel our earlier discussions about skills-management systems. The categories are: (1) skills and objectives; (2) assessment; (3) management; and (4) instruction.

Since many colleges and universities have curriculum resource materials centers and most publishers are interested in providing copies of materials to schools on a loan basis, the most beneficial use of this list of questions is to actually have one or more of the various skills-management systems in front of you as you read the questions. In this way the questions will be more meaningful as you actually evaluate the programs. Furthermore, you may think of additional questions that are pertinent. We hope that you use these questions to help you better understand the distinctions among the various skills-management systems.

Skills and Objectives

1. Are all aspects of reading-skill development covered?
2. Is the number of skills in the program manageable?
3. Are the skills listed in a "commonsense" sequence?
4. Do the skills have a research base?
5. Are the objectives clearly stated in behavioral terms?
6. Are the criterion levels specified in the objectives realistic in terms of expected pupil performance?
7. Are both behavioral (prescriptive) and expressive (descriptive) objectives contained within the program?

Assessment

1. Are the tests group-administerable as well as individually administerable?
2. Does a test manual provide information about test validity and reliability?
3. Are the tests easily scored?
4. Are other means of assessment provided in addition to the paper-and-pencil tests?
5. Are the directions for conducting the assessments clearly stated?
6. Can individual skills be assessed, or must groups or "clusters" be assessed at the same time?
7. Have the tests been field-tested on a large-scale basis?
8. Are technical manuals available for the tests?

Management

1. What type of record-keeping system is provided in the program?
2. Can the records be easily and quickly interpreted?

3. Are there provisions for readily monitoring an individual's skill development? Can progress of the class as a whole be readily monitored?

4. Are records easy to pass on from year to year?

5. Can pupil progress be monitored without using sophisticated hardware?

6. Can the records be easily updated?

Instruction

1. Do instructional materials come with the program?

2. Can the materials be used with any approach to the teaching of reading (e.g., basal reader, language experience, or individualized)?

3. Can supplementary materials be adapted for use with the program?

4. Are materials explicitly keyed by publisher, title, and page number?

5. Are teacher ideas as well as published materials included in the resource listing?

6. Are games and manipulative aids keyed to the skills and objectives?

7. Are audiovisual materials keyed to the skills and objectives?

8. Is there a distinction made between materials that can be used for group instruction and those appropriate for individual instruction?

9. Can additional materials be added easily to the resource list?

SUMMARY: GETTING READY TO TEACH

In this chapter we have introduced you to skills-management systems and how they can help you organize instruction to meet the needs of all students. Although these management systems can be useful in diagnosing students and grouping them for instruction, we have—we hope—alerted you to some of the questions that have been raised regarding their use.

We have also described three popular skills-management systems that are available from publishers. Each of these programs was designed to help you focus reading-skill instruction. These programs are similar in many respects, yet each is unique in one or more ways.

Finally, we provided you with a list of questions for reviewing or selecting a skills-management system. These questions can guide you in making a judicious decision about the strengths and weaknesses of skills-management systems. Now you should be able to organize your instruction as you get ready to teach.

REVIEW QUESTIONS

1. What is objective-based instruction? How does it differ from much of the instruction that takes place in schools you have visited? What first step would you take if you wanted to implement objective-based instruction?

2. If you were explaining the basic characteristics of a skills-management system to a friend, what major points would you touch on?

3. How are most skills-management systems similar? How are they different?

4. Suppose you are trying to convince other teachers in your building to implement a skills-management system. Prepare an outline of the advantages of using such a system. Also include a presentation of potential problems in the use of a skills-management system. For each problem, suggest one or two steps that might be taken to eliminate or minimize the problem.

5. Use the questions in the "Application: Selecting a Skills-Management System" section to evaluate a commercially prepared skills-management system. Then think about which questions were the most valuable to you in making your assessment. Which questions, if any, contributed little to your evaluation?

REFERENCES

Carver, Ronald P. "Two Dimensions of Tests: Psychometric and Edumetric," *American Psychologist* **29**, 7 (1974): 512–515.

Coulson, John E., and John F. Cogswell. "Effects of Individualized Instruction on Testing," *Journal of Educational Measurement* **2**, 1 (1965): 59–69.

Durkin, Dolores. "After Ten Years, Where Are We Now in Reading?" *Reading Teacher* **28**, 1 (1974): 262–267.

Fountain Valley Teacher Support System in Reading. (Fountain Valley, Calif.: Richard L. Zweig Associates, 1971).

Harris, Albert J. "The Effective Teacher of Reading," *Reading Teacher* **23**, 3 (1969): 195–204, 238.

Instructional Objectives Exchange (Box 24095, Los Angeles, California 90024, 1972).

Johnson, Dale D., and P. David Pearson. "Skills Management Systems: A Critique," *Reading Teacher* **28**, 8 (1975): 757–764.

Otto, Wayne, and Eunice Askov. *Rationale and Guidelines*, The Wisconsin Design for Reading Skill Development (Minneapolis: National Computer Systems, 1973).

Powell, William R. "The Effective Reading Teacher," *Reading Teacher* **25**, 7 (1972): 603–607.

Prescriptive Reading Inventory (Monterey, Calif.: CTB/McGraw-Hill, 1972).

Proger, Barton B., and Lester Mann. "Criterion-Referenced Measurement: The World of Gray versus Black and White," *Journal of Learning Disabilities* **6**, 2 (1973): 72–84.

Rude, Robert T. "Objective-Based Reading Systems: An Evaluation," *Reading Teacher* **28**, 2 (1974): 169–175.

Samuels, S. Jay. "Hierarchical Subskills in the Reading Acquisition Process," in John T. Guthrie, Ed. *Aspects of Reading Acquisition* (Baltimore: Johns Hopkins University Press, 1976), pp. 162–179.

Stallard, Cathy. "Comparing Objective-Based Reading Programs," *Journal of Reading* **21** (1977): 36–44.

Stennett, R. G., P. C. Smythe, and Madeline Hardy. "Hierarchical Organization of Reading Subskills: Statistical Approaches," *Journal of Reading Behavior* **7**, 3 (1975): 223–228.

Thompson, Richard A., and Charles D. Dziuban. "Criterion-Referenced Reading Tests in Perspective," *Reading Teacher* **27**, 3 (1973): 292–294.

Part III
Helping Children Develop Reading Strategies: What Children Need to Know

Part II focused on the importance of thinking about the whole reading process in order to better teach to children's individual needs. In Part III we describe what we feel these needs are in the areas of readiness for reading, decoding (saying the words), comprehension, and study skills. We show you what we think needs to be taught and how this content of reading instruction can be measured in order to identify individual needs, and we suggest ways in which these skills can be blended together to provide reading instruction that integrates the parts of reading into a meaningful, fluent whole.

Chapter 5
The Nature of
Readiness

OBJECTIVES FOR THE CHAPTER

After reading this chapter, you will be able to:

1. Describe the "nature/nurture" controversy surrounding reading readiness and explain its implications for teaching.
2. Explain the relationships existing among readiness and chronological age, mental age, sex, experiential background, and language development.
3. Arrive at your own definition of reading readiness.
4. Identify important reading-readiness skills.
5. Select and use readiness tests appropriately.
6. Describe several advantages and disadvantages of using reading-readiness workbooks.
7. Relate how various "training programs" have affected young students' readiness.

Readiness, especially reading readiness, has received much attention from a variety of sources. Parents worry whether their toddlers will be ready for school, and kindergarten teachers fret because not all of their students will be ready for formal reading instruction when they move into first grade. Primary teachers become disturbed if their students do not have the requisite concepts to understand what they read.

Everyone wants children to be "ready." And yet the question remains: "Ready for what?" Before teachers can provide experiences that will lead to "readiness," they must first understand what the objectives of readiness are. They must adopt a definition of readiness on which to build a framework of experiences for developing readiness. They must be aware of factors that affect readiness and of a variety of ways of influencing readiness. In this chapter we discuss each of these topics so that *you* will develop "readiness" for dealing with reading readiness in the classroom.

THE NATURE/ NURTURE CONTROVERSY

Much misunderstanding and confusion surround the concept of readiness. More than almost any other reading-related topic, the question of what to do about readiness has divided educators into two camps. This division of opinion has been termed the nature/nurture controversy. At one end of the continuum are the spokespersons for the developmental, let-the-child-grow-up point of view. They argue: Let maturation take its normal course, and sooner or later the child will be ready for reading instruction. This has become known as the "nature" philosophy. The "nurture" philosophy, found at the other end of the continuum, is based on a more behavioristic theory that teachers should not sit idly by and wait for the child to "become" ready. Those taking the most extreme position on the nurture side of the argument suggest that teachers must provide focused instruction early so that readiness skills can be learned in order that children get the earliest possible start in reading. To help you better understand the underlying reasoning behind these two views of the development of readiness, we will examine each in more detail.

The belief that most children should not be exposed to reading instruction until they are between seven and eight years of age typifies a developmental point of view. This suggested age for beginning reading instruction was determined, in part, from the work of Dr. Arnold Gessell at Yale University. Gessell, a physician, was interested in child behavior and spent many years observing and recording the developmental changes children undergo (Beller, 1970). He was especially interested in children's physical and motor development. The data collected by Dr. Gessell and his associates produced a great deal of interest in child development, and as a result a number of books for parents and educators have been published. Two of the more notable books that have had an effect on educators' views of readiness are *Child Behavior* (Ilg and Ames, 1964) and *School Readiness* (Ilg and Ames, 1972). *Child Behavior* has been read by millions of parents seeking to understand the continual changes that take place as a child grows.

Although the data collected by Gessell were related largely to motor-skill development, educators of the 1920s and 1930s applied his theory of physical development to the development of intellectual functions. Although this application has been questioned (Durkin, 1970), the fact remains that many teachers came to believe that the most important factor in intellectual growth is maturation; in so doing they almost overlooked the interaction between children and their environment. The implication for reading instruction was that if children are not "ready" for reading, they should be allowed to "mature." In essence, many teachers believed that the longer instruction was postponed, the greater were the child's chances of success in learning to read.

During the past quarter of a century additional evidence has been found of the important role that maturation plays in determining whether a child is ready to read. For example, for most preschoolers reading is a mysterious activity. Young children usually have no specific idea of what reading is all about. Downing (1971–1972) and Downing and Oliver (1973–1974) have conducted a series of experiments with young children to better understand four- and five-year-olds' concepts of the terms "word" and "sound." The researchers found that the terms "word," "letter," and "sound" had little meaning to children just entering school. Furthermore, to many of these young children phrases and sentences were synonymous with words. Clearly, these children were not conceptually ready to handle such abstract terminology. By the time these children reached the age of eight, however, this confusion and uncertainty had largely disappeared.

Because young children have only vague notions about the function of reading and writing and have difficulty understanding the terms used in reading instruction, many educators have urged that reading instruction be postponed until children are well into the first grade. Others have argued for postponement because of the evidence presented by Piaget (1954) that children's reasoning powers do not reach a stage of logical operations necessary for reading until children are seven or eight years of age. Still other educators have shown that instruction in decoding before the child is conceptually ready to understand the material is useless (Roberts, 1976). As a

A Nature/Developmental Point of View

result of such premature instruction, children may be able to decode and pronounce words, but may be unable to comprehend what they read (King, 1969). For all of these reasons, those espousing the nature point of view believe that reading readiness cannot be forced or hurried, but will naturally develop as the child matures.

A Nurture/Behavioristic Point of View   Another point of view about readiness is expressed by those who believe that sitting idly by waiting for students to "mature" is wasting valuable time and may also cause some children to become bored with school. Instead, nurture proponents argue, educators should be taking advantage of the insatiable curiosity of young children and should be providing a variety of opportunities for developing their readiness for reading. Such important learning cannot be left to chance. The cognitive development of children must be *nurtured*.

In line with this point of view, many training programs have been developed to teach readiness skills. We discuss some of these efforts in detail later in this chapter. In this section, however, we wish to explain the general theoretical point of view and to present some of the evidence supporting it.

A great deal of evidence has been gathered to indicate that children can learn to read before first grade. For example, Sutton (1965) found that children who had received 15–20 minutes of unstructured reading-readiness training during kindergarten had an increasing advantage in reading over students who had not received such training. At the end of kindergarten, the average score for the readiness group was grade 1.78 on a standardized reading-achievement test. The children in Sutton's program were chosen on the basis of interest and were characterized as "book-hungry." Thus they may not have been representative of kindergartners at large. However, Sutton's study does show that at least some kindergarten children are capable of benefiting from reading-readiness training.

Hillerich (1965) found similar benefits when an unselected group of kindergarten children received training in a structured prereading program. Fowler (1971) demonstrated that even three- and four-year-old children can be taught basic visual and auditory discrimination skills and can in some cases develop a degree of competence in reading sentences and paragraphs.

These three studies are only a small sample of the research that indicates that children *can* develop reading-readiness skills through training in kindergarten. Through *nurture*, these studies claim, nature can be supplemented.

Our Point of View   We believe that reading readiness is a product of both nature *and* nurture. Although this position may be interpreted as a classic example of "fence straddling," we feel that readiness is the product of the interaction between these two variables—"nature" and "nurture." Durkin, who has spent many years investigating readiness for reading, puts it well when she states (1974, p. 123) that "each child's capacity at any given time is the product of both nature and nurture. That is, it is the product of an interplay among genetic endowment, maturation, experiences, and learnings."

Developmental maturation contributes largely to the way young children think and the concepts they acquire. As we have already mentioned, young children do not possess a clear understanding of the technical language of the classroom (i.e., the terms "sound," "letter," "word," or "sentence"). Furthermore, most children do not clearly understand these abstract labels until they have received some type of school training and have reached a chronological age of between seven and eight. Downing (1969) has also suggested that some young children have difficulty understanding the purpose of print. This is not surprising, for two reasons. First, a three- or four-year-old may not be able to conceptualize the idea that the squiggly lines on a page represent the thoughts, ideas, and words of someone else. This *is* a sophisticated concept for a youngster to grasp. Even if young children did perceive the relationship between print and speaking, there is no guarantee that they would understand the *purpose* for print being on a page. These concepts, then, are probably determined largely by maturation *and* exposure to print, or, to put it another way, the interaction between nature and nurture.

Teachers need to be aware that there is little value in trying to teach specific reading skills if the child is not developmentally ready for such instruction. Having students in a class who are "ready" but are not receiving appropriate instruction is equally unforgivable. The teacher must be sensitive to the requirements of each student. This means that a great deal of individualized teaching will be necessary. For example, in almost any kindergarten class there is a good chance that at least one or two of the students will already be reading. Others won't be ready for "formal" instruction until much later. Some students may not be ready for reading until well into first grade—or perhaps not even until second grade. Each of these students needs some type of instruction, however. The teacher must determine how best to develop each child's abilities (nurture) while keeping in mind the child's developmental level (nature).

READINESS AND SOME RELATED FACTORS

In addition to the arguments made for letting the child grow naturally into reading—a nature point of view—and for providing an instructional program designed to enhance readiness—a nurture point of view—many other factors have been suggested as playing a role in readiness for learning to read. We feel that the importance of at least five of these factors (chronological age, mental age, sex, experiential background, and oral-language development) need to be discussed in detail here.

Chronological Age

Because most schools require that children reach the age of six within at least three months of entering first grade, it is quite understandable why being six years old and learning to read have become closely related. The reasoning goes something like this: If you're six years old, you're in first grade; if you're in first grade, you learn to read. Hence, if you are six, you should learn to read. The fallacy of this syllogism lies in the fact that entrance based on chronological age is as arbitrary as the notion that all first graders should learn to read.

Much evidence has been found to indicate that chronological age is not a crucial factor in learning to read (Durkin, 1970, 1974). Simply because the students in a classroom were all born at about the same time does not mean that they possess the same experiences that contribute to a solid readiness foundation or that they have reached the same level of physical or intellectual maturation. Therefore, it is only logical to expect the children in a single classroom to be at many different stages of readiness for reading.

Mental Age Mental age is computed by multiplying a student's chronological age by his or her score on an intelligence test and then dividing by 100. For example, a child with a chronological age of 10 with an IQ of 100 has a mental age of 10. If the child were 10 years old and had an IQ of 120, his or her mental age would be 12. With an IQ of 80, the child's mental age would be 8.

Mental age has long been thought to be closely related to the ability to learn to read. At one time it was thought that unless a student had a mental age of six years and six months, that child was not ready to learn to read. And if the child *was* six and one-half years old, she or he was automatically ready. This "6.5—dead or alive" type of reasoning led some school districts to postpone any type of reading instruction until a student had reached this mental age.

In the past 20 years, however, much evidence has been gathered to indicate that the mental age of a student is only one of many factors that contribute to a successful beginning in reading. A child may be bright but lack a broad experiential background or may have social or emotional characteristics that interfere with learning to read. In addition, the type of instruction the child receives is crucial. To be sure, mental age is important, but it is not the sole determinant of readiness for reading.

Sex Have you ever observed a group of young children engrossed in learning to read? If you have, you've probably noticed how attentive the little girls are when the teacher is presenting a lesson. The boys, however, often seem to lose interest and drift off into their own world. This tendency was evident when one of the authors recently conducted a videotaped demonstration lesson with a group of kindergartners. A review of the videotape soon made clear that the boys in the group were unable to attend to the task for as long as the girls. This phenomenon, as well as girls' generally superior elementary school reading scores, has led some to conjecture that the sex of the student may be closely related to readiness for reading in a *causative* way.

Our position is that although young girls are by and large more ready for school than young boys are, this is not caused by specific genetic factors. Instead, several scholars have demonstrated that sex and reading ability are *culturally* determined. Johnson (1973–1974), for example, demonstrated that in some countries males are better readers than females are. He contends, and we agree, that students will respond to the cultural demands placed on them. In the United States and Canada reading is viewed largely as a female-oriented activity. Hence young boys tend to engage in more nonreading activities than do young girls. When these students enter school, the girls have had more

Children are ready to read at many different ages.

reading-related experiences and are likely to respond better to the instructional program than the boys will. Furthermore, since the majority of primary-grade teachers are women, many boys may fail to identify the teacher as an appropriate model. This may also have some effect on the performance of students.

Experiential background is one of the most important factors in readiness for reading. Parents can play an important part in providing the necessary experiences to ensure a good foundation for reading instruction. Yet the teacher also needs to provide many experiences for students to help them better understand the material they read.

Experiential Background

A broad experiential background can help children become better readers in at least three ways. First, many varied experiences, accompanied by a rich language environment, will help expand students' listening and speaking vocabularies. Later, when the students have acquired sufficient decoding ability to enable them to unlock unknown words, they will have a greater understanding of what the decoded words mean.

A rich background of experiences is also essential for comprehension. A child must have the background of concepts to understand what he or she reads; just being able to say the words is not enough. To illustrate the importance of experiential background, we have constructed the short story below. Undoubtedly, you will be able to read all of the words. You will probably be able to understand the actions that take place. But as you read the story, think about how much you *really* understand of the story.

Raisin Day

Lisa was very excited. Today was Raisin Day, and *she* had been chosen to present the raisins to Grandmother. Of course, she wasn't surprised to have been chosen, because her birthday fell only three days after the first full moon of summer. Lisa carefully washed the raisins in the milk and then put them near the fire to dry. After they were dry, she placed the raisins in the fur-lined egg carton, wrapped the carton in old newspapers, and topped the package with a strand of cold spaghetti. Lisa knew that if she didn't do each step exactly right, she would have to go to her room without brushing her teeth.

Lisa seems to be performing some sort of solemn ritual, but do you understand the significance of the ritual and of each step? Why is the egg carton fur-lined? Since when is going to your room without brushing your teeth a punishment? Who cares what state the moon was in three days before Lisa was born? A child from a restricted background might be similarly confused when reading a story about recycling bottles and cans or having a family portrait taken by a professional photographer (or with a Polaroid camera) or even visiting the dentist. The child is not "ready" to read about and understand such experiences until he or she has at least some basic background in the concepts involved.

Nevius (1977) has suggested a third reason for the importance of a broad base of experiences. Some studies (Siegel, 1972; Wohwill, 1973) have found that emphasizing a multitude of related experiences helped to develop concepts of logical thought. Nevius argues that children who are able to conceptualize the relationships among a set of experiences may also be able to generalize their learnings appropriately to a new set of experiences, thus providing transfer of learning. In this sense a wide experiential background can be considered a prerequisite for the development of certain cognitive abilities.

Oral-Language Development

Without good listening and speaking vocabularies, based on a wide experiential background, a child may have trouble with communication in the classroom as well as with reading itself. Indeed, if the development of any of the three language systems—phonological (sounds), syntactic (grammar), or semantic (meaning)—is delayed, the child may have difficulty in learning to read. (The importance of these language systems to reading is discussed in

Chapter 6.) One of the teacher's most important jobs, regardless of the grade level, is to extend the language development of the students.

Primary-grade teachers can do much to expand the language competence of their students. Reading aloud to children is one of the easiest, yet most effective, ways to develop their experiential background as well as their listening and speaking vocabularies. Providing opportunities for creative play, in which children can explore language freely, is another important means of developing oral-language ability. Modeling, in which the teacher is careful to use the desired language patterns, provides still another way in which language acquisition can be enhanced.

Oral-language development, because it is such an important prerequisite to reading, cannot be overlooked. Many students come to school with large listening and speaking vocabularies. Others come from homes in which language has not been as valued; hence these students will need additional activities to develop their language competence. The teacher must provide the necessary background experiences and opportunities to use language that will enable all students to have a successful beginning when learning to read.

Having talked about two theories of the development of readiness and some factors often thought to be related to readiness, we must now give an operational definition of reading readiness. This leaves us in somewhat of a quandary, because the concept of readiness is so complex that it defies a simple definition. However, we shall try.

AN OPERATIONAL DEFINITION OF READINESS

As you discovered in reading Chapter 2, no one explanation of the reading process (or to be more correct, *processes*) has been widely accepted or empirically validated. This lack of consensus about what constitutes reading makes it difficult to construct a single definition of reading readiness. Just as beauty is in the eyes of the beholder, so too is readiness largely in the eyes of the teacher. Or, to put it another way, readiness for reading will be largely dependent on the reading program the student will be placed in. A student may be ready for one reading program but not for another.

Another difficulty in defining "readiness" is, as we have discussed, that readiness is not a unitary concept. It is not composed of just one factor. Durkin (1970) has suggested that it may be more appropriate to think of several *readinesses* rather than a readiness. Others have also suggested that this may lead to a more enlightened view of reading readiness (Beller, 1970; Cashdan, 1973; Rude, 1975). Therefore, keeping in mind both that little agreement has been reached about what reading is and that readiness appears to be multifaceted, we suggest that readiness for reading be thought of as having those capacities or characteristics necessary for relatively easy acquisition of basic reading abilities in a particular program.

This proposed definition has at least two direct implications for the instructional program. First, a child's readiness program should consist of activities related to the specific beginning-reading program that will be used with that child. If the reading program places great emphasis on sounds, the readiness program should prepare the child to work with sounds. If the reading program involves a great deal of independent work, the child should be helped to develop the ability to work without the continual guidance of the teacher. The teacher should always ask of his or her readiness program: "Readiness for *what*?"

In addition, if the readiness program is directly related to the reading program that is to follow, as it should be, many of the readiness activities will be almost indistinguishable from beginning-reading activities. Readiness will become a natural part of the overall *reading* program, not an entirely separate entity that bears little relationship to the tasks of the beginning-reading program.

To recapitulate, a teacher's concept of readiness should be tied to the overall reading program. "Readinesses" may vary from program to program, depending on the methods and materials a particular school emphasizes. The best way to determine whether students are ready for reading instruction is to provide many and varied opportunities for them to come in contact with words, books, and language. Observing students in a rich learning environment will help the teacher determine whether they are indeed ready for reading.

IMPORTANT READING-READINESS SKILLS

So far, we have been talking about readiness in rather abstract terms. As a person who may be working with five-, six-, or seven-year-olds each day, you're probably anxious for specific advice to help you get students "ready" for reading instruction.

Otto *et al.* (1974) propose a system that we think makes eminent sense. Instead of simply listing a myriad of readiness skills, they suggest that readiness skills be grouped into two categories: high-priority skills and low-priority skills. We will discuss the high-priority skills further in Chapter 6. Rather than elaborate on them here, suffice it to say that the five high-priority skills—letter orientation, letter order, and detail in letter strings (visual skills) and sound matching and blending (auditory skills)—have been demonstrated to be critical ones for success in most beginning-reading programs. Lower-priority reading skills also have a role in learning to read. Ability to attend to a task, linguistic awareness, understanding a task, pattern recognition, and motor skills should be considered when evaluating a student's readiness (Otto *et al.*, 1974; Stanchfield, 1971; and Wanat, 1976).

Visual Discrimination

Since reading is deriving meaning from the printed page, it is only natural that visual discrimination should be considered an important part of any readiness program. Visual discrimination, sometimes confused with visual acuity, is the ability to discern likenesses and differences in shapes. Visual acuity, on the other hand, is "keenness of vision, usually measured at near-point, 14 to 18 inches, and at far-point, 20 feet or more" (Spache, 1976, p. 18). Unless students have good vision, they will be unable to develop adequate visual-discrimination ability. All beginning readers should have their vision checked at both near-point *and* far-point.

We have observed countless lessons in which kindergarten and first-grade teachers doled out worksheets asking students to "put an *X* on the fruit that is different" or "circle all of the triangles in the first row on your paper." These teachers may have good intentions, but their instruction is misdirected. Most young students have little difficulty discriminating shapes and pictures (Hall, 1976; Paradis and Peterson, 1975). Our work with children from affluent suburban homes as well as inner-city schools tends to confirm this. When we do find occasional students who fail to discriminate a triangle from a set of squares, it is usually because they do not understand the assigned task, not because they have some gross visual anomaly. A particular student may have marked a square instead of a triangle because of the *color* of the square, not the shape, or because of its position in the row.

Our point is simply that the teacher probably is wasting a good portion of his or her instructional time by continually asking students to complete visual-discrimination tasks such as those we've just described. Visual-discrimination instruction will be more beneficial if the students are required to discriminate among letters. After all, children read letters, not geometric shapes or pictures!

Although efforts requiring students to discriminate among pictures or geometric forms may have minimal carry-over to later reading skills, having students discriminate between letters or letterlike forms will prove to be very beneficial. However, rather than just having children practice matching letter shapes, the teacher would be wise to point out the distinctive features of the letters. In this way the children will be more likely to learn what aspects of the letters they should be attending to. For example, if a child is just beginning to discriminate letters, the teacher might point out that *t* has all straight lines and *s* has all curved lines. Later, to help the child differentiate between *m* and *n*, the teacher might call the child's attention to the second "hump" in *m*.

Gibson (1965) has done extensive research in the area of visual discrimination. Using letterlike forms, she discovered that visual-discrimination ability improves between the ages of four and eight. She also documented what most experienced primary-grade teachers have said for some time; namely, that some differences between letterlike shapes are more difficult to discriminate than others. Gibson suggests that the best thing to do for children who cannot differentiate among letters is to provide exercises that require the students to discriminate between the specific letters with which they are having problems. For example, if Tom confused *b* and *d*, he might be asked to put a red line under all of the *b*'s in *dbddbdb*. However, if Amanda confused *b* and *p*, not *b* and *d*, she would be asked to put a red line under the *b*'s in *pbpbbppb*.

Careful planning of visual-discrimination activities is important so that there will be carry-over, or transfer, to later reading. Several games and other activities can be used to teach basic visual-discrimination skills to children.

Figure 5.1 shows a board game designed to teach *letter order*. Students are asked to select from the array the letter pair that matches the sample (to the left of the vertical line). The letter pairs in the activity in Fig. 5.1 would probably be relatively easy to discriminate. More similar combinations of letters would require more astute perception, however. For example, the child might have more difficulty discriminating among PB/BP PB BP or TX/TX XT XT. For students who could discriminate among upper-case letter pairs, the difficulty of the activity could be increased again by switching to lower-case letters, such as lt/tl lt tl. Another way of making the activity even more difficult would be to increase the number of letters in each set from two to three. Later, even four letters could be used, such as tmrh/tmhr trmh tmrh.

Other activities might be developed to teach discrimination of *letter orientation*. Letter-orientation training focuses on problems of reversals and rotations of letters such as *b, p, d,* and *q.* Figure 5.2 illustrates some examples of difficult letter pairs that might be used to provide practice in discriminating letter orientation.

A final visual-discrimination skill of importance to reading is *word detail.* The term "word" is used loosely and simply implies that three or more letters can be construed as being a "word" whether in actuality they do or do not constitute a "real word." Since at this stage of instruction students should possess no reading ability, all words are in essence "nonsense" words. (If they *can* read, they have no business doing "readiness" exercises in visual discrimination!) Figure 5.3 shows examples of "words" which could be used to teach word detail.

These activities may be viewed as starter ideas from which to create more activities. Depending on the abilities of the students, the activities may be made easier or more difficult. In addition, many commercial activities are available for visual-discrimination practice. However, care must be taken that commercially prepared activities actually work with letters and not just shapes.

AO	OA	AO	OA
JP	PJ	PJ	JP
LS	LS	SL	SL
VE	EV	EV	VE
PL	PL	LP	LP
QB	BQ	BQ	QB
GH	HG	GH	HG
OS	SO	SO	OS

Fig. 5.1. Letter-order activity

dp	dp	bp	pd
qu	pu	qn	qu
bg	dg	bg	gd
db	bd	dd	db
bu	up	bn	bu
nb	up	bn	nb

Fig. 5.2. Letter-orientation activity.

slu	cml	jul	slu
ess	oss	sme	ess
was	wos	was	waz
mup	mup	mak	sup
klum	mupl	jlum	klum
home	home	name	hone
read	road	reed	read

Fig. 5.3. Word-detail activity.

Acuity and discrimination are separate elements of the auditory process as well as of the visual process. Auditory *acuity* refers to an individual's ability to hear various frequencies at different intensities of loudness (Ekwall, 1976). Frequencies are measured in cycles per second, whereas loudness is measured in decibels. Auditory *discrimination* refers to an individual's ability to hear differences in sounds. Asking a child to tell whether he or she hears the same beginning sound in *fan* and *fat* is an example of requiring a student to use auditory discrimination.

Auditory Discrimination

Another important reading skill that is a prerequisite for good phonic-analysis ability is sound matching—the ability of an individual to take a given sound and match it to an identical sound. For example, a teacher might supply a sound to a child (such as the *s* sound as in *sink*) and have him or her match the sound to the initial sound of a picture, choosing from pictures of a mop, a numeral six, and a dog. This type of matching can be done using pictures having the sound in the initial, medial, or final position.

Sound Matching

Sound blending, another important auditory skill, refers to the ability to take isolated, segmented sounds and blend them into known words. Blending the individual sounds of the word *f-i-sh* into a recognizable word, for example, is a skill that many beginning readers do not have. Yet if students are expected to decode words using phonic-analysis skills, they must be able to blend sounds together.

Sound Blending

The close relationship between auditory discrimination and reading achievement has long been recognized, but only recently have auditory-discrimination skills been taught to very young children (Rosner, 1974). Such training appears to be especially important for children from lower socioeconomic backgrounds, because many of these children do not appear to have adequate auditory discrimination (Paradis and Peterson, 1975). If these children are to succeed in reading programs that use phonics, they must receive instruction in auditory discrimination.

Application: Auditory-Discrimination Activities

In this section we have described several activities that should help generate ideas that you can use in your classroom to teach auditory-discrimination skills. Figure 5.4 illustrates a game that requires the student to look at the pictures of two objects placed on an oaktag card. The student identifies each picture and listens for the first sound in each word. If the two words begin with the same sound, the card is placed in the *yes* pocket of the chart. If the words begin with different sounds, the card is placed in the *no* pocket. If the correct response is printed on the reverse side of each card, the students can check their own work, without teacher help.

Different people or animals can be drawn holding the *yes/no* pockets. When working on the letter sound of *m*, for example, a *mischievous monkey* might be an appropriate figure to hold the pockets. A *silly seal* could be used to help identify the sound of *s*.

Fig. 5.4. Sound-matching activity.

A variation of this type of game would be to ask the student to choose the one picture of three that does not have the same beginning sound as others in the set. Figure 5.5 shows an example of this kind of exercise.

Exercises such as those described will permit the teacher to quickly assess whether students are able to match pictures on the basis of beginning sounds. Several sets of pictures may be grouped together on a worksheet for this purpose. Or, if each set of pictures is attached to oaktag, children can identify the odd member of the set while a teacher, aide, or older student monitors their performance.

To help students learn to blend isolated sounds into meaningful words, the teacher might pronounce individual sounds and ask the children to supply the complete word. Thus the word *sail* might be broken into two parts: *s/ail.** Other words following this pattern are *b/oat*, *p/ile*, or *c/ake.* Each of those examples requires the blending together of two sound units. An advanced skill would require students to blend three separate sounds or sound units: *s/i/t*, *p/e/t*, and *bl/o/ck*.

Of course, once students have mastered the auditory-discrimination skills we have described, they will need to learn to recognize letters in words and to know their representative sounds before they can blend sounds into meaningful words. Activities for developing these skills are presented in Chapter 6.

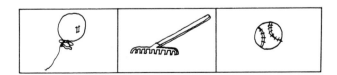

Fig. 5.5. Sound-matching activity.

*Avoid making an "uh" sound after an isolated consonant sound, as in the *s* sound (/s/) in this example.

Readiness tests are instruments that have been developed to help teachers predict which students will be successful in learning to read and to help identify those who may need additional work before they are ready for reading instruction. Although readiness tests can be very helpful to the classroom teacher, users of these tests should be aware of three important generalizations about the use of readiness tests:

1. Readiness tests are predictive, not diagnostic, instruments.
2. One test is not "just as good" as another for assessing readiness for a particular reading program. Different tests assess different skills in different ways.
3. A readiness test should be considered only one source of information about a student's readiness to begin reading instruction.

Because these three generalizations are often ignored by teachers and administrators, we will discuss each of them in detail.

Over the years there has been a growing tendency away from using readiness tests for their original purpose, that is, to predict later success in reading. More and more people now (incorrectly) perceive readiness tests to be diagnostic in nature. Because each readiness test consists of a series of subtests, many teachers have come to believe that each subtest measures a skill prerequisite to reading. If a child does poorly on a subtest of a specific skill, the child is often considered to lack that skill. Most readiness tests, however, were not designed to be used as a set of criterion-referenced (mastery) tests. They were developed to be used as norm-referenced tests. Individual subtests of readiness tests are usually not sufficiently reliable to be used separately for specific diagnosis. The entire readiness battery should be used to provide information about a child's *general* readiness for reading.

Another confusing aspect of readiness tests is that these tests measure many different skills (Rude, 1973). Table 5.1 illustrates this point. Five popular readiness tests are listed: The *Metropolitan Readiness Tests* (Hildreth *et al.*, 1965), the *Murphy-Durrell Reading Readiness Analysis* (Murphy and Durrell, 1965), the *Clymer-Barrett Pre-reading Battery* (Clymer and Barrett, 1969), the *Gates-MacGinitie Reading Test—Readiness Skills* (Gates and MacGinitie, 1968), and the *Harrison-Stroud Reading Readiness Profiles* (Harrison and Stroud, 1950). As you can see, each test battery measures a different set of skills. When selecting a readiness test, the teacher should look at the specific subtests of that battery to see if they evaluate the skills needed for success in the reading program that will be used.

A quick glance at the subtest names may not really tell the teacher what skills are measured. If you examine each of the specific subtests in the five batteries in Table 5.1, you will note that some subtests measure the same skills, yet are labeled differently. For example, the category entitled *Letter recognition* includes subtests labeled *Alphabet, Letter names, Recognition of letters, Letter recognition,* and *Giving the names of the letters.* Unless the teacher

TABLE 5.1 Skills tested by five readiness tests	Skill	Metro-politan	Murphy-Durrell	Test Clymer-Barrett	Gates-MacGinitie	Harrison-Stroud
	Vocabulary development	Word meaning*				
	Listening	Listening			Listening, comprehension, and following directions	Using the context and using context and auditory clues
	Letter recognition	Alphabet	Letter names	Recognition of letters	Letter recognition	Giving the names of the letters
	Numbers	Numbers				
	Visual-motor coordination	Copying		Shape completion and copy-a-sentence	Visual-motor coordination	
	Rhyming words			Discrimination of ending sounds in words		
	Phoneme correspondences		Phonemes	Discrimination of beginning sounds in words		Making auditory discrimination
	Learning rate		Learning rate			
	Auditory discrimination				Auditory discrimination	
	Auditory blending				Auditory blending	
	Word recognition				Word recognition	
	Matching	Matching		Matching words	Visual discrimination	Using symbols and making visual discriminations

*Subtest titles are given in the appropriate cells.

Robert T. Rude, "Readiness Tests: Implications for Early Childhood Education," *Reading Teacher* (March 1973): 574. Reprinted by permission.

examines the tasks the children are required to do, she or he may not get a true picture of what is being tested.

No matter how thorough a readiness test is or how closely related it is to the beginning-reading program, the teacher should keep in mind that readiness tests, like all other tests, measure only a small part of a student's knowledge or overall skill development at a single point in time. Many aspects of readiness, such as attention span, language development, and experiential background, are not assessed by most readiness tests. These readiness characteristics are just as important as those that can be easily measured by pencil-and-paper tests. The teacher must be careful to include his or her personal observation of such traits in the overall assessment of a child's readiness. Reading-readiness assessment must be an ongoing process that includes daily observation of the child. A paper-and-pencil test can be only one part of a more comprehensive readiness evaluation.

One problem with using teacher observation to help assess readiness (or any other aspect of reading behavior) is that the information gained from such observation may be so disorganized that it can never be retrieved. Teachers may help systematize their observations by keeping a file folder for each child with samples of the child's daily work. In addition to gathering work samples, such as completed worksheets or bits of letter copying, the teacher should include anecdotal comments on these samples. A sheet on which Becky got all the answers right might include the notation, "Becky raced through this the first time and had to do it again. It was easy for her once she took her time." Contrast this with the comment on Maggie's perfect paper: "I had to sit with Maggie and help her with *each* example. She just didn't understand!"

A teacher may choose to organize personal observations by using a checklist. The teacher might list the behaviors or characteristics felt to be essential to reading readiness and then place a check (and possibly the date) whenever she or he felt that the child had consistently exhibited that behavior. The *Clymer-Barrett Prereading Battery* (Clymer and Barrett, 1969) includes such a checklist for teachers who do not care to construct their own lists.

Readiness tests are valuable tools for helping a teacher decide if children should begin formal reading instruction. Like all tests, though, reading-readiness tests must be used intelligently and above all must be viewed as contributing only a *portion* of the information needed for deciding if the children are "ready."

USING READINESS WORKBOOKS

Readiness skills are taught to most students by using the structured programs included in basal-reader programs (Paradis and Peterson, 1975). Generally, these programs have been developed to be used by either kindergarten or first-grade teachers. Almost half of the kindergarten teachers in LaConte's (1969) survey used readiness workbooks in their classrooms. We believe that even more first-grade teachers rely on workbook exercises to help their students develop readiness skills.

Since the mid-1960s, there has been a trend toward increasing the number of phonic-related exercises in readiness workbooks. Whereas readiness workbooks used to include many pages requiring students to match geometric shapes or to identify verbally a host of animals or objects in a panoramic scene, today's workbooks are more likely to require students to match letters, group pictures of items beginning with the same initial consonant sound, or to match letters with appropriate sounds. Figures 5.6 and 5.7 depict typical readiness workbook pages.

The advantages of using readiness workbooks are basically those derived from using any workbook. First, directions for using the materials are spelled out in great detail, usually, in an accompanying teacher's manual. In addition to the basic lesson, suggestions are often given for supplementary activities to provide extra practice for students who do not learn a skill during the basic lesson.

Another benefit of using a workbook is that the lessons are arranged in a logical sequence that has been carefully developed so that one skill builds on another. In addition, if the teacher uses the readiness workbook of the basal-

Fig. 5.6. An auditory-discrimination workbook activity. (*Getting Ready to Read*, Teacher's Edition, Boston: Houghton Mifflin, 1971, p. 22. Reprinted by permission.)

reader program that will be used to teach beginning reading, the students will most likely receive a lot of practice with readiness skills necessary for success in *that* program. By checking the child's answers in the workbook, the teacher can evaluate the progress of that child toward beginning reading in a specific program.

There are also disadvantages to using readiness workbooks. First, readiness workbooks can provide only a limited type of readiness. Many readiness workbooks provide good exercises for developing visual discrimination, but do not contain activities that will encourage language development or extend limited experiential backgrounds. Workbooks, in other words, should not be thought of as constituting the entire readiness program.

A second disadvantage to using readiness workbooks is that the teacher may be tempted to assign the same work to all students. The entire class may end up doing the same page, whether or not individual students need work on

Fig. 5.7. A letter-sound matching activity. (*Getting Ready to Read,* **Teacher's Edition,** Boston: Houghton Mifflin, 1971, p. 10. Reprinted by permission.)

that particular skill. Obviously, these materials were not intended to be used in this way, but we have seen dedicated teachers resort to this tactic simply because their work load was so overwhelming.

A third and quite serious limitation of some readiness workbooks involves the kinds of things young children must know in order to complete the assignments they are given. In examining teachers' manuals to determine problems in the instruction of young children due to the abstractness of the reading process, MacGinitie (1976) and his coworkers found that the lessons beginning readers were asked to complete were "absurdly difficult for six-year-old children" (p. 372). Terms such as *words, begins with,* and *ends with* are meaningless to many beginning readers. Some readiness workbooks do devote numerous pages to developing these concepts. Teachers must examine the workbooks they use carefully. If these concepts are not taught through the workbook exercises, the teachers must provide the additional instruction needed.

As you read this book, you will find one theme repeated over and over again: The *teacher,* not the materials, makes the difference. This is true for the teacher and readiness workbooks, too. The workbooks provide carefully structured lessons, *but* the teacher must not assume that these lessons are all there is to readiness instruction. The workbooks have skills arranged in a logical sequence, *but* the teacher should realize that not *every* child needs work on *every* skill. The workbooks include many attractive, ready-made exercises for the students to complete, *but* the teacher must make sure that the children have the underlying concepts needed to understand and complete the tasks. The *workbook* does not provide the readiness training; the *teacher* does.

READINESS TRAINING PROGRAMS

In this chapter thus far we have identified some important aspects of readiness and have discussed the use of workbooks and readiness tests. However, a successful readiness program involves more than just choosing appropriate workbooks and assessment instruments. In this section we identify several broad characteristics of any good readiness program, regardless of the beginning-reading approach that will follow the readiness training. In addition, we describe in some detail four readiness programs that have proved successful.

Characteristics of a Good Readiness Program

Anyone who has worked with young children will quickly agree that preschoolers or kindergarteners have a limited attention span. It is imperative, therefore, that a readiness program be highly motivating in order to keep the children interested. Learning activities should not require the children to remain at any one task for a long period of time. Even ten minutes may be too long if the task involves great concentration and little movement. The tasks should also be varied in format. A pencil-and-paper activity should be followed by a learning game or other task that allows the children to move about. A listening period should be followed by a time in which the children can express themselves through words or movement or song. At times the teacher may feel that he or she has a lot in common with the producers of "Sesame

Street"—trying to put together "a show" that is primarily educational but also entertaining. However, a readiness program *must* take into account that the students are young children, not miniature adults with long attention spans who will sit quietly for long periods.

In a good reading-readiness program children will have many opportunities to see the relationship among speaking, writing, and reading and to practice with the "raw materials" of reading and writing. Providing children with opportunities to print letters and words has been demonstrated to increase attention to the task and to be closely related to learning to read (Durkin, 1974–1975). Labels on objects in the room can help children understand the connection between the written word and the spoken word. For many children, seeing and reading their own names in print is the first step in developing some type of reading ability. Youngsters are usually eager to reproduce their names using crayons, pencils, felt markers, or paint. Children can also be encouraged to dictate captions or short sentences about pictures they have drawn. When the teacher or aide transcribes this language into print, the children are helped to see the relationship among speaking and writing and reading. (This relationship is explored more fully in Chapter 10, which describes the language-experience approach.)

Another characteristic of an exemplary readiness program is that it is "rule free." By this we mean that the natural function of the language is not torn apart and sacrificed for the learning of basic decoding skills (specifically, phonics "rules"). Downing (1969) contends that teaching beginning readers formal rules is unnecessary and may even impede learning to read. Furthermore, he suggests that verbal rules about reading are ritualistic and result in making learning to read dull and boring. We agree that the learning of "rules" has no place in a readiness program. Instead, easy phonics generalizations, such as the association of specific sounds with certain consonant letters, should be learned through a low-pressure, discovery approach. In this manner the learning will be more meaningful, interest in learning to read will remain high, and the children will not become frustrated or bored.

A final characteristic of a good readiness program is that instruction is focused and directly related to the skills necessary for learning to read. Hall (1976) calls this "teaching for the task." Montgomery (1977) stresses the same point, stating that "the training sample must be drawn from the same population as to which one wishes to generalize" (p. 617). In other words, good readiness programs incorporate instruction that will enhance the transfer of learning from the readiness stages to the reading stage.

Effective Readiness Programs

During the past two decades, a number of attempts have been made to design effective readiness programs. This section is not concerned with the commercial materials that usually accompany basal-reader series, but rather with independent efforts to improve the readiness skills of young children through carefully developed programs. We have chosen to describe three such programs, each of which has been evaluated and reported in the literature.

The Denver Study   In the mid-1960s the Denver public school system began to initiate 20 minutes of reading-readiness instruction in selected kindergarten classrooms throughout the district (Brzeinski *et al.*, 1967). Students in the district were divided into four groups. The first, the control group, received "traditional" kindergarten instruction and "regular" instruction throughout the elementary grades. The second group, a delayed-experimental group, received regular kindergarten instruction, but instruction adjusted to individual needs throughout the remainder of the elementary grades. In a short-term experimental group, the third group, children received special instruction in kindergarten, but "regular" instruction in grades 1–5. The final group, labeled the experimental group, received special instruction in kindergarten as well as an adjusted curriculum throughout the grades. No elaborate screening or readiness testing was used to determine which students were ready for the instruction.

Students enrolled in the experimental readiness program received instruction in a number of different areas. There were many opportunities for using and developing language. Teachers spent time improving both auditory and visual-discrimination skills, and training was provided in matching letters and sounds. Students were asked to use the context of spoken sentences in conjunction with consonants to unlock words. Finally, students were asked to read sentences and to use context to independently decode words.

After six years of instruction, Brzeinski and his coworkers (1967) reported, beginning-reading skills could be taught to large numbers of kindergarten students. Second, unless there were adjustments made in instruction during the elementary grades, the gains made by the experimental groups during kindergarten could not be maintained. Third, the more that instruction was adjusted, the better the students who received the special kindergarten program performed. Finally, there was no evidence that early instruction in beginning reading negatively affected visual acuity, created school-adjustment problems, or resulted in dislike for reading. In summary, then, early reading instruction was not harmful to the students; if instruction in the subsequent grades was adjusted to take into account the reading skills the students possessed, the students could maintain their advantage over students who had not had the readiness training.

The Durkin Study   Durkin's (1974–1975) extensive work with children at the reading-readiness level has provided many insights into early reading instruction. One of her most enlightening undertakings was a six-year study to determine if early reading instruction had any lasting positive effects.

After studying children who came to school already reading, Durkin planned a readiness program for four-year-olds. All phases of the language arts were included in the core of the curriculum. Children were given many opportunities to practice writing, and children's dictated stories formed the basis for most of the reading activities. Titles on bulletin boards, food labels, street signs, and children's names were also used to teach basic reading skills.

Phonics skills were taught as the need arose, usually in an informal, nonstructured way. At least 15 minutes a day were also spent reading stories to the students.

After two years in the pre–first grade language arts program, the students were followed through the fourth grade. Durkin discovered that children who received the early training scored significantly higher on tests of reading through the second grade than did students who did not receive the training. Significant differences between the two groups of children were not found in the third and fourth grades, however. Durkin postulated that this may have been caused by the fact that schools are generally unwilling to adjust instruction for the varied individual needs of children—especially in the intermediate elementary school years. Nevertheless, she believes that early instruction in reading is warranted, providing that it is a high-quality language arts–based program that is enjoyable for the students. Furthermore, appropriately adjusted instruction must follow students who have been enrolled in these programs.

"Sesame Street"

Few children or adults in the United States have not seen the television program "Sesame Street." It has been estimated that there are approximately nine million regular viewers of the show, most of whom are under six years of age. Unlike the Head Start program, the primary purpose of "Sesame Street" is to entertain; Head Start programs are more structured, intensive, educational endeavors. Both programs, however, attempt to prepare children for formal schooling.

"Sesame Street" is the result of the joint efforts of both private industry and public education. After extensive planning, the first segment of "Sesame Street" was aired on November 10, 1969, and was an instant success.

The program provides many reading-readiness activities for its viewers. Children are taught a small sight vocabulary in both English and Spanish, simple phonics skills, basic math skills, and problem-solving techniques. Relationships with people are also stressed, as are emotions and the ability to deal with various social situations. Like all good instructional efforts, each of the program's segments is aimed at specific educational objectives. To keep interest high, the producers of the show have relied on a "magazine format" that moves quickly from one topic to another in short, fast-paced sequences.

Educational Testing Service, the firm hired to evaluate the effectiveness of "Sesame Street," has uncovered some interesting, yet not surprising, results (Bogatz and Ball, 1971). Children who viewed the program the most, for instance, learned the most. And skills that were emphasized most over the air (recognizing and naming upper- and lower-case letters, recognizing and naming numbers, and completing simple addition and subtraction) were learned best. Another interesting finding was that the so-called disadvantaged child who watches the program regularly will probably make greater gains in learning than will middle- or high-income children who watch the program only periodically.

"Sesame Street" has also done much to ease the transition from home to school for many students. In addition, children from low-income homes which may not provide the kinds of experiences necessary for success in school may now develop a stronger foundation from which to better compete with students from more advantaged homes.

"Sesame Street" has made a profound impact on the learning of young students and has won more than 100 different awards, including seven Emmys and a Peabody. With these results, "Sesame Street" should be around for some time to come.

SUMMARY: THE NATURE OF READINESS

Like the "nature of the reading process," the "nature of reading readiness" is not easily described. Some authorities in psychology and education caution parents and teachers not to force reading instruction on children before they are ready; others present evidence that teaching young children to read as soon as they are able to has lasting benefits in the early grades. In this chapter we have explored the validity of both points of view, describing some of the difficulties preschoolers, kindergartners, and first graders may have in preparing for reading, but stressing that proper instruction can avoid many of these problems.

In this chapter we have also discussed many factors that have been thought to be related to success in learning to read, including chronological age, mental age, sex, experiential background, and oral-language development. We have shown how each may or may not be related to learning to read. In addition, we have illustrated how two other important factors—visual and auditory discrimination—can be developed.

To help teachers provide readiness instruction of high quality, we have presented the advantages and disadvantages of using commercially prepared workbooks and readiness tests. Furthermore, we have identified what we feel are the characteristics of an exemplary reading-readiness program and have described several experimental programs in detail.

Preparing children for reading is not easy. The teacher must devise a program that is manageable and yet still takes into account the uniqueness of the students involved and the characteristics of the beginning-reading program that will follow. Commercially prepared materials can be very helpful in organizing such a program, but the entire program will succeed only if the teacher chooses and uses these materials wisely.

REVIEW QUESTIONS

1. Prepare your own definition of readiness. This definition should include your understanding of the important aspects of this complex concept and should have logical implications for developing a readiness program.

2. As in so many other areas of education, the pendulum in reading readiness has swung from one extreme ("a nature point of view") to the other ("a nurture point of view"). What specific effects might this have on the kinds of instruction that kindergartners and first graders receive?

3. Over the years, a variety of factors have been thought to be closely related to learning to read. Chronological age, mental age, sex, experien-

tial background, and oral-language development are five such factors. In your opinion, which of these are related primarily with learning to read? Describe how each may or may not influence readiness for reading.

4. To maximize your effectiveness as a teacher, you should identify the readiness skills you plan to teach. List the skills you feel beginning readers must master before they can learn to read. Can you defend your selection?

5. A great deal of controversy has surrounded the use of reading-readiness tests. What precautions would you follow when selecting a readiness test? Might you rely on additional means to assess readiness? If so, describe the procedures you would follow.

6. What factors would influence your judgment of whether to use readiness workbooks? Describe several advantages and disadvantages of using workbooks. How would you overcome these disadvantages if you chose to use readiness workbooks?

7. What are the distinctive features of effective reading-readiness programs? Cite two exemplary readiness programs that were described in this chapter. Explain how you might adapt these programs for your own classroom.

REFERENCES

Beller, E. Kuno. "The Concept Readiness and Several Applications," *Reading Teacher* **23**, 8 (1970): 727–737, 747, 765.

Bogatz, Gerry Ann, and Samuel Ball. "A Summary of the Major Findings in *The Second Year of Sesame Street: A Continuing Education* (Princeton, N.J.: Educational Testing Service, November 1971).

Brzeinski, Joseph E., M. Lucille Harrison, and Paul McKee. "Should Johnny Read in Kindergarten: A Report on the Denver Experiment," *NEA Journal* (March 1967): 23–26.

Cashdan, Asher. "Reflections on the Beginning Reading Program," *Reading Teacher* **26**, 4 (1973): 384–388.

Clymer, Theodore, and Thomas C. Barrett. *Clymer-Barrett Prereading Battery* (Princeton, N.J.: Personnel Press, 1969).

Downing, John. "How Children Think about Reading," *Reading Teacher* **23**, 3 (1969): 217–230.

_____. "Children's Developing Concepts of Spoken and Written Language," *Journal of Reading Behavior* **4**, 1 (1971–72): 1–19.

Downing, John, and Peter Oliver. "The Child's Conception of a 'Word,' " *Reading Research Quarterly* **9**, 4 (1973–1974): 568–582.

Durkin, Dolores. "Reading Readiness," *Reading Teacher* **23**, 6 (1970): 528–534, 564.

_____. *Teaching Them to Read*, 2d ed. (Boston: Allyn and Bacon, 1974).

_____. "A Six-Year Study of Children Who Learned to Read in School at the Age of Four," *Reading Research Quarterly* **10**, 1 (1974–1975): 9–61.

Ekwall, Eldon E. *Diagnosis and Remediation of the Disabled Reader* (Boston: Allyn and Bacon, 1976).

Fowler, W. "A Developmental Learning Strategy for Early Reading in a Laboratory Nursery School," *Interchange* **2**, 2 (1971): 106–132.

Gates, Arthur, and Walter MacGinitie. *Gates-MacGinitie Reading Test—Readiness Skills* (New York: Columbia University, Teachers College Press, 1968).

Gibson, Eleanor. "Learning to Read," *Science* **148**, 3673 (1965): 1066–1072.

Hall, Mary Anne. "Prereading Instruction: Teach for the Task," *Reading Teacher* **30**, 1 (1976): 7–9.

Harrison, M. L., and J. B. Stroud. *The Harrison-Stroud Reading Readiness Profiles* (Boston: Houghton-Mifflin, 1950).

Hildreth, G., N. Griffiths, and M. McGawran. *Metropolitan Readiness Tests* (New York: Harcourt, Brace and World, 1965).

Hillerich, Robert. "Pre-reading Skills in Kindergarten: A Second Report," *Elementary School Journal* **65** (1965): 312–317.

Ilg, Francis L., and Louise Bates Ames. *Child Behavior* (New York: Dell, 1964).

———. *School Readiness* (New York: Harper & Row, 1972).

Johnson, Dale D. "Sex Difference in Reading across Cultures," *Reading Research Quarterly* **9**, 1 (1973–1974): 67–86.

King, Ethel M. "Beginning Reading: When and How," *Reading Teacher* **22**, 6 (1969): 550–553, 581.

LaConte, Christine. "Reading in Kindergarten," *Reading Teacher* **23**, 2 (1969): 116–120.

MacGinitie, Walter H. "Difficulty with Logical Operations," *Reading Teacher* **29**, 4 (1976): 371–375.

Montgomery, Diane. "Teaching Prereading Skills through Training in Pattern Recognition," *Reading Teacher* **30**, 6 (1977): 616–623.

Murphy, Helen, and Donald Durrell. *Murphy-Durrell Reading Readiness Analysis* (New York: Harcourt, Brace and World, 1965).

Nevius, John R. "Teaching for Logical Thinking Is a Prereading Activity," *Reading Teacher* **30**, 6 (1977): 641–643.

Otto, Wayne, Robert Chester, John McNeil, and Shirley Meyers. *Focused Reading Instruction* (Reading, Mass.: Addison-Wesley, 1974).

Paradis, Edward, and Joseph Peterson. "Readiness Training Implications from Research," *Reading Teacher* **28**, 5 (1975): 445–448.

Piaget, Jean. *The Construction of Reality in the Child* (New York: Basic Books, 1954).

Roberts, Kathleen Piegdon. "Piaget's Theory of Conservation and Reading Readiness," *Reading Teacher* **30**, 3 (1976): 246–250.

Rosner, Jerome. "Auditory Analysis Training with Prereaders," *Reading Teacher* **27**, 4 (1974): 379–384.

Rude, Robert T. "Readiness Tests: Implications for Early Childhood Education," *Reading Teacher* **26**, 6 (1973): 572–580.

———. "Can Very Young Children Be Taught to Read?" *Journal of the New England Reading Association* **10**, 1 (1975): 14–18, 64–68.

Siegel, I. "The Development of Classificatory Skills in Young Children," in *The Young Child* (Washington, D.C.: National Association for the Education of Young Children, 1972).

Spache, George D. *Diagnosing and Correcting Reading Disabilities* (Boston: Allyn and Bacon, 1976).

Stanchfield, J. M. "Development of Prereading Skills in an Experimental Kindergarten Program," *Reading Teacher* 24 (1971): 699–707.

Sutton, Marjorie. "First Grade Children Who Learned to Read in Kindergarten," *Reading Teacher* 18 (1965): 192–196.

Wanat, Stanley F. "Reading Readiness," *Visable Language* 10, 2 (Spring, 1976): 101–127.

Wohwill, Joachim. "The Place of Structured Experience in Early Cognitive Development," in Joe L. Frost, ed., *Revisiting Early Childhood Education* (New York: Holt, Rinehart and Winston, 1973).

Chapter 6
The First Step:
Decoding

After reading this chapter, you will be able to:

1. Describe the role of language cues in decoding.

2. Describe specific prereading skills and attitudes that are logical prerequisites to success in decoding.

3. Judge the usefulness of specific phonic skills on the basis of their general utility.

4. Identify structural-analysis skills that are useful for decoding.

5. Describe what is meant by the term "sight vocabulary."

6. Judge the usefulness of the Dolch, Johnson, and Great Atlantic and Pacific sight-vocabulary lists.

7. Develop appropriate activities for introducing and reinforcing decoding skills.

8. Describe the advantages and disadvantages of using three different methods for evaluating decoding skills.

Decoding, or reading what the words say, is not a matter of plodding through a sentence one word or one letter at a time. Mature readers certainly do not read in this manner, and beginning readers should never be taught to think of reading as entailing this kind of activity. In this chapter you will learn that decoding skills are related to three aspects of language: syntax (grammar), semantics (meaning), and phonology (the sound system). You will learn that there are three basic methods of identifying an unknown word—using context clues, phonics generalizations, and structural analysis—and that these three word-identification strategies are not employed one at a time, but in interaction with one another. The importance of a strong sight vocabulary will be discussed, and you will be shown techniques for selecting and teaching sight words to young children. As a result of reading this chapter, you should begin to understand that decoding is a very complex process that must be taught with specific goals in mind. Skill in decoding does not just "happen," but is acquired only as the result of careful instruction based on the needs of individual children.

AN OVERVIEW OF INSTRUCTION IN DECODING

An adult who was attempting to help a youngster read a new book was heard to lament, "But he's not sounding out the words. He's just saying them from memory." Unfortunately, this well-meaning but unenlightened soul missed the whole point of teaching a child to learn to decode. "Sounding out" by using phonics cues is only one method of identifying words, and most important, such a laborious strategy should be used only when the reader fails to recognize the word at first glance. The child in this instance had achieved success—he recognized words by sight, immediately. That is the goal of all the instruction in word-identification strategies. The child is to use mediating strategies, such as phonics or structural analysis, only until the word has become part of his or her sight vocabulary and is recognized instantly when encountered.

No one method of decoding, or word identification, is "best." The strategy for identifying *enough* in "I had enough cake," for example, is not the same strategy as would probably be most successful for identifying *cake*. There is no way to sound out *enough*, but phonics cues are very helpful for identifying *cake*. Teaching a child to rely primarily on one method of attacking new words is inefficient at best. A child who relies mainly on phonics cues may become a "word caller," insisting that every word conform to the rules of phonics. *Have* would rhyme with *save*, *could* with *toweled*, and *enough* would be practically unpronounceable. On the other hand, a child who uses only context cues to identify an unknown word may seriously distort the author's meaning by replacing the author's words with ones that are based entirely on the reader's expectations and experiences. The child who relies solely on configuration, or shape, is in real trouble, unable to distinguish between *went* or *want*, *have* or *here*, *mommy* or *swing*.

Children need to develop flexible repertoires of decoding, or word-attack, skills that equip them to take advantage of all of the cues within a sentence for identifying an unknown word. This means that readers must have an array of skills that enables them to use syntactic, semantic, and graphophonic cues within the language as these cues are appropriate.

Any language has certain restrictions that enable a reader to predict or anticipate what is to follow in a meaningful string of words. The syntactic cues within the language are those usually thought of as related to grammar. One such cue is word order. If a reader comes to an unknown word, he or she should be able to use an innate sense of the language to predict which part of speech the unknown word must be. For example, in "Henry wants a new _____," only a noun can fit in the blank. In "My sister _____ the pie," the missing word could only be a verb. Abstract though this ability may be, it is not above the competence of a six-year-old. Brown (1966) found that even four-year-olds were able to classify parts of speech by their use. Beginning readers should be given practice in using this competence in identifying unknown words.

Other types of syntactic cues are helpful. The redundancy of the English language means that cues are often given more than once in a sentence. In "Five dogs eat their bones," there are five cues to plurality: the word *five*, the plural marker in *dogs*, the absence of the third-person singular marker on *eat*, the plural possessive pronoun *their*, and the plural marker on *bones*. A reader who relies on only one method of word identification may fail to make use of these cues, and the task of reading will become unnecessarily difficult. For example, try the following exercise.

Self-Check Quiz: A Breather (Gasp!)

To help you determine if you understand the nature of syntactic cues, complete the short quiz below:

1. Identify the part of speech of each italicized word:

   a) The red *spandorg* was delicious.

     b) I washed my *flez* sweater.

     c) After Diana *gloobed,* she *thracked.*

2. Identify the indications that the action took place in the past in: "Yesterday Mark went to New York."

Similarly, semantic, or meaning, cues will help the reader. Only one word can possibly make sense in "The capital of Wisconsin is _____" or "Every person has only _____ nose." Even if the meaning cannot be narrowed down to one specific word, as in "He was hot, so he opened the _____," the use of semantic cues enables a reader to limit the many possibilities to a few that are meaningful, based on the reader's own experiential background.

The English language, like all languages, has phonological restrictions that limit the permissible sequences of sounds and prescribe other sequences. Berko (1958) found that very young children could correctly add phonemes to construct plurals and past-tense forms of nonsense words. The children added /əz/* to a nonsense word such as *putch* to form the plural, /s/ to a word such as *wat*, and /z/ to a word such as *lig*. No one had taught these children the way to form plurals for words ending with different kinds of consonants. Indeed, few adults could even verbalize the rules governing such a procedure. And yet these children intuitively knew the correct procedure. Such knowledge should be put to use when a reader is attempting to recognize an unknown word.

English has sequences of phonemes that are not permissible, even though they are common in other languages. No English word ends with /hw/ or beings with /mb/. A child who attempts to use such sounds in "sounding out" a word must be repressing his or her own good sense about the language.

Children must be taught to use their innate understanding of all three of the cue systems—syntax, semantics, and phonology—to help them read. Overreliance on any one of these systems can lead to inaccurate decoding and distortion of meaning.

Psycholinguistic Theory and Reading

Goodman (1976, p. 497) has likened reading to a "psycholinguistic guessing game." A fluent reader does not use cues in isolation, applying them sequentially or singly. Rather, according to Goodman (1976, p. 497): "Reading is a selective process. It involves partial use of available minimal language cues selected from perceptual input on the basis of the reader's expectation. As this partial information is processed, tentative decisions are made to be confirmed, rejected or refined as reading progresses."

Goodman is describing the mature, successful reader. Beginning readers are usually not skilled enough to interact so fully with their language. But this type of reading should be the goal as one teaches a child strategies for identifying words. Children must learn to relate their reading to their own language and to pick and choose the strategies that are most appropriate for dealing with a particular segment of language. Goodman (1976, pp. 507–508) has suggested a series of steps that may describe this process.

*Slashes, //, are used throughout the text to indicate phonemes, or sounds.

1. The reader scans along a line of print from left to right and down the page, line by line.

2. He fixes at a point to permit eye focus. Some print will be central and in focus, some will be peripheral; perhaps his perceptual field is a flattened circle.

3. Now begins the selection process. He picks up graphic cues, guided by constraints set up through prior choices, his language knowledge, his cognitive styles, and strategies he has learned.

4. He forms a perceptual image using these cues and his anticipated cues. This image is then partly what he sees and partly what he expected to see.

5. Now he searches his memory for related syntactic, semantic, and phonological cues. This may lead to selection of more graphic cues and to reforming the perceptual image.

6. At this point, he makes a guess or tentative choice consistent with graphic cues. Semantic analysis leads to partial decoding as far as possible. This meaning is stored in short-term memory as he proceeds.

7. If no guess is possible, he checks the recalled perceptual input and tries again. If a guess is still not possible, he takes another look at the text to gather more graphic cues.

8. If he can make a decodable choice, he tests it for semantic and grammatical acceptability in the context developed by prior choices and decoding.

9. If the tentative choice is not acceptable semantically or syntactically, then he regresses, scanning from right to left along the line and up the page to locate a point of semantic or syntactic inconsistency. When such a point is found, he starts over at that point. If no inconsistency can be identified, he reads on seeking some cue which will make it possible to reconcile the anomalous situation.

10. If the choice is acceptable, decoding is extended, meaning is assimilated with prior meaning, and prior meaning is accommodated, if necessary. Expectations are formed about input and meaning that lies ahead.

11. Then the cycle continues.*

When one teaches a child a strategy for identifying words, the ultimate process, that of reading and of interaction with language in print, should always be kept in mind. This point is stressed by Hall and Ribovich (1973, p. 164), who state that "isolated word and letter study is not communication, and emphasis on fragmented language leads to a gross neglect of language cues that cannot be taught in isolation from language context." A strategy should always be placed back into the total language, where it can become part of the total process. If strategies are practiced only in isolation, the child may have great difficulty melding them together again when reading real language.

*Kenneth S. Goodman, "Reading: A Psycholinguistic Guessing Game," in Harry Singer and Robert B. Ruddell, eds., *Theoretical Models and Processes of Reading,* 2d ed., Newark, Delaware: IRA, 1976. Reprinted with permission of the International Reading Association.

PREREQUISITES TO DECODING WORDS

In Chapter 5 readiness for beginning-reading instruction was discussed. Here more specific prerequisites will be presented that relate directly to decoding or word identification. Two kinds of prerequisites will be outlined: a set of attitudes that must be developed in the child and three visual and auditory skills specifically related to decoding words in print.

Attitudes

One of the most important responsibilities of the teacher of reading is to develop within the student a confidence in his or her own ability to deal with printed words. This involves establishing a climate of acceptance and encouragement in which the child is rewarded for a good try. The child must be encouraged to take risks, to make a "good guess" based on all of the data that are available and that the child knows how to use.

Biemiller (1970) analyzed the oral-reading errors of first graders, finding that beginning readers initially used primarily contextual information to guide their guesses. For example, a reader might substitute *sweater* or *gloves* for *hat* in *John was cold, so he put on his hat.* In such a case the reader is making no use of letter cues when guessing *sweater* for *hat,* but is using meaning as the only basis for the guess. However, in the next phase of reading development nonresponse errors became very prevalent. That is, the children simply would not even make a guess. In the third phase the readers began using both contextual and graphic restraints (letter cues) and usually had fewer nonresponse errors.

The results of Biemiller's research seem to indicate that children initially approach the reading task with confidence and a set for getting meaning. However, as they become aware of the constraints that are placed on a word, the children become less willing to risk errors. Eventually they are able to overcome this hesitancy and to use several kinds of cues to identify a word. But many children have difficulty escaping from the second phase, becoming bogged down and overwhelmed by the whole process. These children often need a great deal of encouragement and may even require training in making educated guesses.

A second attitudinal set that is necessary for success in reading is that of self-monitoring of what one decodes. A reader who blithely reads "Mary went to the birthday pretty," "Mitsy had eggit [for *eight*] kittens," or "The eagle coaches lizards" is not demanding meaning from the words. When a child supplies a word that is syntactically or semantically inappropriate or provides a nonsense word, that child is not doing any self-monitoring. Children must develop the habit of "listening" to what they themselves read, always checking that a meaningful response has been given. A reader, of course, will not be able to use this procedure to discover that Mitsy had eight kittens and not seven, but at least reading will be maintained as a process of getting ideas, not just sounds, from print.

A third set is for working with a word or a sentence until it makes sense. Some poor readers will read "Mary went to the birthday pretty," and their self-monitor will sound the alarm. But too often the only response is a bewildered expression and a determined attack on the next sentence. Children must be taught from the very beginning to use correction strategies. They must be taught to reread the entire sentence, or even the preceding one, to find clues to meaning that were missed the first time. Children can use this strategy before they have been taught any phonics generalizations at all. If they have been taught phonics generalizations, they should develop the habit of consciously reapplying these rules to the troublesome word. If the word still does not sound right, the children should learn to try different variations of sounds, paying the most attention to the consonant sounds and the context. Skill at working with a word until it makes sense will improve as the children learn more ways in which letter patterns vary, but the basic concept of trying alternative strategies should be taught as soon as children learn more than one cue to word meaning.

Barrett (1965) found that knowledge of letter names is the best single predictor of reading achievement at the end of first grade. He suggested, however, that *teaching* children the names of the letters of the alphabet does not lead to greater success in beginning reading, and further research (Johnson, 1970; Samuels, 1970) has confirmed this. Furthermore, the ability to name the letters of the alphabet in itself has no logical relationship to the task of learning to read.

Specific Prereading Skills

However, several important prereading skills do underlie this ability. If the child can name the letters of the alphabet, she or he must already possess: (1) adequate visual-discrimination skills to differentiate among the graphic symbols; (2) the ability to hear the differences among the names of similar-sounding letters, such as *b, d,* and *p* (auditory discrimination); (3) the ability to learn names for abstract symbols; (4) serviceable visual memory; and (5) an interest in working with the raw material of printed matter.

Knowledge of letter names can be a good predictor of first-grade reading achievement, but the research has shown that this knowledge itself is not the important factor. Instead of beginning reading-readiness instruction by attempting to teach all children the names of the letters of the alphabet, the teacher of young children might do well to work on improving their more basic reading-readiness skills, such as specific visual- and auditory-discrimination skills, the ability to work with abstract symbols, and visual memory. Attention should also be paid to developing an interest in reading in the young child.

In attempting to describe precisely the skills that underlie the ability to decode printed symbols, Venezky (1974) delineated three skills—one visual and two auditory: matching letters and words visually, matching sounds, and blending sounds. The skills were derived through a logical analysis of what a child actually has to do when learning to deal with printed words. To date, no empirical validation of the importance of these skills has been done, but work in this area is planned.

The skills identified by Venezky have a logical relationship to learning to decode, and they can provide specific goals for teachers of beginning readers. Broken into five subskills and stated as prescriptive objectives, they can bring focus to readiness instruction.

1. Visual skills
   a) *Letter orientation:* The learner matches identical letters when distractors are present that are similar in form but different in regard to orientation in space (e.g., b/d, p/q, u/n).
   b) *Letter order:* The learner matches identical words when distractors are present that have the same component letters in a different order (e.g., arts: rats, star, arts, tras).
   c) *Detail in letter strings:* The learner matches identical words when similar distractors are present (e.g., clear: cleat, clean, clear).

2. Sound skills
   d) *Matching:* The learner matches phonemes in isolation with the same sounds in words (e.g., /s/ some).
   e) *Blending:* The learner blends isolated phonemes into words (e.g., /p/ /i/ /t/ ⟶ pit).

According to Venezky's analysis, the most important visual skill is the ability to match letters and words. The reader must be able to compare letters or strings of letters and tell whether they are identical. This one visual skill is made up of three subskills. One subskill is the ability to attend to letter orientation. That is, the child is able to tell that *b* and *d*, *d* and *p*, and *u* and *n* are different. This concept is often a difficult one for young children, and reversals of *b* and *d* are common in beginning readers. The child has learned to deal with a world in which an object does not change its identity just because it is oriented in space in a different manner. Winnie the Pooh is still Pooh whether he is sitting, standing on his head, or tumbling end over end down the stairs. And yet a ball and a stick make a *b* when placed in one relationship to each other, but a *d* or *p* when placed in another relationship. The child must learn to attend to these details in order to deal successfully with those letters in the alphabet that are made of identical components.

A second visual subskill identified by Venezky calls for the ability to attend to letter order. The beginning reader must understand that a change in the order of the components of a string of letters results in a change in the identity of that string. *Was* is not the same string as *saw; rats* is not the same as *star* or *arts.* The ability to detect these differences includes the habit of always scanning a word from left to right. Again, such an orientation is not "natural" or "normal." It is an arbitrary standard of the English language, but it is one that must be adhered to if reading is to be successful.

The third visual subskill identified by Venezky is the ability to attend to essential details within letter strings. The child learns to look carefully at all of the word and not just at the initial or final letters, noting that *went* and *want* are not identical, nor are *cat* and *cats* or *best* and *bent*. Too often beginning readers learn just to identify words by configuration or beginning letter. These strategies work for a short time, but as soon as words of similar configuration are introduced, the child must learn to attend to all of the components of the word.

Venezky suggests two important auditory skills that are prerequisites to success in early reading: sound matching and sound blending. These two skills appear to be needed before a reader can use phonics to identify words. Both of these skills are often difficult for beginning readers to develop because of the abstract nature of the skills. Particular attention may be needed to develop these skills before any phonics instruction is given.

Readiness for decoding involves preparation in both skills and attitudes. If children do not have attitudes that enable them to use a variety of skills and strategies to identify words, teaching skills will be of little utility. If children do not have the basic prerequisite skills that underlie the ability to deal with words in print, they will be unable to profit from instruction in more sophisticated skills that require readers to see differences among words or to hear and blend phonemic elements.

WORD-IDENTIFICATION STRATEGIES

Fluent readers do not pause to identify each word they read. As Goodman (1976) has described reading, mature readers sample only enough of the printed cues to allow them to make and to confirm guesses about words and meanings. However, all readers do encounter words that they do not recognize immediately. When this happens, three kinds of strategies are available to help readers decode unknown words: the use of context clues, phonics cues, and structural analysis.

Context Clues

Context clues are cues to a word's meaning contained in the context that surrounds the unknown word. These cues may be within the same sentence or in preceding or following sentences. For example, cues to the meaning of *burga* are contained within one sentence: "The burga swept in from the northeast, dumping 15 inches of snow on the town." However, to identify the meaning of *lugubrious* in the paragraph below, one must read on for several sentences after the word has been used:

> The old man had a lugubrious expression. We didn't know what had caused it. He didn't usually look that way. In fact, his mournful appearance today was an unpleasant shock for us.

Context clues are meaning cues and as such are dependent on the reader's own experiences and interpretations. Few mature readers would be able to define *apneustic* in a meaningful manner even after reading that "the tracheal system of the larva was apneustic because it had no open spiracles." Nor would a fifth grader be helped to identify *lugubrious* by "his lugubrious expression, the most dolorous in the room, surprised me." To a city-bred first grader, "We gathered up the alfalfa and took it to the barn" contains few context cues for *alfalfa*. Alfalfa could be anything able to be gathered up. Similarly, "We rode on the escalator in the department store" has no context clues for a rural child who has never seen moving stairs. When teachers ask children to use the context clues in a sentence to identify the meaning of a word, they must be sure that the children have the experiential background to profit from those clues.

Not all sentences contain context clues. Teachers must be wary of asking a reader to identify a word from a context such as "Susan is _____" or "Paul _____ the dog." The reader can limit guesses in the second sentence to verbs, but that does not narrow the choices down a great deal. Using context in the first sentence is almost totally useless, for syntactic cues are not even helpful. The missing word could be a participle *(running)*, noun *(captain)*, or adjective *(happy)*. Before suggesting that a reader use context clues, a teacher should be relatively certain that the sentence or sentences do offer such cues.

Context clues may not always help the reader to identify the unknown word exactly. Often the reader can come close to guessing the meaning of a word even if the precise word itself remains elusive. Sometimes the problem is merely a matter of pronunciation. Often we mumble a word to ourselves that we find difficult to pronounce. The pronunciation is not important as long as we know the meaning. A reader does not need to be able to pronounce *La Jolla* in order to know that it is the name of a city in the sentence "My cousin lives in La Jolla, California." Similarly, we all have had those unfortunate experiences in which we can "decode" a word and know its meaning, but habitually pronounce it incorrectly. For one of the authors *disheveled* was such a word. She knew that it meant unkempt or messy, but pronounced it as dis-heveled rather than as di-sheveled. The word's meaning was known, but its pronunciation was not.

In other cases neither the pronunciation nor the precise meaning may be identified, but the reader is able to get a general idea of the meaning of the word. In "He was embarrassed to have made such a *fatuous* remark," the reader can use the context to recognize that *fatuous* has a negative meaning. The reader may not know if *fatuous* means stupid or silly or crude, but he or she does know that it is the kind of remark that causes the speaker embarrassment. Often that amount of information is enough for the reader, and he or she continues reading, having only a general idea of the meaning of the unknown word.

Context clues are not the only cues to word identification. The use of phonics generalizations and structural analysis are also valuable aids. But we suggest that children be taught that the first cue to word identification that they should try to use is context and that context should always be used to confirm a guess made through phonics generalizations or structural analysis. Children should be encouraged to automatically use the following strategies each time they encounter an unknown word in context:

1. First, read the rest of the sentence, skipping the unknown word. If that word is at the end of the sentence, reread the entire sentence.
2. Next, use phonics or structural-analysis cues to attempt to identify the word. Try to think of a word that makes sense and fits the phonics cues.
3. If neither of these strategies works, ask for help or put in a word that makes sense, even if it doesn't match the phonics cues, and read on.

Reading should always be a process of meaning getting. If children are taught to use context cues to make and to confirm guesses about words, they will be unlikely to see decoding as a game of simply pronouncing words.

Phonics

If one were to observe a parent helping a child with reading, chances are that the words "sound it out" would be heard again and again as the child stumbled over words. Often the first question a parent asks a teacher about a child's reading instruction is, "Are you teaching phonics?" Perhaps this concern with phonics is still a result of Flesch's *Why Johnny Can't Read* (1955). This book contained an indictment of American schools for using a look-say approach to reading instruction rather than a phonics approach. Whatever the reason, phonics is revered by the public.

Unfortunately, that reverence for phonics by the public is somewhat misplaced. Phonics is often perceived as the magic key to unlock every word. "Sounding it out" is indeed useful when attempting to identify *run*, *scratch*, or even *happiness*. However, a problem arises with common little *put*, *what* and *cold*. An unknown author describes the problem well:

Hints on Pronunciation for Foreigners

I take it you already know
Of tough and bough and cough and dough?
Others may stumble but not you,
On hiccough, thorough, laugh and through.
Well done! And now you wish, perhaps,
To learn of less familiar traps?
Beware of heard, a dreadful word
That looks like beard and sounds like bird,
And dead: it's said like bed, not bead—
For goodness' sake don't call it "deed"!
Watch out for mean and great and threat
(They rhyme with suite and straight and debt.)

A moth is not a moth in mother
Nor both in bother, broth in brother,
And here is not a match for there
Nor dear and fear for bear and pear,
And then there's dose and rose and lose—
Just look them up—and goose and choose,
And cork and work and card and ward.
And font and front and word and sword,
And do and go and thwart and cart—
Come, come, I've hardly made a start!
A dreadful language? Man alive.
I'd mastered it when I was five.

T. S. W. (only the initials of writer are known)

Utility of Phonics Generalizations

One may wonder why phonics is taught at all if English is so filled with irregular spellings. Clymer (1963) attempted to answer this question by rating the utility of commonly taught phonics generalizations. Of the 45 generalizations examined, only 33 held true for at least 60 percent of the words found in primary-grade materials to which these generalizations could be applied. For 5 of these 33 generalizations, fewer than ten words could be found in the primary materials to which the generalizations could be applied. Emans (1967) found only 18 of these generalizations to be useful with materials above the primary grades. The results of these studies and another by Bailey (1967) seem to indicate that teaching children long lists of rules to use to decode words is not productive.

Although memorization of a myriad of rules is not helpful, at least three interrelated arguments may be put forth in defense of teaching some phonics generalizations. First, phonics is a useful tool when used in conjunction with other cue systems in the language. Sounding out is not an efficient way to decode every word. The first attempt to identify an unknown word should always be through context, with the sounds of the letters* providing confirmation of the guess. This procedure keeps meaning getting as the primary focus and takes into account that sounding out a word may or may not work. Phonics generalizations by themselves often do not work, but they are frequently useful in confirming a guess based on meaning.

Bukovec (1973) suggests an extension of this argument. Granting that phonics generalizations do not always work, Bukovec states that "it is not uncommon for an imprecise pronunciation to be sufficiently close to the correct sound as to spark recognition on the part of the reader" (p. 272). Experienced teachers are familiar with this phenomenon. A student who has incorrectly placed an accent, pronounced a vowel wrong, or misread an entire syllable will often repeat the word once or twice, varying different

*Letters don't have sounds, but only represent sounds. However, to be completely and repetitively accurate in discussing grapheme patterns that represent sounds is needlessly precise and awkward.

aspects of the word until, with a smile, he or she pronounces the real word triumphantly. This procedure is especially successful if the consonants of the word are pronounced correctly. Something about the miscue (the incorrect response) is close enough to the real word to jog the reader's memory and to encourage her or him to keep working with and altering the sounds. Of course, the word must be in the child's oral (speaking) or aural (listening) vocabulary in order for him or her to recognize when the real word has been pronounced. Readers will often reject the *correct* pronunciation of a word initially because that word is not familiar to them. They will keep trying alternative pronunciations because they are unable to recognize the correct one. In cases like this, the teacher should immediately intervene and tell the reader the correct pronunciation.

A third, and related, reason for teaching some phonics generalizations is that many of the generalizations commonly taught to beginning readers *are* consistent, or at least provide the reader with clues for a guess that is fairly close to the real word. For example, phoneme-grapheme (sound-letter) correspondences for consonants are very stable and can give quite reliable cues to a word's identity. Another commonly taught rule states that when a vowel is in the middle of a one-syllable word, that vowel is short. Clymer (1963) found that this generalization could be correctly applied to 328 words in primary materials, but would be incorrect for 119 other words. To state this another way, a beginning reader could use that rule alone to identify 328 words likely to be encountered while reading, but would have to make a second guess using other cues to identify the other 119 words. A few phonics generalizations are reliable enough, especially with many of the simple words found in beginning-reading materials, to enable a child to identify hundreds of words correctly. These few rules, listed on the following pages, can help to give beginning readers confidence that they can have success in decoding.

Once having decided to introduce selected phonics generalizations to the class, the teacher must be aware of the problems inherent in teaching children that certain letters or letter combinations represent specific sounds. Some of these pitfalls have already been mentioned. Below are several guidelines to help ensure that phonics instruction will be successful. Several of these guidelines are followed by an activity so that you can check on your understanding of the main points.

Instructional Guidelines for Teaching Generalizations

1. Children (and teachers and parents) must become aware that not all words can be "sounded out." Beginning readers need to learn to switch strategies if a phonics-based guess doesn't fit. In addition, teachers must be extremely careful in choosing words to exemplify rules and when urging children to use phonics cues. Many of the most common words follow the *graphemic* pattern for some very useful phonics generalizations, but are in reality exceptions.

Activity: Which of the following words from the Great Atlantic and Pacific Word List can be identified by the rule that states that when a vowel is in the middle of a one-syllable word, that vowel is short?*

that	what	just
was	then	find
for	put	much
with	told	most
his	her	well

(The answers are at the bottom of the page.†)

2. The use of phonics should be taught as a strategy to be applied in conjunction with cues from the other aspects of language—syntax (grammar) and semantics (meaning). The three cue systems of the language should be used together to identify an unknown word.

3. Conscious attention must be given to providing opportunities for the youngsters to transfer the phonics rules they are taught to real reading situations. Too often beginning readers do not make the connection between learning about sounds of letters and what to do with this knowledge when reading. This connection has to be made explicit. After a phonics generalization has been introduced, the children should always work with the generalization within the context of complete sentences. Since many published materials for phonics instruction provide for little practice in using phonic generalizations in context (Groff, 1973), teachers will often need to construct their own materials and practice exercises. For example, if the silent *e* generalization‡ has been taught, the following sentence and others like it might be written on the board:

The dog will <u>bite</u> the cat.

A student could be asked to read the sentence, skipping the underlined word if it is not immediately recognized. Then the class could be asked to identify the underlined word. Individual students could be asked how they had recognized the word, why "bit" is not correct (it doesn't make sense with "will," and the *e* makes the *i* long), and why "chase" is wrong (it doesn't have the right sounds). Discussing all of the steps used to identify the word will help the students realize how their phonics knowledge fits into reading whole sentences.

In addition to using instructional procedures such as those sketched above, the teacher must seize every opportunity during the entire day to urge the students to apply their word-attack skills. Phonics and all word-identification strategies must not be perceived only as tools used to read

---

*The following words may be used as key words for the short-vowel sounds: *cat*, *bed*, *dish*, *top*, *duck*.

†The words that follow the generalization above are: *that*, *with*, *his*, *then*, *just*, *much*, and *well*.

‡If a word or syllable has two vowels and the second vowel is a final *e*, the *e* is silent, and the first vowel is usually long.

lists of words during reading class; children must see that these skills help them read words everywhere—in social studies books, during free-reading time, on signs, on recipes.

4. The teacher must be aware of dialectal differences, both within the class and between the major dialect of the classroom and the materials being used. If a teacher in the Midwest were using a lesson dealing with the short sound of *a*, *bath* and *cat* would be appropriate examples. This is not true for many New England areas, where *bath* and *laugh* have the same vowel sound as the *a* in *father*, not *cat*. Similarly, *root* and *food* have the same vowel sound in many dialect areas; in other regions the vowel sound of *root* is the same as that in *good*. In many areas *pen* and *pin* are virtually indistinguishable.

Forcing students to pronounce words in a way that is not consistent with their own dialect is self-defeating, as well as degrading. There is no one "correct" dialect. To be sure, some dialects are more prestigious than others, but each dialect is a fully formed grammatical system itself and not just the result of sloppy speech or ignorance.

Activity: Say each of the word groups below aloud. Circle the words in each group that have the same vowel sound in your own dialect. Compare your lists with those of a friend who has the same dialect as your own. If possible, compare your lists with someone who has a different dialect.

a) been, bit, creek, meal, chief
b) all, oil, saw, Don, hop
c) car, bath, cat, laugh, stand
d) ten, hem, tin, him, seen
e) route, news, ouch, move, owl

5. When isolating consonant sounds for the purpose of class discussion, one must guard against putting an artificial "uh" after the target sound. The sound of the letter *b* is not "buh" and a child who is told to blend "buh" "ă" "tuh" will have difficulty arriving at *bat*. When saying isolated consonant sounds, one should try to pronounce the sounds of continuants and nasals (such as /m/, /n/, /s/, /f/, and /w/) in a drawn-out manner. Stops (/b/, /p/, /t/, and /g/, for example) should be produced quickly, in a clipped manner.

Activity:

a) Say the beginning sound of *man*, drawing out the sound as long as you can. Do *not* open your mouth; produce the /m/ sound through closed lips. Opening your mouth will add a vowel sound to the /m/ phoneme.

b) Follow the same procedure with the first sound in:
   (1) *net* (Keep your tongue behind your upper teeth for the duration of the sound.)
   (2) *sand* (Keep your teeth touching.)

(3) *fun* (Keep your upper teeth on your lower lip.)

(4) *win* (Keep your lips rounded.)

c) Say the beginning sound of *bug* as quickly as possible, just letting your lips pop out the sound. Avoid opening your mouth widely. Poking yourself sharply in the stomach helps to produce the sound with the needed brevity.

d) Follow the same procedure with:

(1) *pan*

(2) *tip* (The lips are not involved in this sound.)

(3) *go* (The lips are not used with this sound either.)

What to Teach   All published materials for instruction in phonics have a predetermined scope and sequence of skills. Although some of these programs appear to be more logically organized than others, no one specific sequence of phonics skills has been agreed on by all reading theorists.

CONSONANTS   Most phonics programs suggest teaching the consonant sounds first. There are three good reasons for this:

1. The consonant sounds are more regular than the vowel sounds. Most consonants usually represent one phoneme. Several represent two or even three phonemes, such as *s* (*hats*, *dogs*, and *sure*) and *d* (*had* and *jumped*), but these phonemes are very similar. If the reader ascribes the /s/ sound to a letter or sequence of letters when the /z/ sound is proper, the /s/ sound is usually close enough to the correct one to enable the reader to identify the word.

2. Many consonant sounds can be identified by the names of the consonant letters. That is, the sound of the name of the letter also contains the sound the letter usually represents. For example, in saying the name of *m* or *b*, the speaker is also saying the sound of the consonant. Of course, a vowel sound is spoken with the consonant when the name is pronounced, but most children do not have difficulty deleting the vowel sound when asked just to give the consonant sound. With the advent of educational television, most children come to school knowing many of the names of the letters of the alphabet. A teacher can put that knowledge to use when teaching consonant sounds.

3. The consonant letters are usually the most useful in identifying a word. *R-m-mb-r*, *st-rt*, and *fr-nt* are more easily recognized as specific words than *-a-*, *-o-ey*, or *--oo-*.

Consonants, however, do not always have the same sound. Sometimes these letters are silent, as in *knot*, *light*, or *write*. Sometimes these letters have two sounds. *C*, for example, has the /s/ sound in *city*, but the /k/ sound in *cat*. Children do need to be taught these regular variations.

Although the sounds of most consonants are given by their names, this is not true for *w, y, x, q, h,* or hard *g* (*go*) and hard *c* (*cat*). Not surprisingly, these letters are among the most difficult when beginning readers are learning phoneme-grapheme correspondences. Children often suggest /d/ as the sound of *w* and /č/ (*church*) for *h*. These are logical though incorrect extensions of the generalization that the name of the letter indicates its name. Special attention needs to be given to these letters.

Instruction about consonant sounds may be categorized into four major areas: single consonants, consonant digraphs, blends, and silent letters. For single consonants children should be taught that generally the following consonants represent the sounds heard at the beginning of the key words.

Single Consonants

	Key word		*Key word*		*Key word*
b	book	k	kite	s	six
c	cat, city	l	leaf	t	top
d	dog	m	mask	v	vest
f	fish	n	net	w	web
g	goat, giraffe	p	pig	x	fox, xylophone
h	hat	qu	queen	y	yarn
j	jeep	r	rope	z	zebra

Many other key words are possible, of course. Whatever words are chosen, the teacher should provide a key word for each letter. The key word and its picture should be displayed with the consonant letter in the room, and the children should be encouraged to refer to the key word and picture when they forget a letter-sound correspondence. Because the key word is pictured and not written, a good practice is to choose a key word that is easily illustrated, such as *book* or *bed,* rather than *by* or *big*. The key word should be of only one syllable, if possible. If the word is of more than one syllable, the children may attend to the beginning sound of the second or third syllable rather than to the beginning sound of the word itself. In addition, the word should represent an object that has only one possible identity. For example, a picture of a *jet* that the teacher uses to illustrate the /j/ sound could be called a plane by the child, thus causing confusion.

You will note that three of the listed consonants—*c, k,* and *x*—have two key words. Children need to be taught these sounds and how to predict which of the two sounds is the better "first guess." Fortunately, fairly reliable generalizations do exist to help readers with these predictions.

1. *C* and *g* usually have their their "soft" sounds (as in *city* and *gym*) before *e, i,* or *y* and their "hard" sounds (*cat, goat*) before other letters.

2. *X* usually has the sound of /ks/ when at the end of the word and the sound of /z/ when at the beginning. *X* usually takes the /gs/ sound when in the medial position. However, this sound is so close to the /ks/ sound that

children do not need to be taught this variation as a separate rule. If the children are aware of the /ks/ and /z/ variants, they will have little trouble arriving at the correct pronunciation of *exit*.

Consonant Digraphs   Consonant digraphs are pairs of dissimilar consonants that together represent a sound unlike the sound of either of the two component letters. These sounds and suggested key words are listed below:

	Key word		*Key word*
sh	shoe	ph	phonograph
ch	church	wh	wheel
th	thumb	ng	king (*Note: -ng* appears only at the ends of syllables in English words.)

    Wh is usually included as a digraph even though in some dialects *wh* is pronounced as /hw/, which is the component letter sounds but in reversed order. In other dialects *wh* has the /w/ sound, and *which* and *witch* are pronounced alike. We feel that *wh* should be taught as a digraph to encourage children to think of the *wh* grapheme cluster as a unit and not as two successive letters, each to be sounded in order.

    Th has both a voiced (*this*) and voiceless (*think*) variation. Some phonics series give children practice in distinguishing between these two sounds. As with the /gs/ sound of *x*, we feel that although children should be aware that the two variations exist, they do not need to practice differentiating between the two sounds.

    The most common sound of *ch* is that heard in *church*. However, *ch* does represent other sounds, as in *Chicago* and *charade* or *character* and *chemistry*. Children should be taught to try the /č/ (*church*) sound first and then to try the /š/ (*Chicago*) or /k/ (*chemistry*) sounds if needed.

Blends   Blends are clusters of two or three consonants in which the resultant sound is made up of the sounds of each of the individual component letters. Examples are found in *frog*, *strap*, *glove*, and *mist*. Beginning readers need to be given practice in applying the concept of blending adjacent consonants. However, teaching each consonant blend separately does not appear to be an efficient procedure. Once children have the concept of a blend, they can apply this knowledge without explicit instruction for each blend.

Silent Consonants   The fourth major area of consonant generalizations is that of silent letters. Children need to learn that in certain combinations some letters will not be sounded. The most common silent consonant letters or combinations are:

kn knot   *tch* match
wr write   *h* honest
ght light

In addition to learning these specific letter combinations, the children should develop the set that other consonant letters may be silent, as in *fasten*, *doubt*, and *lamb*. If an attempt to sound out a word does not result in a recognizable word, children should learn to try varying or deleting the consonant sounds as well as those of the vowels.

Learning to identify the sounds of the vowels is usually much more difficult for young learners than learning the consonant sounds. The vowel letters (*a, e, i, o, u,* and sometimes *y* and *w*, as in *pay* and *know*) all have more than one sound associated with them. In fact, vowels are not even just long or short. A vowel letter can also be *r*-controlled (*car, bird*), silent (*road, hope*), or a component of a diphthong (*oil, new*). The vowel letter can even have the sound commonly associated with another letter. For example, in many dialects the *a* in *father* sounds like the vowel in *hop;* in *what* the *a* sounds like the *u* in *cup.*

VOWELS

In spite of the seemingly endless variation of vowel letter-sound correspondences, several reliable phonics generalizations may be taught to help the child predict which sound a given vowel will have in a sequence of letters. The purpose of teaching these generalizations is to provide the reader with a basis for a good first guess. Each generalization given below has many exceptions, but we feel that the seven suggested generalizations have high enough utility, especially in words used in beginning-reading materials, to justify teaching them to children.

The words listed below may serve as key words for the long- and short-vowel sounds referred to in generalizations 1–4:

	a	*e*	*i*	*o*	*u*
short	cat	bed	dish	top	duck
long	cake	bee	bike	rope	{ mule { tube

1. *If a word or syllable has only one vowel and that vowel is in the middle or at the beginning of the word or syllable, the vowel usually has the short sound.*

The following words illustrate this generalization and provide examples of the five short-vowel sounds:

a	*e*	*i*	*o*	*u*
at	elf	it	odd	up
cab	jet	pin	top	but
land	melt	list	bond	jump
scrap	bled	slip	prop	drum
rabbit	better	pillow	robber	punish

2. *If a word or syllable has only one vowel and that vowel is at the end of the word or syllable, the vowel usually has the long sound.*

Some examples are given below:

a	e	i	o	u
	be	hi	go	gnu
bacon	recent	silent	sofa	tulip

3. *If a word or syllable has two vowels and the second vowel is a final* e, *the* e *is silent and serves as a marker to signal that the first vowel is usually long.*

Some examples follow:

a	e	i	o	u
bake	Pete	like	rope	rule
paste	these	tie	hoe	cute
escape	compete	retire	parole	excuse

Note that *u* has two long vowel sounds, one more rounded than the other. Students should be made aware that long *u* may have the vowel sound in either *use* or *June* and must learn to vary their guess if the first attempt does not seem quite right.

4. *When a word or syllable has two adjacent vowels, the first vowel is often long and the second silent.*

Some examples are:

rain, daisy
boat, toaster
seed, beetle
beat, feature
day, layette

Generalization 4 is often attacked because of the many exceptions. Smith and Johnson (1976) state that the rule should never be taught, because it is so unreliable. However, we feel that the generalization has sufficiently high utility to provide readers with a good first guess. The alternative is to teach *ai, oa, ee, ea,* and *ay* as five separate generalizations. It seems more practical to teach beginning readers generalization 4 as a useful strategy and to let them learn the vowel pairs that cannot be identified in this manner later.

5. *When a vowel is followed by* r, *that vowel has neither a long nor a short sound and is said to be* r-*controlled.*

ar	er	ir	or	ur
far	her	sir	for	fur
barn	germ	girl	short	curve

Note that *er, ir,* and *ur* all have the same sound. Children will find it easier to remember the *r*-controlled vowel sounds if *ar* and *or* are taught as distinct sounds and *er, ir,* and *ur* are all grouped together.

6. *When certain pairs of vowels occur, the sound of neither of the vowels is heard. Rather, a new sound, unpredictable from the sound of either component letter, occurs.*

house	*saw*
now	*cause*
oil	*new*
bo*y*	

These vowel pairs have to be taught as separate entities, because the reader has no way of identifying the vowel sound from the sounds of the component letters.

7. *The vowel sound in an unaccented syllable usually has the* schwa *sound. The* schwa *sound is symbolized by* ə *and has the sound heard in the underlined vowels below.*

a	*e*	*i*	*o*	*u*
about	effect	dentistry	offend	upon
china	market	easily	carrot	circus
machine				

The *schwa* sound is often difficult to teach. A great deal of time should not be spent on generalization 7. The students should learn that any vowel can have the "uh" or *schwa* sound and that if the vowel sound they try first doesn't sound right, they should try the *schwa*.

After the students have learned to identify the major sound-letter correspondences and have learned to use phonics generalizations to identify one-syllable words, phonic syllabication may be taught. The purpose of using the rules of phonic syllabication is to divide an unknown word into smaller, pronounceable units to which the phonics generalizations can be applied. To do this the students must know both the syllabication rules for dividing a word and the generalizations that will enable them to pronounce the individual syllables. The following three phonics syllabication generalizations should be taught:

PHONIC SYLLABICATION

1. *In vowel-consonant-consonant-vowel (VCCV) words, divide between the two consonants, unless the two consonants form a digraph.*

    Examples: ham/mer, whis/per, con/cern
    Digraph exception: tea*ch*/er

2. *In VCV words, divide after the first vowel.*
    Examples: ba/by, to/ken, pu/pil

3. *When a word ends in a consonant plus* le, *the final syllable is made up of the consonant and the* le.

   Examples: bun/dle, sta/ple, tri/fle

These three generalizations will enable a reader to divide most words into pronounceable units.

Syllabication should never be practiced by dividing known words. (If the word is known, the generalizations aren't needed!) Of course, when providing practice, the teacher will undoubtedly suggest some words that a few of the children recognize by sight. This is unavoidable if real words are used. Nonsense words, such as *napsin, rabin,* or *trindle,* may be used to avoid this. Most important, the students must realize that phonic syllabication generalizations *are* to be used with unknown words. We have often heard children refuse to try dividing a word into syllables, saying, "But I don't know what the word is." The children must be given guided practice that shows them just how these generalizations can be applied to unknown words.

Teaching Phonics Generalizations

The two basic approaches to teaching phonics are analytic phonics and synthetic phonics. Analytic phonics instruction starts with whole, known words and asks the child to induce generalizations based on these words. For example, if the words *bed, Bill, be,* and *tub* were in the children's sight vocabularies, these words would be written on the board, and the children would be asked to tell how the words are all alike. The class would be led to the conclusions that all of the words have *b* in them and that *b* has the /b/ sound. This approach has the advantage of teaching children to use phonics within the context of words. The children are more likely to see phonics as something to be used when reading than as a game of making sounds. Another advantage of this method is that sounds are not artificially isolated. The sounds are first heard as they appear within words and not in isolation.

In the synthetic phonics approach, children learn the sounds of letters as separate units and then practice blending these sounds together. If the child knows the sound of *b,* the short sound of *a,* and the sound of *t,* the child could blend these sounds to produce *bat.* One disadvantage of this kind of phonics instruction is that the sounds are artificially isolated from the very beginning. Isolating a sound distorts the sound and may make blending very difficult. In addition, reading is often perceived as making noises or sounding out every word or letter. The meaning-getting aspect of reading may be lost. So are the additional cue systems in the language. One of the authors actually heard a child trained by this approach read correctly "This is the right way to do it," and then go back and "correct" *right* to something like *rig-hut.* That child had had so much phonics instruction that the method—sounding out—was indeed the message.

One useful approach often found in primary reading instruction combines both analytic and synthetic phonics. This approach makes use of phonograms, or word families. Several known words that contain a common spelling pattern are written on the board—for example, *at, fat,* and *cat.* The children are led to induce the sound of *-at,* and then they are asked to suggest other words that follow this pattern. The children may also be asked to synthesize new words by the process of consonant substitution. That is, *at* is written on the board, and then *b* is placed in the initial position. After *bat* has been identified, the *b* is erased and replaced with *m* or *p,* and so on.

The phonogram method has the advantage of using real words. Individual sounds are not presented in isolation as much as in the synthetic method. The phonogram approach is very enjoyable for beginning readers because they are able to read many words quickly. However, this method is useful only as a supplement to another, more inclusive approach. To teach *-an, -at, -ab, -ad, -ap, -am,* and *-azz* as separate phonograms is inefficient. For these letter combinations the children should eventually be led to the short-vowel generalization (generalization 1).

Suggested Activities for Teaching Phonics Generalizations
ACTIVITIES FOR INSTRUCTION IN DISCRIMINATING BEGINNING SOUNDS

1. To help children hear similar beginning-consonant sounds, sorting activities may be used. Pictures of various objects, some beginning with the target sound and some beginning with other sounds, are placed before the class. The children are to say the name of each picture and tell if the picture begins with the target sound.

2. After the children have learned several beginning sounds, they can be asked to place all of the pictures that begin with the /b/ sound in a paper bag labeled *b,* all those beginning with /s/ in the *s* bag, and so on. The children can do this individually or as a class. (This activity also helps establish letter-sound correspondences.)

3. Fruit Basket Upset can be adapted for work with beginning consonants. Each child is given a picture card. Chairs are placed in a circle. The teacher or leader says, "All those with pictures beginning with /m/ (or, 'like *mouse*") change places." As soon as the appropriate children have left their places, the teacher removes one chair so that one child will be left without a seat. That child is out of the game. The game continues, with the teacher removing one chair each turn. "Alphabet Upset" is the signal for *all* children to change places.

Note: For all activities designed to practice hearing sounds, the stimuli should be mainly auditory. The word for each picture should *not* appear on the card. Otherwise, the children may just match visual symbols, not auditory ones. Care must also be taken that each child knows the name of each picture.

ACTIVITIES FOR TEACHING CONSONANT LETTER-SOUND CORRESPONDENCES

1. Activities can be developed in which the child progresses along a path of a game board by naming a picture pasted on the path, giving its beginning sound and identifying the beginning letter (see Fig. 6.1). Each player would roll a die or whirl a spinner to determine how many spaces could be moved. If the player comes to a picture for which he or she cannot give the beginning letter, the teacher tells the player the correct answer. The player must then leave his

Fig. 6.1. Board game for consonant-sounds practice.

or her marker on the last picture for which the beginning letter was success-fully identified, and the next player takes a turn. If the player cannot identify the picture itself, the teacher or another player should tell the player what the picture is, without penalty.

2. Lotto or Bingo games can be used to practice consonant sounds. Each child is given a card that has been divided into 9 or 16 squares. A different picture is on each square of a card, and each player's card has a different arrangement of the pictures (see Fig. 6.2).

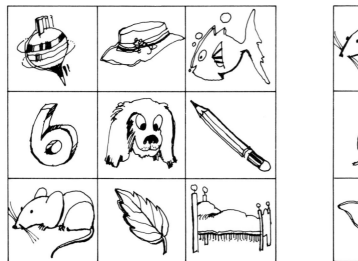

Fig. 6.2. Bingo cards for consonant-sounds practice.

One player serves as caller. The caller has a deck of letter cards, each of which has one letter on it. The letters represent the beginning sounds of the pictures on the players' cards. The caller shuffles the letter cards and displays them one at a time. As each letter is displayed, the players place a small paper marker over the picture on their card that has that beginning sound. For example, if the card is *d*, the players would cover the picture of a dog. (The cards may use the same picture or different pictures for each sound. However, each sound should have a representative picture on each player's card.) The first player to cover all of the pictures in a row vertically, horizontally, or diagonally shouts "Lotto" or "Bingo."

3. A Trip to the Market game can be used to practice associating sounds with letters. Each child is given a large letter card. The first child shows his or her card and says, "I went to the market and bought a *fan*." The item bought must begin with the letter the child holds. The second player says, "I went to the market and I bought a fan and a bun." Each child must repeat all of the previous items and add a new item. To help the children remember the words, each letter card should be held in the lap throughout the game as a memory jogger. (It is not a good idea to eliminate those who fail from the game. If these children are out of the game, they get no more practice, and they are obviously the ones who need practice most!)

4. To help students see the connection between phonics and reading, the teacher can write the following sentence on the board:

I love to eat c_____.

The students are to suggest as many words beginning with the two sounds of *c* (/k/ and /s/) as possible. These words are written on the board. Some examples are listed below.

cucumbers	celery	cinnamon	candy
cereal	cake	caramels	crackers
carrots	cookies	coconuts	crab

(Words that the children suggest that begin with *k* or *s* should be written to one side. The teacher should indicate that although these words are not wrong, they aren't spelled with *c* at the beginning.) Then the teacher adds the words *angel food* to the sentence: I like to eat angel food c_____. The students are asked to cross out each word that no longer fits the sentence. The same procedure is followed with other sentences and for other consonants. For variety the teacher can suggest words that do not fit, either because they begin with the wrong sound or because they don't make sense.

1. After the students have learned several long- and short-vowel patterns, they can play games in which they have to match the vowel sounds in written words. For example, *rain* and *day* would be a pair, as would *boat* and *go*. The games could follow the Go Fish, Dominoes, or Concentration formats described below. Words must be read to be played.

For Go Fish a deck of cards is needed that contains three cards for each vowel sound being practiced. For example, *main, say,* and *take* would form a set of three, and *noise, coin,* and *boy* would form another set. The object of the game is for each player to get rid of all of the cards in his or her hand. The cards are shuffled, and each player is dealt four cards. The remaining cards are

ACTIVITIES FOR TEACHING VOWEL GENERALIZATIONS

placed face down in a stack in the center. Players discard in front of themselves all sets of cards that have the same vowel sound that they have been dealt. They must name the cards as they discard them. Then the first player (the caller) displays a card from his or her hand, names another player, and asks if that player has a card with the same vowel sound as the word on the card. If that player does have a card that matches the vowel sound on the displayed card, he or she must give the card to the caller. If the player has more than one of the requested card, he or she must give up only one card per request. If the caller is successful in the request, he or she continues making requests until a "Go Fish" answer is given, signifying that the player does not have a matching card. Then the caller draws the top card from the pack. If the word on the card drawn does match the vowel sound requested, the caller gets another turn. If not, the player on the caller's left becomes the caller. Play continues in this manner, with triplets being placed on the table and named whenever they are assembled, until one player has no cards left in his or her hand. The game then ends. The first player to be without cards is designated as the winner.

In Dominoes, as in Go Fish, the object of the game is for each player to get rid of all of his or her dominoes. The dominoes are 2" × 4" cards divided into two equal spaces. Each card has a different word written in each space. The words should contain the vowel sounds being practiced. The dominoes are shuffled, and each player is given four dominoes. The remaining dominoes are placed in a stack, face down on the table. The top domino is placed face up in the middle of the table. The first player matches one end of a card from his or her hand with either end of the starter card. Cards match if they have the same vowel sound (see Fig. 6.3). If the player cannot make a match, he or she draws from the pack of dominoes until a match can be made. Then the next player follows the same procedure, matching a domino to the free end of either domino on the table (see Fig. 6.4). Play continues until one player plays the last domino in his or her hand.

The object of Concentration is to match words with the same vowel sound. A set of 16–24 cards is needed in which each vowel sound being practiced is represented by two or four words. For example, for the long *o* sound, *coat, hope, go,* and *show* might be written on separate cards. The cards are

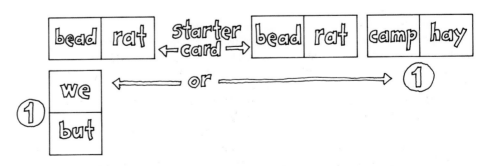

Fig. 6.3. **Examples of first play in Dominoes.**

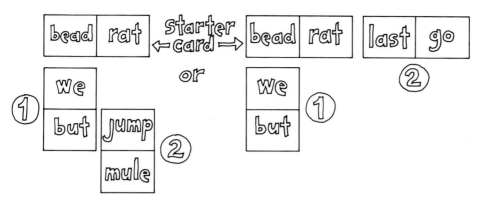

Fig. 6.4. Examples of second play in Dominoes.

shuffled and placed face down in rows. The first player turns over one card in its place, reads the word, and then turns over a second card and reads the word on that card. If the two words have the same vowel sound, the player places the pair of cards to one side and repeats the procedure. If the vowel sounds do not match, the cards are returned to their face-down position, and the next player takes a turn. Play continues until all the cards have been matched. The winner is the player with the most cards. (*Note:* Be sure that the cards are returned to their original places in the rows after each unsuccessful turn.)

2. Bingo may also be used for practicing vowel generalizations, such as the CVC pattern for short vowels. The words used should all differ minimally. For example, the Bingo squares could contain *big, bag, bug, beg; pin, pan, pen.*

3. Fill-in-the-blank exercises can be used to help children make precise differentiations among vowel sounds. For example:

The _____ ran away.
(big, bug, bag)

The word choices should differ only in the vowel.

ACTIVITIES FOR TEACHING PHONIC SYLLABICATION

1. Card games may be played in which the pairs match because they have common first or last syllables (*bacon* and *baby* or *whistle* and *bustle*) or similar inflectional endings (*sits* and *runs* or *jumping* and *gardening*). The student must be able to say the words to claim the pair.

2. Students can work with nonsense words to practice phonic syllabication. The group should be divided into teams and each team given a different list of nonsense words. The lists must be of comparable difficulty. Each team is to decide as a group how to pronounce its words. Then the words from each list are written on the board, and the team responsible pronounces the words, one at a time. The other teams may challenge a pronunciation, and the presiding

team must defend its answer by citing a rule. The team with the most correctly pronounced words wins. (The teacher is the final arbiter.) Some examples:

> pable
> spumey
> gummot
> shiker
> wimdan
> flarnabble

Structural Analysis Syllabication generalizations provide the reader with the ability to divide a word into pronounceable units. Structural-analysis skills enable the reader to divide a word into morphemes, which are the smallest units of meaning. *Duck* is one morpheme; *ducks* is made up of two morphemes—*duck* and the plural morpheme *s*. Similarly, *unfriendly* has three morphemes. A successful reader is able to identify morphemes in words and use this knowledge to both decode the words and gain insight into their meanings.

Instruction in structural analysis should help the student to identify the following word parts:

1. inflections
   a) plural (cat*s*, match*es*, hobb*ies*)
   b) past tense (jump*ed*, greet*ed*)
   c) continuous tense (walk*ing*, speak*ing*)
   d) comparison (redd*er*, rich*est*)
2. compounds: *side/walk, foot/ball*
3. root words: *help*s, *help*ed, *help*ing, *help*er
4. prefixes and suffixes: *bi*cycle, *bi*noculars, *bi*nary; farm*er*, report*er*, danc*er*
5. contractions: *is/n't, they/'ll, we/'ve, you/'re*

We do not recommend teaching children long lists of prefixes and suffixes and their meanings. However, recognition of some of these word parts as units of both pronunciation and meaning is useful.

The following prefixes, chosen because of their frequency and relative familiarity to elementary-age children, may be worth teaching.*

ab (from)	en (in)	phono (voice, sound)
ad (to)	ex (out)	pre (before)
anti (against)	in (into)	pro (in front of)
be (by)	in (not)	re (back)
bi (two)	inter (between)	sub (under)
com (with)	mis (wrong)	trans (across)
de (from)	mono (one)	un (not)
dis (apart), (opposite of)	non (not)	

*Reduction of a listing in Emerald Dechant, *Reading Improvement in the Secondary School,* Englewood Cliffs, N.J.: Prentice-Hall, 1973, pp. 221–223.

In addition, even beginning readers are able to deal with the more simple aspects of structural analysis, such as plurals and past-tense markers, and to take delight in identifying long compound words.

Word-identification strategies, such as the use of context, phonics generalizations, and structural analysis, are necessary so that a reader can decode unknown words. Throughout instruction in these strategies, however, the teacher and the child must keep in mind that the ultimate goal of all such instruction is that the child eventually learn to recognize words as wholes, immediately. These words are now *sight words,* and the child no longer has to analyze them in order to identify them.

SIGHT WORDS

A large sight vocabulary is necessary for even a beginning reader. If a reader has to spend a great deal of time and effort identifying individual words in a sentence or passage, she or he will be unable to attend to the meaning of the passage. Most theorists agree that if a reader cannot recognize 95 percent of the words in a passage, it is too difficult for that reader.

Importance of an Adequate Sight Vocabulary

Furthermore, unless the reader has a large enough sight vocabulary to recognize nearly all of the words in a sentence, the reader will lose the use of one of the most important of all word-identification cues—context clues. Many words can be identified by using meaning clues from the context that surrounds them, but only if the words in that context can be read. A meager sight vocabulary prevents an already struggling reader from using context clues.

A large sight-word vocabulary is also useful for developing another word-identification strategy, the use of phonics generalizations. One practice in common use is to teach children several sight words that begin or end with a certain letter and then to use these known words as a basis for teaching a generalization about sound-letter correspondences. For example, if the children have learned *my, me, Mother,* and *Mike,* these words might be used to help the children learn the sound of *m*.

Some words need to be taught early as sight words because of their frequency in printed materials and because they are phonically irregular. Words like *what, they,* and *of* cannot be "sounded out." They can only be recognized as wholes or identified by the context in which they appear. Most reading programs recognize that at least a certain number of these frequently occurring words need to be taught early in the reading program in order for the student to be able to read meaningful sentences.

How is a teacher to decide which sight words should be taught? One procedure is to refer to a sight-word list that has been developed on the basis of frequency. A second procedure is to allow the students to choose the words they would most like to learn.

Selection of Sight Words to Teach

The most widely used of all sight-word lists is the one published by Dolch (1941). Dolch identified the 220 most frequent words in children's vocabularies and in beginning-reading materials, according to the International Kinder-

Sight-Word Lists

garten Union Vocabulary List, the Gates Primary Word List, and the Wheeler-Howell First Grade Vocabulary List. These three lists were compiled during the 1920s. Recently more current lists of the speaking vocabularies of children and of the most frequently occurring words in printed materials have been made available. Johnson (1971) compared the Kučera-Francis list (1967), which provides a rank-ordered list of 50,406 different words found in a wide variety of adult reading materials, with the Dolch list. Johnson found that 37 percent of the words on the Dolch list were not among the first 220 words of the Kučera-Francis list. This finding led Johnson to conclude that the Dolch list was out of date.

To develop a more current list, Johnson then compared the 500 most frequent words on the Kučera-Francis list with a list developed by Murphy and her associates (1957) of the words in the spontaneous-speaking vocabularies of primary-grade children. Johnson found 306 words that had been used at least 50 times by kindergarten or first-grade children that also appeared among the first 500 words of the Kučera-Francis list. He suggests these words as a basic sight vocabulary for beginning reading because the words are common in both the speech of children and printed materials and because the words are based on the results of relatively recent studies.

Otto and Chester (1972) examined Johnson's criteria for selecting words, questioning whether spoken vocabulary provides a sound basis for a beginning-reading vocabulary. Furthermore, they do not feel that it is appropriate to base a beginning-reading vocabulary on adult reading materials. Otto and Chester suggest that an initial sight-word vocabulary should be drawn from printed materials designed to be read by young children. According to Otto and Chester, the American Heritage *Word Frequency Book* (Carroll, Davies, and Richman, 1971) provides such a basis. This publication includes a list of the 23,477 different words found in samples of 215 texts designed for use by third-grade readers in 20 different subject areas. Using this list, Otto and Chester rank-ordered the third-grade words by frequency and identified the 500 most commonly occurring words. The authors suggest that these words provide a basis for a beginning-reading vocabulary and have dubbed their list the Great Atlantic and Pacific Sight Word List.

The Great Atlantic and Pacific Sight Word List includes all of the most frequent graphic words from the American Heritage computer-assembled list. No alterations were made. For this reason proper names, digits, and inflected forms are included on the list. Thus *word* and *words* are listed as two different entries. The authors make several suggestions for pruning or organizing the list, but have chosen to present the list in its complete form until empirical bases for such changes can be established.

The Dolch list contains 220 words; the Johnson list, 306 words; and the Great Atlantic and Pacific list, 500 words. The lists do differ in some degree because each was derived from a different source. However, a great deal of overlap exists among these three lists and among all sight-word lists. Otto and Stallard (1977) compared 16 sight-word lists based on oral or written language of children or adults. They identified 100 words common to all of the lists. These words are listed in Table 6.1.

a	down	it	out	three
about	for	just	over	to
after	from	know	put	too
again	get	like	right	two
all	go	little	said	up
an	good	look	saw	us
and	got	made	say	want
any	had	make	see	was
are	has	me	she	we
at	have	my	so	went
away	he	new	some	were
be	her	no	take	what
big	here	not	that	when
but	him	now	the	where
by	his	of	them	who
came	how	off	then	will
come	I	old	there	with
could	if	on	they	would
did	in	one	think	you
do	is	our	this	your

Wayne Otto and Cathy Stallard, "One Hundred Essential Sight Words." Reprinted with permission from *Visible Language* **10**, 1 (Summer 1976): 251. Box 1972 CMA, Cleveland, Ohio 44106. Copyright 1976 by *Visible Language*.

TABLE 6.1
One hundred essential sight words

Sight-word lists can be useful in helping teachers plan for instruction in reading. Words from a list may be used to illustrate phonics lessons. Teachers may wish to compare periodically the words they have taught their classes with the words on a sight-word list to ensure that the children are being taught the most common words. However, we do not suggest that teachers begin with the first word on a list and "teach the list." A sight-word list should serve only as a guide and as a source of comparison of what words the children have been taught and what words they may be expected to meet in printed material.

Self-Selection of Words

An alternative to teaching all children a specific set of words is to allow the children themselves to choose words that they would like to learn. This procedure is espoused by Ashton-Warner (1963) and other proponents of a language-experience approach. According to these writers, a child is likely to learn a word that is meaningful to the child and that he or she wants to learn. The children are encouraged to identify these words and to place them in word banks for easy access. The obvious drawback of this approach is that few children are going to choose such frequent but intrinsically uninteresting words as *to, of, for,* or *what.* Function words, such as prepositions and conjunctions, are necessary for stringing words together, and unless children learn words of this type as well as *giraffe, satellite,* and *jogging,* they will never learn to read printed material.

We suggest that teachers combine the two methods for choosing words. The children may be encouraged to choose words that they have an interest in learning. But they will also need to learn the more frequent and less tangible function words. These additional words may be chosen from a sight-word list and introduced gradually so that the children steadily increase their stock of words that they recognize instantly.

The teacher must be careful not to overload beginning readers with too many new words at one time. Words should be introduced gradually and reviewed often. New words should always be presented in a meaningful context, not in isolation. This is especially important for words that lack a concrete referent and for function words. This procedure will help the students to perceive these words as part of a flow of language and to help them concentrate on chunks of meaningful language, not just isolated bits. Care should also be taken that the students learn to transfer their knowledge to new situations. Learning to recognize a new word in a specific context is not particularly useful. What the student must learn is to recognize the word in all possible contexts. The teacher must provide opportunities for the child to practice recognizing new words in varied reading materials. Practice sessions should also require that the child differentiate the new word from words of similar appearance. For example:

> Susan _____ into the big house.
> (want, went, what)

One common but inappropriate practice for reviewing sight words is to have the child flip through a set of word cards, saying the words silently. This procedure is ill-advised because the student has no feedback about the correctness of the response. It does only harm for little Sam to sit by himself at his desk and practice saying *went* for *want* ten times. All such practice should take place only with another person who can monitor the responses. The monitor can be an aide, the teacher, or even another child. But the response *must* be monitored.

Word cards *can* be useful as a reference source for the beginning reader. A sentence containing a word in a meaningful context can be placed on the back of the card. Then the child can use the context to confirm the word's identity. However, the student must be able to read the words in the context, and the context must help identify the word. "I like my new _____" is not a particularly enlightening context. Nor is "David is _____." "I rode my _____ to school" and "Dan read the _____" do provide context clues for identifying the missing words. Choosing precise contexts can be difficult, but without such precision using context to review words is not very useful.

1. Many games can be adapted to provide practice with sight words. Concentration, Go Fish, and Bingo are three such games. Instead of using isolated words, these games should require the students to read the words in phrases. A Bingo or Lotto game could look like the one shown in Fig. 6.5.

When playing games like Concentration that require visual matching of identical words, the students should always be required to name the words before claiming them as a pair. Otherwise, the game involves nothing more than matching words by the way they look.

in my house	on our house	at his house	under our house
at her house	in his house	at my house	under her house
in our house	under my house	on my house	on his house
at our house	in her house	on her house	under his house

Fig. 6.5.   Bingo card for sight-word practice.

2.   Activities played on a teacher-made game board can also be used to provide practice in identifying sight words. In such games the students move markers along a path. Players can move their markers only if they correctly identify a word or phrase. There are two basic variations of board games. In one, the player throws a die or whirls a spinner in order to find out how many spaces may be moved. Then the player moves along the path for that many spaces, reading the phrase or word on each space (see Fig. 6.6). If the player comes to a phrase that he or she cannot read, the teacher or another person serving as a monitor tells the player what the phrase is. Then the player has to leave the marker on the last space successfully read, and the next player takes a turn.

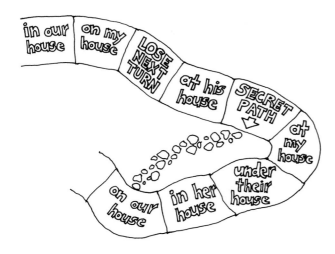

Fig. 6.6.   Game board for sight-word practice.

The type of game board shown in Fig. 6.6 requires a new path for each new set of sight words. As an alternative the phrases can be written on small cards that can be attached by paper clips to the path. In this way the cards may be easily interchanged (see Fig. 6.7).

Fig. 6.7. An alternative format for constructing a game board.

A second kind of board game uses an unmarked path. (Special messages, such as "Take another turn" or "Go back three spaces," may be written on certain spaces permanently. These messages usually add extra excitement to the game.) From a deck of cards the players draw cards with numbers on the back, one card per turn. On the face of each card is a sentence, with one sight word underlined. The student must identify the underlined word. If the player does not know any word in the context, that word should be provided. In this way the student is assured of being able to use the context to identify the word. If the student is able to identify the underlined word, he or she then moves along the path for the number of spaces indicated on the back of the card. Then the next player takes a turn.

3. Primary children enjoy taking a project home to show their parents. Sight words can be tested or practiced by many art-type activities. The children can identify words or phrases printed on feathers and then paste these feathers on a turkey at Thanksgiving time. The same procedure can be used with spring flowers, valentines, snowflakes, or countless other seasonal symbols. Of course, this practice is time-consuming, requiring a great deal of advance preparation and one-to-one work during class time, but it also provides a novel break from more routine practice.

EVALUATION OF DECODING SKILLS

Veterans of the classroom are well aware that simply teaching a skill or an idea does not guarantee that all, or even some, of the students have learned anything. We are always amazed by teachers who assume that they do not have to teach something because the students "had that" last year. What they *had* was an *opportunity* to learn the skill; there can be no blind assumption that the children availed themselves of this opportunity.

Constant evaluation needs to be carried out in order for teachers to know if children have learned what has been taught. Further evaluation is required later to determine if the students have retained their knowledge. In addition, evaluation is necessary at all stages of skill development to find out not only if the students *can* use the knowledge, but also if they *do* use it.

Evaluation is discussed in depth in Chapter 12. Here, however, we wish to suggest three methods of assessing word-identification skills.

Criterion-referenced measures, such as those found in skills-management systems, can be very useful for measuring the effectiveness of objective-based instruction. Most criterion-referenced measures attempt to isolate a decoding skill as much as possible in order to determine if the student has mastered that particular skill. Criterion-referenced tests usually involved paper-and-pencil tasks in which the student chooses the answer from several choices. However, some criterion-referenced tests are performance tests. For these tests the student supplies the answer without being given choices from which to select the answer, not just recognize it. (See Fig. 6.8 for examples of criterion-referenced test items for knowledge of beginning consonant blends, recognition of possessive forms, and use of context clues.)

Of course, few (if any) word-identification skills can truly be isolated. For example, in order to correctly answer the context-clue item in Fig. 6.8, the student must be able to read the context. That is, the student must have the sight vocabulary and phonics skills needed to read the words surrounding the nonsense word. In addition, because reading abilities often build on one another, a teacher may unwittingly evaluate a whole series of underlying abilities when supposedly measuring just one reading skill or task. Furthermore, a reader does not use skills one at a time when actually reading. Nonetheless, we feel that measuring mastery of discrete skills in reading can be a useful part of measuring reading ability and that criterion-referenced tests, properly constructed, can fulfill that function well.

Criterion-referenced tests have several advantages for measuring word-identification skills. Because they test individual skills, criterion-referenced tests can help the teacher distinguish between a student who knows a skill and doesn't apply it and a student who has not yet even learned the skill. Pencil-and-paper criterion-referenced tests also are easy to administer and are often suitable for groups rather than just individuals. (Performance tests, however, must be given to students one at a time.) Because of this characteristic, teachers can monitor the skill development of many children without investing a great deal of time in individual testing. Furthermore, because criterion-referenced tests do deal with individual skills, teachers are able to use these instruments to identify the specific skill needs of their pupils and therefore to focus instruction more precisely.

Strangely enough, many of the disadvantages of using criterion-referenced tests for assessing decoding skills are related to the advantages. Although criterion-referenced tests can help pinpoint specific needs by testing mastery of isolated skills, one does not read by using skills separately. Teachers who use criterion-referenced skills must keep in mind the artificiality of the tasks used to test skill development and must remember that these tests can give only *part* of the information needed to assess reading development.

Consonant blends

Directions:
Listen carefully to each word I say and decide what the first letters of the word are. Then fill in the circle for that choice on your answer form. The first word is *sprej*:

Test item:
A. spl
B. spr
C. sch
D. str

Possessives

Directions:
Read the four phrases for each item. Decide which underlined word shows that something belongs to someone or something, and then fill in the circle for your choice on the answer form.

Test item:
A. *let's* find
B. that *book's* good
C. my *brothers*
D. *birds'* nest

Context clues

Directions:
Read the first paragraph in each item carefully and use the context clues to determine the meaning of the nonsense word. Then read the second paragraph and fill in the circle for the answer choice that best completes the last sentence.

(1) Mr. Green was teaching Sally how to *mup.* He held her hand around the pencil and helped her make the letters on the paper. The lines of each word were wiggly, but Mr. Green could read the whole sentence.

(2) Because we were very noisy, Ms. Martin made the whole class *mup* for the rest of the hour. To do this, we

A. put our heads down
B. took out paper and pencils
C. got out our reading assignment
D. folded our hands

Fig. 6.8. Sample items from criterion-referenced tests. (Adapted by permission from R. Klumb, J. Thompson, and D. Spiegel, *Design II: A Post-Elementary Reading Program, Proficiency Test,* **Minneapolis: NCS Educational Systems, 1977.)**

Similarly, although criterion-referenced tests are good for identifying which skills a student *can* use, tests of this type do not determine if a student *does* use the skills. The reading tasks in criterion-referenced tests are often so removed from "real" reading that application of learned skills cannot really be judged.

A third disadvantage of paper-and-pencil criterion-referenced tests is that mastery of a word-identification skill is measured through recognition of the correct response and not through unprompted production. That is, when the teacher pronounces the word *damp* and the student is asked to circle the letter (*b, d, p,* or *t*) that represents the beginning sound of *damp*, he or she is provided with the sound and must choose from only four letters. Similarly, if a student is asked to underline *want* (without seeing the word) from the choices *when, went,* and *want,* the student not only has a 33 percent chance of simply guessing the right answer, but also has only to recognize the word, not produce it from his or her own memory. Teachers should be aware that such recognition tasks are different from the tasks of independent silent reading.

If one were to develop a continuum for describing methods of evaluating decoding skills, one endpoint of the continuum would probably be criterion-referenced tests, and the other endpoint might be procedures for analyzing oral-reading errors. These two evaluation methods differ widely in many respects, and we feel that both of them have a place in efforts to determine reading-skill development.

Analysis of Oral Reading

The term *analysis of oral-reading errors* describes the process well: A student reads aloud, and the teacher records exactly what the child says and then analyzes any deviations from the printed text. The most common procedure for gathering the oral-reading data is to use an informal reading inventory (IRI). In an IRI the student reads aloud short, graded passages and then answers questions about what has been read. The teacher uses a recording system, such as the one shown in Fig. 6.9, to indicate what the student read. Then by looking at how the student's responses agreed with and differed from the text, the teacher can make determinations of what skills and strategies the student is or is not using while reading. For example, if a student read *The dog ran ask the cat* for *The dog ran after the cat,* the teacher might suspect that the student was using some letter-sound (graphophonic) cues, but was not using semantic (meaning) and syntactic (grammar) cues. If the student read the sentence as *The man ran around the house,* the teacher might be concerned about the student's sight-vocabulary level and his or her ability to use phonics cues.

One of the most important advantages of using oral reading to assess word-identification skills is that the teacher can determine if the student actually *applies* these skills. Some children do not connect skill-development activities with reading at other times. As a consequence, these students do not put to use those skills they actually have mastered. Using an IRI or similar oral-reading task can help the teacher find out if the pupils have indeed made the connection.

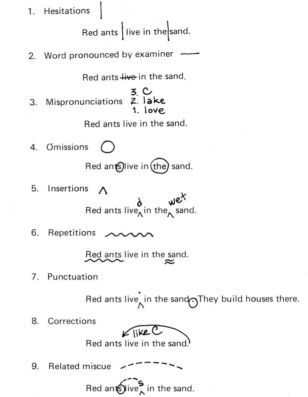

Fig. 6.9. Marking oral-reading performance.

A second important advantage of measuring skill development through oral-reading performance is that the skills are not isolated. The task the student is asked to perform more nearly resembles "real" reading than do the tasks in most criterion-referenced tests. Skills are not isolated, but are used (or not used!) in conjunction with all of the available cue systems of the language.

The most important disadvantage of this method is obvious: The effectiveness of analyzing oral-reading errors to determine word-identification skill development depends almost entirely on the teacher's expertise. The teacher has to record the data accurately and to interpret the data perceptively. No manual exists to indicate exactly what a particular miscue (deviation from the text) means, although the *Reading Miscue Inventory* developed by Goodman and Burke (1972) does provide useful guidelines for analyzing children's oral-reading miscues. Most often the teacher alone searches for patterns of response and interprets the relative importance of various responses. Clearly the teacher must feel confident about his or her knowledge about reading and the reading process.

Criterion-referenced tests can be given to groups. Informal reading inventories and other oral-reading measures must be given individually. Furthermore, the analysis of oral-reading errors can be very time-consuming. Many teachers do not wish to use oral-reading measures, simply because of the large amount of time needed to administer and interpret them properly.

As with criterion-referenced tests, the results of an analysis of oral reading should be used cautiously. A student's oral reading may not accurately reflect his or her silent-reading strategies and skills. An analysis of oral-reading errors should be viewed as just one piece of information about a student's reading ability.

Assessment procedures that involve the formal collection of information about a student's decoding skills are a necessary part of the evaluation of instruction. However, teachers can informally gather data throughout the entire school day to help determine if their students have developed the ability to use decoding skills. *Any* activity in which a child has to read can be used for assessment. For example, the child's performance on a workbook page should be viewed as an indication of his or her ability to use certain skills. The child's ability to do the necessary reading in math or social studies reflects on his or her decoding skills. When reading a library book, does the child ask for help with a word that follows a common vowel generalization taught the week before? Does the child consistently choose "easy" books when given a free choice of reading material?

Just as the teaching of reading should not be confined to the 8:30–10 A.M. time slot alone, the assessment of reading cannot be limited to specific situations in which the teacher announces (aloud or silently) *"Now* I am going to evaluate my students' decoding skills." *Any time* a child reads *anything*, the teacher can make such an evaluation. Limiting evaluation of decoding skills to formal assessment means closing your eyes to what the children are really *doing* with reading during their daily lives, and that is, after all, where your success as a teacher will ultimately count.

Informal Assessment of Decoding Skills

You probably have figured out already what our suggestion is going to be for evaluating word-identification skills. Table 6.2 gives you one more gigantic hint.

As you no doubt suspected, we recommend using both criterion-referenced tests and analyses of oral reading, supplemented by informal evaluation of daily reading performance. Criterion-referenced tests can give teachers the confidence that they have specific, objective-based information by which they can focus their instruction. Oral-reading analyses can help teachers

Application

Type of assessment	Mastery and application	Isolation and recombination	
Criterion-referenced tests	Indicates if skill mastered	Identifies specific skill weaknesses	**TABLE 6.2** **Advantages of using criterion-referenced tests and analyses of oral reading**
Oral-reading analyses	Indicates if skill applied	Identifies weaknesses in using skills in combinations	

determine how effective their instruction has been in guiding their pupils toward becoming fluent, mature readers. Informal evaluation can give teachers information about what the students are doing when they read in "real-life," functional reading situations.

SUMMARY Teaching children to decode is more than helping them learn sight words and sound-letter correspondences. Children must be taught to use multiple cue systems of the language and must learn that meaning is as much a cue to word identification as sounds are. Good instruction in decoding provides practice with many different word-identification strategies and helps the students relate these strategies to "real" reading situations.

REVIEW QUESTIONS
1. We have stated that children need to develop a flexible repertoire of decoding skills. Relate this statement to the three cue systems of the language: the semantic, syntactic, and graphophonic systems. How does the child's knowledge of these systems help him or her in decoding?

2. Review the section entitled "Prerequisites to Decoding Words." Why is each of the attitudes describing a logical prerequisite to successful decoding? What kinds of decoding problems might result if a child has not developed the five prereading subskills identified by Venezky?

3. Clymer investigated 45 phonics generalizations that have been included for decoding instruction in different reading programs. Develop a set of criteria to help you make decisions about what generalizations are appropriate for teaching your class.

4. Distinguish between phonic syllabication and structural analysis. Why does a young reader need to develop skill in using both of these areas?

5. What are the reasons for combining self-selection with the use of a sight-word list for choosing words to enlarge a child's sight vocabulary?

6. Read again the sections on teaching different decoding skills. Then list five criteria for judging effective lessons in decoding skills.

7. Complete the following chart to show the advantages and disadvantages of the three methods given below for evaluation decoding skills. (You will have to come to your own conclusions about the advantages and disadvantages for informal assessment, because *we* didn't discuss them!)

Method	Advantages	Disadvantages
Criterion-referenced tests		
Analyses of oral reading		
Informal assessment		

Ashton-Warner, Sylvia. *Teacher* (New York: Simon and Schuster, 1963).

Bailey, Mildred. "The Utility of Phonics Generalizations in Grades One through Six," *Reading Teacher* **20** (1967): 413–418.

Barrett, Thomas C. "Visual Discrimination Tasks as Predictors of First Grade Reading Achievement," *Reading Teacher* **18** (1965): 108–117.

Berko, Jean. "The Child's Learning of English Morphology," *Word* **14** (1958): 150–177.

Biemiller, Andrew. "The Development of the Use of Graphic and Contextual Information as Children Learn to Read," *Reading Research Quarterly* **6** (1970): 75–96.

Brown, Roger. "Linguistic Determinism and the Part of Speech," in S. Sapporta, ed., *Psycholinguistics* (New York: Holt, Rinehart and Winston, 1966).

Bukovec, Joseph. "Usefulness of Phonic Generalizations: A New Formula," *Reading Teacher* **27** (1973): 270–283.

Carroll, John B., Peter Davies, and Barry Richman. *Word Frequency Book* (Boston: Houghton Mifflin, 1971).

Clymer, Theodore. "The Utility of Phonic Generalizations in the Primary Grades," *Reading Teacher* **16** (1963): 252–258.

Dechant, Emerald. *Reading Improvement in the Secondary School* (Englewood Cliffs, N.J.: Prentice-Hall, 1973).

Dolch, Edward. *Teaching Primary Reading* (Champaign, Ill.: Garrard Press, 1941).

Emans, Robert. "The Usefulness of Phonics Generalizations above the Primary Grades," *Reading Teacher* **20** (1967): 419–425.

Flesch, Rudolph. *Why Johnny Can't Read* (New York: Harper and Bros., 1955).

Goodman, Kenneth. "Reading: A Psycholinguistic Guessing Game," in Harry Singer and Robert Ruddell, eds., *Theoretical Models and Processes in Reading*, 2d ed. (Newark, Delaware: International Reading Association, 1976).

Goodman, Yetta, and Carolyn Burke. *Reading Miscue Inventory: Procedure for Diagnosis and Evaluation* (New York: Macmillan, 1972).

Groff, Patrick. "Fifteen Flaws of Phonics," *Elementary English* **50** (1973): 35–40.

Hall, MaryAnne, and Jerilyn Ribovich. "Teaching Reading in Reading Situations," *Reading Teacher* **27** (1973): 163–166.

Johnson, Dale D. "A Basic Vocabulary for Beginning Reading," *Elementary School Journal* **72** (1971): 29–34.

Johnson, R. J. "The Effect of Training in Letter Names on Success in Beginning Reading for Children of Differing Abilities." (Paper presented at the 1970 convention of the American Educational Research Association.)

Kučera, Henry, and W. Nelson Francis. *Computational Analysis of Present-day American English* (Providence: Brown University Press, 1967).

Murphy, Helen *et al.* "The Spontaneous Speaking Vocabulary of Children in the Primary Grades," *Boston University Journal of Education* **140** (1957): 1–105.

Otto, Wayne, and Robert Chester. "Sight Words for Beginning Readers," *Journal of Educational Research* **65** (1972): 435–443.

Otto, Wayne, and Cathy Stallard. "One Hundred Essential Sight Words," *Visible Language* **10**, 1 (Summer 1976): 247–252.

Samuels, S. Jay. "Letter-Name vs. Letter-Sound Knowledge as Factors Influencing Learning to Read." (Paper presented at the 1970 convention of the American Educational Research Association.)

Smith, Richard J., and Dale D. Johnson. *Teaching Children to Read* (Reading, Mass.: Addison-Wesley, 1976).

Venezky, Richard. "Prereading Skills: Theoretical Foundations and Practical Applications," Technical report no. 54 (Madison: Wisconsin Research and Development Center for Cognitive Learning, 1974).

Chapter 7
Understanding
What You
Decode:
Comprehension

After reading this chapter, you will be able to:

1. Discuss characteristics of written material that affect comprehension.
2. Discuss characteristics of the reader that affect comprehension.
3. Compare and contrast theories of comprehension.
4. Describe what is meant by literal, inferential, and critical comprehension (evaluation).
5. Describe what is meant by appreciation.
6. Describe several important aspects of preparing children for comprehension.
7. Develop appropriate activities for furthering comprehension abilities.
8. Discuss procedures for assessing comprehension.

Recently one of the authors evaluated the reading skills of a third-grade student, Mark, a delightful child with whom it was easy to gain rapport. Allowed to choose the order in which he would complete the diagnostic activities, Mark chose the visual-discrimination tasks, then the copying task, and next the auditory-discrimination test, followed by the lists of nonsense words designed to test knowledge of vowel generalizations. Mark did well on all of these tasks. Next, he read a graded list of sight words and performed satisfactorily even at the fifth-grade level. And his teacher said he had a reading problem! The only activity left was oral and silent reading of short selections, followed by questions about what he had read. We began with a selection at the first-grade level, just to ensure success. Mark read the selection perfectly, confidently, and with good expression. But when reminded that now he would be asked a few questions about what he had read, Mark grinned sheepishly and responded, "Gosh, that's going to be hard." And it was. He could answer only two of the five questions correctly, even with encouragement and a little prompting.

Children like Mark are found in nearly every classroom. They can say the words, but are unable to gain meaning from the words. They cannot comprehend what they read. In this chapter we explore the nature of reading comprehension and the factors that affect it. We suggest some instructional practices that will help to develop comprehension abilities, and we examine several techniques for assessing comprehension. As you read this chapter, you may become discouraged about "the state of the art." Research has provided definitive answers to few of the important questions about reading comprehension. However, comprehension can be enhanced by good instructional practices and can be assessed, albeit imperfectly, in a variety of ways. Although theorists don't have *the* answers, we do know enough about comprehension to permit classroom teachers to proceed thoughtfully and with purpose in guiding and evaluating comprehension.

DEFINING COMPREHENSION

Too often teachers, parents, and indeed children themselves equate reading with decoding. If a reader can pronounce the words on the page, the listener often assumes that the reader must understand what he or she has just pronounced. This confusion is apparent in the following statement from Flesch (1955, p. 23): "I once surprised a native of Prague by reading aloud from a Czech newspaper. 'Oh, you know Czech?' he asked. 'No, I don't understand a word of it,' I answered. 'I can only read it.' "

Reading is not just saying the words. Reading must always be a meaning-getting process. Many children can read the words in a passage perfectly, but are unable to answer questions that call for making inferences or for identifying the main idea. Some of these children are not able to answer even the most simple questions ("What color was Mary's dress?" or "Where did the dog find the lost kitten?"), even though the answers were directly contained in the words they pronounced. Other children will stumble over many of the words in the passage, skipping some words, repeating others, and substituting words for the ones that appear in the text. And yet these children may understand much of what they are reading and may be able to answer questions about both minor details and major concepts contained in the passage.

Even the ability to repeat verbatim words from the passage does not necessarily indicate that the passage has been comprehended. To illustrate this, we ask you to read the sentences below and to answer the questions that follow them.

1. Maria chose the puce sweater instead of the taupe one.

   Question: What kind of sweater did Maria choose?

2. The sample variance of estimate for standardized scores is:

   $$S^2_{z_y \cdot z_x} = \frac{\Sigma_i (z'_{yi} - z_{yi})^2}{N} \quad \text{(Hays, 1963, p. 498)}$$

   Question: Write the formula for the sample variance of estimate for standardized scores.

Could you point to the sweater that Maria chose if the two sweaters were presented to you? Could you make any use of the formula you so effortlessly copied in question 2? The ability to recognize or repeat the exact words of a selection does not guarantee understanding, as those of us who have taken multiple-choice tests will agree. The ability to verbalize is not necessarily an indicator of comprehension.

The teacher of reading must always keep in mind that reading is more than decoding. Unless the meaning-getting aspect of reading is consistently used as the criterion for success, both the teacher and the students will become susceptible to accepting pleasant pronunciations as evidence of successful reading.

Factors Affecting Comprehension

Many factors affect comprehension of printed materials. Some of the factors are characteristics of the material to be read; others are related to the reader. When attempting to guide comprehension, the teacher should consider both kinds of factors.

Characteristics of the Material

Consider the following sentences:

Consciousness is a being such that in its being, its being is in question in so far as this being implies a being other than itself. (Sartre, 1966, p. xxiv)

Distortion of the renal pelvis with "clubbing" is a common finding. . . . but is not pathognomonic for pyelonephritis. . . . (*Kidney and Urinary Tract Infections*, 1971, p. 47)

The innings opened briskly. Mr. Barrow, who was rather a showy bat, though temperamental, took the bowling at the factory end of the pitch and cheered the spirits of his side by producing a couple of twos in the first over. Mr. Garrett, canny and cautious, stonewalled perseveringly through five balls of the following over and then cut the leather through the slips for a useful three. (Sayers, 1967, p. 250)

In the bosom of one of those spacious coves which indent the eastern shore of the Hudson, at that broad expansion of the river denominated by the ancient Dutch navigators the Tappan Zee, and where they always prudently shortened sail, and implored the protection of St. Nicholas when they crossed, there lies a small marketplace or rural port, which by some is called Greensburgh, but which is more generally and properly known by the name of Tarry Town. (Irving, 1974, p. 59)

Very likely your comprehension of these sentences was poor, but for a different reason for each quotation. In the Sartre quote the words themselves were not particularly difficult. No doubt you were able to read them easily. But the concept being expressed is an extremely abstruse one. Familiar words were used to express a philosophical concept, and it is the concept itself that provides the barrier to comprehension.

A different problem exists with the second quotation. In that sentence from a medical textbook the concept itself is not complex; however, unless the specialized vocabulary—*renal, pathognomonic,* and *pyelonephritis*—is familiar to the reader, the concept itself will remain elusive.

The third quotation illustrates yet another barrier to comprehension. No doubt you know not one but several meanings for *innings, bowling, pitch, over,* and *slips*. However, none of the common meanings of these individual words seems to fit within this particular passage. An American reader would most likely conclude that a game is being played with a bat of some kind and a ball. But beyond that a mental image of the game is probably blank. Unless one were familiar with cricket and the special meanings of these very common words within the context of that game, comprehension of the quoted sentences would be extremely limited.

The Irving quotation, which begins that old favorite *The Legend of Sleepy Hollow,* was probably the most easily understood by the readers of this text. The concepts are not difficult, the vocabulary is familiar to the reader, and the words are not used in unusual ways. And yet you may have had to reread the sentence at least once in order to comprehend it because of the tortuous grammatical structure. Irving has crammed 78 words into just one sentence. If the sentence had been divided into several sentences of less complex grammatical structures, you might have had no trouble understanding Irving's message at a glance. Research by Ruddell (1965) and Tathum (1970), among others, has shown that using children's own language patterns in written materials can lead to improved comprehension by young readers. If Irving had used language patterns that more nearly reflected the patterns of adult oral language, his writing would probably have been more easily understood.

Characteristics of the material being read can be a major block to comprehension. We have shown you passages in which concepts, technical vocabulary, special meanings for words, and unfamiliar syntactical structures can limit comprehension. When assigning passages for children to read, teachers must be aware of these potential roadblocks and must prepare the students to deal with them.

As illustrated in the preceding section, one of the most important prerequisites for understanding written material is familiarity with both the concepts and vocabulary contained in the material. In the examples given above, some of the concepts were very esoteric, and much of the vocabulary was extremely specialized. If an adult had difficulty comprehending any of the sentences, we are not surprised. The same principle of familiarity also applies to comprehension by children, but teachers often assume that their students have the necessary background for comprehending the simple stories found in basal readers and other material written for children. What child would not understand a story about getting stuck in an elevator? Who could be confused by a story describing a trip to a museum? How could a second grader fail to understand a story about a trip to the seashore? If the child has never been in an elevator or a museum or has always swum in a farm pond or a city pool, she or he will probably have some difficulty understanding these stories. Teachers must not take for granted that their pupils have had the same experiences, either vicarious or real, that they have had in 20 or 30 or more years of living, reading, and traveling.

Characteristics of the Reader

Another important factor in a reader's ability to comprehend is the decoding skill of the reader. Proponents of using an informal reading inventory (in which the student reads aloud a short passage and answers questions about it) to determine a level of reading ability have long suggested that a passage is probably too difficult if the reader cannot read about 95 percent of the words (Betts, 1957; Harris, 1970). Samuels (1976) has labeled this level of proficiency "automaticity in decoding." Samuels warns that if readers have to use most of their available attention for the purpose of decoding, an insufficient quantity of attention will be left for processing the meaning of the passage.

The purpose the reader sets for reading the passage or selection will also affect his or her comprehension. If the reader is attempting to get only a general idea of what the passage is about, the comprehension of small details incidental to the main idea or topic will most likely be low. On the other hand, if the reader is interested primarily in details, he or she may lose the overall theme of the selection. If, as is too often the case, the reader's only purpose for

Reading can take place almost anywhere.

reading a selection is to complete a class assignment, comprehension may be minimal, because no real focus has guided the reader.

A fourth important characteristic of the reader is the attitude he or she holds about reading itself. If reading is perceived as a chore and something to be done only under duress, comprehension may suffer, because the reader's only purpose is to get done. If reading is seen as pronouncing words, comprehension will be minimal, because the reader's attention is on accuracy of decoding and not on meaning getting. However, if reading is looked on as an enjoyable experience and as a way of gathering information, comprehension will most likely be at a high level, because the reader is interested in what is being read and *wants* to read the material.

The *reader* is the one who must be doing the comprehending, and therefore the characteristics of the reader as an individual must be considered when assigning materials. The reader's familiarity with the concepts and vocabulary presented, decoding ability, purpose for reading, and attitude toward reading itself all will influence comprehension.

Comprehension does not just happen because a reader's eyes move across a page of print. Understanding of written material depends on the characteristics of both the material and the reader. Therefore, teachers must choose reading materials for their students wisely. They must make sure that their students have the skills necessary for both decoding and understanding the materials.

Unlike many aspects of decoding, comprehension remains in the minds of many a mystical process. Theories of the nature of the decoding process have been developed and have been subjected to a great deal of research. Much has been learned about decoding, even though many questions remained unanswered. To date, however, theories about the nature of comprehension have been for the most part unsatisfactory. No theory has been acclaimed by more than a few theorists, and research in comprehension has been confused by both the lack of an adequate theoretical base and problems with methodology. No wonder, then, that comprehension is often ignored, or at least slighted, in classroom instruction. Teachers have little on which to base their understanding of comprehension and their instructional practices for developing comprehension. They often do not feel confident in teaching comprehension skills and at times have little focus for their efforts. In this chapter we hope to provide a framework of skills or tasks for dealing with comprehension that will make it less mystical and more teachable.

Theories of Comprehension

Some theorists perceive reading comprehension in global terms. According to the view of these educators, comprehension cannot be divided into distinct skills. Goodman defines reading comprehension as "interaction between thought and language" (1966, p. 188) and bases evaluation of success in comprehension on "the extent to which [the reader's] reconstructed message agrees with the writer's intended message" (p. 188). Thorndike (1973–1974) equates reading comprehension with verbal reasoning. He bases this assumption on two kinds of evidence. In the first place, factor-analytic studies (Davis, 1972; Spearritt, 1972) have not been able to identify any set of distinct comprehension skills. In the studies cited, most of the variance in comprehension scores was accounted for by a single factor, generally identified as word meaning or vocabulary. Second, reading tests correlate highly with tests purporting to measure general intelligence. For these reasons Thorndike suggests that

Looking at the Whole

reading comprehension should be considered in global terms. Efforts to increase comprehension should concentrate on improving thinking abilities and should not attempt to deal with hypothesized separate subskills that research has failed to validate.

One advantage of viewing comprehension as a whole is expressed by Beery (1967) when she stresses that skills are not used in isolation but in combination. A reader does not read just to get the main idea or to read details; rather, "a flexible reader shifts from one skill to another as he gains insight into the nature of the problem, the difficulty of the reading matter, and its development by the author and as he develops and rejects 'hunches' he has concerning the best solution" (p. 110).

The most important disadvantage of looking only at the whole of comprehension is that the theory provides no focus for instruction and keeps comprehension at a mystical level. What does the teacher *do* when the reader fails to reconstruct the author's meaning? If reading is viewed as reasoning, how does one teach "reasoning" without breaking down the task in some way?

Looking at the Parts as Well as the Whole

A second view of reading comprehension suggests that separate skills or tasks can be identified which, when used singly or in concert, lead to understanding of a passage. To comprehend written material, according to these theorists, readers must use a variety of skills. For example, readers must be able to draw conclusions, identify main ideas, and recognize details from the selection. Not all skills are used for comprehending every passage, and as Beery has noted, the skills are not used in isolation. But many educators believe that several specific skills or tasks can be identified that are important in the comprehension of written material.

Several taxonomies of comprehension skills or tasks have been developed. Smith (1969), for example, suggests that reading comprehension may be divided into four categories: literal comprehension, interpretation, critical reading, and creative reading. She defines literal comprehension as "the skill of getting the primary, direct literal meaning of a word, idea, or sentence in context" (p. 255). Literal comprehension is generally accepted as the most simple, or basic, comprehension skill and one that requires little thinking or reasoning.

Smith's next level is interpretation, which definitely involves thinking skills and requires readers to identify ideas and meanings that are not explicitly stated in the written text. Within the interpretive level, readers may make generalizations, determine cause and effect, identify motives, find relationships, predict endings, and make comparisons.

Critical reading, the third category of skills in Smith's paradigm, includes both literal comprehension and interpretation, but also goes beyond these two levels of comprehension. When individuals read critically, they evaluate what is read. That is, they examine critically the thoughts of the writer, which have been identified through the two lower levels of comprehension, and judge their validity, or worth.

The fourth level of comprehension that Smith identifies is creative reading—going beyond what the author has written, applying ideas from the text to new situations, and recombining the author's ideas with other ideas to form new concepts or to expand old ones. Through creative reading the reader *creates* something new—an idea, the solution to a problem, a new way of looking at something—from the ideas gleaned from the text.

Smith's levels of comprehension can be summarized as follows:

1. Level 1—*literal comprehension*—getting the direct meaning that has been explicitly stated;
2. Level 2—*interpretation*—identifying ideas not explicitly stated;
3. Level 3—*critical reading*—evaluating what is read;
4. Level 4—*creative reading*—applying ideas read to new situations.

Barrett (1972) also has divided reading comprehension into four taxonomic levels, but in addition has proposed some specific tasks that might be found within each of these levels:

1.0 Literal recognition or recall

    1.1 Recognition or recall of details
    1.2 Recognition or recall of main ideas
    1.3 Recognition or recall of sequence
    1.4 Recognition or recall of comparisons
    1.5 Recognition or recall of cause-and-effect relationships
    1.6 Recognition or recall of character traits

2.0 Inference

    2.1 Inferring supporting details
    2.2 Inferring the main idea
    2.3 Inferring sequence
    2.4 Inferring comparisons
    2.5 Inferring cause-and-effect relationships
    2.6 Inferring character traits
    2.7 Predicting outcomes
    2.8 Inferring about figurative language

3.0 Evaluation

    3.1 Judgments of reality or fantasy
    3.2 Judgments of fact or opinion
    3.3 Judgments of adequacy or validity
    3.4 Judgments of appropriateness
    3.5 Judgments of worth, desirability, or acceptability

4.0 Appreciation

    4.1 Emotional response to plot or theme
    4.2 Identification with characters and incidents
    4.3 Reactions to the author's use of language
    4.4 Imagery*

*From *A Taxonomy of Reading Comprehension* by Thomas C. Barrett. Used by permission of the publisher, Ginn and Company (Xerox Corporation).

Barrett warns that although the tasks within each category have been logically ordered from easiest to most difficult, no such hierarchical ordering has been empirically validated (Smith and Barrett, 1974, p. 53). He also urges that the taxonomy be viewed as a teaching tool and not as an exhaustive "classification of comprehension abilities and tasks" (1974, p. 52).

At the literal level Barrett distinguishes between recognition tasks and recall tasks. Recognition tasks require readers to be able to recognize a statement that has been drawn explicitly from the text. Recall tasks require readers to reconstruct an explicit statement from memory.

Barrett's second level of comprehension is inference, which he defines as a synthesis of the student's prior knowledge, intuition, and imagination with the literal content of the text. Inferential comprehension may involve combining two literal statements to reach an unstated conclusion. Readers use inferential-comprehension skills when drawing on their own experiential background to fill in facts not expressly given in a passage. For example, if the text stated that "her dress was the color of ripe strawberries," even a young reader should be able to infer that the dress was red.

The third level of Barrett's taxonomy is evaluation, which roughly corresponds to Smith's third level, critical reading. According to Barrett, when students evaluate while reading, they compare the information contained in the selection with external criteria, such as outside authorities, or with internal criteria, such as personal knowledge.

Appreciation, the fourth level, involves a reaction to the aesthetic aspects of written communication. Barrett emphasizes the students' responses to the craft involved in writing, such as style, use of language, and the ability to create believable characters.

Smith and Barrett have divided reading comprehension according to the kind of response required by the reader. A different approach to identifying manageable elements of reading comprehension is to base levels of comprehension on the unit of comprehension as well as on the response required by the reader. Carver (1973), analyzing Spache's description of reading comprehension (1963), suggests four levels of comprehension. Level 1 is the word level. Before one can understand a complete sentence, one must know the meanings of at least most of the words in the sentence, as they are used in that sentence.

The second level described by Carver is the sentence. The reader must combine the words in the sentence and understand what the whole sentence means. The process of combining is not simply additive. Fluent readers do not read or comprehend one word at a time, in a linear fashion, and then add up the meanings. Furthermore, the meaning of a particular sentence, as with a particular word, depends in part on the meanings of the sentences that surround it. For example, "She got it for him" contains three pronouns whose antecedents the reader must comprehend before the sentence can be understood. "Sam cleaned up" has a different meaning if the rest of the paragraph is about a messy room than if the paragraph has been describing a particularly exciting poker hand.

The third level involves the unit of the paragraph. Readers comprehend the words and sentences in a paragraph and also develop an understanding of the meaning of the paragraph itself. This third level of reading comprehension, like the other levels, does not involve just one skill. In comprehending a paragraph a reader may, for example, identify the main idea, draw an inference, or use the information in the paragraph to determine cause and effect.

Carver suggests that the fourth level of comprehension contains a large element of reasoning. As Spache describes this level, reasoning resembles the critical and creative levels of Smith's analysis of reading comprehension. According to Carver, "Level 4 is associated with no particular unit and may involve thinking activities which are not at all associated with literal, implied, or tangential meanings of the prose" (p. 46).

In order for an analysis of reading comprehension that uses the units of word, sentence, and paragraph to be useful for instructional purposes, specific subskills within these levels of comprehension must be identified. Comprehending words does not just involve a unitary skill. Different kinds of words and different kinds of relationships among the words in a sentence will call for varying word-comprehension skills. Similarly, sentences vary in structure and complexity, and diverse skills may be needed to understand these varying structures. Different relationships among information within paragraphs may call for a variety of comprehension skills.

One possible breakdown of literal and inferential comprehension skills based on a division by word, sentence, and paragraph is given below. This division of skills is from a skills-management program, the *Wisconsin Design for Reading Skill Development* (1977). Note that only skills at the literal and inferential levels are included in this list. We have included objectives for the first set of comprehension skills, "Determining Word Meaning," so that you can see how objectives may be expressed for comprehension.

1. Determines word meaning
   a) Identifies word parts
      (1) Prefixes
          Objective: The child recognizes that a prefix is a meaning-bearing unit that can modify the meaning of a word by: (a) signifying range (e.g., sub-, super-, inter-); (b) indicating time (e.g., pre-, post-); (c) signifying approval or support (e.g., pro-); (d) signifying opposition (e.g., anti-); (e) signifying number (e.g., bi-, tri-).
      (2) Suffixes
          Objective: The child recognizes that a suffix may serve to: (a) modify the meaning of a base word and/or (2) identify the grammatical function of that base word.
      (3) Combining forms
          Objective: The child recognizes that combining forms (e.g., bio, graph) are meaning-bearing units that join together to constitute new words.

(4) Word roots

Objective: The child recognizes that some words consist of prefixes or suffixes combined with word roots (e.g., fac, sta).

b) Identifies context clues

(1) Direct context clues

(2) Direct context clues—application

(3) Indirect context clues—application

(4) Obscure meanings

2. Derives meaning from sentences

a) Notes detail

(1) In simple sentences

(2) In positive and negative sentences

(3) In active- and passive-voice sentences

(4) In sentences with more than one subordinate clause

b) Paraphrases

(1) Positive and negative sentences

(2) Active- and passive-voice sentences

(3) Complex sentences

(4) Complex sentences with two or more prepositional phrases

(5) Long sentences by rewriting them into shorter sentences; short sentences by rewriting them into a single long sentence

3. Derives meaning from passages

a) Identifies central thought

(1) Identifies a topic

(a) Pictures

(b) With organizer

(c) Without organizer

(2) Identifies relevant information

(3) Identifies central thought

(a) With organizer

(b) Without organizer

(4) Generates central thought

b) Identifies relationships and conclusions

(1) Identifies relationships

(2) Predicts outcomes

(3) Identifies conclusions

(a) One relationship

(b) Direct relationships

(c) Indirect relationships

      (4) Identifies cause-effect relationships

      (5) Recognizes supported and unsupported conclusions

      (6) Modifies conclusions

  c) Determines sequence

      (1) First or last event

      (2) Event before

      (3) Event after

      (4) Event before or after

      (5) Calendar markers

      (6) Explicit cues

      (7) Implicit cues

      (8) Implied and stated events

Summary

We have presented three different approaches to categorizing subtasks within the overall task of comprehension. Smith's division of tasks is quite broad; the *Wisconsin Design* list of skills is very specific; Barrett's taxonomy lies somewhere between the other two. We ask that you consider all three approaches carefully. The differences among the three taxonomies may provide you with insight into the complexities of reading comprehension.

When discussing the holistic view of reading comprehension, we listed one primary advantage and one main disadvantage. The skills or task approach to reading comprehension is almost the complement of the global view in respect to advantages and disadvantages. The most salient advantage of looking at components of comprehension as well as at the whole is that focused instruction is possible. The task for the readers may be objectively stated, and instruction may be given that centers specifically on that task. Teachers who include a consideration of skills or tasks in their view of comprehension have a way of organizing their instruction and assessing the effects of that instruction.

The primary disadvantage is that reading comprehension may become so fragmented that the reader cannot put the pieces back together again. Mature readers do not use skills one at a time. If instruction is given on pieces of comprehension, no one can be sure that ability to deal with the parts will ever add up to ability to deal with the whole.

Application

Several theories of reading comprehension have been described. No theory has been shown to provide the magic key to understanding the complexities of comprehending written matter. However, we feel that viewing reading comprehension as including several specific skills or tasks will provide teachers with a way of organizing instruction in a meaningful way. The final goal may indeed have been well described by those who have a global, or holistic, view of reading comprehension, but these theorists have given no suggestions for attaining this goal. Instruction in specific skills may provide a way of achieving this final goal.

To help you decide if any of the theories described can be useful to you as a teacher, read the selection on p. 159, entitled "Seals" (Eklund and Beckman, 1963, pp. 26–27). When you have finished reading, write six questions for the selection. Then for each question, identify the taxonomic level of the question according to Smith's paradigm. Then identify the specific subtasks from Barrett's taxonomy that have been tapped by your questions. Finally, try to identify the specific skills from the *Wisconsin Design* list that would be needed to answer the questions. Compare the degree to which each of the three taxonomies or skill lists was used when you decided on important comprehension questions to ask. (Use the grid in Fig. 7.1 to help you make these comparisons.) This exercise will help you to consider how these varied approaches to comprehension tasks may be used, either together or separately, to think about the nature of reading comprehension.

Question	Level of Smith's paradigm	Level of Barrett's taxonomy	Wisconsin Design skill
1.			
2.			
3.			
4.			
5.			
6.			
Total number of separate levels or skills used			

Fig. 7.1. Question-analysis grid.

Seals

Seal hunters risked the stormy Antarctic waters in their small ships for over 100 years in search of these animals which supplied profitable oil and furs. The fur seal was nearly exterminated by the middle of the last century, and almost no sealing is carried out in the area today. From 1820–22, 320,000 fur seals were reported slaughtered in the South Shetlands. Today this seal, which inhabits the sub-antarctic regions, is protected by the countries having jurisdiction over the various islands where it breeds. Fortunately, the populations are building up despite their earlier destruction, and with proper management, sealing may some day again be a profitable industry.

There are five species of seals in the Antarctic—the crabeater, Weddell, leopard, Ross, and elephant seals. All are hair seals, and all but the elephant seal are unique to the Antarctic. This last species breeds in colonies on subantarctic islands, but occasionally is found on the continent as a summer visitor.

The most common seal is the lithe and active crabeater. Our knowledge of its life history is limited, but it is circumpolar in distribution, probably migratory in movements, and inhabits the pack-ice year-round. Averaging seven to eight feet in length and weighing about 500 pounds, its name is misleading since it feeds almost exclusively on red krill. Recent studies indicate a probable population of from 5 to 8 million in Antarctic waters. Interesting collections of this species have been made in the ice-free areas of the McMurdo Sound region, where 90 mummified carcasses were found 30 miles from the sea at an elevation up to 3000 feet above sea level. One carcass was dated by radio-carbon analysis and found to be between 1600 and 2600 years old.

The Weddell is the second most common species of seal. The most southern of all in distribution, it usually occupies the fast-ice along the coast. Eight to nine feet in length and averaging 900 pounds, the adult Weddell on the ice looks like a huge, lethargic garden slug. Its sluggishness and lack of fear make the species easy to kill for biological specimens or food. The single pup is born in the Spring (October), averaging about 60 pounds in weight and 3½ to 4 feet in length. In winter, the animals usually stay under the ice, where the water temperature never falls below 28°F, and it is warmer than the surface temperatures. The Weddell exists by cutting breathing holes from the underside of the ice with its sawlike teeth, the only Antarctic seal with such a habit. It feeds on fish and cephalopods.*

IMPROVING COMPREHENSION SKILLS

Deciding which comprehension skills are going to be stressed is important, but just asking children comprehension questions and then giving them feedback about the correctness of their responses is not *teaching* comprehension. Children must be prepared for the comprehension tasks they will be asked to perform, and they must be guided through these tasks and not just told to practice them.

*C. Eklund and J. Beckman, *Antarctica*, New York: Holt, Rinehart and Winston, 1963, pp. 26–27.

Preparing for Comprehension

The most important step in preparing children to comprehend written material is to help them understand that reading is a communication process. The symbols printed on the page are supposed to give a message to the reader. Tovey (1976) suggests that one important component of this process is helping children to understand *why* they are reading. The "why" of reading is not always obvious, even to adults. Many adults who are able to both decode and comprehend well do not think of turning to written materials when seeking a solution to a problem. To go to the library for a book on training that new puppy or installing a windshield in their car simply does not occur to them. Similarly, reading the written directions for assembling their child's new bicycle is the last resort for many individuals.

Children must be taught from the beginning that reading can provide the answers to many questions. They should learn to follow printed instructions, whether these instructions are found in the basal text workbook or in a recipe. Cooking in class or building a model can help to provide even very young children with practice in using the written word to achieve a goal. We have

Reading serves many purposes.

had elementary grade children make brownies, apple pies, taffy apples, and pizzas from scratch by following carefully the directions that have been written on the board.

Sometimes failure to follow directions can have unfortunate results. One teacher we know was too optimistic about the results of her lesson in following directions. Instead of melting the chocolate, cooling it, and then adding the raw eggs, her little cooking group blithely put the chocolate and the eggs together and turned on the heat. Yuck! The children must be taught to read the whole recipe or other set of directions first, to get an overall picture of the processes involved.

Children must learn to be aware of the many uses for the written word. Talking to kindergarten children about signs they can read (STOP, McDonald's, Parker School, Boys' Room) will help them to realize that messages are contained in printed words. Even preschoolers can learn to identify the most favored jobs on the "helpers list" and can immediately recognize if they have been given an interesting or boring task for the day. Written messages between teacher and student or between students are an enjoyable way of showing that reading means communicating. Imagine a first grader's joy at receiving a secret note: "You did very good work today" or "You may be first in line. Get in line right now." Imagine a teacher's delight in receiving a note from a child: "I love you" or, in an actual case, "Theres a bug on my papr." Misspellings are of no importance; what is important is that a message has been offered and received.

Children should also be taught to see reading as a source of information. The teacher can do the reading for very young children who cannot yet read themselves. For example, if a youngster wants to know if butterflies sleep in the winter like squirrels, the teacher can show the child that this information can be obtained by reading a science book or an encyclopedia. Of course, the teacher will not have time to refer to a book for every question, but this procedure should be followed often enough for the children to perceive that written material can be a source of information. Older children can be led to materials that they can read themselves to find the answers to their questions.

Much preparation for comprehending written material can be done through exercises in which the children listen to orally presented information or respond to questions orally. Listening-comprehension activities can help children practice many of the thinking strategies that they will also use in reading comprehension. However, important differences do exist between listening comprehension and reading comprehension. Reading comprehension, of course, depends a great deal on decoding ability. This intermediary step, decoding, between the presentation of the ideas of the author and the reception of those ideas by the reader, can often prevent comprehension from taking place. If the information or problem is given orally, the child's ability to decode is not a factor. This means that children who can't read above a minimal level, whether because of age or reading disability, can still practice many of the skills of reading comprehension without the interference of undeveloped decoding ability.

On the other hand, the reader has an advantage over the listener because the reader can control the rate of input of the words and ideas and can even go back and review them, whereas the listener is most often at the mercy of the speaker. The listener must attend carefully and at the pace at which the speaker chooses. Then again, the listener receives intonation cues that can be only imperfectly represented in print by italics and marks of punctuation. In addition, the listener has the cues of facial and body language—a grimace, a pointing finger, a clenched fist—that are totally lacking in print.

Just as listening has advantages and disadvantages when compared to reading, oral presentation of answers differs in important ways from written responses. The most obvious difference is that oral responses are not dependent on a student's composition or handwriting skills. Perhaps the most important difference between oral and written responses, insofar as *teaching* comprehension is concerned, is that when a child responds orally, the teacher can follow the child's patterns of responses and can interact with the child to help him or her reach the correct response. If the child answers a question in written form, only the final answer is available to the teacher, and the processes of arriving at that answer are not evident.

Cunningham (1975) emphasizes that teachers should provide for transfer between listening activities and reading activities. She suggests that teachers develop two parallel lessons—one a listening activity and the other a reading activity. In the listening activity the children are guided through the steps needed to reach a particular solution to a problem or answer to a question. Immediately after the children have finished the steps orally, they are asked to do a reading activity in which they will need to follow the same kinds of procedures to find the answer. Cunningham stresses that what the students are asked to do in the reading task must parallel what they did in the listening task. Furthermore, the students must be made aware of the similarities between the two tasks. In addition, the teacher must set specific purposes for each task and must probe and question in order to get the children to explain verbally how they arrived at certain answers.

Well-chosen oral-comprehension exercises help children gain confidence that they *can* think of answers to questions that appear to be very complex. Many children are unaware that reading comprehension involves not only understanding what they read, but also integrating this new information with what they already know. The printed word is often perceived as "the Truth," and children (and adults) sometimes forget that they also have information on a topic themselves. A belief in one's own power of thinking is especially important in critical or evaluative reading and thinking. Oral-comprehension work, during which the teacher urges children to bring their own experiences to bear on a problem and helps them to challenge information that is presented to them, can help to prepare children to read printed materials critically. For example, kindergarten children could see a cartoon about a dog who helped his mother clean up the house. The children might be asked if they thought the story could really have taken place. They might be asked to give evidence to support their point of view. The children could suggest other ways the dog

Gaining self-confidence in their ability to think independently can help children learn to read printed material critically.

could have helped his mother and could tell how they help their own mothers. They could compare the ways in which they helped with the ways in which the dog helped. Older children could listen to a debate between two classmates on a topic of special interest and then could evaluate the information presented by each debater. Such oral practice in reasoning and evaluating will help the children be able to apply these skills when reading.

Even though children perceive reading as a form of communication and even though they have practiced many comprehension skills orally, if children choose or are assigned books that are much too difficult for them to decode, they will not be able to comprehend. Of course, children do not need to be able to read every word in a book in order to comprehend it. Furthermore, great interest in a book or a strong background in the subject will make comprehending it easier. Hunt (1970) talks about transcending the frustration level through pupil interest and by accepting less than total comprehension. Nevertheless, the teacher can help ensure comprehension by attempting to make reading assignments that are within the capabilities of the students. Sometimes textbooks, especially in the intermediate and secondary levels, are too difficult for even the average reader in the grade for which the books are ostensibly written. Asking a reader to complete an assignment in a book that he or she cannot decode easily is fruitless and needlessly frustrating to both the child and the teacher. To help match a child with a book, the teacher can use a readability formula to identify the reading level of the book. (The concept of readability and examples of readability formulas are presented in Chapter 8.) Often textbook publishers will provide information about levels that is based on application of a readability formula.

Another way of matching child and book is to have the child read aloud a passage of approximately 100 words from two or three places in the text. If the child misses more than five words in 100, the text is most likely too difficult.

The teacher can also prepare children for improved comprehension by giving them ways to identify by themselves books that they are likely to be able to read. The children need not use the criterion of readability for every book they choose, but they should have techniques for determining if they will be able to read a book when they want to use that criterion. One such technique is the "Five Finger Rule" (Tovey, 1976, p. 289), which has been used by elementary school teachers for years to guide children in selecting books and is based on the guideline described above—95 percent accuracy in oral reading of a short passage. The children are taught to choose a page or several pages in a book, totaling about 100 words in length. (The children do not need to count the words. With practice using teacher-selected passages, the children can develop a general feel for the length of passage required.) Then as each child reads silently, he or she is to hold up a finger on one hand every time a word is encountered that cannot be decoded. If, at the end of the passage, five or more fingers are "up," the book is too difficult.

Much work in building comprehension skills can be done outside of a structured reading lesson. The teacher who helps children to see reading as a process of getting meaning, who prepares children for reading comprehension by working orally with "thinking" skills, and who makes sure that children have the decoding ability to read something they are expected to comprehend will have done a great deal toward ensuring that children will comprehend what they read.

Guiding Comprehension

Guiding children to comprehend what they read involves more than asking them yes-no questions or putting check marks and smiling faces in their workbooks. Knowing the "rightness" or "wrongness" of an answer is only a beginning. In fact, in some of the most valuable comprehension exercises, there are no definite right answers. What the student really needs to know is how to arrive at an answer and how to support that answer.

Teacher Questions

Probably the most important means of guiding children's comprehension is questioning by the teacher. Through questions, teachers can help children refine their answers, find support for their hypotheses, and look at problems in new ways. The *quality* of the questions is all-important. "What color was Spot?" does not really help children develop their powers of understanding. A better question might be: "Why do you think Rob named his dog Spot?" This question could be followed by: "What do you think he might have named his dog if it were all brown?" and "Do you have a dog? What is the dog's name? Do you remember why you gave your dog that name?"

According to Hoskisson, "The purpose in asking questions about stories read by pupils should be to foster reflective thinking" (1973, p. 159). Hoskisson distinguishes between "true questions," for which the teacher does not already know the answer (Why ask a question if you already know what the answer should be?), and "false questions," for which there is only one right answer. Of course, readers need to be able to understand the literal content of a selection before they can make inferences or evaluate this content. However, too often teachers never move beyond the literal level. When Guszak (1967) studied teacher questioning in three grades, he found that over 70 percent of the questions asked were at the literal level. The children had only to locate or recall explicitly stated information. Less than 14 percent of the questions asked the children to make any kind of an inference, and only about 15 percent required the students to make a judgment or evaluation. With questioning patterns like these, it is not surprising that children often perceive reading only as parroting back exactly what has been written down. Melnick (1965, p. 36) warns that teacher questions influence children's perceptions of reading. If the teacher only asks the children to repeat what is in the book, that is all they will learn to do. As they read, they will attend only to the details they feel the teacher is likely to ask about. Experienced teachers have all seen the blank faces or even panic-stricken expressions that occur when they ask an inferential question of children who are not used to thinking while they read. "But, Teacher," one brave soul will respond with a bewildered look, "the book didn't say!" And as far as the child is concerned, that's that.

Teacher questioning is extremely important, but the goal of such questioning should be to develop questioning habits within the students themselves. Stauffer (1970) has described activities to help children become independent critical readers. These Directed Reading-Thinking Activities (DRTA's) are developed through teacher-pupil and pupil-pupil interaction. The teacher serves as an "intellectual agitator" (p. 137) to guide the pupils' reading and thinking.

The DRTA has three basic steps. The first step is to develop purposes for reading. The teacher helps the children set their purposes for reading and helps them think about what they are going to read even before they begin. The children learn to predict what they are going to read, perhaps by skimming or by reading titles, headings, and picture captions. They learn to pose questions about what they are going to read and to set up hypotheses. Through questioning, the group, not just the teacher, helps each child to set goals and form reasonable hypotheses before reading begins. The group determines which hypotheses are reasonable, asking a student to give evidence that a specific

Directed Reading-Thinking Activities (DRTA)

conjecture may have merit. For example, if Ruthie examined the chapter entitled "Bees and Their Community" in her science book and predicted that she would learn about different kinds of insects, another student, Arthur, might logically ask, "Why do you think you are going to find out about any insects besides bees?" Ruthie might have a perfectly good defense for her hypothesis ("The picture on p. 48 shows ants and beetles and wasps"). On the other hand, she may not be able to give any reasonable justification for her prediction, and as a result of Arthur's challenge, Ruthie may choose to change her prediction.

The second step of the DRTA is to develop habits of reasoning while reading. As the children read, they are to use both their own experience and the information given by the author to refine their preconceived ideas. While they read, the children will reject some of their hypotheses, confirm others, and even develop new hypotheses to be confirmed or rejected by further reading. The children are not just passively moving their eyes across the page, but are engaged in a search for evidence.

The third step is to develop the habit of testing and proving predictions. This step is built on the first two, in which the children make predictions and read to find evidence. In the last step the children offer proof to the group for their final hypotheses, and the group judges the worth of the evidence. The children will learn that sloppy reasoning or evidence based on "just because" will not pass the group's inspection. They will learn to offer valid proof for their conjectures.

Let's return to Ruthie and Arthur for the moment. In spite of Arthur's questioning, Ruthie has insisted on including her prediction that she will learn about different kinds of insects. After reading, Ruthie is asked if she did learn anything about ants or wasps. She responds that the picture was the only place in which other insects were found in the chapter and that nothing in the text ever mentioned other insects. Ruthie is not particularly embarrassed by this, because she felt that she had had valid reasons for making the prediction in the first place.

All of the students are asked to provide proof for their hypotheses. Arthur had predicted that the story would tell about how honey is made, and now he reads aloud the two paragraphs that describe this process.

The Directed Reading-Thinking Activity should help children to see reading as a process of combining their own ideas and the ideas of an author in order to solve a problem or to find the answer to a question. The DRTA should help students to become critical questioners of their own ideas, the ideas of their peers, and the ideas of the "experts." The DRTA can provide a bridge between the teacher as a guide to understanding written material and the student as an independent critical reader.

Guidelines for Teaching Comprehension Skills

Teacher questions and Directed Reading-Thinking Activities are two examples of important kinds of oral teacher-pupil interactions that can lead to improved comprehension. We will now suggest five specific guidelines for planning and carrying out comprehension activities in general. Application of these guidelines to all activities designed to improve comprehension should help to provide a well-balanced program through which children learn to comprehend a variety of kinds of materials in a variety of ways.

1. *Teach. Don't just provide opportunities for practice.* The scene described below is unfortunately all too common.

> *Ms. Whiz:* Today we are going to do an exercise on finding the main idea. The main idea tells you what the *whole* paragraph or story is about. Open your workbooks to p. 52. Now, Sally, read the first paragraph aloud and then tell us which of the four choices given after the paragraph tells us the main idea. (Sally reads and then incorrectly identifies the main idea.) No, Sally, that's a good guess, but it's not quite right. Juan, can you help? (Juan responds with the right answer.) Great! That's right. Now, class, finish the rest of the page by yourselves. Any questions?

What is wrong with the teacher's strategies? Ms. Whiz did several things right. She gave praise for a good guess; she defined the main idea for her pupils; she made sure that the students were on the right page. Great. But she didn't *teach* anything. Sally and all of the other students who also chose a wrong answer have been given no clues as to why that answer was wrong and no direction on how to find the right answer. Juan may have an equally vague notion about how he arrived at the *right* answer. It may have just been a lucky guess.

Guiding comprehension means just that. The students are guided step by step through the processes by which one finds the right answers. Wrong answers are analyzed to see how the student went astray. Students who give right answers are asked to defend those answers and to explain how they happened to choose them. Just giving examples of right and wrong answers usually is not enough.

Similarly, that time-honored dictum "Correct the ones you have wrong" is useless unless the student receives further instruction in how to find the right answer. If he or she did not know how to find the answer before, the bluebird of happiness is not going to arrive now and give the child the right answer. Of course, no further instruction is needed if the answers were true/false. The child returns to the desk, erases the T's and writes in F's and vice versa. If the child is really clever, he or she just draws a cross bar on the T, instantly and mindlessly transforming it into the right answer without even having to erase!

2. *Use reading materials of varied styles and formats, covering a wide range of topics.* Children can become very adept at finding the main idea in a short factual paragraph or putting the events from a 100-word narrative in order. However, these same children may be unable to transfer these skills to longer selections or to passages in which the style differs markedly from the materials on which they have practiced these skills. The wise teacher provides opportunities for practicing skills with varied materials. When working with identifying details, for example, the children could read single paragraphs from science books, short chapters in social studies texts, recipes, directions for

building models, poems, newspaper articles, menus, catalogs, detective stories, and so on. Learning to identify details in just one kind of material is not a particularly useful skill. Learning just to identify details in a reading selection on a workbook page is even less useful. Children need explicit practice in applying skills to the vast array of reading matter they will be meeting in daily life.

3. *Provide practice in using several comprehension skills at one time.* One of the major arguments against separate skills for reading comprehension is that mature readers do not use skills discretely. When drawing a conclusion, the reader will also need to attend to details; when identifying a sequence, the reader may have to infer that one event took place after another. We feel that it is appropriate to separate comprehension skills for instructional purposes. But we also feel that children should then be given specific practice in using several of these skills to solve a single problem or to find a set of answers.

Just as children become skillful at identifying details in a particular kind of passage, so they also do well when they are required to account for only one kind of comprehension. For example, the child who has been told to read to find the main idea may pay little attention to the sequence of events in the selection or may not read critically. The child has been given a set to use only one kind of comprehension, and that is all that is used. In addition, there is no guarantee that the child could find the main idea or draw a conclusion without an explicit set for performing that particular task.

The teacher must provide opportunities in which the child must use several different comprehension skills in order to find an answer or to solve a problem. Furthermore, this practice should be done without giving an explicit skill set. That is, the child should be told what the problem is that is to be solved or what question will be asked, but the child should not be told that the solution involves "finding the main idea" or "reading for details." Without direction, the child should be able to apply the different comprehension skills needed to arrive at the right answer.

4. *Set the stage and set a purpose for reading.* Comprehension will be enhanced if the reader has an idea of what he or she is going to be reading and if a purpose has been set for reading. In Stauffer's Directed Reading-Thinking Activity, the students preview the reading selection in order to make hypotheses and to set purposes for reading. Many other techniques are available to acquaint the reader with the selection. For example, the teacher may provide an oral or written advance organizer that presents both the concepts that must be dealt with in the reading selection and related concepts that are relevant to an understanding of the passage. The advance organizer brings to the reader's attention what he or she already knows about the concepts of the passage and indicates how the new information in the passage is different from what is already known (Ausubel, 1964). An advance organizer for a passage about a new process for making steel, for instance, might review current steel-making processes. The organizer might then explain that the passage would be describing a new way of making steel. Through the advance organizer, the reader is prepared for the passage before beginning to read.

Another way to prepare the reader and also to set a purpose for reading is to let the reader know what questions will be asked after the passage has been read. This technique is especially helpful when working on improving reading in the content areas, such as science or social studies. One disadvantage of allowing the reader to see the questions ahead of time may be that the student reads only enough to answer the specific questions that will be asked. If that happens, incidental learning of information not relevant to those questions may decrease.

Few teachers will have the time to prepare an advance organizer or to lead a DRTA for each selection the students read. Nor will these activities be appropriate for every selection. Similarly, teachers will not want to create a specific set of questions for every passage in order for the students to see the questions ahead of time. Often the class discussion will lead to questions which the students themselves wish to answer. But a purpose of some kind and a general introduction should be given for each reading selection. "Turn to pages 52–56 and read the story" does nothing to guide children toward better comprehension.

5. *Probe, pry, and pick.* We have mentioned before in several contexts that comprehension is best taught through person-to-person interaction. Children must be asked to give reasons for their answers; they must be asked to expand their answers; they must be given opportunities to defend seemingly incorrect statements. Without exploring the thought processes by which the child has come to an answer, the teacher cannot know where to intervene when a wrong answer has been given. If the child has responded correctly, the exploration of the source of the answer may be of benefit to a listener who was not able to find the right answer. For example, consider the following scene:

Mr. Kool Class, I'd like you to read this paragraph about a very interesting bird called the emu. After you have read the paragraph, read the four sentences marked A, B, C, and D. Read each sentence and decide if it is true or false. (The students all read the passage):

> The emu is the second largest living bird. It is found in Australia, where it causes a lot of problems for the farmers. The emus come in large numbers and invade the farmers' fields. They eat the wheat and trample down what they don't eat. In spite of traps, poisons, and fences, the farmers can't seem to get rid of these large birds.
>
> A. Emus usually travel alone.
> B. Poison has been very effective in getting rid of these pests.
> C. Emus eat only meat and berries.
> D. There is another bird larger than the emu.

Paula Choice D isn't true.

Mr. Kool How do you know that, Paula?

Paula The first sentence said so.

What is the problem here? The first sentence gives specific evidence that choice D *is* true. Why doesn't Paula understand that? The scene continues:

Mr. Kool   Paula, why don't you read that sentence out loud to us?

Paula   Sure. "The emu is the largest living bird."

What has Mr. Kool learned? Does Paula have a severe comprehension problem that prevents her from understanding what she reads?

Mr. Kool   Paula, you skipped a word in the sentence. Can you read this word? (Points to *second*.)

Paula   Of course. That's *second*. Oops! I really blew it, didn't I? If the emu is the *second* largest bird, there must be a first largest bird, and D is true.

Whew! Paula's apparent comprehension problem was simply due to the careless omission of one word. The result would probably have been the same if Paula had been unable to read the word *second*. Let's investigate another young learner.

Scott   I know A's false. Emus travel in flocks or herds or whatever you call them.

Mr. Kool   Very good, Scott.

Scott has given a correct answer. Is there any point to questioning him further? Yes!

Mr. Kool   How do you know that emus don't usually travel alone?

Scott   I saw this neat show on "Wild Kingdom," and they showed these herds of emus ruining a farmer's field.

Aha! Readers should use their previous experience to help them understand a selection. But let's probe further.

Mr. Kool   Good. I'm glad you remembered that, Scott. Now, can you find a sentence in the paragraph that gives more proof that emus don't usually travel alone?

Scott   Hmmm. Yeah. It says, "They trample down what they don't eat," and it says that they "cause a lot of problems for the farmer."

(Huh? Those aren't the sentences with the proof. What's the matter with that kid?)

Mr. Kool   Why do you think that those sentences prove your point?

Scott   Well, one lonely emu isn't going to do a lot of trampling. I mean, it might hurt a garden or something, but the story's talking about damaging wheat. Wheat grows in big fields, and one emu at a time isn't going to make much of a dent in a wheat field.

(Maybe there's hope for the kid yet!) If Mr. Kool had accepted only "Emus come in large numbers" as proof, Scott's answer would have been considered wrong. Scott chose to combine different elements of the sentence to come to a correct conclusion, but he was still right and for valid reasons.

Let's view one more interchange:

Mr. Kool   Kim, what about choice C? Is that statement true or false?

Kim   It's not true.

Great! Another right answer. Surely Mr. Kool isn't going to badger this child, too!

Mr. Kool   Show me some proof!

Kim   Aw. I just guessed. I can't prove it.

Now is the opportunity to do some teaching. Mr. Kool can either dismiss the rest of the group to work on a follow-up exercise, or he can ask some or all of the other students to stay for a little more work.

Mr. Kool   Okay, Kim. Let's find the proof. You're right, you know. C isn't true. What does choice C talk about?

Kim   What emus eat.

Mr. Kool   Right. Now skim through the paragraph and find something about eating or food. As soon as you spot a word about food or eating, say that word.

Kim   (Skims the paragraph.) Eat. Wheat.

Mr. Kool   Now read that whole sentence and see if it gives any proof that emus don't eat just meat and berries.

Kim   (Reads the sentence.) Yeah. It says that they eat wheat, and I know that wheat ain't meat or berries.

Mr. Kool has not just provided Kim with the right answer. He has shown Kim a technique for finding that answer himself. If Mr. Kool had not probed into Kim's original answer, he would never have known that Kim had no idea of how to find the proof of a statement.

No teacher has time to investigate every answer, right or wrong. But such interchanges should take place often, when right as well as wrong answers have been given.

Application: Some Activities for Improving Comprehension Skills

Comprehension instruction should not be didactic and routine. We have suggested several guidelines for effective teaching of comprehension. In this section we describe several techniques for developing selected comprehension skills. We have not followed any one taxonomy or list of skills in developing this list; rather, we have chosen only a few categories of activities that reflect some of the tasks or skills described in both Barrett's taxonomy and the *Wisconsin Design* list of skills. In fact, few of the activities can be described by just one label. For example, in one activity the students are to use the clues given in a riddle to infer what object is being described. This activity could also be used to reinforce the task of understanding literal details. Teachers must be aware that several skills are often involved in any one comprehension activity. The interrelationship of skills is one of the problems that opponents point out to those who attempt to identify subskills of reading comprehension. However, as the activities given in the following pages illustrate, one skill can be the focus for explicit instruction even though it is combined with many other skills. By choosing several activities that show a common skill in combination with many other skills, the teacher will be able to help the students learn to use the skill in a variety of reading situations.

Comprehending Words That Identify Relationships

A reader must be able to understand words that determine relationships before he or she can use these words to identify conclusions. The activities given below are examples of exercises that would give students practice in using *whether, all, only, some,* and *no.*

1. Ammon (1975) suggests that "in teaching new vocabulary to children, definitions are of minimal value. Children learn vocabulary through usage" (p. 247). This is especially true for words that are difficult to define other than by example of proper usage. Relationship words are of this type. Ammon suggests using the technique of "oral bombardment" to demonstrate the correct usage of a particular word or term. For example, to teach the use of *whether,* Ammons proposes that the teacher give a test frame sentence, such as "I don't know whether to go to the movies or _____" (p. 248). The children are to complete the sentence in an appropriate manner. Any answer that makes sense is acceptable. The gamelike atmosphere and the admissibility of any logical answer can remove the tedium of practice from vocabulary study and can help children gain confidence in their ability to use the vocabulary word in a meaningful way.

2. Present a picture of several blue boats on a lake. Ask the children to tell which of the following sentences are true about the picture. (The sentences may be given orally or in written form.) Ask the students to defend their answers. In some cases, such as "All of the blue boats are on the lake," students may decide that not enough information has been given to determine if the sentence is true or false.

All of the boats are blue.

All of the blue boats are on the lake.

Only green boats are on the lake.

Only blue boats are on the lake.

Some of the blue boats are on the lake.

Some of the boats on the lake are blue.

No blue boat is on the lake.

No green boat is on the lake.

3. Ask the students to draw pairs of pictures that illustrate the differences between conditions, such as "Some of Nancy's sweaters are green" and "Nancy has only green sweaters." The finished pictures should be discussed. Other students could be asked to match each picture with the appropriate sentence.

4. For each set of relationship sentences below, ask the students to choose the correct conclusion—A or B.

_____ All of the girls in my math class wear glasses. Jane is in my math class.

_____ The only girl in my math class who wears glasses is Maria. Jane is in my math class.

_____ No girl in my math class wears glasses. Jane is in my math class.

Conclusions

A. Jane wears glasses.

B. Jane doesn't wear glasses.

In order to be able to make inferences or to identify a main idea, the reader often needs to understand the details that support the inference or that add up to the main idea. The activities given below provide practice in attending to details.

Comprehending Details

1. Either read aloud or give the students a written copy of a paragraph that gives a detailed description of an imaginary creature or object. Ask the students to draw a picture of the creature, using all of the details given in the paragraph. Compare the finished pictures and discuss how the same details may be illustrated in varying manners. Ask the students to judge if each picture accurately depicts every detail that was provided. An example follows:

The Whiffling Marfweezel

The whiffling marfweezel is a very strange animal. Its body is shaped like an apple, and its head looks like a triangle. It has long, pointed ears. The whiffling marfweezel's nose is perfectly round, and its eyes are striped. The whiffling marfweezel is very cheerful and always has a smile on its face.

2. Show the students a picture. Then provide three short descriptive paragraphs (in either written or oral form) and ask the students to identify which one accurately describes the picture. The paragraphs should differ in minor details so that the students have to attend carefully to small distinctions. Ask the students to support their choices. Some examples follow.

a) The house was small and had been painted yellow. The two downstairs windows had shutters. The door, which was between the two windows, was open. The owner had planted bushes around the house, and a tall maple tree shaded the front lawn.

b) The small yellow house was surrounded by bushes. The tall maple tree on the front lawn was beautiful. The house had two windows upstairs with shutters. The two downstairs windows did not have shutters. The windows were all closed. Only the front door was open.

c) The owner had painted the small house yellow and had put shutters next to the two downstairs windows. To the left of these windows was a door. The door was open today to catch the summer breezes. The bushes around the house and the maple tree on the lawn helped to make the little house appear cool on this hot day.

3. Have the children go on a treasure hunt, using clues that give detailed descriptions of the hiding places.

- This clue is in a blue book near the biggest desk in the room.
- The third clue will be found under a chair. The chair is six long steps from the doorway.

Identifying Sequence   Children should learn to use their intuitive knowledge of what step might be next to help them follow the sequence of events in a reading selection. Students also need to learn to follow a sequential plan that does not necessarily have a logical order that can be based on their own experiences.

1. Read a short story to young children and then ask them to arrange pictures that illustrate events in the story in the proper sequence.

2. Recipes and directions for making simple items can be used to provide practice in following a set of sequential steps. Put the various steps on individual sentence strips. Ask the students to recreate the correct sequence after reading or listening to the recipe or the directions by placing the strips in the right order. The strips can also be ordered by the students on the basis of a logical sequence before they read the recipe or directions. In that case, ask the students to compare their intuitive order with the real order. After the students have determined the proper order, have them follow the directions without further guidance.

3. Read or have the students read a paragraph in which a logical sequence of events has been violated. Ask the students to reorder the events into a more plausible sequence and to give their reasons for their order. Different orders may be acceptable because of different experiential backgrounds. An example follows:

He brushed his teeth.

He got dressed.

He ate breakfast.

He got on the school bus.

He got out of bed.

He raced out of the front door.

Many children have difficulty distinguishing between important details and overall main ideas; some are even unable to identify the specific topic of a selection easily. These children must be taught to read beyond interesting details in order to combine these details into a central thought.

Identifying Topics or Main Ideas

1. Reproduce a short news story and ask the students to choose a title or headline for the story from several similar titles. For example, if the story were about a new hospital for children in Greenville, the headline choices could be: New Children's Hospital in New York, Remodeling the Greenville Children's Hospital, New Children's Hospital in Greenville, and New Hospital for the Elderly.

2. Reproduce a short news story and explain to the students that they are to write a five- to ten-word telegram or a headline giving the main idea of the story.

3. Math problems often give a lot of information about a topic. Sometimes it is hard for the student to decide exactly what question is being asked in a math problem. This question is really the main idea of the problem.

Give the students several math problems and ask them to underline the main idea in each problem. Then have them find the answer to the problem. Two examples follow:

   a) Phil has $37.23 in his savings account. He used to have $43.59, but he spent part of his savings on a new shirt. Phil earned this money by mowing lawns in July. He wants to buy a new tape recorder that costs $58.89. Find out how much money Phil still needs to earn.

   b) Who earns the most money in a week? Bob earns $10 a day, Monday through Friday, by raking leaves for the city. Diane sells cosmetics and earns $20 each afternoon she works. She usually works Saturday and Sunday afternoons. Paula makes $3 an hour and works 15 hours a week as an assistant in a florist's shop.

4. Play the Topic Game.

Materials: game board with a path to follow (see Fig. 7.2), topic cards (see Fig. 7.3), paragraph cards (see Fig. 7.3), three to six persons

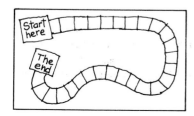

Fig. 7.2. Game board for the topic game.

Fig. 7.3.   Examples of paragraph and topic cards.

Object of the game: to give students practice in identifying the topic of a paragraph

Procedure: The paragraph cards are shuffled and placed face down in a pile. The topic cards are shuffled, and each player is dealt five cards. The reporter (leader), who gets no topic cards, is to read the paragraph cards to the players. The rest of the topic cards are placed face down in a pile.

The reporter draws the first paragraph card, making sure that no player can see the face of the card, and reads the paragraph aloud. The player who has the topic card for that paragraph may move the number of spaces indicated on the topic card. If a student incorrectly identifies a topic, he or she must move back one space. If no student holds that topic card, the reporter draws another paragraph card. If a student does correctly identify a topic, he or she discards that topic card and draws a new topic card to replace it. The first player to reach the end of the path wins.

Making Inferences   Students often need help in using information to make valid inferences. Sometimes students are simply unaware of how to use information in a logical manner. Other problems with inferential comprehension may be due to a lack of confidence by the reader in his or her own ability to go beyond what the author has explicitly stated.

1.   Give the students a sentence that states a condition, such as: "Whenever John has a test, he gets nervous." Then give the students one more piece of information and a conclusion. Ask the students to tell if the conclusion is true or not true or if the validity of the conclusion cannot be determined by the information given. For example:

Given	*Conclusion*
John has a test.	John is nervous.
John has a test.	John is not nervous.
John is nervous.	John has a test.

2.   Read a familiar story, such as "The Three Little Pigs" or "Little Red Riding Hood," to a group of young children. Stop before the final outcome of the tale is given and ask the children to predict what will happen. Most of the children will probably suggest the usual ending. Ask the children what other endings

might make sense for the story and ask them to give reasons for their answers. If the children cannot suggest alternative outcomes, make some suggestions yourself and ask the children to judge if the facts warrant each prediction.

3. Play the Riddle Game.

Materials: a set of riddle cards (see Fig. 7.4), four to ten players and a leader, a watch or clock with a second hand.

1. It has four legs.
2. It eats eucalyptus leaves.
3. It lives in Australia.
4. It looks like a teddy bear.

1. It is something to wear on your feet.
2. It is worn only in winter.
3. It makes travel on snow easy.
4. It looks like a tennis racket.

Fig. 7.4. Examples of riddle cards.

Object of the game: to give the students practice in inferring the topic of riddle.

Procedure: One student is chosen as leader, and the remaining students are divided into two teams. The leader shuffles the set of riddle cards, draws the top card, and reads the first sentence of the riddle. Each team is given 30 seconds to agree on one guess about the identity of the topic described by the riddle. If neither team guesses correctly, the next sentence is read, and again each team has one guess. (The teams alternate making the first guess.) This procedure is repeated until the riddle has been guessed correctly or all four of the clues for that riddle have been given. The game then continues with the drawing of a new card.

A team gets 30 points for guessing the riddle after hearing only one clue, 20 points after two clues, 10 points after three clues, and 5 points after four clues. The team with the most points at the end of the game wins.

Many readers are not "discriminating consumers" of what they read; instead, they accept many ideas that appear in print simply because the ideas *are* in print. Practice in evaluating what is read should begin very early so that readers develop the habit of reading critically.

Evaluating What Is Read

1. Read a fairy tale or other make-believe story to young children. Ask them to judge if the story really could have taken place. Have the children give specific reasons for their answers. (This activity is not appropriate for very young children, who are still unable to distinguish between reality and fantasy, even after explanations are given.)

2. Collect several versions of one news story, which may be taken from different newspapers, news magazines, and even radio and television broadcasts. Ask the students to compare the different versions of the story, identifying

conflicting information, completeness and accuracy of the information given, and signs of bias or prejudice on the part of the reporter.

3. Discuss propaganda techniques, such as the use of loaded words ("un-American," "racist"), testimonial statements, or "jump on the bandwagon" appeals, with the students. Have them read or listen to advertisements for products and then ask them to identify the specific propaganda technique used. The students may even be asked to create their own advertisements, using one or more propaganda techniques.

Developing
Appreciation of
What Is Read

Too often teachers do not give children opportunities to "stop and smell the roses" when they read. Children need planned activities that point out for them the different ways in which an author may convey the same meaning. Understanding the options should help the students appreciate the subtle craft of authorship.

1. To help children gain an appreciation of the use of figurative language (such as similes and metaphors—"I was as hungry as a bear" and "That car is a lemon.") and to assess their understanding of figurative language, ask them to rewrite a short paragraph that uses figurative language. The new paragraphs are to contain no figures of speech, but are to retain the original meaning. Compare versions written by several children. Ask the students to judge if each child retained the author's meaning. Then ask the students whether they preferred the original version or one written by a student. Have each student tell the reasons for his or her preference.

2. Ask the students to describe a single scene or object in two different ways for different purposes. For example, show the class a picture of a dog. Ask the children to describe the dog first as if they were trying to sell it to a prospective buyer for $100. Then ask them to write a paragraph describing the same dog from the point of view of a person who has just been bitten by the dog. The students must not alter characteristics that are apparent in the picture.

3. Find or write several descriptions of the same or similar scenes or events. Ask the children to compare their responses to the different descriptions and to try to tell why their reactions varied. Then have the students use their reactions as the bases for identifying each author's purpose in describing the scene or event in that particular manner.

ASSESSING
COMPREHENSION

Assessing comprehension, especially beyond the literal level, is often difficult. Many factors need to be considered in choosing an assessment instrument. Furthermore, teachers will need to be sure that failure to respond correctly to a comprehension task is indeed the manifestation of a *comprehension* problem. Several complicating factors that may cause what seem to be comprehension problems are presented in this section. In addition, we describe several techniques for evaluating comprehension and the strengths and limitations of each.

Many children have difficulty comprehending what they read. These children need guidance in thinking and in developing skills that will help them understand what they have read. However, many apparent comprehension problems are really due to much more prosaic causes and are much more amenable to correction. Here we will describe some of the "masqueraders" and suggest a series of questions teachers should ask themselves when attempting to evaluate comprehension problems.

1. *Could the reader decode most of the words in the selection?* We have mentioned this before, and we emphasize it again here: If children cannot read most of the words in the selection, they will be so involved in the decoding process that they will be unable to attend to comprehension. Furthermore, if too many of the words are unknown, the reader will have too little information on which to build comprehension.

2. *Did the reader understand the specialized vocabulary of the selection?* Sometimes failure to understand only one or two key words can prevent comprehension. What may appear to be a severe inability to understand written materials may dissolve entirely once the reader understands just one or two important words. The message here to teachers should be obvious: Introduce specialized vocabulary *before* the students begin reading.

3. *Was the reader interested in reading the selection?* Many times failure to comprehend what was read is simply a problem of motivation. The reader just didn't give a hoot and was merely playing the "move-the-eyes-across-the-page" game. Discriminating between students who can't and those who won't comprehend is not always easy, and trying to motivate the disinterested learner can be very frustrating. Teachers may help minimize the problem of lack of motivation by helping their students set purposes for reading and by introducing a reading assignment in a manner calculated to pique interest and instill enthusiasm.

4. *Did the reader's experiential background interfere with comprehension?* If the reader is familiar with the concepts involved in the selection, comprehension will be enhanced. If the reader has no experiential background to which he or she can relate what is read, comprehension becomes more difficult. In addition, dissimilar backgrounds can lead to different interpretations of the same passage. If the child's background and the teacher's are much alike, the child's interpretation may agree with the teacher's "right" answer. However, many "wrong" answers are really right in light of the child's unique background and expectations.

5. *Did the reader follow directions?* The ability to follow directions is a very important comprehension skill. However, a failure to follow directions should not be misinterpreted as a problem in other areas. Teachers must be especially careful of this when evaluating performance on independent written assignments, although this can also be a problem in oral-comprehension work.

6. *Could the reader express the answer correctly?* Some children have very poor composition skills. However, inability to write down an answer in a coherent manner does not necessarily mean that the child does not know the answer. Too often teachers confuse composition disabilities with reading disabilities.

Teachers should also be aware that some children have difficulty expressing their ideas orally, even though they know what they want to say. Distinguishing between problems with oral expression and genuine comprehension difficulties may be difficult, but teachers should consider a student's expressive abilities when evaluating comprehension.

7. *Did the reader understand the question?* Sometimes a seemingly incorrect answer will be given merely because the question was misunderstood. Whenever a student gives an apparent *non sequitur*, the teacher should be alerted to the possibility that it is the question, not the answer, that is causing problems. Often a simple rephrasing of the question will clear up the confusion.

8. *Did the reader forget what he or she read?* Of course, if the reader cannot remember what was read, momentary understanding of the passage is not very useful. However, remediation of comprehension difficulties will be different for cases in which memory is the primary stumbling block and those in which the reader never did understand what was read. The teacher should investigate the source of the problem by allowing the student to refer back to the selection in order to find the answer. If the student still cannot easily identify the right answer, the problem is more severe than just poor memory or inattentiveness.

9. *Could the reader's answer be right and the teacher's wrong? Could both answers be right?* Horrors! Experienced teachers can provide numerous examples of incorrect answers given in teacher's manuals. Furthermore, children with divergent minds or different experiential backgrounds may provide entirely new responses that are based on perfectly sound reasoning and on the information from the text. The creative child or one with a different cultural background should not be penalized by the narrow restrictions of someone else's background or uncreative mind. On the other hand, not every creative answer can be justified. The child must be able to offer logical support for any answer.

These nine questions should help teachers "clear away the underbrush" in order to identify real comprehension problems. Too often teachers get sidetracked by peripheral problems that are not really problems with comprehension at all.

Measuring Reading Comprehension

Reading comprehension may be measured in several different ways. In this section we describe briefly five of the most common of these assessment techniques. We also show how the teacher can gather information informally about a child's ability to understand what has been read. Evaluation in reading will be discussed more fully in Chapter 12.

Standardized tests of reading comprehension, through which a student's performance on comprehension items is compared with the performance of other students from a larger population (the norming group), are common. Typically, standardized tests require the student to read a variety of selections silently and then to choose an answer from several choices. Usually the passages are organized roughly in order of increasing difficulty, and a time limit is prescribed. A comprehension score is derived from the student's performance on a standardized test. This score is usually reported in raw score, percentile, and grade-equivalent forms.

Teachers wishing to use a standardized test to measure reading comprehension should examine the test critically. The test should have been normed on a very diverse population or on a population similar to the children who will be taking the test. A variety of kinds of reading selections should be included in the test, and these selections should be of different lengths. Teachers should also note if the time limit seems realistic.

Most standardized reading tests are not intended to be diagnostic. That is, they are designed to identify a level of reading achievement and do not claim to pinpoint specific comprehension difficulties.

As with standardized tests, most criterion-referenced tests require the student to read passages silently and to respond to multiple-choice questions. However, criterion-referenced tests do not compare a student's performance with the performances of other students. The student's score is based instead on achievement of a certain criterion of success. The student either achieves this level of success, and is therefore considered to have mastered the skill, or does not reach this level. Criterion levels for mastery or success vary, usually between 80 and 90 percent.

Criterion-referenced tests are usually skill-oriented. A reader is tested on various reading subskills or tasks and is judged to have mastered these skills or not. When the focus is on individual skills, criterion-referenced tests may be used diagnostically. (Criterion-referenced tests are discussed more fully in Chapter 12.)

The value of a criterion-referenced test depends on the degree to which the test measures the specific skill it purports to measure. Proponents of a global view of reading comprehension would deny that this can be done. Even theorists who believe that subskills or tasks of comprehension can be identified warn that some tests may not really evaluate the skill they were designed to assess. Teachers should examine tests carefully in order to judge if such problems exist.

A cloze test measures the student's ability to comprehend a written prose selection by his or her ability to supply words that have been deleted from the passage. The underlying assumption of the cloze procedure is that if a reader can reconstruct the author's exact words, the reader has understood the author's meaning.

Usually every fifth or tenth word is deleted to form a cloze passage. The reader is required to write in or to supply verbally the missing word. In order for a response to be counted as correct, the exact missing word must be supplied; synonyms are not acceptable. This restriction may seem unnecessarily harsh, but it is balanced by the fact that the criterion for success or comprehension is only 40 percent.

Cloze measures are very useful for assessing if a particular instructional material is of the appropriate level of readability for a certain student. As measures of comprehension, cloze tests can give only an overall estimate of comprehension ability. They cannot be used diagnostically except as indicators of the student's ability to attend to semantic and syntactic restraints of the language.

Informal Reading Inventories

Informal reading inventories (IRIs), in which a student reads a short, graded selection aloud and then responds orally to questions about the selection, are useful for diagnosing decoding problems. If comprehension is based only on oral reading, however, IRIs may be of limited utility for identifying comprehension problems, although they can help to identify an appropriate level for instruction. Comprehension should be assessed by silent reading because silent reading is more common than oral reading in real life. When using an IRI to assess both decoding and comprehension, some of the selections should be read silently rather than aloud, followed by questions designed to assess comprehension of the selections. These questions should include questions at least at the literal and inferential levels. Many published IRIs have questions primarily at the literal level. Teachers would be wise to augment the literal questions with their own questions at higher levels of comprehension.

Teachers can create their own informal reading inventories to assess both decoding and comprehension abilities. Using the actual reading materials the students will most likely be using, the teacher should choose three selections from each book under consideration. One selection should come from the beginning of the book, one from the middle, and one from the end. For pre-primers, selections should be of about 50 words in length. For primers and first-grade readers, passages of approximately 100 words are appropriate. Reading selections for higher grade levels should be longer, about 200–300 words.

After identifying the selections, the teacher should write several comprehension questions for each selection. These questions should tap both literal and inferential questions. The teacher must be very careful that the questions are passage-dependent. That is, the student should have to have *read* the passage in order to answer the questions. For example, questions such as "How did Ethelbert feel when the lion bit his arm?" or "What color were the strawberries?" can be answered from general knowledge (we hope vicarious in the case of the lion and Ethelbert). One way to test for passage dependency is to ask someone to answer the questions without ever having seen the passage. Under such circumstances, if a question can be answered, it should not be included in the IRI.

An informal reading inventory can provide useful information about a student's comprehension. However trite this may sound, an IRI is only as good as the questions that are asked. If the questions are only at the literal level of comprehension or if they are not passage-dependent, the IRI will be of only limited value.

Three of the four kinds of comprehension measures already described assess understanding by asking the student to answer specific questions. Retelling measures comprehension by asking the student to tell as much of the story as he or she can recall, usually without referring back to the text. The examiner prepares an outline of the text that is used to evaluate the retelling performance. Goodman and Burke (1972, p. 24) suggest guidelines for outlining reading material. A total of 100 points is divided among four major categories for story material and among three different categories for informational material (see Table 7.1). Within each category the points are allotted among specific items. A careful outline should cover a wide range of understandings, both specific and general.

Retelling

Story material	Maximum points	Informational material	Maximum points
Character analysis:			
Recall	15	Specifics	40
Development	15	Generalizations	30
Events	30	Major concepts	30
Plot	20		
Theme	20		

TABLE 7.1
Point distribution for retelling formats

From Y. Goodman and C. Burke, *Reading Miscue Inventory Manual: Procedure for Diagnosis and Evaluation* (New York: Macmillan, 1972), p. 24. Copyright © Carolyn L. Burke and Yetta M. Goodman 1972. Reprinted by permission.

According to the Goodman-Burke model, the reader is invited to tell as much as he or she can remember about what has just been read. After the student has completed this task, without aid from the text and without prompting from the teacher, the teacher may ask questions. These questions should not introduce new information, but should encourage the student to expand on statements previously made. General questions, such as "When did the story take place?" or "What point do you think the author was trying to make?" are permitted. The teacher is to give the reader every opportunity to exhibit understanding of the passage, but without providing information that the reader had not assimilated through reading.

Goodman and Burke (1972) suggest that a reader whose retelling covers 50 percent of the points in the outline (that is, has a score of 50 or better) has been highly effective in the use of reading strategies. A score of 40–80 points indicates moderately effective strategies; 20–60 points signals some effective use of strategies; and a score of fewer than 25 points is a sign of ineffective reading.

Using retelling to measure comprehension permits the student to show fully the extent of his or her understanding of the passage. The student is not restrained by being allowed to answer only a small, preselected set of questions. In addition, the reader and the examiner can interact, thus preventing misinterpretations of both questions and answers. In guiding the retelling, the teacher can direct the questions in order to assess the reader's understanding of a variety of comprehension tasks. Furthermore, retelling measures a different kind of comprehension than do tests that call for responses to specific questions or recognition of answers in a multiple-choice format.

As with any measure of comprehension, there are disadvantages to the use of retelling. The outline of the text and the questioning during the retelling are dependent largely on the skill of the teacher and on the teacher's subjective judgment. For example, a teacher may emphasize understanding only at the literal level or may unwittingly provide additional information to the reader through questions. The teacher may lack skill in eliciting further information. Another disadvantage to using retelling is that it is a time-consuming, individualized procedure. The retelling and the questioning that guides it cannot be rushed, or the score will not truly reflect the depth of the reader's understanding of the passage.

Informal Daily Observation

Unfortunately, many teachers do not have confidence in their own ability to make judgments about how well their students understand what they read. Such teachers have been overwhelmed by the mystique of tests. Surely the person who works with a child six hours a day for 180 days ought to be qualified to form valid opinions about that child's comprehension. Observation of the child during the day can provide a great deal of information. The teacher can note if the child participates in class discussions of an assignment in the social studies book. The student's performance in a reading workbook can give information about his or her comprehension. The child's ability to tell about a book just read can provide data. Throughout the day there are many opportunities for the teacher to observe the ability of the students to understand what they have read. The teacher simply has to be aware of these opportunities and make use of them.

APPLICATION

In the preceding pages we have explained in great detail what is *not* a comprehension problem, and we have been fairly pessimistic about the value of many kinds of assessment techniques for measuring reading comprehension. You may have been left with the feeling that you know what *not* to do and what *not* to use, but that you still have not been told what you *should* do. That's right, and we are not going to step forth now to the blare of trumpets and announce that at last we've found the answer.

However, we do have two pearls of wisdom to offer in concluding a discussion of evaluating reading comprehension. First, *use a variety of measures.* All of the testing procedures we have described have merits, and teachers should consider using several of these techniques in order to get as full a picture as possible of their students' comprehension abilities. The deficits of one test may be remedied by combining the information gleaned from that test with the information from another. In addition, many students will do better on some kinds of measures than on others. Using a variety of assessment techniques will permit students to display their comprehension abilities fully.

Second, *always confirm the information given by the tests through personal observation.* Never accept unquestioningly the information provided by a test. If the information does not match the child's actual performance on a day-to-day basis, investigate further.

A great deal of research is currently being carried out to investigate many aspects of comprehension. Ideally, these investigations will help teachers become even more effective in guiding the comprehension of their students. In the meantime, enough is known about the nature of comprehension, effective strategies for improving comprehension, and techniques for measuring comprehension to enable teachers to focus their instructional efforts. Improving comprehension abilities is not easy; there is no magic way that will work for all teachers and for all children, and research is never going to establish that one magic way exists. Teachers will always have to combine the suggestions and ideas generated by research with their own common sense and their ability to interact with children.

1. Review the characteristics of materials that can cause poor comprehension. Do the same for the characteristics of the learner. Which of these possible roadblocks to comprehension can be removed relatively easily? Which are very difficult to overcome? Which of these remedies involve a great deal of teacher preparation time and/or expense? Which involve fairly simple teaching techniques that require only a little preplanning and investment of time?

2. Two basic theoretical approaches to reading comprehension, "looking at the whole" and "looking at the parts as well as the whole," were described. Think about the advantages and disadvantages of each approach. Then think about how you could combine aspects of both approaches in helping your students develop their comprehension abilities. How would you reconcile the "Humpty Dumpty" aspects of separate-skill development with the "undifferentiated blob" aspects of viewing comprehension as a whole?

3. Read the following passage about Abraham Lincoln (Foster, 1952) and the questions that follow it. Decide if each question is at the *literal, inferential, evaluative,* or *appreciation* level of comprehension. Write your decision on the line next to each question. Compare your answers with a friend.

A whole year passed in misery and loneliness. Then Abe's father couldn't stand it any longer. He went back to Kentucky, leaving Abe and Sarah alone with Dennis Hanks. Dennis had come to live in their cabin after Aunt Betsy died.

One dismal December day, Abe sat by the fire, scratching all the letters he could remember in the ashes, wishing he knew how to read. Every day seemed like a week, waiting for his father to come back. Abe knew why he'd gone, but that didn't make waiting any easier. Dennis had just come in with his gun, bringing a squirrel for dinner. Sarah said she'd cook it and try to make it taste good. Abe said he couldn't eat. He couldn't even swallow.

What if nobody would come? he thought. Or what if somebody came, and she didn't like them—him and Sarah? What if . . . . All of a sudden he heard horses' hooves. He ran outside. And, almost before he knew it, SHE was there. His stepmother, Sarah Bush Lincoln. He saw her first, sitting beside his father on the seat of a big wagon, piled so high with furniture that it took four horses to pull it.

On top of the pile sat two girls and a boy. They jumped down as the wagon stopped and stood staring at Abe and Sarah in their dirty, ragged clothes. Then the tall, straight woman came and stood beside them.

"These are my children," she said. "John and Sarah and Matilda Johnston." Her voice was warm and friendly. "And I suppose you are Sarah Lincoln? And you," she added slowly, "you must be Abraham."

Abe looked up. Her eyes were as friendly as her voice. She didn't even seem to see that he was too tall, or mind that he was homely. She just smiled, and so Abe smiled, too. From then to the end of his life, this second mother was to be "the best friend he had."*

_____ 1. What famous person is this story about?

_____ 2. What time of year was it?

_____ 3. There are three Sarahs in this story. How was each related to Abe?

_____ 4. How did Abe feel as he waited for his father's return?

_____ 5. Why did he feel this way?

_____ 6. How would you feel in this situation?

_____ 7. Why did the author write SHE in capital letters?

_____ 8. How do you know that Sarah Bush Lincoln was still alive when Abe died?

_____ 9. Why was the wagon piled high with furniture?

_____10. What words does the author use to make the reader think of Sarah Bush Lincoln as a nice person?

Now put a check in front of each question you think is passage-dependent. Base your decisions on what you think a fourth-grade student, not an adult, would have as general knowledge. Again, compare your answers with a friend.

*Genevieve Foster, "His Good Stepmother," in *Abraham Lincoln*, New York: Scribners, 1950. Reprinted with the permission of Charles Scribner's Sons.

4. Four important aspects of preparing children to read with comprehension were given in this chapter. Which of these are of importance primarily in the readiness stage of reading? Which are important to stress at every stage? Think of suggestions you might give to parents who wished to help prepare their children for understanding what they read.

5. Suppose that you are a member of a committee to help teachers assess the reading comprehension of their elementary-school students. One member of the committee insists that teachers need "hard data" and that standardized tests are the only way to gather these data. Another committee member feels that formal tests do not give a true picture of actual student reading competence. You take the eclectic position: Some assessment techniques are good for certain purposes, and different techniques are more appropriate for other purposes. To help prove your point, you outline the advantages and disadvantages of each of the assessment techniques described in this chapter. Prepare that outline now.

REFERENCES

Ammon, Richard. "Generating Expectancies to Enhance Comprehension," *Reading Teacher* **29** (1975): 245–249.

Ausubel, David. "Some Psychological Aspects of the Structure of Knowledge," in S. Elam, ed., *Education and the Structure of Knowledge*, Fifth Annual Phi Delta Kappa Symposium on Educational Research (Chicago: Rand McNally, 1964).

Barrett, Thomas C. "Taxonomy of Reading Comprehension," *Reading 360 Monograph* (Lexington, Mass.: Ginn, 1972).

Beery, Althea. "Clustering Comprehension Skills to Solve Problems," in *Forging Ahead in Reading* **12**, pp. 109–111 (Newark, Del.: International Reading Association, 1967).

Betts, Emmett. *Foundations of Reading Instruction* (New York: American Book, 1957).

Carver, Ronald. "Reading as Reasoning: Implications for Measurement," in W. MacGinitie, ed., *Assessment Problems in Reading* (Newark, Del.: International Reading Association, 1973).

Cunningham, Patricia. "Transferring Comprehension from Listening to Reading," *Reading Teacher* **29** (1975): 169–172.

Davis, F. "Psychometric Research on Comprehension in Reading," *Reading Research Quarterly* **7** (1972): 628–678.

Eklund, C., and J. Beckman. *Antarctica* (New York: Holt, Rinehart and Winston, 1963).

Flesch, Rudolph. *Why Johnny Can't Read* (New York: Harper and Bros., 1955).

Foster, Gertrude. *Abraham Lincoln* (New York: Scribner, 1950).

Goodman, Kenneth. "A Psycholinguistic View of Reading Comprehension," in G. Schick and M. May, eds., *New Frontiers in College-Adult Reading: Fifteenth Yearbook of the National Reading Conference* (Milwaukee: National Reading Conference, 1966).

Goodman, Yetta, and Carolyn Burke. *Reading Miscue Inventory Manual: Procedure for Diagnosis and Evaluation* (New York: Macmillan, 1972).

Guszak, Frank. "Teacher Questioning and Reading," *Reading Teacher* **21** (1967): 227–234.

Harris, Albert. *How to Increase Reading Ability*, 5th ed. (New York: McKay, 1970).

Hays, William L. *Statistics* (New York: Holt, Rinehart and Winston, 1963).

Hoskisson, Kenneth. " 'False' Questions and 'Right' Answers," *Reading Teacher* **27** (1973): 159–162.

Hunt, Lyman. "The Effect of Self-Selection, Interest, and Motivation upon Independent, Instructional, and Frustrational Levels," *Reading Teacher* **24** (1970): 146–158.

Irving, Washington. *Rip van Winkle and the Legend of Sleepy Hollow* (Tarrytown, N.Y.: Sleepy Hollow Restorations, 1974).

Kidney and Urinary Tract Infections (Indianapolis: Lilly Research Labs, 1971).

Melnick, Amelia. "The Formulation of Questions as an Instructional-Diagnostic Tool," in *Reading and Inquiry* 10, pp. 36–39 (Newark, Del.: International Reading Association, 1965).

Ruddell, Robert. "Effect of the Similarity of Oral and Written Patterns of Language Structure in Reading Comprehension," *Elementary English* **42** (1965): 403–410.

Samuels, S. Jay. "Automatic Decoding and Reading Comprehension," *Language Arts* **53** (1976): 323–325.

Sartre, Jean-Paul. *Being and Nothingness*, trans. H. Barnes. (New York: Washington Square Press, 1966).

Sayers, Dorothy. *Murder Must Advertise* (New York: Avon, 1967).

Smith, Nila B. "The Many Faces of Reading Comprehension," *Reading Teacher* **23** (1969): 249–259.

Smith, Richard J., and Thomas C. Barrett. *Teaching Reading in the Middle Grades* (Reading, Mass.: Addison-Wesley, 1974).

Spache, George. *Toward Better Reading* (Champaign, Ill.: Garrard, 1963).

Spearritt, D. "Identification of Subskills of Reading Comprehension by Maximum Likelihood Factor Analysis," *Reading Research Quarterly* **8** (1972): 92–111.

Stauffer, Russell. *The Language Experience Approach to the Teaching of Reading* (New York: Harper & Row, 1970).

Tathum, Susan. "Reading Comprehension of Materials Written with Selected Oral Language Patterns: A Study of Grades Two and Four," *Reading Research Quarterly* **5** (Spring 1970): 402–426.

Thorndike, Robert. "Reading as Reasoning," *Reading Research Quarterly* **9** (1973–1974): 135–147.

Tovey, Duane. "Improving Children's Comprehension Abilities," *Reading Teacher* **30** (1976): 288–292.

Wisconsin Design for Reading Skill Development (Minneapolis: National Computer Systems, 1977).

Chapter 8
Learning
How to Learn:
Study Skills

After reading this chapter, you will be able to:

1. Discuss the importance of study skills in the elementary school.
2. Discuss techniques for determining the readability of printed materials.
3. Discuss the importance of reading in different ways for different purposes.
4. Discuss the importance of instruction in identifying appropriate resources.
5. Identify important locational skills.
6. Identify important interpretation skills.
7. Discuss the importance of outlining and note-taking.

Elementary-school teachers sometimes get so caught up in teaching decoding skills and in using basal readers or story books to teach comprehension that they forget one of the primary goals of reading instruction: to prepare students to be independent learners, not just completers of workbook assignments or readers of fiction. Junior high and middle-school teachers often complain that their students "can't read." By this they usually mean that the students are unable to complete independent-study assignments that require them to extract information from a variety of sources, interpret that information, organize and store the information, and then retrieve it in some meaningful form. Elementary-school teachers often do not see study skills as their responsibility, and junior high and middle-school teachers expect students to come to them already knowing these skills. Unfortunately, the development of study skills does not suddenly just "happen" in the carefree summer between elementary school and entry into junior high or middle school. The development of study skills is the responsibility of *both* sets of teachers, but instruction must begin in the elementary school, in the primary grades.

In this chapter we discuss five important aspects of developing independent learners. First, students must be provided with materials that they can decode. With this in mind, we have presented four different procedures for assessing the readability of printed materials so that the teacher will have a better basis on which to assign materials to students. Next, techniques for varying rate when reading for different purposes are described, and a study method, SQ3R, is suggested. Then the importance of helping students select and use appropriate resource materials is outlined. Fourth, skills needed for interpreting maps, graphs, and tables are suggested, and techniques for developing these skills are given. Last, the case for the necessity for giving children a great deal of practice in outlining and taking notes is argued. If students cannot organize, store, and retrieve the information they have gathered and interpreted, this information is of little use to them.

That best of all students, the independent learner, does not spring forth from the elementary school spontaneously. Elementary-school teachers must understand that the responsibility for developing study skills does indeed begin in the elementary school and that they must provide students with guidance and focused instruction in the study skills. The independent learner is not "created" overnight, but develops from several years of careful encouragement and instruction.

Studying study skills may not seem particularly exciting. Few theoreticians have devoted their lives to the complexities of alphabetizing; the question of whether to use a bar graph or a line graph may not seem very important to many readers. And yet study skills are crucial if a reader is going to be able to *do* anything with what is decoded and comprehended. Study skills enable a reader to locate and interpret information from a variety of sources and to synthesize that information into the solution to a problem. Study skills are *useful*; they are not just hoops through which a reader must jump passively, but rather tools that enable the reader to find an answer to a problem. Artley (1967, p. 12) expresses the character and the importance of study skills well:

> First, there was a problem, a question, or an issue. Second, there was the securing and marshalling of facts and information needed to solve the problem. Third, there was the evaluating and weighing of the bits of information, since each bit was not necessarily of equal value or merit. Finally, there was a resolution of the problem. All of these together composes the acts of study.
>
> Take note, if you will, of the second step in the study act. We called it the securing and marshalling of facts and information. There is no doubt that this was a very important part of the study process; but there would have been very little, if any, reason for it *had there not been a problem to resolve.* *

If teachers can instill in their students a sense of excitement about the problem-solving process, the teaching of study skills will be simplified. If students see the value in being able to interpret different kinds of graphs, to read maps of various kinds, to locate information to support their point of view, they may "learn to learn independently."

The first step in teaching study skills, however, is not to convince the students of the value of those skills. Rather, the first problem is to convince the *teachers*. Too often teachers do not see the teaching of study skills as their job. Reading teachers assume that social studies teachers are showing the students how to read maps and that math teachers are instructing their charges in the interpretation of tables and graphs. Unfortunately, many social studies, science, and math teachers feel that their job is to teach content, not study skills. Teachers in self-contained classrooms often do not make a connection between reading in the content areas and reading itself. The many excellent techniques used to introduce a selection and to guide the students through it in reading class are abandoned from 2:15–3 P.M. in "Social Studies Class." Skill develop-

---

*A. Sterl Artley, "Effective Study—Its Nature and Nurture," in J. Allen Figurel, ed., *Forging Ahead in Reading*, Newark, Delaware: IRA, 1968, p. 12. Reprinted with permission of the International Reading Association.

ment, a regular part of the reading curriculum, is not always perceived as a part of the social studies or science lesson. The focus is primarily on content.

Many teachers are guilty of what Herber calls assumptive teaching (1970, p. vii). These teachers assume that the students have the skills needed to study content-area matter. Such teachers ignore the signals that indicate that the students really do not have these skills, and they continue to make assignments that require use of the skills, without providing any instruction for developing the skills.

Study skills need to be taught by someone. No teacher should assume that students have already been taught these skills or that some other educator is taking the responsibility for this teaching. A teacher in a self-contained classroom should make specific plans for teaching study skills, whether these skills are taught during reading class, during one of the content-area classes, or in a separate skill-development period. Teachers in a departmentalized or team-teaching situation should plan as a group to divide the responsibility for teaching the study skills. In this way the teachers can not only be assured that the students will have had instruction in these skills, but also will be able to provide opportunities in all the subject classes for the students to apply the skills they have learned.

Once a teacher has taken the responsibility to provide instruction in the study skills, the process need not be dull or routine for either the pupils or the teacher. Artley (1967) has expressed the key to exciting instruction in study skills: The students and the teacher identify a problem and then gather information to solve that problem. Consider the following "problems":

- *Grade 1:* The children are going to study about fire safety in social studies. As part of the unit, they are going to walk to the local fire station. The problem identified is: How do the firefighters help our community?
- *Grade 5:* The students have been studying American history and will be reading about the Lewis and Clark expedition to explore the Northwest Territory. The problem identified is: Write the final report that Lewis and Clark might have presented to President Jefferson about their trip.

For the first grade, the following study skills (and many others) might be taught, reviewed, or practiced through the activities described:

1. *Using the card catalog and the Dewey decimal system:* The teacher or librarian could ask the class under which topic in the card catalog they might find books about how firefighters help the community. Then the librarian or teacher could look up *firefighter* in the card catalog and show the children all of the cards that contain books on the topic. Next, each child or small groups of children could be given the name of a book and the Dewey decimal number of the book on a slip of paper and be asked, one at a time, to find the book on the shelf, after the adult has shown them the general section in which the book could be found. (This would not involve reading necessarily, but just visual matching of the symbols on the paper with the symbols on the spine of the book.)

2. *Preparing and interpreting graphs:* At the fire station, the firefighters could be asked to tell how many fire calls they had answered on each day of the previous week. Then the class could prepare a picture graph (see Fig. 8.1) depicting the number of fire calls responded to in one week.

Fig. 8.1.   A picture graph.

3. *Reading maps:* Before starting on the trip, the teacher would show the children a simple map illustrating the area between the school and the fire station. The children would use the map, which contained picture symbols for the school fire station and other points of interest, to plan the safest route. Each child would then be given a mimeographed copy of the map, with the route penciled in, to carry on the trip for reference. On the trip the children would consult their maps frequently to make decisions about directions.

The fifth-grade class might utilize the following study skills:

1. *Using reference sources and taking notes:* The students could be asked to identify and consult different reference sources to find out the details of the Lewis and Clark expedition. They would use their note-taking abilities to record these details for later use.

2. *Preparing and interpreting graphs:* Using information gleaned from various sources, the class could prepare a bar graph that showed how many miles the expedition traveled in each month of the journey.

3. *Using maps:* The class could plot the trip on a large United States map, marking the route and significant events that took place along the way.

For both the first- and fifth-grade problems, many other skills and activities might be chosen. Regardless of the specific skills, however, the point is the same: Study skills can be taught and practiced through imaginative and interesting activities designed to teach the skill *and* the content being studied.

READABILITY: PROVIDING MATERIALS STUDENTS CAN READ

A teacher may pose the most interesting problem of the year in the most enthusiastic manner, but if a student cannot read the assigned material, all effort on the part of both the teacher and the student is wasted. If teachers wish to advance the study skills of their students, they must be able to supply a variety of materials which the students can read. A sixth-grade student who is reading at the third-grade level can still receive instruction in study skills, but the student must have materials with which to practice these skills at the third-grade readability level, not the sixth.

Many publishers identify reading levels of their textbooks. These designations may or may not be accurate, depending on the manner in which the reading levels were identified. Furthermore, most trade books (books not designed as texts or parts of series) have no designated level of readability. Teachers need to know techniques for identifying the readability levels so that they can guide their students to materials with which they can be successful. In this section we describe four formulas or techniques that may be used to assign readability levels to printed materials.

An Overview of Readability

Most common readability formulas take into consideration the number of difficult words and sentence length in order to determine readability. Klare (1974–1975, p. 96) suggests that consideration of these two elements is sufficient. Taking into account the number of difficult words, whether by counting the words not on a list of familiar words or by calculating word length through a syllable count, ensures that a semantic (word-meaning) component has been included in the determination of readability. Taking sentence length into account brings the component of syntactic complexity into the determination, since sentence length correlates highly with syntactic complexity. After reviewing more than 30 readability formulas, Klare concluded that techniques that attempt to include more variables or to measure the semantic and syntactic variables more precisely are not significantly better than the more simple measures, especially when the additional time needed to apply these techniques is considered.

The Spache and Dale-Chall Formulas

The Spache formula (Spache, 1970) was designed to be used with primary-level materials, up to a 3.9 grade level. The Dale-Chall formula (Dale and Chall, 1948) is most appropriate for use with materials of a fourth-grade readability or higher. Both formulas use percentage of difficult words and average sentence length to compute readability. For the Spache formula, the percentage of difficult words is determined by counting the words in a sample of approximately 100 words that do not appear in Stone's revision of the Dale list of 769 easy words and by dividing by the total number of words in the sample (Stone, 1956). For the Dale-Chall formula difficult words are those in a

100-word sample that are outside the Dale list of 3000 familiar words (Dale and Chall, 1948). In both formulas average sentence length is determined by dividing the number of words in the sample by the number of sentences in the sample. Then the percentage of difficult words and the average sentence length are each multiplied by a constant and added together with a third constant. The resulting number is the approximate grade level of the 100-word sample.

These procedures are carried out on several 100-word samples, chosen from the beginning, middle, and end of the book being assessed. The average readability level of the book is determined by adding the estimated level for each sample and dividing by the number of samples.

Application of the Dale-Chall Formula

To help you understand how to use the Dale-Chall formula, we have applied it to three 100-word samples from this book. (We have chosen the Dale-Chall rather than the Spache formula because we assume that the readability of this text is at least at fourth-grade level!) The first sample, from the beginning of the book, consists of 81 words in the section entitled "Objectives in Perspective" (Chapter 3, p. 34). The sample is not exactly 100 words, because whole sentences must be used. The second sample, of 106 words, is from this chapter, p. 190. The third sample (95 words) is from Chapter 12, p. 323. The authors of the Dale-Chall formula suggest taking a sample from every ten pages of a book. Naturally, we did not feel compelled to follow their instructions to the letter in order to construct this example!

Next, we counted the number of words not on the *Dale List of 3000 Unfamiliar Words*. We are not including this list or the special rules for determining what is or is not a familiar word, because of space limitations. Trust us. The unfamiliar words for each sample are listed below each sample.

Then we determined the number of sentences in each sample. The next step for each sample was to put the appropriate numbers into the proper places in the formula and to average the results. Finally, we converted the formula raw score to the corrected grade level and got a readability level of grade 13–15 for this text. (All computations are shown below each passage.)

PASSAGE ONE

Objectives can shackle spontaneity and creativity if they are treated as absolutes and applied with a heavy hand. But they can be beneficial if you use them to provide direction. Perspective makes the difference.

If you search the literature for the pros and cons of instructional objectives, you are likely to be struck by the extreme positions of the proponents and critics. Consider, for example, a brief quotation from James Popham, one of the most outspoken advocates of objectives in education. . . .

Unfamiliar Words

The unfamiliar words in the quote above are: objectives, shackle, spontaneity, creativity, absolutes, applied, beneficial, provide, perspective, literature, pros, cons, instructional, objectives, struck, extreme, positions, proponents, critics, consider, example, brief, quotation, outspoken, advocates, objectives, education (27 words).

Number of Words in the Sample	81
Number of Sentences in the Sample	5

Formula

$$\left[.1579 \times \left(\frac{\text{Number of words not on list}}{\text{Number of words in sample}} \times 100 \right) \right] + \left(.0496 \times \frac{\text{Number of words in sample}}{\text{Number of sentences in sample}} \right)$$

$$+ 3.6365$$

Application of Formula

$$\left[.1579 \times \left(\frac{27}{81} \times 100 \right) \right] + \left(.0496 \times \frac{81}{5} \right) + 3.6365 = 9.70$$

PASSAGE TWO

Elementary-school teachers sometimes get so caught up in teaching decoding skills and in using basal readers or story books to teach comprehension that they forget one of the primary goals of reading instruction: to prepare students to be independent learners, not just completers of workbook assignments or readers of fiction. Junior high and middle-school teachers often complain that their students "can't read." By this they usually mean that the students are unable to complete independent-study assignments that require them to extract information from a variety of sources, interpret that information, organize and store the information, and then retrieve it in some meaningful form.

Unfamiliar Words

The unfamiliar words in the quote above are: elementary, decoding, skills, basal, comprehension, primary, instruction, students, independent, learners, completers, workbook, assignments, fiction, complain, students, usually, students, unable, complete, independent, assignments, require, extract, information, variety, sources, interpret, information, organize, information, retrieve, meaningful (33 words).

Number of Words in the Sample	103
Number of Sentences in the Sample	3

Application of Formula

$$\left[.1579 \times \left(\frac{33}{103} \times 100 \right) \right] + .0496 \times \frac{103}{3} + 3.6365 = 10.25$$

PASSAGE THREE

Most standardized tests are norm-referenced. That is, a given individual's performance is examined in relation to the performance of other individuals. Keep the following points in mind when you select a standardized test.

Define your purpose for testing. Standardized tests may be given for any number of reasons—to compare class achievement with local or national norms, to determine the current achievement status of classes or individuals in order to learn whether corrective or remedial steps should be taken, to screen in order to determine the need for further testing, or to evaluate the program.

The unfamiliar words in the quote above are: standardized, norm-referenced, individual's, performance, examined, relation, performance, individuals, standardized, define, purpose, standardized, compare, achievement, local, national, norms, determine, current, achievement, status, individuals, whether, corrective, remedial, determine, evaluate, program (28 words).

Unfamiliar Words

95   ***Number of Words in the Sample***

5   ***Number of Sentences in the Sample***

$$.1579 \times \frac{28}{95} \times 100 + .0496 \times \frac{95}{5} + 3.6365 = 9.23$$ ***Application of Formula***

1. Average for three samples—9.52.

2. Conversion of raw score to corrected grade level—13–15th.

SUMMARY

Fry (1968, 1977) has devised a graph designed to identify the readability of materials from first grade through college level. The graph considers two easily identified variables: sentence length and word length (calculated by number of syllables). Three 100-word samples are chosen from the beginning, middle, and end of the book. For each sample the total number of sentences is calculated. If the sample does not terminate at the end of a sentence, the length of the final sentence fragment is estimated to the nearest tenth of a sentence. The total number of sentences for the three samples is found and divided by three, giving the average number of sentences per 100 words. Then the total number of syllables in each sample is ascertained. As Fry suggests (1968, p. 514), this is most easily done by counting every syllable over one in a word and then adding 100 to the total. Thus for *bread*, a one-syllable word, no count would be made; for *baby*, a two-syllable word, one extra syllable would be counted, for *disappointed* three extra syllables would be added in. The total number of syllables for the three samples is averaged. These two variables— average sentence length and average number of syllables per 100 words—are then plotted on the graph (see Fig. 8.2) to determine approximate grade level of the book.

The Fry Graph

To give you practice in working the Fry graph, we suggest that you apply it to the three passages on pp. 195–196 and compare your results with the readability estimate determined by the Dale-Chall formula. We have done the work for the first sample for you. You will need to fill in the information for passages two and three and make the final computation.*

---

*According to our computations, the readability level based on the Fry graph is grade 15.

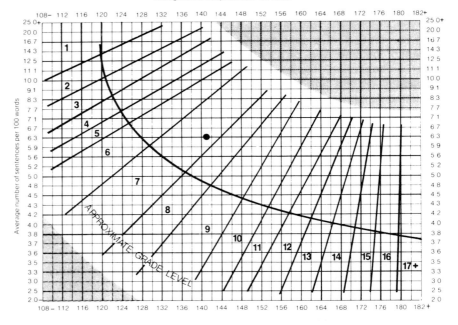

Average number of syllables per 100 words

Expanded Directions for Working Readability Graph

1. Randomly select three (3) sample passages and count out exactly 100 words each, beginning with the beginning of a sentence. Do count proper nouns, initializations, and numerals.
2. Count the number of sentences in the hundred words, estimating length of the fraction of the last sentence to the nearest one-tenth.
3. Count the total number of syllables in the 100-word passage. If you don't have a hand counter available, an easy way is to simply put a mark above every syllable over one in each word, then when you get to the end of the passage, count the number of marks and add 100. Small calculators can also be used as counters by pushing numeral 1, then push the + sign for each word or syllable when counting.
4. Enter graph with *average* sentence length and *average* number of syllables; plot dot where the two lines intersect. Area where dot is plotted will give you the approximate grade level.
5. If a great deal of variability is found in syllable count or sentence count, putting more samples into the average is desirable.
6. A word is defined as a group of symbols with a space on either side; thus, *Joe, IRA, 1945,* and *&* are each one word.
7. A syllable is defined as a phonetic syllable. Generally, there are as many syllables as vowel sounds. For example, *stopped* is one syllable and *wanted* is two syllables. When counting syllables for numerals and initializations, count one syllable for each symbol. For example, *1945* is four syllables, *IRA* is three syllables, and *&* is one syllable.

Fig. 8.2. **Fry graph for estimating readability—extended. (From Edward Fry, "Fry's Readability Graph: Clarifications, Validity, and Extension to Level 17,"** *Journal of Reading* **21, 3 (December 1977): 249.)**

1. *Passage One*
   a) *Number of sentences for 100-word sample:* 5.48. (To get 100 words, you must go 19 words into the next sentence, which is 40 words long. Hence the 19 words —I believe that those who discourage educators from precisely explicating their instructional objectives are often permitting, if not promoting—are .48 of the next sentence.
   b) *Number of syllables:* 178
2. *Passage Two*
   a) *Number of sentences:* _____
   b) *Number of syllables:* _____
3. *Passage Three*
   a) *Number of Sentences:* _____
      (*Hint:* The next sentence is 24 words long and begins with "With the purpose for testing . . .")
   b) *Number of syllables:* _____
4. *Averages*
   a) *Number of sentences:*
      (1) Passage 1 ___5.48___ +
      (2) Passage 2 _____ +
      (3) Passage 3 _____

      _____ divided by 3=_____
      (number of
      passages)
   b) *Number of syllables:*
      (1) Passage 1 ___178___ +
      (2) Passage 2 _____ +
      (3) Passage 3 _____

      _____ divided by 3=_____
5. *Intersection on graph:* _____ grade level

Fry suggests that the scores thus found should be accurate within one grade level (1968, p. 514). The Fry graph correlates highly with the Dale-Chall and Spache formulas, and although Fry does not claim that his graph is as accurate as these formulas, the graph does save a great deal of time. Spache (1970, p. 210) has criticized the Fry graph because it gives only whole-grade level estimates. However, when one considers that reading ability itself can be only measured roughly, a readability level that is accurate within one grade level appears to be sufficient.

The cloze procedure, first developed by Taylor (1953), measures readability in a manner very different from the formulas described above. In a cloze procedure words are regularly deleted from a passage (usually every fifth word), and the student is required to supply the missing words. A sample follows:

Cloze Procedure

The loud horn signaled _____ the race was starting. _____ cyclists burst forward and _____ climbing the first steep _____. Two of the racers _____ almost immediately because they _____ flat tires. The others _____ were all trying hard _____ win, pedalled furiously up _____ hill and over the _____. Next they came to _____ sharp curve and there _____ more riders dropped far _____. The last problem was _____ narrow wooden bridge. Two _____ approached the bridge at _____ same time and neither _____ give way. Suddenly there _____ a tremendous crash that _____ be heard a half-mile _____.

(The missing words are: that, The, began, hill, quit, had, who, to, the, top, a, three, behind, a, riders, the, would, was, could, away.)

If the student can supply 44–57 percent of the exact missing words, the material is considered to be of an appropriate readability level for the student to read with supervision. If the student can supply over 57 percent of the missing words, the material is assumed to be at a suitable level for independent study (Bormuth, 1968, p. 434).

The cloze procedure was described in Chapter 7 as a comprehension measure. Its use as a readability measure should not be surprising, since the concept of readability is based on comprehension: If a student can comprehend a passage, the passage is at an appropriate readability level for that particular student.

Bormuth (1968) outlines very stringent requirements for constructing a cloze test in order to obtain a readability level for a text. This procedure involves selecting from 6 to 12 passages from the text, constructing cloze passages from these selections, and administering these cloze tests to 25–30 students at the grade level at which the text is usually read. We do not feel that many classroom teachers will be willing to follow such a time-consuming procedure to identify a readability level. Rather, teachers might choose to use a formula such as the Dale-Chall or the Spache or the Fry graph. All of these methods for determining readability would be less time-consuming than following Bormuth's strict requirements. However, teachers may choose to use a cloze test on an informal basis as a means of matching a particular student with a particular reading material, without trying to ascertain a specific grade-level number for the material. In such instances one or two cloze passages of approximately 100 words in length may be constructed from the text, and the child's success would be based on the criteria mentioned above. Used in this way the cloze procedure resembles the Five Finger Test described in Chapter 7 as a technique that children may use to decide if a book is too difficult.

Limitations of Readability Measures

Readability measures are useful for estimating a general level of reading difficulty. However, these measures must always be considered to be only estimates. Many factors that contribute to the understanding of a reading selection are not taken into account by the most commonly used readability measures. For example, the interest of a reader in a particular topic and the reader's background knowledge in the topic are not measured by a readability formula. Teachers have often found that a student who is interested in a topic will be able to read and understand easily a selection that supposedly is much too difficult. Interest and prior experience enable the student to decode long words and to deal with even quite complicated concepts, because these words and ideas are familiar to the student at the oral/aural level.

Readability measures also fail to take into account the complexity and density of the concepts presented in the selection. Most readers would find a passage about different kinds of cats easier to read than a passage dealing with Einstein's theories, in spite of the fact that the two passages might have the same readability, based on the Dale-Chall or Fry methods. Concept density also has an effect on readability. Some passages and books are loaded with important ideas piled one upon another; other reading matter, especially fiction, introduces new ideas at a more leisurely pace. Selections with only a few major concepts are undoubtedly easier for the average reader to understand than are selections with many ideas.

Sentence complexity is assumed by the authors of many formulas to be measured by sentence length. This is not always the case. "Aunt Jane's large red car was parked near the dilapidated gray garage" and "Unlike Jack, who had understood why Mother was late, Sam was worried" are of the same length (12 words) and contain the same number of syllables (17). The second sentence, however, is more complex than the first and would no doubt be more difficult for many readers, especially elementary-school children, to understand. Botel, Dawkins, and Granowsky (1973) have developed the Syntactic Complexity Formula intended to help evaluate readability by giving different weights to various syntactic elements. However, we feel that in spite of the validity of the assumptions behind this instrument, most classroom teachers will not have the time to use such a complicated, time-consuming formula. Teachers would be better advised to use a more simple readability measure and to interpret the results of such measure with caution.

The readability measures we have discussed all suffer from the limitations mentioned. Teachers must keep these limitations in mind when assigning grade levels to written materials and must understand that all readability measures provide only estimated levels of readability. Teachers can make a good guess when assigning a material, but they must also be flexible enough to change an assignment when the child and the "readability level" just do not match.

VARIATION: READING IN DIFFERENT WAYS FOR DIFFERENT PURPOSES

A good reader does not read every type of material in the same way. A novel is usually read more quickly than a science text. Sometimes the reader is interested in getting only a general idea of what a selection is about. At other times the reader may be looking for the answer to a specific question. The manner in which an individual reads a particular selection should depend on the purpose for reading that selection and the nature of the selection. Many students do not automatically vary their reading to accommodate changes in the materials and in their own purposes for reading; they must be taught these skills.

Rate   According to Braam (1963, p. 247), the rate at which an individual can and should read a particular selection is dependent primarily on three factors: "the purpose for reading, the degree of familiarity or prior knowledge concerning the subject, and the level of difficulty of the material." Shores (1968, p. 24) also points out the contributions of both the material and the reader in determining rate. Among the important characteristics of the material that Shores identifies are the kind of type and paper used, the format of the page, the clarity of the ideas, the author's style, and the density of the ideas. The effect of the reader on the rate of reading depends on the individual's background of experience, purpose for reading, interest, mental set, familiarity with the author's style, ability to accommodate the new ideas to his or her own existing cognitive framework, reading skills, and general health at the time of the reading. In light of this multitude of contributing factors, to talk about an "average" rate of reading seems superficial. The more important concept is that of *flexibility of rate:* The reader should learn to vary the rate of reading in accordance with the factors listed above.

Research about the effectiveness of teaching students to vary their rate of reading has been contradictory. McDonald (1960, pp. 29–35) suggests that reported research showing that most readers had very limited ability to vary their reading rate, in spite of explicit instructions to do so. However, Braam (1963) found that high school students were able to increase both their rate and their flexibility of rate through repeated practice, guided by the instruction: "Read as quickly as you can and still understand the general content of this selection."

Braam measured both gross rate and effective rate. Effective rate was determined by multiplying gross rate by percentage of comprehension. Rate per se is of little value if comprehension suffers. Reading then becomes a game of moving one's eyes across the page as fast as is physically possible. When measuring rate, teachers should always include a comprehension measure.

We suggest that students be given instruction in varying their rate according to their purpose for reading and the nature of the material. However, we would like to interject some cautions. The first one was given above: Comprehension should always be measured along with rate. Second, work on increasing rate and flexibility of rate should not be begun until a student has mastered most decoding skills. A student whose energy is still required to identify a great number of the words in a selection will have little excess energy to devote to increasing speed, especially when she or he is also having to attend to comprehension. Third, a balance must be struck between emphasis on rate and emphasis on flexibility. Students (and teachers!) may become so enamored with speed that they forget to vary their speed and instead strive for the maximum at all times. Careful instruction in reading a variety of materials for a variety of purposes should help students improve both their rate and their flexibility of rate.

Skimming and Scanning   Two specific procedures for varying rate according to differing purposes are skimming and scanning. These two techniques involve selective focusing on the pages of print. The goal of skimming, according to Durkin (1974, p. 487), is getting "the general gist of content." The reader moves the eyes quickly over the printed page, looking for key words and making use of organizational cues, such as headings, and other aids, such as graphs and pictures. Students who are practicing skimming techniques must keep in mind that their purpose is not to identify details, but to get an overall picture of what the selection is about and how it is organized. Teachers may guide students in their practice by asking them, after they have finished skimming, to generate broad questions that might be answered by the selection or to suggest a title for the selection. The students may also be asked to give a short summary of what they *think* the selection is mainly about. Students should understand that at times these predictions will be wrong. They might have given improper importance in their skimming to a word or phrase or might have missed other key words. Such inaccuracies are a natural by-product of the process of skimming. In order to ensure completely accurate predictions, skimming would need to be replaced by more careful and therefore less rapid reading.

Scanning is rapid perusal of the print in order to find a particular piece of information. The students should be taught to move their eyes down the page, in a search for the answer to a specific question. They must also be taught to confirm their answer. Too often readers (young and old) think that they have found the answer and do not bother to read the entire context in which the "answer" appears. Thus in searching in the paragraph below for the most important industry in New City, a careless reader might choose *meat-packing*. However, careful reading of the sentence containing the word *meat-packing* would uncover the important word *not*. Similarly, if asked to identify the head of the New City Tool and Die Works, the reader must choose between two names. The choice can be made only by carefully reading to confirm the selected answer.

> The most important industry in New City is not the meat-packing plant, as many suppose. The biggest industry is the tool and die works. The New City Tool and Die Works, founded by Hiram Babcock in 1946, is now run by Art Evans, a New City native.

Beginning "scanners" may need hints about what kind of an answer to look for. For example, if the question to be answered is "What kind of a pet did Vicki have?" the children should be led to the understanding that through their scanning, they will be looking for the name of an animal. If the question were "Who ate the apple pie?" the children should understand that they might be looking for a person's name (signaled by a capital letter).

Skimming and scanning are important study skills. Children should be taught to both skim and scan while using a variety of resource materials. Effective study cannot take place if the search for information involves the laborious reading of every word about a topic. Only through guided practice can students learn to skim and scan effectively, avoiding the compulsion to read every word on the one hand and eluding the dangers of superficial glances on the other.

SQ3R   Some students may need to learn a highly structured technique for using vary-ing reading rates for different purposes. The SQ3R method, first introduced by Robinson (1946), is a systematic reading-study procedure designed to be used with content-area materials that are organized through the use of headings, underlinings, and other format cues that highlight important topics. SQ3R stands for the five steps of the process: survey, question, read, recite, and review. In the first step the student glances quickly through the selection, look-ing at key words and headings in order to get a general idea of the important concepts covered by the selection. If a summarizing paragraph is included, that paragraph should be read during the initial survey. This step, of course, is skimming. Robinson suggests that the survey step should take no more than one minute; however, we feel that the amount of time spent will depend on the length of the selection and on the density of ideas. Regardless of these consid-erations, however, the survey step should be completed quickly.

The second step is to turn the first heading into a question. This technique will help the reader focus precisely on what is to be found in that section and will also help to bring to the reader's mind the information he or she already knows about the topic. The question step helps to set the reading task for the student.

The third step, read, involves reading the first section in order to answer the question posed in step 2. The reader is to focus only on the main topic and the important supporting details that are needed to answer the question fully. Because the reader is seeking the answer to a specific question through this reading, she or he is actively involved in the perusal of the section and is not just passively moving the eyes across and down the page.

In the fourth step, recite, the reader attempts to reconstruct the answer to the question, without looking back in the text. The recitation may be oral, but Robinson suggests that jotting down brief notes in outline form can be a very useful form of recitation. He also recommends that the reader paraphrase the important points of the section instead of just reciting parts of the text verba-tim. In this way the reader must *process* the information, not just recall it. If unable to recite the major points of the selection without looking at the text, the reader should glance at the section again and then once more attempt to complete step 4.

Steps 2–4 (question, read, recite) are repeated for every subsection of the selection. Then step 5, review, is followed. The reader looks through the notes that have been made, noting again the key points and the supporting details. Then the reader should assess how well he or she has remembered the material, by attempting to recite the information found in the notes. Robinson suggests that the review step should take about five minutes.

The SQ3R method is often thought of as a study technique for secondary-school students rather than for elementary-level learners. However, we feel that students in fourth and fifth grades, and even third, can learn to use the SQ3R method when dealing with content-area materials. Students must be taught early that they must be active participants in reading and that they should read content-area materials differently from the way in which they read narrative material. Too often secondary-school teachers must overcome their students' concept that all reading is done in essentially the same way and at the same rate. Instruction in the elementary grades can help prevent this.

Objectives for Variation Skills

In Chapter 3 we presented two kinds of objectives: prescriptive and descriptive. We suggested that prescriptive objectives are most appropriately used when an expected outcome can be precisely stated. Descriptive objectives were recommended for use when the outcome cannot or should not be precisely delineated. The reading behaviors described above—varying rate, skimming, scanning, and using the SQ3R study method—are best stated in terms of descriptive objectives. To try to construct an objective that describes an exact outcome for these skills, such as "The learner will read science materials at one-half the rate with which she or he reads prose materials," is obviously ridiculous. Rate depends on the characteristics of both the reader and the reading material and cannot be dictated purely on the basis of subject matter. A more general, descriptive objective is needed: "The learner varies the reading rate in accordance with the nature of the material and his or her own characteristics."

Teachers should be wary of slighting the study skills that involve variation in reading simply because these skills cannot be stated in precise terms. Descriptive objectives can be used to give the necessary focus to instruction without artificially circumscribing the reading behavior. And focus *is* necessary. Perhaps conscious focus is even more crucial when outcomes are not easily measured, especially by paper-and-pencil tests. Special efforts involving personal observation of student performance will have to be made to assess if students are using the variability skills. Study skills such as the ones described in this section are not "mastered" unless the student independently puts them to use in appropriate reading situations.

LOCATIONAL SKILLS: FINDING INFORMATION

Anyone who has watched students pull books at random from library shelves will recognize that one of the most important tasks in solving a problem is to locate needed information. Students must be able to predict which sources of information are most likely to contain the necessary information, and they must be able to use these sources efficiently.

Identifying the Appropriate Resource

Many students, even in high school, do not have a thorough knowledge of the resource materials available to them, both in school and out. They are probably aware of the encyclopedia and the atlas in the school's instructional materials center (IMC), but may not really understand the kinds of information that can be derived from these sources. Furthermore, students are often unfamiliar with many other sources of information. They have no knowledge of how to use the newspaper effectively to gather information; they may not even know of the existence of the *Reader's Guide to Periodical Literature*; they may not think of using the filmstrip library or magazines as sources of information for solving a problem. When asked to find information about a specific topic, these students may begin aimlessly thumbing through the reference materials in the library, hoping that they will chance on the needed information, or else they will immediately go to that one source (in their minds) of all human knowledge—the encyclopedia. The teacher's task is to provide students, even at the elementary level, with guidelines for predicting which sources of information are most likely to contain the needed information and to give the students practice in using and confirming these predictions.

The second step in helping students predict which resource materials might be useful is to tour the school's IMC. But the first step might be to have a brainstorming session in which the class identifies resource materials of which they are aware. The final list should include materials found not only in school but also outside of school. The list should contain community resources for information as well as printed materials. If the students are unable to generate a list without help, the teacher should give them several specific problems, such as "Where would you go to find information about the court system in Idaho? Where would you find information about food additives? How could you learn about child abuse in our state?" The list that evolves might include such diverse resources as the *Congressional Record,* the evening network news broadcast, the *Guinness Book of Records,* and the mayor. Then, armed with a copy of *their* list of resources, the students could go on a guided tour through the IMC. The librarian or IMC director should be asked to point out the less well-known reference sources, such as *Shepherd's Historical Atlas* or *Bartlett's Familiar Quotations.* In addition, the unique value of each resource should be explained and exemplified. Students should be asked to add these resources to their lists.

Just talking about what resources are available is, of course, not enough. Students must be given many opportunities to predict which resources will supply certain information and then to confirm these predictions. Students can be asked to compare the type of information given about a topic in different sources. They can have races to find specific information, using resources of their choice. Treasure hunts can be conducted during which the students have to find clues in a variety of resource materials. Only through actual use of resource materials will students become familiar with these materials and learn to use them appropriately.

Using the Appropriate Resource Efficiently and Effectively

Once students have identified the resources that are most likely to contain needed information, they must be able to use an index and a table of contents. They must also have the ability to use alphabetical order, guide words, pronunciation guides, and glossaries.

Alphabetical Order

Skill in using alphabetical order to locate information is essential to the use of a great variety of resource materials, from the dictionary to the encyclopedia. Even first graders can learn to alphabetize and to use alphabetical order to find words in picture dictionaries. Young children can organize small cards containing words they can read by placing all of the cards beginning with A together, followed by those beginning with B, and so on. Older elementary students can learn to alphabetize by second, third, and fourth letters and to use alphabetical order to locate words in dictionaries, indexes, the telephone directory, and other resource materials.

When providing instruction in alphabetizing, teachers must be sure to include practice both in placing words in alphabetical order and in retrieving information from sources that have been alphabetized. In addition, the teacher must be certain to provide opportunities to use alphabetizing in a great many learning situations, not just through worksheets that have nothing to do with actually *using* alphabetical order.

Once students have learned the rudiments of alphabetizing, they are ready to learn to use guide words. In order to use guide words effectively, children must really understand their purpose, which is to speed up location of a word or topic, and then practice using guide words for this purpose. Races in which students compete with one another or with their own record can be used to emphasize the speed element of using guide words. Students should also learn which resource materials are likely to have guide words and should receive many opportunities for using the guide words found in a variety of materials. Only through repeated actual utilization of these guides will the students develop the habit of making use of these aids when using resource materials.

Guide Words

Pronunciation guides, such as |gī'gər|, are often found in resource materials to help readers pronounce unknown words properly. However, these guides are of little value if the students cannot read the phonetic symbols. Unfortunately, agreement has never been reached on a set of symbols to be used in all texts. As a result, one text may suggest that *blockade* is pronounced blŏ kād', and another may reproduce the phonetic pronunciation as bläk-'ād. Students can learn to circumvent this confusing lack of agreement by consulting the pronunciation key that is almost always found at the beginning of a text or a glossary. In some dictionaries the key is found at the beginning, and in others it is printed at the bottom of every page (see Fig. 8.3). Students should receive practice in interpreting several different keys so that they are not defeated when they meet an unfamiliar key. Students will also need reminders to *use* the pronunciation guides themselves. They should be held responsible for figuring out the pronunciation of any word that has the phonetic respelling given.

Pronunciation Guides

Glossaries are dictionaries of the technical or specialized terms found in a particular text. Glossaries are usually found in the back of a text and often have pronunciation guides with them. Students should be taught to automatically examine a resource material or other text to determine if a glossary has been included. Too often students (and teachers!) are completely unaware of a glossary's existence. Other readers may know that the glossary is there, but may not recognize its value as a quick reference source of word meanings.

Glossaries

One way to stress the value of a specialized glossary over a conventional dictionary is to have students compare the amount of time it takes to look up a word in the glossary (which is immediately at hand) with the amount of time it takes to get up, find the dictionary, and look up the word needed among the several thousand words contained in the dictionary (as compared to the 100–200 in the glossary). The students should also be led to note that in the glossary the particular meaning of the word as it is used in the text is given, whereas in the dictionary the student must frequently choose from among several definitions.

PRONUNCIATION KEY

ă	pat	m	am, man, mum	v	cave, valve, vine	
ā	aid, fey, pay	n	no, sudden	w	with	
â	air, care, wear	ng	thing	y	yes	
ä	father	ŏ	horrible, pot	yōō	abuse, use	
b	bib	ō	go, hoarse, row, toe	z	rose, size, xylophone, zebra	
ch	church	ô	alter, caught, for, paw	zh	garage, pleasure, vision	
d	deed	oi	boy, noise, oil	ə	about, silent, pencil, lemon, circus	
ĕ	pet, pleasure	ou	cow, out			
ē	be, bee, easy, leisure	ŏŏ	took	ər	butter	
f	faste, fife, off, phase, rough	ōō	boot, fruit			

FOREIGN

œ	*French* feu
ü	*French* tu
KH	*Scottish* loch
N	*French* bon

g	gag	p	pop	
h	hat	r	roar	
hw	which	s	miss, sauce, see	
ĭ	pit	sh	dish, ship	
ī	by, guy, pie	t	tight	
î	dear, deer, fierce, mere	th	path, thin	
j	judge	*th*	bathe, this	
k	cat, kick, pique	ŭ	cut, rough	
l	lid, needle	û	circle, firm, heard, term, turn, urge, word	

STRESS

Primary stress ´
  bi·ol´o·gy |bī ŏl´ əjē|

Secondary stress ´
  bi´o·log´i·cal |bī´ əlŏj ´ĭkəl|

Note: A detailed explanation of the pronunciation key starts on page xxviii of the Dictionary.

(a)

fat, āpe, cär, ten, ēven, hit, bīte, gō, hôrn, tōōl, book, up, fūr;
get, joy, yet, chin, she, thin, *then*; zh=s in pleasure; ´ as in able (ā´b'l);
  ə=a in ago, e in agent, i in sanity, o in confess, u in focus.

(b)

Fig. 8.3. Pronunciation keys: (a) *American Heritage School Dictionary*, **1972,** © **1969, 1970, 1971, 1973, 1975, 1976, 1978, Houghton Mifflin Company. Reprinted by permission from the** *American Heritage Dictionary of the English Language;* **(b)** *Webster's New World Dictionary,* **Elementary Edition, with permission, from** *Webster's New World Dictionary, Basic School Edition,* **copyright** © **1976 by William Collins+World Publishing Co., Inc.**

The index is another special study aid that is designed to speed up the locating of specific information. As with the glossary, students need to develop the habit of checking for an index automatically. To use the index to find the location of a certain topic, readers need two special skills: They must be able to use alphabetical order, and they must be able to think of alternative headings or topics if the heading they are searching for is not listed. Brainstorming sessions can help children develop the ability to choose synonyms (or near-synonyms) for topics. In these sessions pairs of students might be given one minute to name as many different headings for "chief crop of Bolivia" as possible, for example. As with guide words, practice in using indexes should stress speed.

Indexes

Most texts and other resource materials include a table of contents. The table of contents differs from the index primarily in the fineness of its information. The index is to be used to locate specific, narrow topics; the table of contents, found in the front, rather than in the back, of the book, is used to show the organization of the entire text and the location of broad topics. Students should have much practice in predicting whether they should be consulting the index or the table of contents to solve a particular problem. In addition, they should learn to use the table of contents to preview how the author deals with a certain subject and to help them organize their own reading of the text. Frequently neglected, the table of contents can be a useful locational tool, if students develop the habit of consulting it.

Tables of Contents

Unlike the skills involving variation in rate, locational skills can be stated in terms of prescriptive objectives. The *ability* to use these skills can be measured by paper-and-pencil tests, and specific outcomes can be identified. The following objectives, taken from the *Wisconsin Design for Reading Skill Development* (1977), indicate how selected locational skills may be stated objectively:

Objectives for Locational Skills

Skill: Applies basic alphabetizing skills

Objective: The child alphabetizes words by attending to first and second letters.

Skill: Begins to use indexes

Objective: Having identified a general topic, the child uses the indexes of books to locate information about the topic.

Skill: Uses tables of contents

Objective: The child refers to the table of contents
- to determine if a book is relevant to his specific purpose
- to locate a particular chapter or section in a book.

Skill: Selects relevant sources

Objective: Given several topics, the child chooses from among a list of available sources those that are likely to include relevant information on the topics.

The usual warning that paper-and-pencil tests determine only if a student *can* use a skill and not if the student *does* use the skill is especially pertinent for study skills. Focused instruction in the locational skills should emphasize not just acquisition of the skills, but also their practical uses for finding information. Practice must be provided in which the students actually use the locational skills to solve problems and not just to complete worksheets at their desks.

INTERPRETATION SKILLS: USING MAPS, GRAPHS, AND TABLES

Maps, graphs, and tables are often incorporated into content-area materials and reference sources. Instruction in the use of these graphic aids should have two primary emphases. First, students must learn to consult these aids when they are available. Usually maps, graphs, and tables present information in a highly compressed form. If readers will learn to attend to these aids, they will find them extremely useful as quick sources of information.

The second emphasis with maps, graphs, and tables should be on developing the skills of interpretation. Weintraub (1967) points out that because these graphic aids "distill" a great deal of information into a small space, their interpretation is frequently difficult. Students must discover what kind of information they can and cannot glean from maps, graphs, and tables and must learn to extract this information accurately and with ease.

Using Maps

The use of map skills can begin on the first day of school. Kindergarten and first-grade children can be helped to locate bathrooms or the exits to the playground by referring to simple maps (see Fig. 8.4). They can begin to learn that symbols, such as

can be used to represent real objects. They can begin developing the ability to describe relative distances between things, noting that the red chair is closer to Ms. Garver's desk than the blue chair is or that they must take about five giant steps to go from the piano to the painting easel, but only three giant steps to get to the door from the piano.

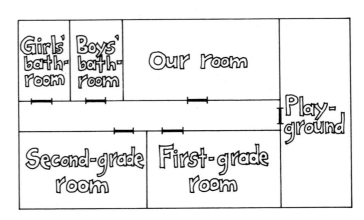

Fig. 8.4. Simple map.

Older elementary-age children can learn to use maps and globes to locate places mentioned in the news or in their social studies lessons. They can make their own maps of their neighborhood and of larger geographical areas, such as their state. These maps can be used to plan trips and to discuss their own environment.

Because of the breadth of the category of study skills designated as "map skills" and because of the abstract nature of many of these skills, developing the ability to use map skills requires careful planning. Askov and Kamm (1974) warn that map skills are often taught as though they were unrelated to one another. They argue that this haphazard, hit-or-miss approach may result in children's receiving instruction in skills for which they have not developed the necessary prerequisite concepts or skills. For example, children who are learning to use abstract map symbols should first be able to understand the use of picture symbols as representations of real objects. Students should not receive instruction in the intermediate directions (southeast, northwest, and so on) until they are able to use the cardinal directions with ease. To avoid haphazard skill development, teachers would be wise to take two steps. First, all of the teachers in the elementary school should be involved in designing a suggested sequence of map skills to be taught, so that the necessary prerequisites are introduced to the students in an orderly manner. Second, teachers should pretest their students to check if they indeed *have* learned the needed skills before moving on to more difficult skills. Just because the teachers in the primary grades have taught certain skills does not necessarily mean each child has learned those skills.

Askov and Kamm (1974) suggest that map skills can be divided into three strands: representation, location, and measurement. The representation skills are used to interpret symbols used in maps, ranging from the realistic, such as small pictures of trees and houses, through the very abstract, such as dots for cities and stars for county seats. The locational skills involve being able to use grids, which divide maps into cells, and to use directions. The measurement skills, according to the Askov-Kamm framework, enable students to approximate distances and to use standard and nonstandard units of measurement. The measurement skills also involve an understanding that because the earth is too big to be seen all at one time, it must be represented as smaller than the real earth, but with the same proportions. That is, the earth, or the part of it being represented on the map, is drawn "to scale."

Because of the abstract nature of many map skills, teachers should take care to relate the study of maps to the real environment as much as possible. Activities in which students actually construct maps are especially useful. For example, when teaching students that dots of various kinds are used to represent cities of varying populations, the children might construct a map of their own area, representing the largest town in their environment with one kind of dot and several smaller towns with approximately equal populations with dots of another kind. Young children learning to use grids might divide their classroom into cells by the use of crepe paper streamers and grid labels. They could then play a riddle game in which objects would be identified according to their color and their grid location. One riddle might be: "I see something blue in C-4." Intermediate-grade students might be interested in developing an "official" map of their school, drawn to scale, to be used to guide visitors. A resourceful teacher can find many opportunities to teach map skills by relating these skills to the environment that surrounds the class and the needs of the children in moving about in and using that environment.

Using Graphs

Graphs, like maps, are used to present information in a succinct, manageable form. And, like maps, graphs are useful only if readers refer to them and know how to use them. There are four basic kinds of graphs (see Fig. 8.5), and students must learn to interpret each kind. Weintraub (1967, pp. 347, 349) cites evidence that children can be taught to use these aids and lists a suggested order of teaching the interpretation of graphs, based on research: picture graphs, circle or pie graphs, bar graphs (first vertical and then horizontal), and line graphs.

Picture graphs can be used even by very young children to illustrate quantitative information. Elementary-school teachers do this all the time when they make charts showing how many books each child has read, with one small book or star representing one book read. Picture graphs could be used to show how many pets are owned by each child in the class (see Fig. 8.5a) or how many apples were eaten each week by the class for a month. Older students can learn that one symbol can represent more than one object and that one-half of a symbol indicates one-half of that amount. For example, in preparing a picture graph to show the number of records sold by different salespersons in one month, it would not be practical to have one symbol for each record; the graph would probably be huge. A better solution would be to have each symbol represent ten records, so that if a salesperson sold 45 records in the month, $4\frac{1}{2}$ record symbols, not 45, would appear after that person's name.

When a symbol stands for more than a one-to-one correspondence with the object represented, a key must be included to show the relationship between the symbol and the number of objects it represents. Furthermore, students must practice *referring* to this key and using it to interpret graphs. Elementary-age (and even older) students often fail to refer to the key when working with graphs and will even miss noting the absurdity of such an answer as "Mark sold $6\frac{1}{2}$ cars in one month."

Circle graphs are used to show the parts into which a whole has been divided. Primary-age children might construct a simple circle graph to show approximately what part of their school day is spent in certain activities (see Fig. 8.5b). Older children, who have a rudimentary knowledge of fractions and percentages, may work with more complex graphs.

Bar graphs can be used to illustrate how one variable fluctuates in relation to another variable. For example, the high temperature might be charted on a daily basis for a week. The graph would contain seven bars, each labeled with one day of the week. The height of each bar would indicate the number of degrees of the highest temperature for that day. Bar graphs give readers a "picture" of such comparisons and help them to visualize the relationship between

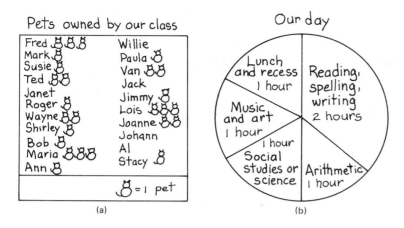

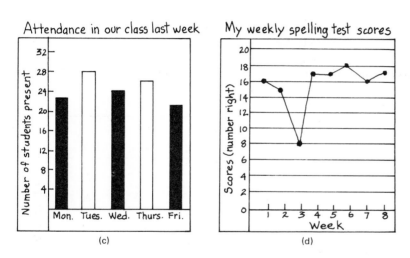

Fig. 8.5. Graphs: (a) picture graph; (b) circle graph; (c) bar graph; (d) line graph.

the two variables. Line graphs present the same information, but use points connected by lines to show the relationships.

Instruction in interpreting all forms of graphs should emphasize that students must always read the title and labels on the graph in order to know what the graph is representing. Amazingly, students frequently resist employing such a sound practice, assuming that they know what the graph is representing without bothering to check their intuitive judgment. Some students may even need to give themselves a mechanical procedure to follow, such as drawing a ring around the title and labels, in order to develop the habit of consulting these aids.

Using Tables   Tables are used to convey information that has three dimensions. Table 8.1 shows students' scores on each of eight tests. Three dimensions are included: the student, the test taken, and the score on each test. Information that includes so many dimensions cannot be easily portrayed graphically, but can be exhibited clearly in the form of a table. Even primary-level children do not find it particularly difficult to interpret tables once they learn to work carefully in finding the appropriate intersection of row and column.

TABLE 8.1
Student scores on weekly test

Student	Test							
	1	2	3	4	5	6	7	8
Betty	78	85	77	89	82	76	88	97
Sally	92	97	89	88	82	95	96	97
Brian	88	79	80	91	86	80	92	93
David	69	75	79	77	82	85	90	94
Kim	73	68	75	75	80	91	83	74

The totals row and column (note Table 8.2) can present problems in some cases simply because the student does not understand how that column has been formed. As with maps and graphs, actual construction of tables can help overcome student confusion about the totals row and column, as well as other problems in the interpretation of tables.

TABLE 8.2
Steel production for first six months (in thousands of tons)

Company	Month						Total
	Jan.	Feb.	Mar.	Apr.	May	June	
American Steel	15	25	23	26	22	20	131
Grade A Steel	10	11	10	10	12	11	64
Best Steel	28	32	38	39	37	38	212
National Steel	5	8	7	8	7	6	41
Penn Steel	25	27	28	28	28	26	162
Total	83	103	106	111	106	101	610

Objectives for Interpretation Skills   The skills needed to interpret maps, graphs, and tables may be stated in terms of prescriptive objectives. Teachers must be careful, however, to be specific when writing objectives for interpretation skills. "The student can read maps" and "the student is able to use graphs to obtain information" are too broad to be of any use. The map skills will need to be identified specifically: "The learner can use coordinates on a grid to locate points and to describe the location of points" or "The learner can use nonrealistic symbols, as identified in a key, to interpret maps." For graphs the type of graph will need to be specified. Objectives for the interpretation of tables may be broader, although teachers may consider writing objectives that distinguish among tables of varying complexity. However, "reading maps" and "interpreting graphs" are not unitary skills, and instruction will not be able to be focused with precision if they are treated as such.

Most teachers who have asked students to write reports for social studies or science have had the unrewarding experience of receiving at least one beautifully written, well-organized report—that has been copied word for word from the encyclopedia. Other reports will just as obviously not have been copied, because they are merely jumbled collections of facts, apparently arranged at random. Instruction in the skills of storing and organizing information will not, of course, prevent students from copying encyclopedias or turning in stream-of-consciousness reports, but if students have developed skills that enable them to organize information and to store it in a meaningful manner, they may be less likely to resort to these abhorrent practices.

When confronted with the task of storing and organizing information from a reference source, many students are unsure of what to do. They have no method for selecting information. They may randomly write down interesting facts; they may copy whole paragraphs in order not to miss any information. These students have an equally vague notion of what to do with the information they have selected. They have no method for organizing the mass of information into a report that conveys what they have learned in any meaningful way. Teaching students to outline material from which they are seeking information can help them to store material in a manner that is easy to use and to think about the information as they are storing it. Outlining forces the reader to focus on the author's organizational scheme. As the reader completes the outline, he or she must note the relationship of ideas and facts to one another as well as noting the facts themselves. The reader must decide which are the important topics in the selection and which are the supporting details. Having to make decisions like these helps to involve the reader in what is being read and should make the material easier to remember.

Outlining

Teachers can help students to develop outlining skills through shaping procedures. That is, the students can be given partial outlines, such as the one shown below:

Antarctic Seals

1. Crabeater seals
   a) most common kind
   b)
      (1) 7–8 feet long
      (2) weighs 500 pounds
   c) eats red krill, not crabs
2.
   a) second most common seal
   b) lives farthest south of all seals
   c) appearance
      (1) 8–9 feet long
      (2)
      (3)

As the students become more adept at filling in the missing topics and details, less and less information can be given. Next, the students would be given only the organizational framework for the outline and would have to fill in all of the information themselves, as follows:

1.
   a)
      (1)
      (2)
      (3)
         (a)
         (b)
   b)
      (1)
      (2)
2.
   a)
   b)
      (1)
         (a)
         (b)
      (2)

Finally, the students would be asked to make outlines of material with no guidance at all.

Of course, providing outlines for student use is very time-consuming. However, if this technique is used in conjunction with social studies, it can help students to learn the social studies content as well as the skills of outlining. Such joint programing can also help the students to recognize the value of outlining as an information-storage system and not just as an exercise in reading class.

A second way in which teachers can help students to develop outlining skills is to point out to them the organizational cues that are often used in informational writing. Students should be led to discover that headings in the text will often be major topics in the outline. Main-idea statements should also be seen as potential major or minor topics. Students should learn to note such cues as "There are two reasons for . . ." or "The whiffling marfweezel differs from the snuffling marfweezel in five important ways." Most well-written selections are written from outlines and contain cues to their inner organization. Readers need to learn to recognize and utilize these cues.

Note-taking   Once students have developed the ability to make and use formal outlines of what they are reading, they can practice the less formal procedures of note-taking. Like outlining, good note-taking involves making use of the organizational structure of a selection, but the format of putting down the information is not as rigid as with outlining. Harris (1970, p. 438) suggests that one of the greatest values of note-taking is that it forces "selective, thoughtful reading." This is especially true if the reader paraphrases the information rather than just copies down selected information word for word. Paraphrasing requires the student to process the information, to think about it, and to integrate it with already existing concepts.

One good way to show students the value of taking well-organized (and legible) notes is to have them take notes about a common reading selection, turn in their notes (with their names on them), and then use these notes at a later date to answer questions about the selection. For example, the students in the class might read about the agricultural products of several South American countries in their social studies books. The students would be told to take notes about the important facts that they thought they should remember from their reading. The children would also be told that they would have a quiz two or three days later and that they could use their notes to help them answer the questions on the quiz. After the students had finished with their note-taking, the notes would be collected by the teacher. Then, as announced, the notes would be returned to the authors and the quiz distributed. Students who had taken functional notes would be able to answer such questions as "What is the most important agricultural product of Bolivia?" and "Which South American country produces the most coffee?" Students with less effective note-taking skills might have jotted down notes such as the ones shown in Fig. 8.6a and would be unable to answer the questions. Through procedures such as these, students should quickly learn that "tin" or "10,000 in the summer" are not very useful notations unless they are related to the rest of the passage in some way.

Students often have problems in deciding the right amount of notes to take. Some students will jot down almost every fact mentioned in the selection; others will note only the most general information. The quantity of notes will vary according to the students' purpose for reading the selection, and lots

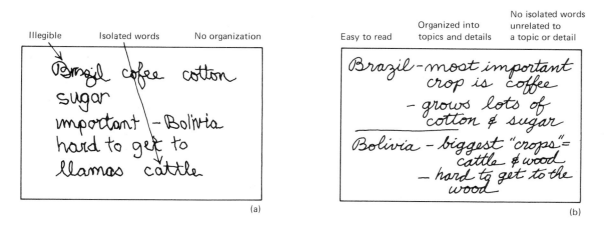

Fig. 8.6. Taking notes: (a) ineffective notes; (b) effective notes.

of practice with using notes for different purposes will help students adjust their note-taking practices. Certain characteristics, however, are of universal importance in note-taking: The notes should be legible (to the student), written in a specific, permanent place and not on a handy scrap of paper or on the back of an old test, and convey information to the student even after a lapse of time.

Choosing Objectives for Skills for Organizing and Storing Information

In order to be complete, an outline of a specific selection must contain certain pieces of information. Thus there is, more or less, a "right" answer. Therefore, a prescriptive objective, such as "The learner organizes a selection into major and minor topics in a formal outline," seems to be appropriate. Note-taking, on the other hand, varies according to the requirements of the reader and the purpose for which the notes are taken. A descriptive objective ("The learner takes notes in a form that is useful to him or her and that can be used to retrieve information at a later date") would be appropriate for focusing instruction in note-taking.

APPLICATION: PUTTING STUDY SKILLS TO USE

In this chapter we have described several study skills we feel young readers need to develop: choosing resource materials likely to contain the information sought, locating that information, reading materials at different rates for varied purposes, interpreting graphic aids, and organizing and storing information in a meaningful way. However, the most important aspect of instruction in study skills is not which *skills* to teach, but the ultimate *goal* of teaching study skills, which is to develop independent learners. A natural corollary of this goal is that students must use study skills *independently*, not just to complete artificially contrived worksheets, but to *learn* something.

Study skills may need to be taught in isolation, but they should be used together for the purpose for which they were intended: to gather and use information. Sterile, desk-bound exercises that are completed only because they were assigned cannot help students to truly develop study skills.

Teachers can help students see the utility of study skills by designing exciting projects in which the students will have to put their study skills to use. A class project on endangered species or world sources of energy would surely be more motivating than answering questions about the relative sizes of mythical cities or putting a list of unrelated words in alphabetical order. In addition, if children are constantly using study skills to complete interesting class projects, they will be likely to call on these skills when seeking information outside of school. Education is really of little value if the students see no connection between what they do in school and the "real world." Intelligently designed information-seeking projects can aid students in making this connection.

REVIEW QUESTIONS

1. You are part of a districtwide committee to develop a study-skills curriculum, kindergarten through twelfth grade. Some members of the committee believe that instruction in study skills should not begin until junior high or middle school. Outline your arguments for including study skills in the elementary-school curriculum.

2. Several limitations to readability formulas were given in this chapter. List these limitations and then decide how you would take these limitations into account when estimating a book's readability. Which of these limitations can be overcome with a minimum of teacher time or effort? Which are the most serious? With these limitations in mind, do you think that readability formulas have any validity? Why or why not?

3. Review the sections of this chapter related to reading in different ways for different purposes.

   • Con Mann, a salesperson, has come to your school to try to interest you in purchasing his speed-reading program. He promises that every student who completes this program will be able to read all materials at an average rate of 700 words per minute. Mr. Mann further promises that your students will love his program because all of the reading selections are interesting, "true-life" stories about events in the lives of three ten-year-old children. In addition, students will enjoy the program because they will not get bogged down by having to answer boring questions after they read; they can concentrate just on speed.

   Would you buy Mr. Mann's program? Why or why not?

4. Which resource materials in the library would you teach fifth graders to use? What kinds of information would you have them seek in each resource material?

5. For a third-grade class studying the planets in our solar system, design an activity for each of the following locational and interpretation skills.

   • putting words in alphabetical order
   • using a glossary
   • using an index
   • understanding map symbols
   • approximating distances
   • using scale
   • interpreting a bar graph
   • retrieving information from a table

   Ask a friend to critique your activities. Are they interesting? Do they ask the student to apply the skills in a meaningful way? Do they seem too easy or too difficult?

6. Complete the following outline of pp. 210–212, "Using Maps."

   1. Need for Careful Planning in Teaching Map Skills

      a) Primary reason:

      b) Ways to avoid problems
         (1)

(2)

(3)

2. Map-Skill Strands

    a) Representation skills (interpretation of symbols)

    b) Locational skills (   )

    c)   (   )

Now take notes on the section entitled "SQ3R," pp. 204–205. Which technique would you, as an adult learner, find more valuable for preparing for an essay question on a test? For a multiple-choice or short-answer quiz? Is your answer dependent in any way on the type of information in the passage? How would you choose selections for teaching your students outlining skills? Note-taking skills? Would you motivate your students differently for the two kinds of skills?

REFERENCES

Artley, A. Sterl. "Effective Study—Its Nature and Nurture," in *Forging Ahead in Reading* **12**, Part I (1967 Convention Proceedings) (Newark, Delaware: International Reading Association, 1967).

Askov, Eunice N., and Karyln Kamm. "Map Skills in the Elementary School," *Elementary School Journal* **75**, (1974): 112–121.

Bormuth, John R. "The Cloze Readability Procedure," *Elementary English* **45**, (1968): 429–436.

Botel, Morton., J. Dawkins, and Alvin Granowsky. "A Syntactic Complexity Formula," in W. MacGinitie, ed., *Assessment Problems in Reading* (Newark, Delaware: International Reading Association, 1973).

Braam, Leonard. "Developing and Measuring Flexibility in Reading," *Reading Teacher* **16**, (1963): 247–254.

Dale, Edgar, and Jeanne S. Chall. "A Formula for Predicting Readability," *Educational Research Bulletin* **27**, (1948): 11–20, 37–54.

Durkin, Dolores. *Teaching Them to Read*, 2d ed., (Boston: Allyn and Bacon, 1974).

Fry, Edward B. "A Readability Graph that Saves Time," *Journal of Reading* **11** (1968): 513–516, 575–578.

⸻. "Fry's Readability Graph: Clarifications, Validity, and Extensions to Level 17," *Journal of Reading* **21** (1977): 242–252.

Harris, Albert J. *How to Increase Reading Ability*, 5th ed. (New York: McKay, 1970).

Herber, Harold L. *Teaching Reading in Content Areas* (Englewood Cliffs, N.J.: Prentice-Hall, 1970).

Klare, George R. "Assessing Readability," *Reading Research Quarterly* **10** (1974–1975): 62–102.

MacDonald, A. S. "Factors Affecting Reading Test Performance," *Ninth Yearbook of the National Reading Conference*, (1960): 29–35.

Robinson, F. P. *Effective Study* (New York: Harper and Bros., 1946).

Shores, J. Harlan. "Dimensions of Reading Speed and Comprehension," *Elementary English* **45** (1968): 23–28, 43.

Spache, George D. *Good Reading for Poor Readers*, rev. ed. (Champaign, Ill.: Garrard, 1970).

Stone, C. R. "Measuring Difficulty of Primary Reading Material: A Constructive Criticism of Spache's Measure," *Elementary School Journal* 57 (1956): 36–41.

Taylor, Wilson L. "Cloze Procedure: A New Tool for Measuring Readability," *Journalism Quarterly* 30 (1953): 415–433.

Weintraub, Samuel. "Reading Graphs, Charts and Diagrams," *Reading Teacher* 20 (1967): 345–349.

Wisconsin Design for Reading Skill Development (Minneapolis: National Computer Systems, 1977).

Part IV Helping Children Develop Reading Strategies: What Teachers Need to Know

A general framework for reading instruction was described in Part II, and in Part III the content for reading instruction was given. In Part IV (Chapters 9–11) we describe the three most commonly used approaches to reading instruction: the basal reader, language experience, and individualized approaches. In discussing these approaches we show how each can be an appropriate setting for focused instruction that takes into account both the holistic nature of the final reading product and the individual skill needs of students.

Chapter 9
Making the Most of the Basal Reader

After reading this chapter, you will be able to:

1. List and discuss the basic components of a basal-reader system.
2. Describe how contemporary basal-reader programs differ from programs published before 1970.
3. Describe how to conduct a Directed Reading Activity.
4. Describe how to conduct a Directed Reading-Thinking Activity.
5. Compare and contrast the Directed Reading Activity and the Directed Reading-Thinking Activity.
6. List the advantages and disadvantages of basal-reader programs.
7. Explain how to implement a skills-management system in conjunction with a basal-reader program.
8. List important factors to consider when selecting a basal-reader program.

We hope that after you have read this chapter, you will have a good understanding of the most popular way of teaching reading in American schools—the basal-reader approach. We explain why this approach is used so widely in our country. To help you view the contemporary programs used in today's schools within the perspective of their historical development, we compare reading programs of today with those published before 1970. We also give the details of two basic procedures for developing a basal-reader lesson: the Directed Reading Activity and a derivation of this procedure, the Directed Reading-Thinking Activity.

The advantages and disadvantages of using the basal-reader are described so that you will be able to adjust your instruction accordingly. We also present six procedures for using a skills-management system in conjunction with a basal-reader program in order to have organized, focused skill instruction. To conclude the chapter, we have prepared a short list of questions intended to help you evaluate available basal-reader programs or to assist you in selecting a new program. The questions should prove to be especially useful as you examine some of the new programs being marketed.

BASAL-READER PROGRAMS IN PERSPECTIVE

The basal reader has increased in popularity since its introduction in the late 1800s. In a comprehensive study of instructional practices in the United States, Austin and Morrison (1963) found that at that time 95 percent of all primary-grade teachers used basal readers. There are numerous reasons for this popular appeal.

First, a basal-reader series is designed to provide a set of graded readers and corresponding materials which will ensure that students receive sequential instruction. Children are introduced to new concepts and skills by the teacher, according to the plan set out in the publisher's scope-and-sequence chart. The students then apply these concepts and skills when reading the story in the graded reader and practice them again when completing workbook assignments or duplicated worksheets. The idea that a series provides carefully sequenced instruction has appeal to parents, teachers, and school administrators. There is comfort in the feeling that the "experts" (presumably the authors of the series) have carefully delineated a step-by-step program of reading instruction.

A second reason for the widespread use of basal-reader programs is that they offer guidance and direction to the teacher. This guidance is especially important for inexperienced teachers, but it can also be very comforting to experienced teachers who lack confidence. A typical elementary school teacher's undergraduate training consists of only one course in reading; these 30–50 hours of instruction can only introduce a prospective teacher to the intricacies of teaching children to read. It is not surprising, therefore, that most teachers turn to the basal reader for assistance. And even for those individuals who take more than one reading-methods course, the field of reading is so broad and complex that it is difficult to keep abreast of all the new developments in the field.

A third reason for the widespread use of basal-reader programs is the statewide text-adoption policies that are followed in many states. When a policy of statewide adoption is used, the state department of education suggests that schools within its jurisdiction purchase one or more department-recommended basal-reader programs. School districts that choose to buy these recommended series are partially subsidized by state funds. The economic benefit derived from these subsidies, therefore, is a strong factor contributing to the continued use of basal-reading programs in our country's schools.

Taken together, these three factors have contributed much to the widespread use of basal-reader programs across the nation. Unless palatable alternatives are made available, basal readers will probably continue to be the most widely used teaching materials in the years to come.

BASAL-READER PROGRAMS

According to Harris (1970), the overall organization of basal-reader programs has not changed significantly since the first McGuffey Readers were introduced in the mid-1800s. However, although the basic concept of the basal reader has not been altered much, the components of basal programs and the characteristics of some of these components have changed greatly. Some of these changes occurred in the period between the appearance of the first basal-reader programs and the 1960s. Others have been introduced only in the last 10 or 20 years.

The earliest basal-reader programs introduced words at a gradual pace, starting with short, monosyllabic and often phonically regular words. Longer and more difficult words were introduced as the students became more proficient readers. Often, handwriting exercises were introduced in the stories in an attempt to interrelate the language arts. Engraved illustrations were used to stimulate discussion about the stories (see Fig. 9.1). The stories were usually moralistic or patriotic.

During the 1940s and 1950s, there was a significant change in basal readers. Reading-readiness books appeared for the first time (Smith, 1965). Preprimers also appeared more frequently in many of the series. Stories became more realistic (see Fig. 9.2), and color illustrations became the rule rather than the exception. Workbooks and teacher manuals helped teachers organize their lessons more systematically.

Tŏm   tŏp   Kĭt′tў′s

ăt

băck

lŏŏk

gōŏd   dŏll   thĭn̲k   spŏt

th   n̲   ŏŏ

Look at Tom and his dog.
The dog has a black spot on
his back. Do you think he is
a good dog?
Tom has a big top, too. It
is on the box with Kitty's doll.

Fig. 9.1.   An early basal-reader story. (From *McGuffey's First Eclectic Reader*, **rev.**
ed., 1879, p. 19. New York: American Book Co., reprinted by permission.)

The Ducks Go for a Swim

One day when Dick and Nancy were taking the ducks for a walk, Dick said, "Let us take them down to the pond."

When they came to the pond, Dick pointed to the water.

"I see a tadpole over there," he cried. "I am going to catch it."

He rolled up his overalls.

Fig. 9.2. A 1940s basal-reader story. (*Neighbors on the Hill,* the Alice and Jerry Books, New York: Harper and Bros., 1943, p. 137. Reprinted by permission.)

Over the past two decades other important changes have taken place in basal-reader programs. We will look at five major areas in which significant changes have occurred: physical appearance and components, vocabulary control, skill development, representation of minority groups and women, and story content.

Physical Appearance and Components

Whereas basal-reader programs of the 1950s and 1960s consisted primarily of readers, teacher manuals, and student workbooks, contemporary basal-reading programs include a much broader array of materials. The *Holt Basic Reading System* (1977), for example, includes: (1) 17 student readers (grades K–8); (2) skill pretests; (3) unit tests (tests on sections of books); (4) level tests (tests used to determine the child's reading level); (5) teacher manuals; (6) student workbooks; (7) a skills-management system; (8) an audiovisual kit; and (9) a collection of paperback books (see Fig. 9.3). Other publishing companies offer equally comprehensive reading programs.

Fig. 9.3. The Holt Basic Reading System. This kindergarten and first-grade program includes eight different titles, numbered to reflect increasing difficulty. Ancillary materials provide additional practice on skills. (Courtesy Holt, Rinehart and Winston, CBS, Inc., 1977.)

Students' readers have also changed considerably over the years. In addition to those changes we have already mentioned, colorful photographs, woodblock prints, watercolors, and cartoons are often included to make the texts attractive. Furthermore, there has been a noticeable improvement in the type of print used and typesetting style (see Figs. 9.4 and 9.5).

Vocabulary Control

Harris (1970) observed that the restricted vocabulary control that existed between the 1920s and 1950s has been reversed. Today not only are more words introduced at an earlier stage, but also there is less frequent repetition of words once they have been taught. Barnard and DeGracie (1976), for example, state that only 324 different words were found in seven K–1 basal readers that were used ten years ago. After studying the vocabulary load of eight new reading series, they learned that there has been a 56 percent increase in the average number of words used in today's basal readers. Clearly, more words are being introduced in the beginning readers in the newer reading series.

Skill Development

In 1967 Jeanne Chall published *Learning to Read: The Great Debate.* Chall emphasized the view that reading programs that included a phonics orientation seemed to produce better readers. Since then there has been a significant increase in the number of skill-development exercises included in basal-reader programs. Decoding skills, and especially phonics, have received a renewed emphasis. At one time phonics was not emphasized in elementary schools, but today almost all teachers devote much time to phonics instruction.

Other skills are also receiving increased attention. Comprehension skills and study skills, for example, are now playing an important part in most basal-reader programs. Study skills especially have been long overlooked, but now they are becoming more important in contemporary reading programs.

The renewed emphasis on the systematic teaching of specific skills has led many publishers to include a skills-management system as one of the components of their basal-reader systems, and the trend seems to be toward an increase in the number of basal-reader programs that utilize skills-management systems to help teachers focus their reading instruction.

Representation of Minority Groups and Women

Stories about blacks, Mexican-Americans, and other ethnic minorities are increasingly found in newer basal readers. Not long ago minorities were virtually omitted from the basal-reading series used in this country. To receive instruction in reading meant to read mainly about the "adventures" of a middle-class white family as the children grew up in the suburbs of American cities. In addition, the women in these series were shown only in stereotyped roles (usually wearing an apron).

Fortunately, a more realistic representation of life is presented in today's readers. Ethnic as well as environmental pluralism is shown. Basal readers published after the 1960s usually include stories and biographies of many famous men and women from a variety of ethnic backgrounds. Furthermore, women are shown in more varied roles. Instead of being exclusively mothers, nurses, or teachers, they now are also portrayed as doctors, lawyers, or veterinarians.

Paddy the Penguin

Paddy Wants to Fly

One morning Paddy was playing
a game with the other penguins.
It was called "King of the Mountain."
In this game one penguin would be
on top of a mountain of snow.
But the other penguins wanted to be
on top too.
The penguin who could stay on top
without being pushed off was called
"King of the Mountain."
Paddy got to be King.

Fig. 9.4.   A contemporary basal-reader story. (From *Seven Is Magic* of the **Reading 360** series by Theodore Clymer and others, © Copyright, 1969, by Ginn and Company (Xerox Corporation). Used with permission. Text portion a selection from *Paddy the Penguin* by Paul Galdone, as adapted by Ginn and Company. Copyright © 1959 by Paul Galdone. By permission of Thomas Y. Crowell.

It was one o'clock in the morning on Friday, May 5, 1961. In Hangar S at Cape Canaveral in Florida a man was asleep in a bunk. Someone went in to waken him. The man got up at once, for this was to be the most important day of his life.

Fig. 9.5. A contemporary basal-reader story. (From *With Skys and Wings* of the Reading 360 series by Theodore Clymer and others, © Copyright, 1969, by Ginn and Company (Xerox Corporation). Used with permission.)

New programs also devote a greater percentage of their content to women. Whereas only 28 percent of the illustrations of pre-1971 basal-reader programs included pictures of women, today's readers devote roughly 33 percent of their illustrations to women (Martin and Matlin, 1976). There has also been a 9 percent increase in the stories that portray women as the main character.

We think that much progress has been made in representing minority figures and women in a more realistic fashion. There is still much that needs to be done, but we are encouraged by what we see. Ideally, as reading series continue to undergo revision, even greater progress will be made in this area.

Story Content

We are also delighted with the changes in the types of stories that can be found in today's basal readers. Poetry, folk tales, mysteries, space stories, and riddles can be found in most contemporary readers. The number of nonfiction selections is also increasing (Durkin, 1974). This is a positive trend because one of the weaknesses of older basal readers was that they failed to sufficiently catch the interest of reluctant readers—especially boys. The vivid illustrations and lively style of today's basal readers should help to reduce the number of boys who never get interested in reading. Instead, we think that more boys will take more interest in reading as a leisure-time activity, a trend, we hope, that will result in a reduction in the number of boys who eventually end up in remedial-reading programs.

COMPONENTS OF BASAL-READER PROGRAMS TODAY

To help you better understand basal programs, we will examine the main components: (1) the basic texts read by the students; (2) teacher manuals; (3) text-related workbooks; and (4) supplementary materials.

Student Texts

Each text, or reader, consists of a collection of stories. Usually both fiction and nonfiction selections are included, and many readers also contain poetry, short plays, and "how-to-do-it" selections. The texts are organized so that pupils move through a graded series of readers that have increasingly large vocabularies, longer selections, and more advanced concepts.

Because the students in a single reading group usually read the same stories at the same time, these texts permit students to have common reading experiences on which to base group discussions and skill-building activities. Some reading series are organized as follows:

Readiness workbook(s)—kindergarten or first-grade level

Preprimer ⎫
Primer 1 ⎪
Primer 2 ⎬ First-grade level
Primer 3 ⎪
1¹ Reader ⎪
1² Reader ⎭

2^1 Reader ⎫
⎬ Second-grade level
2^2 Reader ⎭

3^1 Reader ⎫
⎬ Third-grade level
3^2 Reader ⎭

4th Reader—Fourth-grade level

5th Reader—Fifth-grade level

6th Reader—Sixth-grade level

Although variations of this organizational pattern exist, most basal-reader programs published prior to the 1970s are organized in this fashion. Systems developed during the 1970s have changed considerably, however. The *Holt Basic Reading System* (1977), for example, consists of 17 different books designed to be used from the reading-readiness level through the eighth grade. The texts are referred to as levels, thereby encouraging teachers to think in terms of continuous progress rather than to assign books to students on the basis of grade level alone (see Fig. 9.6).

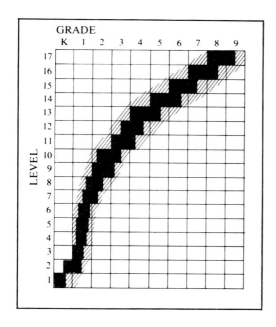

Fig. 9.6. Graph of levels in the Holt Basic Reading System. (Courtesy Holt, Rinehart and Winston, CBS, Inc., 1977.)

Teacher Manuals

Teacher manuals have been designed to help the teacher implement the basal-reader program. The manuals usually include a copy of the student text, as well as a statement of the program's philosophy and an overview of the entire basal program. To go with each story in the reader, specific directions are given for conducting a lesson designed to further the students' decoding and comprehension skills. Often an appendix is included to indicate the placement of particular skill activities and exercises at that particular level.

For each lesson, specific objectives and materials are listed (see Fig. 9.7). Teaching procedures are also spelled out in detail (see Fig. 9.8). Finally, suggestions on how to adapt the lesson to fit the individual needs of each student are given (see Fig. 9.9).

In many cases these directions are so explicit that teachers may find them objectionable. Some teachers are offended when told to say *exactly*, "Now, boys and girls, today we are going to learn about an interesting way to figure out a word's meaning." Stauffer (1971), in criticizing such directions, asserts that many teachers have become "enslaved" by these manuals. In visiting a number of school systems across the country, however, Austin and Morrison (1963) found wide variations in the use of teacher manuals. We believe that *good* teachers will modify these directions and suggestions whenever appropriate and not merely parrot the questions found in them.

Workbooks   Reading workbooks are designed to accompany the students' basal readers. These collections of activities are usually completed by the students independently and are used to reinforce the skills presented by the teacher. Accordingly, the workbooks are sequentially organized, gradually increasing in difficulty. The intent of the workbooks is to provide sufficient practice so that by the time the students finish a workbook, they have mastered the skills presented during the reading lessons. Some programs provide for even more practice by including materials for duplicating individual skill-related worksheets for the students to complete.

At the readiness level, workbooks usually provide activities for prereaders for developing visual- and auditory-discrimination skills and for learning letter-sound relationships. Furthermore, readiness workbooks often provide pictures that can serve as a basis for oral-language stimulation. At the later levels, workbooks provide activities designed to develop decoding, comprehension, and study-skills abilities.

According to Austin and Morrison (1963), workbooks were not in as widespread use as basal readers; they found that only about 50 percent of the systems they surveyed used workbooks. Still, almost half of the teachers did rely heavily on these materials to help them reinforce the skills taught during the reading period.

Supplementary Material   Traditionally, supplementary materials (e.g., library books, films, and recordings) were thought of as materials that were not actually part of the basal-reader program per se. These materials would have to be procured from other publishers, film companies, and educational supply houses. Recently, however, publishers have included a wide variety of supplementary materials as an integral part of their basal-reader programs. Today, it is not unusual to find criterion-referenced tests, spelling books, audiovisual kits, paperback books, and readiness kits included in a basal-reader program. The advantage

PAGES 50-51

SPECIFIC OBJECTIVES

Vocabulary development
   Learning to read the word T<u>ed</u>

Phonemic analysis
   Reviewing phoneme-grapheme correspondences / t / <u>T</u>, / b / <u>B</u>

Comprehension development
   Using picture clues to develop sentence meaning

NEW WORD	DECODING SKILLS
Ted	<u>Elements</u> <u>Reviewed</u>
	Correspondences / t / <u>T</u>, / b / <u>B</u>

SPECIAL MATERIALS

Word card: T<u>ed</u>
Picture card: Ted
Book markers

50 Visual-auditory-kinesthetic practice: **Ted, T**

Fig. 9.7.   List of specific objectives and materials for a basal-reader lesson. (From *My Sound and Word Book, Teacher's Edition* of the Reading 360 series by Theodore Clymer and others, © Copyright, 1969, by Ginn and Company (Xerox Corporation). Used with permission.)

TEACHING THE LESSON

INSTRUCTIONAL PROCEDURES

Place Ted's picture and name card in the card holder. Tell the children the boy's name is Ted and that he is Bill's friend. Write on the chalkboard:

Ted

Bill

Read the names and ask the children why there is a capital letter at the beginning of each one. Have the capital letters named and the words read in unison.

Comprehension Development

Locate page 50 and have the first sentence read. Tell the children that Ted lives near the park and often plays there.

Ask them if they can guess why Ted has come to the park on this day. Develop the sequential action suggested by the pictures.

The action in the pictures on page 51 is not sequential. Have the first sentence read. Help the children discover that Ted is modeling a clay animal, probably at school. Discuss the action and possible settings suggested by the remaining pictures. Identify the people in the second picture as Ted's father and his younger sister, Nan.

Kinesthetic Reinforcement

Write the word Ted on the chalkboard and have it read. Below the model write _ed. Have the capital letter written. Draw three horizontal lines to indicate the letters needed for writing the entire word. Ask a child to write Ted; then have the word read in unison. Anticipate the writing needs for

Visual-auditory-kinesthetic reinforcement: **Ted, T**

Fig. 9.8.   Procedures for teaching a lesson. (From *My Sound and Word Book, Teacher's Edition* of the Reading 360 series by Theodore Clymer and others, © Copyright, 1969, by Ginn and Company (Xerox Corporation). Used with permission.)

completing the sentences on pages 50 and 51. After the writing is completed, have the sentences read and the relationship with the accompanying pictures established.

ADJUSTING TO INDIVIDUAL NEEDS

DECODING ACTIVITY 1

Specific Objective

Phonemic analysis: Strengthening the perception of the sound / t /

Read the words listed below. Ask the children to identify the words in each group that begin with the same sound.

Ted, sail, tank	tooth, orange, tail
toe, table, queen	mask, tear, talk
porch, toy, tongue	teacher, taxi, snow

DECODING ACTIVITY 2

Specific Objective

Phonemic analysis: Reviewing phoneme-grapheme correspondence / t / t

Special Materials

Picture cards for / t /

Distribute the picture cards. Name one of the pictures and have it placed in the card holder. Write the corresponding word on the chalkboard and have it read. Continue until all of the cards are in the holder and the words are listed vertically. Read each word again and ask a child to underline the letter that stands for its beginning sound. Call attention to the initial letters and help the children recall that names of objects are usually written with small beginning letters.

> **PRACTICE BOOK**
> Pages 29, 30

Fig. 9.9.   Individualizing the lesson. (From *My Sound and Word Book, Teacher's Edition* of the Reading 360 series by Theodore Clymer and others, © Copyright, 1969, by Ginn and Company (Xerox Corporation). Used with permission.)

of purchasing such a package is that the teacher has a wide range of inter-related materials readily at hand to help each child reach his or her reading potential. As you might expect, the cost of these complete programs can be thousands of dollars.

THE DIRECTED READING ACTIVITY (DRA)

Typically, the *Directed Reading Activity,* or *DRA*, is the procedure used to teach the lessons in the basal reader. Usually, the DRA consists of four or five specific subsections: the introduction of new vocabulary and/or concepts, guided silent reading (and sometimes oral reading for specific purposes), skill-building exercises, and supplemental enrichment activities. Although publishers may use different terminology to describe each of these subsections, most teacher manuals divide the lessons into these general categories. To understand how each of these parts contributes to the lesson, let's look at each in more detail.

Introduction of New Vocabulary and/or Concepts

Many basal-reader programs instruct the teacher to introduce new vocabulary words to the students before they encounter them in the context of their stories. New words are usually introduced on the chalkboard by including the word(s) in a sentence. Children are asked to read the word by using contextual clues to help them decode it and comprehend its meaning. This practice permits the student to easily decode and comprehend the word when it is encountered later in the story.

When introducing new words, it is important that the teacher spend sufficient time developing not only the decoding abilities of the students, but also their understanding of the words. One of the authors still vividly remembers when as a child, one of his elementary school friends interpreted the sentence "The men took the *ivory* home with them" as meaning that the men took the *soap* home instead of the tusks of an elephant. This student had no difficulty decoding the word, but had obviously misinterpreted its meaning. This illustration emphasizes the fact that unless a student possesses the necessary store of concepts, simply preteaching the pronunciation of new words will do little to increase the child's ability to deal with their meanings (Kingston, 1965).

Guided Silent Reading   After the new vocabulary and concepts have been introduced, the next step is guided silent reading. Before beginning the silent-reading portion of the lesson, it is important to motivate the students so that they are eager to read the story. The teacher manual often has suggestions for providing such motivation, including questions designed to arouse student interest. Examples of motivational questions typically found in manuals are: "What do you think the children will do at the zoo?"; "What do you suppose Ms. Johnson had in the box?"; "Do you think that this story will be about something real or make-believe?" Once their interest in reading the story is high, students are asked to read a portion of the story silently, stop, and discuss their answers to the motivational questions. Then several additional questions are raised—usually by the teacher—and silent reading continues. This pattern is repeated until the students have read the entire story. Throughout the lesson, the teacher may ask students to read orally portions of the story that substantiate answers to the questions.

The guided silent-reading portion of the DRA is often abused through the substitution of oral reading for silent reading. As long ago as 1908, Huey urged that oral reading be discouraged and that it be replaced by the silent reading of meaningful material (Schreiner and Tanner, 1976). Yet many teachers continue to require excessive amounts of oral reading from their students.

Fortunately, however, there has been a gradual increase in the amount of guided silent reading and a decline in oral reading (Rubin, 1975). Teachers who want their students to be fluent oral readers should remember that fluency can be improved if a child is first permitted to read a selection silently and then to reread the passage orally (Rowell, 1976; Heinrich, 1976). Oral reading really has only two main purposes in the classroom. The first is sharing a sentence or selection with other class members or with the teacher through *good* oral reading. The oral reading of poetry or specifically prepared choral reading (group oral reading) materials is often delightful and can help to stimulate interest in reading and in the use of language.

The second, and more important, purpose of oral reading is diagnosis of a student's decoding ability (see Chapter 6). By analyzing the types of errors or miscues that a child makes when reading aloud, the teacher can learn much about a child's reading strategies. When the purpose for asking children to read orally is to diagnose their decoding ability, however, they *should not* be allowed to read the passage(s) silently beforehand. To do so allows them to practice the passage, and hence their oral rereading results in a more "polished" representation of their actual reading ability.

Skill development takes place after the completion of the silent and/or oral reading of the lesson. Typically, the lesson would be presented on the chalk-board or with a correlated handout. Usually these lessons focus on decoding or comprehension skills. Occasionally, however, specific study skills may be taught. After completion of a teacher-directed exercise, students are usually asked to return to their desks and to complete appropriate skill-building exercises in their reading workbooks. Workbook pages generally reinforce the skills that have been taught in the group setting.

    Although there is little disagreement that reading skills need to be taught, there is disagreement as to *when* and *how* those skills should be presented. Stauffer (1969), for example, contends that the basal readers should not present skill-development training, but rather should concentrate on providing children with highly motivating and captivating stories. However, we believe that skills can be taught in many different instructional contexts. What *is* important is that the teacher provide focused instruction attuned to the skill needs of students rather than chance overlooking them altogether. This instruction might be presented through careful use of the suggestions in a basal manual. Another procedure for developing reading skills while using a basal series will be explained later in this chapter.

With the development of contemporary basal-reader systems, the number of supplementary materials and activities to enrich the reading experiences of children has increased. Whereas in the past, teachers were merely encouraged to go to the library to find books that could be read by the students, today's reading programs offer much broader guidelines and more specific suggestions for supplementary activities. Many programs provide these supplementary books and other materials. One publishing company, for instance, has integrated its spelling program with the basal-reading system. Another publisher includes paperback books designed to be read after students finish assignments in their readers and workbooks. No longer is the teacher expected to develop materials to extend children's basic reading experiences. Instead, publishers now offer paperback books, spelling programs, picture cards, specific skills worksheets, audio cassettes, and filmstrips to supplement their basic reading program. Only the school budget limits what types of materials can be purchased to supplement the students' readers and workbooks.

The Directed Reading-Thinking Activity, or *DRTA*, was conceptualized and refined by Stauffer (1969). He popularized the DRTA until today it is thought of as a viable alternative to the Directed Reading Activity. According to Stauffer (1969, p. 38): "Reading, like thinking, is a mental process. It requires symbols (words) that stand for ideas or concepts produced by a writer. It requires a reader's use of his experience and knowledge to reconstruct the ideas

Skill-Building Exercises

Supplementary Activities

THE DIRECTED READING-THINKING ACTIVITY (DRTA)

or concepts produced by the writer. The process of reconstruction begins, goes on, and is in continual change as long as a person reads." Writing with Cramer (1968, p. 3), he further states: "It is apparent, therefore, that both reading and thinking start with a state of doubt or of desire. It is apparent also that the process of reconstructing goes on as inquiry or discovery, until the doubt is resolved, the perplexity settled, or the pleasure attained."

In accordance with Stauffer's philosophy, the DRTA demands that children become active participants in the reading process, first by raising questions about the selection, then by processing the information as they read, and finally by receiving feedback relating back to their original questions. Good readers learn and utilize this three-step process as they read materials on a day-to-day basis; unskilled readers most likely do not.

The primary goal of DRTA training is to develop critical readers; following the three steps outlined below can help students reach this goal.

1. *Setting a purpose.* This first step, developing purposes for reading, is the most important part of the DRTA. During this portion of the lesson, students, at first with teacher direction and later by themselves, establish their reasons for reading. You might think of this as the "what are we reading for" section. Accordingly, questions such as "What do you think the title of this story means?" or "Why do you think the girl is holding the dog the way she is?" may be asked of the group.

The teacher's job is to elicit a number of *diverse* responses. The greater the number of responses, the more chance there is of student involvement when the story is read. Once a sufficient number of plausible answers have been given, the group is ready to move on to the next step.

2. *Thinking.* In this portion of the lesson, the students silently read the selection, relating both personal and vicarious experiences to the story. While the students read, some of their earlier expectations will be rejected, and others will be confirmed. Students are asked to stop reading at selected spots in the story and to conjecture about what might happen next. By following this procedure, students actively engage in a search for evidence to confirm their earlier expectations.

3. *Testing hypotheses.* This is the culminating step of the DRTA and is intimately linked with the other two steps. At this point students present the evidence that supports or rejects their earlier conjectures (Stauffer, 1961). It is not really important that some of the hypotheses will be retained and others will not. In the DRTA "right" answers are not the ultimate goal. Instead, the teacher encourages students to explore why some hypotheses might be more acceptable than others. Thus the negative connotation of being "wrong" is eliminated. Furthermore, students will learn not to be afraid of supplying more than one answer to questions that have been raised.

This is not to imply that "anything goes." To the contrary! Answers to questions must be based on sound reasoning and must have a logical basis. Those that are not Stauffer and Cramer (1968) call ignorant mistakes. Intelligent mistakes, on the hand, are based on clear reasoning, but may be less appropriate than some other explanation. Students should be asked to prove or disprove earlier predictions by finding the sections in the story that support or reject their earlier hypotheses and reading these sections aloud. In this way oral reading serves a meaningful purpose—proving or disproving an earlier hypothesis.

Like the DRA, the DRTA process can be used with basal readers as well as with other types of materials. Science and social studies texts, for instance, lend themselves to this approach. Fiction as well as nonfiction materials can be used. The DRTA approach is usually applicable whenever several students are reading the same material and have about the same level of competence. Ideally, the size of the group should be large enough to permit sufficient interaction and yet not so large that some students do not participate in the group discussions. Seldom should groups exceed 10 or 12 members. Teachers must also ensure that all members of the group are actively involved in the reading of the story.

COMPARING THE DRA AND THE DRTA

To better understand the major differences between the DRA and the DRTA, let's examine four ways in which these two approaches differ. As we look at these two approaches, try to think of ways you might use them when you teach reading and also how you might use them outside of your reading class.

Materials Used

One of the major differences between these two approaches is in the materials used for the lessons. Most basal-reader programs use the DRA, and specific instructional materials have been prepared following the DRA format. Questions are explicitly laid out in the manual, and the teacher need only follow these guidelines in order to complete the lesson.

Having such explicit teacher manuals can be a great boon to the teacher, especially when using a basal program for the first time. However, teachers need to be aware that following the suggested format religiously is not always warranted. For example, we have seen teachers insist on reading every question from a manual even though students have already supplied the answers to some of the questions earlier in the lesson. Such slavish adherence to the guidelines set down by the "experts" is unwise and reduces the effectiveness of a potentially valuable reading program.

The DRTA, by contrast, provides fewer explicit guidelines for the teacher. The teacher is free to allow the needs and interests of the students to guide the development of the lesson. This "materials-free" (or at least manual-free) approach has the advantage of permitting flexibility so that the teacher may respond to the needs of the children. It also has the disadvantage of leaving the teacher solely responsible for the development of the lesson, and that is a responsibility some teachers are reluctant to take.

To our knowledge, there are no basal-reader manuals currently available that strictly follow the DRTA approach. However, the DRTA can easily be implemented in a program that follows the DRA model. In addition, because the DRTA is not "materials-oriented," it can be used in teaching any of the other elementary school subjects that require reading, such as social studies and science.

The Teacher's Role   In the DRA the teacher's role is to direct students to find answers to teacher-supplied questions. Unfortunately, these questions are often only at the literal level, such as "What was the boy's name?" or "Where were Dick and Alice going?" Asking questions at the literal level leaves little opportunity for divergent thinking.* Teachers using basal materials should critically examine the questions suggested in the manual to determine if these questions require varying levels of comprehension. If the questions are primarily at the literal level, additional questions should be supplied.

The DRTA, on the other hand, requires the teacher to assume a different responsibility. While the teacher continues to focus the group's attention on the story, this is done by asking questions that require *divergent* thinking rather than *convergent* thinking.* Questions such as "What do you think the title of this story means?" or "Why do you feel the children did the correct thing?" or "What do you think will happen next?" are typically asked in DRTA lessons. Clearly, this type of question requires a higher level of thinking than do literal-level questions seeking a convergent answer.

When using the DRTA, the teacher moves beyond literal questions and leads children to discover that reading is a dynamic and enjoyable activity, one that transcends simply answering literal questions. The comprehension skills developed during the DRTA lesson are more like those that will be used outside of the reading class. They are the higher-level questions that children will be confronted with throughout their lives.

Vocabulary Development   In the DRA the first procedure followed is to introduce the "new words" the pupils will encounter when they read the story. These words are usually underlined and placed in a sentence context on the chalkboard. Prior to having the students read the story, time is spent making sure that all students can decode, as well as understand, these words.

In the DRTA, however, there is no preteaching of vocabulary. Stauffer and Cramer (1968, p. 25) assert: "In situations where the teacher writes all new words on the chalkboard and tells the children what the words are, or helps them analyze the words before they meet the words in context, the pupils do not have an opportunity to use the skills they have been taught. The teacher short-circuits pupil learning."

Thus, in the DRTA new words are encountered for the first time in the context of the story. The child must use previously taught decoding skills to unlock unknown words. When this occurs, students decode in a more realistic situation. Practicing decoding in this fashion will enable them to transfer their

*Divergent thinking explores the validity of several answers or points of view. Convergent thinking focuses on finding a single "correct" answer or solution.

Reading involves both convergent—literal-level—and divergent—interpretive-type—thinking.

word-attack skills to situations outside of the reading class. The four-step decoding process students in the DRTA are encouraged to use to identify an unknown word is, according to Stauffer and Cramer (1968):

1. Read to the end of the sentence.
2. Look for picture clues in the story.
3. Try to decode the unknown word with phonics skills.
4. Ask for help.

Teachers should consider carefully using the DRTA approach for dealing with new vocabulary. In addition to the sound reasoning put forth by Stauffer and Cramer, empirical support exists for this practice. Groff (1964), for example, attempted to determine the value of preteaching vocabulary words to 347 second-grade students. To his surprise, he discovered that almost 60 percent of these "new" words were recognized before they were "taught." In addition, the preteaching of words didn't seem to reduce the number of mispronunciations later on. This evidence suggests that the traditional practice of preteaching vocabulary words before guided silent reading may not be accomplishing its intended purpose, or even be necessary.

Comprehension Skills   Even a casual glance at reading workbooks will reveal that numerous pages are devoted to teaching comprehension skills. Sentence interpretation, picture interpretation, following directions, understanding details, drawing conclusions, identifying the main idea, and recognizing sequence are just a few of the skills most programs include. Others include such "skills" as empathizing with story characters, determining the author's style, accepting personal behavior, and accepting others in one's environment. Selection of which comprehension skills to teach at what time is based on the basal-reader program's scope and sequence of comprehension skills and on the nature of each story itself. In the DRA the manual prescribes which skills will be taught when. In the DRTA, on the other hand, no prescription for teaching comprehension skills is given. Rather, when using the DRTA, the teacher must learn the art of good questioning and be willing to accept possible alternative answers to questions in order to develop a variety of comprehension skills.

A talented teacher using the DRTA can create an atmosphere that can be distinctively different from one in which only convergent responses are acceptable. Davidson (1970), for example, found that teachers using the DRTA procedures asked more interpretive and inferential questions than did teachers who used the DRA. Teachers relying on DRA procedures asked questions of a more factual nature. The responses of students in each type of group were also noticeably different. In the first group there was a predominance of critical-level responses, whereas in groups in which the DRA was used, responses were chiefly noncritical and were categorized as being at the literal level of comprehension. Fortunately, many newer basal-reader programs have begun to incorporate some of the questioning techniques used with the DRTA. We think that this trend will enhance the DRA as a means of improving the comprehension of elementary school students.

By now it should be clear that there are significant differences between the DRTA and the DRA. Teachers who use basal-reader programs will most likely find the DRA a valuable and readily available teaching strategy. However, we also think that the DRTA has much to offer teachers who are willing to devote the additional energies and creative talent needed to implement it correctly. We have just touched the surface of how to use the DRTA approach. If you are interested in learning more about it, the most authoritative and comprehensive description of this approach can be found in Stauffer's *Directing Reading Maturity as a Cognitive Process* (New York: Harper & Row, 1969). We encourage you to explore it in more detail if you are contemplating using the DRTA in your classroom.

ADVANTAGES AND DISADVANTAGES OF BASAL-READER PROGRAMS

Basal-reader programs are used by more teachers than is any other approach. Because basal readers are so popular, it is important to evaluate their benefits and limitations. To better understand the advantages and disadvantages of this approach, we need to look at some of the concerns that have been raised.

Teacher Directions

As a beginning teacher, you will probably find the basal-reader program to be your primary vehicle for teaching reading. Inexperienced teachers find that the many suggestions offered in the teacher manuals often mean the difference between a successful lesson and a dismal failure. The teacher is led, step by step, through the Directed Reading Activity, supplied with the necessary guiding questions, and finally told which kinds of activities to use to reinforce skill development. Literally everything is laid out for the teacher.

Valuable as the manuals are, however, teachers should not become unquestioning "slaves" of these materials. They should consult the teacher manuals for suggestions, but should not view these suggestions as being prescriptions. If, for example, the manual specifies that today's lesson should center on teaching the skill of recognizing plural forms of words and if the students already know this skill, time should not be wasted in drilling them on this skill. If, on the other hand, a teacher encounters a situation that would lend itself to the spontaneous teaching of a specific skill, she or he should not hesitate to depart from the explicit directions in the manual, but should instead "seize the moment" to teach a meaningful lesson when the need occurs.

Sequential Skill Development

Every basal-reader program has a carefully sequenced list of reading skills. These skill lists are developed after the authors have considered the recommendations of experts in the fields of reading, psychology, linguistics, and child development. The lists represent what these experts feel are the skills needed to learn to read. Once a list has been drawn up, materials are produced to aid children in learning the skills. Additionally, teaching ideas are included to help teachers do a better job of teaching. The expectation is that any child who completes the assignments specified in the program should develop into a competent reader.

The highly structured sequential development of skills that helps many children learn to read may, however, prove to be disadvantageous to others. This can happen in two ways. First, because some children learn to read before they come to school, they may have learned how to decode and comprehend without formal skill instruction. These students have developed their own effective strategies for unlocking and comprehending words. To subject these students to lock-step instruction in the basal-reader program is to require them to do many assignments that will be meaningless because the children already possess the abilities taught in those lessons. Instruction becomes boring for these students.

The other type of student who may not benefit from the structured skill instruction in basal-reader programs is the student who fails to learn a skill in the allocated time. This student may need additional instruction and reinforcement on a skill before moving on to the next lesson in the program. Sometimes less capable students fail to learn to read because instruction has proceeded at too rapid a pace. Unfortunately, most basal-reader programs are geared for the "average" learner. If instruction were at a slower pace, many of these students would learn to read and to enjoy reading, too.

Shared Reading Experiences

One often overlooked advantage derived from using the basal reader is that the stories provide a common experience for all students in the reading group. These readings permit individuals to benefit from the insight and perceptions of their peers. Group discussions can lead to interest in other topics, too. When the Directed Reading-Thinking Activity is used, students are given an opportunity to see how they can transfer divergent comprehension strategies to independent reading. Group instruction, then, can be regarded as a positive feature of a reading program.

Unfortunately, group instruction sometimes may result in students' being placed in reading groups that are too high or too low for their ability. With the wide range of reading abilities in most classrooms, it is almost impossible to have all children in a group reading at a level commensurate with their abilities. Nevertheless, this does not justify forcing students to remain in groups in which the work is too easy or too difficult. Because children learn at different rates, the teacher must constantly be aware of changes in reading ability. Children who were appropriately placed in a group in September may have fallen behind by December or may have leapt ahead by January. The teacher must be flexible enough to move these students into different groups rather than have them remain in the same group throughout an entire school year. By occasionally administering a quick screening test to the students, however, the teacher can check periodically that they are placed in a group in which the work will be neither too easy nor too difficult.

Students' Perceptions of Reading

Contemporary basal-reading programs are attractive in appearance, provide a wide variety of reading material that is often rich in literary content, and offer many suggestions for follow-up activities. Yet teachers need to be aware that even with these laudable features included, reading instruction should consist of more than the lessons supplied in a basal-reader program. Unless the teacher provides ample opportunities for recreational reading, students may eventually acquire inaccurate perceptions of what reading actually is. We have seen second graders, for example, who think that reading is phonics instruction, the completion of workbook pages, or a subject that usually is taught early in the school day. Children need to think of reading as an enjoyable *process* rather than as a *subject*.

Teachers can do much to foster this concept of reading as a process: They can read books to their students during the day; they can help children search for answers in reference materials; and they can provide for visits to the school library. These activities will demonstrate to children that reading is really more than the basal-reading program.

Using a skills-management system with the basal-reader approach can provide precise information about each student's skill development. When a skills-management system is integrated with a basal-reading program, a greater degree of flexibility and individualization can be attained than if all children are routinely asked to complete the same assignments. Many publishers of basal-reader programs now include skills-management systems with their programs. In addition, there are a number of separate skills-management systems available from other publishers.

Unfortunately, few publishers of either basal-reader programs or skills-management systems have provided sufficient guidance on how these two sets of educational materials can be effectively integrated—one reinforcing the other. We feel that there are six viable alternatives to choose from when integrating skills-management systems with basal readers.

APPLICATION: USING A SKILLS-MANAGEMENT SYSTEM WITH THE BASAL READER

To show you how to use a skills-management system to enhance a basal-reader daily lesson, we will assume that you are a beginning teacher who is eager to provide focused skill instruction for your students, within the context of your favorite basal-reading program. Naturally, you would have already administered the appropriate criterion-referenced pretests to students and have up-to-date information describing each student's skill-development profile. Furthermore, all students would have been given informal reading inventories or similar placement tests and would be reading in basal groups at their instructional level. In other words, the students should have no major difficulty in decoding the stories in their readers. Furthermore, they should have relatively good comprehension when reading this material. The following sequence, then, is one you might follow to focus the skill instruction of each child in the basal-reader group.

First, you need to familiarize yourself with the story the children will be asked to read. You can do this by skimming the story, reading the accompanying teacher manual, and surveying any corresponding workbook pages which later may be assigned. Then you would be ready to check the skill-development records for each child in the reading group. Since the teacher manual has specified the skill(s) that will be taught in the lesson, your purpose in examining the skill profiles of the students is to see how many children in the group have deficiencies in the skills the lesson covers. In this way you can make appropriate assignments for each child.

The Daily Basal-Reader Lesson

Next, you must decide what instruction individual members of the group need. If most of the students in the group need instruction on a particular skill, you should plan on presenting the teacher-directed lesson for that skill to those students and assigning the appropriate workbook pages. If you felt that the group could benefit from additional practice beyond that provided by the workbook, you could consult your resource file of commercially available materials and teacher ideas. You might decide, for example, that two additional worksheets plus a board game would help reinforce the skill taught in the workbook.

Now let us assume a different situation. After consulting your basal-reading materials and skill-development records, you may have learned that only two of eight students in the reading group needed instruction on the skill to be covered. In this situation you might not spend much time on the skill in the group session. Instead, you might decide to check informally each child's mastery of the skill during the group session. Then you might assign the suggested workbook pages to the two students who demonstrated a weakness in the skill, perhaps after introducing the skill to these two students after dismissing the rest of the group. The other children would be permitted to do independent reading instead of the workbook pages, thereby freeing them from "busy work" on material already known. Instead, they would be given an opportunity to broaden their reading tastes by reading material of their choice. Furthermore, they would be involved in applying already learned skills while reading independently.

The Basal Reader and Separate Skills Groups

Another alternative procedure for implementing a skills-management system along with the basal reader is to alternate the teaching of reading groups and skills groups. In this plan you schedule meetings of the basal-reader groups two or three times per week. When these groups meet, you provide instruction as specified in the teacher manual, omitting skill-development exercises. On two or three days a week, you would not meet with the basal-reading groups, but instead would form skills groups based on student needs.

Typically, a skill group remains together long enough to permit roughly two hours of skill instruction each week. At the end of two or three weeks, each student's knowledge of the skill is assessed. Students who have mastered the skill should be regrouped in newly formed groups. Students who had not learned the skill might remain in the original group for further instruction and practice.

As you can see, this plan really results in two separate instructional groupings: achievement grouping (based on overall reading level) and skills grouping. The advantages and disadvantages of each grouping plan are beyond the scope of this chapter, but are explained in detail in Chapter 13.

The Basal Reader with Concurrent Skills-Group Instruction

This plan is a derivation of the preceding one. Unlike the separate-skills-groups plan, however, teachers who choose this option have daily instructional sessions with both the basal-reader groups *and* skills groups. In other words, if you decided on this plan for your classroom, you would continue to meet with the regular basal-reader groups for between 60 and 90 minutes every day. In addition to this instruction, though, you would schedule an extra 30 minutes of skill instruction a day, with students grouped for instruction on the basis of skill need, according to the skill-development profiles.

Learning centers are activity centers in which students work independently at tasks designed to reinforce learnings of various kinds. Using learning centers to reinforce specific skills has great appeal to teachers in open classrooms. These classrooms are usually organized to include several learning centers or skill centers. Using a skills-management system allows the teacher to better organize these centers according to student needs and thereby provide focused reading instruction on specific skills—something that all too often has not been done in some open classrooms.

The Basal Reader with Learning Centers

As a beginning teacher using a skills-management system to help structure learning centers, you would conduct the daily basal-reader lessons in the usual fashion, minus the skill-development portions of the lessons. In order to decide what kinds of learning centers were needed for skill development, you would use the record-keeping portion of the skills-management system to determine the specific skill needs of the entire class. For example, the records might indicate that several students needed further instruction in long and short vowels and that a few others had not mastered consonant variants (the "hard" and "soft" sounds of c and g). If you had five learning centers in your classroom, you might decide to design two of them to reinforce the short-vowel generalizations, one to reinforce the long-vowel generalization, and two to provide practice with consonant variants. A quick glance at the class skill-development profile would indicate which children needed each of these skills. Students would then be assigned to the centers based on their specific skill needs.

Whenever possible, learning centers should be self-instructing as well as self-correcting. This will free the teacher to circulate around the room or to work with individuals or groups when other students are at the centers. When students working in the learning centers feel capable of passing the postassessment for a particular skill, they should come to the teacher for an informal, performance-type test or a more formal, paper-and-pencil assessment.

The Basal Reader and Skill Contracts

Although the term "contract" may have a negative connotation to some, we believe that the use of contracts with intermediate-grade students is a viable instructional procedure, provided that sufficient classroom routines have been established and that students have been led to be accountable for completing their assignments. We are not recommending this plan for everyone. But if the students in a particular classroom are responsible and mature, the use of skill contracts allows instruction to be flexible and individualized.

If, in your hypothetical classroom, you had chosen to use skill contracts with the basal program, the basal-reader lesson would remain the primary means of daily instruction. As with the previous plans, the individual skill-development records would allow you to determine what skill instruction would be most appropriate for each student. Skill contracts would then be developed. After consulting the resource file of instructional materials, you would choose suitable tasks for helping students learn the skills. In some instances assignments might be made to individual students. In other cases small groups might receive the same assignment or assignments. A "contract" would be drawn up between you and the student(s). This contract does not necessarily have to be written, but might simply be verbal, provided that both teacher and students understand when the assigned work is to be completed. After completing a contract satisfactorily, a student would be given a new contract, based on another demonstrated skill need.

The Basal Reader and Criterion-Referenced Posttests

A final option for implementing a basal-reader program with a skills-management system is to eliminate any type of pretesting and rely instead on posttesting to determine student mastery of skills. In this plan instruction would continue in the basal reader, and the skill-development lessons in the basal program would be implemented. If you chose this plan, however, you would periodically administer criterion-referenced tests to assess whether students were making satisfactory progress in skill development. Those who were not doing well would be grouped for additional skill instruction as needed, outside of the regular basal-reading groups.

The advantage of using this plan is that the necessity of pretesting is eliminated; hence the time needed to administer and score tests is reduced considerably. The disadvantage, of course, is that without pretesting, teaching lacks the focus that it would normally have. Nevertheless, students' skill development is being monitored by posttests, and instruction is given to students who have failed to grasp skills through their regular developmental reading instruction.

APPLICATION: CHOOSING A BASAL READER

To help you *really* understand basal-reader programs, you might carefully examine an actual set of these materials. By doing this, you will also prepare yourself to make a more intelligent decision when you are faced with selecting a program. To guide you in this process, we have prepared a series of steps you might follow:

1. Starting at the readiness level, list the titles, levels, and/or grade-level designations of all the readers (include readiness materials) in the program.
2. If workbooks accompany the readers, list them as you did for question 1.
3. If separate skill-development workbooks or worksheets are supplied with the program, list the name and general skill categories covered in each workbook or set of worksheets.
4. Identify any additional teaching aids that are available as part of the series (e.g., skills-management systems, games, manipulative materials, audio cassettes).
5. Examine the children's readers and answer these questions:
    a) Are the readers attractive and capable of stimulating student interest?

b) Are multicolor illustrations and/or photographs used?

c) Do the stories represent a wide range of student interests, and will they be of interest to boys as well as girls?

d) Do the stories reflect our pluralistic society?

e) Will students be given opportunities to read content-area materials in the readers?

6. Examine the teacher guides and answer these questions:

a) Are the objectives of the program explicitly stated?

b) Are adequate suggestions given for relating story content and vocabulary to students' prior experiences and vocabulary?

c) Are appropriate and adequate suggestions offered for skill-development exercises?

d) Are appropriate and adequate suggestions offered for follow-up or enrichment activities?

e) Are the guides sufficiently detailed to permit teachers to easily follow the specified recommendations?

7. Examine the student workbooks and answer the following questions:

a) Are decoding, comprehension, and study skills given adequate representation?

b) Are the activities closely correlated with the skills taught during the DRA or DRTA lessons?

c) Are the activities of high interest and meaningful, or do they simply represent "busy work"?

d) Can the activities be completed with only a minimum of teacher supervision?

SUMMARY: MAKING THE MOST OF THE BASAL READER

In this chapter we have described the most popular approach for teaching reading in the United States: the basal reader. During the approximately 100 years that publishers have been marketing these programs, they have evolved from relatively simple readers to complex, complete teaching/learning systems. Because basal-reader programs have undergone significant changes in just the past 10 to 20 years, we have alerted you to some of the recent developments that may influence your choice if you should ever serve on a textbook-selection committee or be in a position to order new readers for your classroom. We think that you should now be able to intelligently discern between "good" and "poor" basal-reader programs.

We have also pointed out the advantages and disadvantages of using these programs. Regardless of which basal-reader program you use, you should be aware of the strengths and the limitations of this approach, including ways in which teachers sometimes misuse basal readers.

We have presented several methods of using basal readers, including two ways of conducting lessons while using the basal reader: the Directed Reading Activity and the Directed Reading-Thinking Activity. By now you should be familiar with how these two kinds of lessons differ in materials, procedures, and the role of the teacher.

Six ways in which you might implement a skills-management system with a basal-reader program were also described in order to familiarize you with techniques for focusing skill instruction within a basal program. Finally, we have given you a list of questions to help guide you in the wise selection of a basal-reader program.

Too often classroom teachers are lulled into a false sense of security when they are surrounded by the warm blanket of a basal-reader program. Basal programs *can* be very effective, but they must be used intelligently and in a manner that still treats children as individuals with specific needs, not just members of a basal group.

REVIEW QUESTIONS

1. Visit a local school or a university instructional materials center. Select a contemporary basal-reader system to review and identify the specific components of that program. Can you explain how each part of the program contributes to a child's learning to read?

2. Since the 1960s, basal-reader programs have undergone considerable change. Compare and contrast reading programs before the 1960s with those available today. Do you think that contemporary basal-reader programs might foster better reader habits than those used in the past? Why or why not?

3. List the steps a teacher would follow using the Directed Reading Activity. Can you explain how a teacher could use the DRA approach when teaching a science or social studies lesson? Might these content areas present any unique problems for teachers using the DRA?

4. Outline the procedures a teacher would follow in using a Directed Reading-Thinking Activity. Compare these procedures with the directions given for a lesson in a basal teacher's manual. How would you modify the directions in the teacher's manual to include important components of the DRTA approach?

5. How does a Directed Reading-Thinking Activity differ from a DRA? Are there any similarities in the approaches? Which do you think might help you reach your teaching objectives most effectively? Why?

6. Although basal-reader programs have received much criticism, they continue to be widely used. Why do you think this is so? Can you cite the advantages and disadvantages of using a basal-reader system? When might a basal reader be inappropriate for a child?

7. Describe the different ways a skills-management system can be implemented with a basal-reader program. Imagine that your principal has asked you how and why these two systems might be implemented simultaneously. Choose one or more of the implementation options you have described and defend your choice.

REFERENCES

Austin, Mary C., and Coleman Morrison. *The First R: The Harvard Report on Reading in Elementary Schools* (New York: Macmillan, 1963).

Barnard, Douglas P., and James DeGracie. "Vocabulary Analysis of New Primary Reading Series," *Reading Teacher* **30**, 2 (1976): 177–180.

Chall, Jeanne. *Learning to Read: The Great Debate* (New York: McGraw-Hill, 1967).

Davidson, Jane L. "The Relationship Between Teachers' Questions and Pupils' Responses During a Directed Reading Activity and a Directed Reading-Thinking Activity," Ph.D. diss., University of Michigan, 1970.

Durkin, Dolores. *Teaching Them to Read* (Boston: Allyn and Bacon, 1974).

Groff, Patrick J. "Readiness for Reading Vocabulary with Ability Grouping," *Journal of Educational Research* **58**, 3 (1964): 140–141.

Harris, Albert J. "Evaluating Reading Readiness Workbooks," in *Problem Areas in Reading . . . Some Observations and Recommendations,* Rhode Island College Reading Conference Proceedings, 1965, ed. Coleman Morrison. (Providence: Oxford Press, 1966), pp. 26–31.

———. *How to Increase Reading Ability,* 5th ed. (New York: McKay, 1970).

———. "New Dimensions in Basal Readers," *Reading Teacher* **25**, 4 (1972): 310–315.

Heinrich, June S. "Elementary Oral Reading: Methods and Materials," *Reading Teacher* **30**, 1 (1976): 10–15.

Holt Basic Reading System (New York: Holt, Rinehart and Winston, 1977).

Kingston, Albert J. "Research for the Classroom: Vocabulary Development," *Journal of Reading* (March 1965): 265–269.

Martin, Laurel A., and Margaret W. Matlin. "Does Sexism in Elementary Readers Still Exist?" *Reading Teacher* **29**, 8 (1976): 764–767.

Rowell, E. H. "Do Elementary Students Read Better Orally or Silently?" *Reading Teacher* **29**, 4 (1976): 367–370.

Rubin, Rosalyn A. "Reading Ability and Assigned Materials: Accommodation for the Slow but Not the Accelerated," *Elementary School Journal* **75**, 6 (1975): 373–377.

Schreiner, Robert, and Linda R. Tanner. "What History Says about Teaching Reading," *Reading Teacher* **29**, 5 (1976): 468–473.

Smith, Nila Banton. *American Reading Instruction* (Newark, Delaware: International Reading Association, 1965).

Stauffer, Russell G. *Directing Reading Maturity as a Cognitive Process* (New York: Harper & Row, 1969).

———. "Reading and the Educated Guess." Address given at the Seventeenth Annual Conference and Course on Reading, University of Pittsburgh, 1961.

———. "Slave, Puppet or Teacher?" *Reading Teacher* **25**, 1 (1971): 24–29.

Stauffer, Russell G., and Ronald Cramer. *Teaching Critical Reading at the Primary Level* (Newark, Delaware: International Reading Association, 1968).

Chapter 10
Expanding
Horizons:
The Language-
Experience
Approach

After reading this chapter, you will be able to:

1. Describe the three-step process for conducting a language-experience lesson.
2. Explain how a skills-management system can be integrated with the language-experience approach.
3. Recall four special uses of the language-experience approach.
4. List several advantages and disadvantages of using this approach.

Almost all children come to school with well-developed language abilities. The language-experience approach takes advantage of these language strengths by using the child's oral language to form the material for the reading lesson. During a language-experience lesson, the child (or a group of children) dictates a story to the teacher, who transcribes the story for the child and then helps him or her read the story aloud. These dictated stories are the core of the reading lesson.

In this chapter we outline the three steps usually used to conduct a language-experience lesson. In addition, we show how this approach to reading instruction can be modified to use with kindergarten children and with dialectally different students. We also describe how skills instruction can be handled within the language-experience approach.

The language-experience approach to teaching reading is a flexible method of instruction that requires a great deal of teacher expertise and confidence. Its greatest asset is its adaptability to individual needs. But that asset can be utilized fully only if the teacher understands the program thoroughly and is willing to invest a great deal of time to make the program work.

THE LANGUAGE-EXPERIENCE APPROACH IN PERSPECTIVE

In the language-experience approach the speech of the students is transcribed into print and used as the primary material for teaching reading. This approach is perhaps the most natural way for teaching children to read, because it takes advantage of many characteristics of beginning readers. First, almost all children come to school with the expectation that they will begin to learn to read. Transcribing their speech into sentences and encouraging the students to read the sentences back is a quick way to show these eager students that reading (even if just a word or two) can be easily learned. Second, young children bring a variety of experiences to school and are eager to share these with their classmates and teachers. These experiences can form the basis of much of the students' reading material. Furthermore, by using the actual speech patterns of the children to create a story, the teacher can be assured of a close syntactic match between speech and print. If such a match does exist, there is greater likelihood of more fluent oral reading and greater comprehension than if the students read materials that do not resemble their own syntactic patterns (Ruddell, 1965; Tathum, 1968). These factors are important influences in learning to read. As Goodman (1971, p. 46) states:

The five- or six-year-old child coming to school for the first time is not a beginner because he has already learned his native language. He has learned to communicate his needs, wishes, feelings, and his wonder. He has learned to use language, not only to relate his experiences to others, but also to organize, manipulate, and reflect on those experiences.

Thus it seems only reasonable that children be taught to read by transcribing their thoughts into print. In the language-experience approach this is precisely what is done. As a result, reading is treated more as a thinking process (Thorn, 1969), and decoding and comprehension are learned together, one reinforcing the other. The integration of these two components of reading is important if reading is to be meaningful.

Another important advantage of the language-experience approach is that children quickly learn that contextual clues can help them decode many words that they would be unable to "unlock" in isolation. In addition, Hall (1972) contends that reading their own transcribed speech greatly simplifies reading for the children. Because the oral and written language patterns involved are similar and therefore can be anticipated, children taught by the language-experience approach can make successful initial progress in reading (Goodman and Burke, 1972, p. 11).

Although it might be argued that an objective-based approach to reading instruction is incompatible with the language-experience approach, we disagree. To be sure, it is indeed difficult to express behaviorally the outcomes of language-experience lessons in advance, but we feel that prescriptive objectives can be used to guide the teaching of specific decoding skills and that descriptive objectives can be useful for characterizing expected student behaviors in the areas of interpretive comprehension and attitude toward reading.

To summarize, we are suggesting that the language-experience approach, supplemented by focused skill instruction, can serve as a basis for learning how to read. With the wide variety of experiences children bring to school and with the oral-language abilities young children have, the language-experience approach to teaching reading has much to offer.

Children bring to school many exciting experiences which they are eager to share and to write about. Their friends, family, pets, hobbies, and travels all are meaningful to them and are potential sources of stories. Grandmother's visit may provide an opportunity for a child to dictate a very personal, individual story to the teacher or may even become the basis for a group story as the other children relay information about *their* grandparents.

CONDUCTING A LANGUAGE-EXPERIENCE LESSON

The teacher may also provide additional experiences for the class. The class may tour a local bakery, listen to the mayor tell about managing city government, or taste fresh pineapple and avocado. Even seemingly routine activities within the school can be used to generate stories. The children could write or dictate stories about events that happened on the playground or in art class. They could tell about class news or about something they have read. The variety of experiences that can serve as the bases for stories to be dictated is limitless.

One useful source of topics for language-experience stories is *Language Experiences in Reading: Teacher Resource Books* (Allen and Allen, 1970*a*, 1970*b*). Step-by-step directions are provided in these books to illustrate how the teacher can lead children to write stories on a variety of topics, ranging from introspective themes, such as "About Myself," to topics that integrate the language arts and the content areas, such as "All Kinds of Weather."

Experience stories may be written by whole classes, small groups, or individuals. Whole-class experience stories are often appropriate for beginning instruction with this approach. Class discussions, field trips, movies, games, songs, and teacher-read stories can be used to stimulate stories in kindergarten or first grade. Students can then dictate sentences, and the teacher can transcribe the words onto newsprint, the chalkboard, or an overhead transparency.

Although whole-class stories are often created, the most common practice is to generate stories within small groups of children (Henderson, 1973).

Children can "translate" their own experiences into meaningful stories to be used for reading material.

Because of the small size of the group (four to eight students is a good size), all students can be given an opportunity to contribute to the story. Personal involvement runs high when everyone has many opportunities to help develop the story. Furthermore, the small-group model permits the teacher to call on all members, rather than just a few, of the group for a rereading of the story.

The third type of language-experience story is the individual story. Individual language-experience stories are written by only one child and are used most frequently after students have mastered a beginning sight vocabulary and can proceed to develop and write their own stories. However, the students will still need many kinds of teacher assistance. The teacher may, for example, take dictation from students, help them with the spelling of a word, or suggest additional ideas for stories. Eventually, however, most students should be able to reach a level at which they can write stories independently.

Language experience can be the basis for whole-class, small-group, or individual stories.

Since most experience stories are written by small groups of students, we will present a set of procedures to follow when working with a few children at a time. You may choose to modify these procedures after you have gained experience with the approach. To begin, however, these three steps may provide valuable guidelines.

The First Step   The first step in implementing the language-experience approach with a small group of youngsters is to stimulate discussion about a topic of common interest. In this way all the students will have something to contribute when the story is being constructed. With beginning readers, a joint experience, such as a field trip to the dairy farm, or a concrete object that the group can touch, smell, and see may serve as a starting point for discussion. Thus something as simple as a bunch of grapes, an umbrella, or a statue can form the focus for the story. Discussion of the stimulus or stimulus event should be informal and wide-ranging, with the teacher and the students exploring the topic thoroughly. The teacher should encourage each student, even the most shy, to participate in the discussion. The concepts that are examined during the discussion and the words that are used to express these concepts will form the basis for the story that the children dictate later.

To help you get a clear picture of the first, and very important, step in the formation of a language-experience story, let us observe Ramon, Candy, Beth, and Billy and their first-grade teacher, Ms. Alvarez. Ms. Alvarez has brought a pair of wooden shoes to class, and the children are discussing the odd footwear. Ramon has some difficulty expressing himself in English, but Ms. Alvarez gently supplies some of the English vocabulary for which Ramon is searching. Beth tends to want to be the center of attention, explaining at length how she thinks the shoes were made. Ms. Alvarez suggests that Beth let Billy and Candy have a turn, but that then Beth may have another turn herself. Billy seems quite happy to give his views on the topic, now that Beth has moved from center stage. Candy, however, says nothing. In an attempt to draw the shy Candy into the discussion, Ms. Alvarez suggests that the youngster try on the shoes and tell the others how the shoes feel. Candy agrees and is soon clumping about the room, giggling. She gleefully reports that the shoes are too big, but that they really don't hurt her feet like she thought they would. The others insist on trying on the shoes, too, and discussion continues on a lively note.

More sophisticated discussions can occur when the language-experience approach is used with older students. A third-grade teacher might have a small group of students dictate a story about the statues found on Easter Island. As the students pass around a model of one of the statues, the teacher might lead a discussion of such questions as: "How do you think the actual statues were made?"; "What were they used for?"; "When were they made?"; "What do you think the people were like who made these statues?"

After everyone in the group has been given an opportunity to contribute to the discussion, students are asked to dictate sentences for the story. Some teachers like to ask students for a story title first. Our preference, however, is to wait until the story has been completed. Then students have to synthesize the main idea of the story before they can provide an appropriate title. Each student should be urged to contribute at least one sentence. The story dictation continues until the group concludes that enough sentences have been offered and the story seems complete. However, sometimes the students will need urging to expand a story beyond a few sentences, and at other times the teacher will need to limit their enthusiastic responses in order to keep the story to a manageable length.

Let us return to Ms. Alvarez and her first graders. The children are ready to dictate a story, and Ms. Alvarez has taped two pieces of large chart paper to the chalkboard, one on top of the other, so that her felt-tip marker will not soak through onto the chalkboard. Beth (naturally) has contributed the first sentence: "I like the wooden shoes." Ms. Alvarez has printed the words carefully on the chart paper. Now Billy offers: "Them shoes are hard." Ms. Alvarez smiles and repeats Billy's sentence as she writes it on the paper. She does not mention that "them shoes" is not standard English. She knows that if she corrects Billy now, he will probably be reluctant to contribute any more to the story. Furthermore, she is very sure that even if she writes "the shoes" or "those shoes," Billy will *read* "them shoes." Ramon wants Ms. Alvarez to write: "I like the wooden shoes." Ms. Alvarez points to the first sentence and asks Ramon if he knows what it says. He grins and reads "I like the. . . ." Ms. Alverez supplies "wooden," and Ramon finishes the sentence successfully. Realizing that his sentence is already part of the story, Ramon stops and thinks and then says, "Put down 'We walked in the shoes.'" Ms. Alvarez cheerfully complies and then turns to Candy, who is sitting attentively but silently. Ms. Alvarez asks Candy if she remembers how she felt when she had the shoes on. Very shyly, Candy says, "The shoes didn't hurt my feet," and Ms. Alvarez records the words on the chart. Then she asks the children to suggest a title for the story. Not surprisingly, they choose "The Wooden Shoes." The whole story is thus:

> The Wooden Shoes
>
> I like the wooden shoes.
>
> Them shoes are hard.
>
> We walked in the shoes.
>
> The shoes didn't hurt my feet.

After the story has been completed, the teacher should read the story to the group, being careful to move his or her hand under each word as it is read aloud. This movement should be smooth, and the teacher should avoid pointing to each word separately. Moving the hand across the page helps to emphasize that the teacher is reading the specific marks in that line and that reading moves from left to right.

After the teacher has read the story to the group one or two times, the children may be asked if they remember any of the words in the story. Words known by the students can be underlined; in this way, each child has an opportunity to show what he or she knows. If the group is advanced, the children may be asked to read the entire story with the teacher. In addition, individual students may be asked to find a favorite sentence and read it out loud for the rest of the group.

Impromptu skill instruction is usually conducted next. This skill instruction can deal with problems encountered by the children when reading the story. In addition, the story itself may present an opportunity to teach specific decoding or comprehension skills. If a child experiences difficulty pronouncing a word, for example, the teacher could show the group how to use context clues to help unlock the word. Or, perhaps the story would lend itself nicely to an explanation of how compound words are formed. The wooden-shoes story might provide an opportunity to teach the /sh/-*sh* letter-sound correspondence or the use of the plural marker *s*. Because the stories will be spontaneous, the teacher must be alert and ready to provide instruction on specific skills whenever problems occur or whenever the stories present opportunities for skill instruction.

Before the children return to their seats, the story is read again—by either the teacher or the students. This rereading of the story reinforces the skills and words that were taught earlier in the lesson and also marks the end of the group's activities for the first session.

Sometime before the next session, the teacher will need to make arrangements to have the dictated story reproduced so that each student will have his or her own copy. The stories are usually copied by either printing or typing them on ditto masters, with enough space left for children who care to illustrate their stories.

The Second Step   The next meeting of the reading group is usually held the following day. At this time, the teacher reviews the events of the first day. Next, she or he may read the story to the students. This rereading serves as a review for those who may have forgotten part of the story. Then either the entire group or selected individuals may read the story aloud. While all of this rereading may seem redundant, you should remember that these children are only learning to read and usually benefit from the continual rereading. The process of learning to read is so exciting to most children that they are far from bored by this repetition. In fact, with each rereading the children become more and more successful with reading the story and more confident in their emerging reading abilities.

After the story has been reviewed, the teacher should distribute the stories that have been duplicated. Each child thus receives a personal copy. Stauffer (1970) suggests that each child should now underline any words on the personal copy that he or she might know. Once the known words have been underlined, the children can illustrate their story. While the children are drawing or underlining words, the teacher needs to meet individually with each student. During this individual conference, the teacher should check the student's sight vocabulary by listening to the child read the story aloud. To determine whether a word is known in isolation as well as in context, the teacher can use his or her hands as a mask to block out the contextual clues available to the child. The teacher can also assess the word-identification strategies the child used while reading the story.

Once the teacher has met individually with each member of the group, the stories are collected and students return to their seats. This concludes the activities for the second session.

The third, and final, time students meet with the teacher, the whole group may be asked to orally reread the story, first as a group and then individually. Again, the teacher should carefully note any problems one or more children may be having while reading the story. Once the story has been read, students are given the copies of the story on which they underlined the words they knew. During this session the children are asked to draw a second line under words that they still recognize. While the group is doing this, the teacher meets individually with students to assess whether the words that have been underlined twice are indeed "sight words." If a child knows a word without the use of contextual clues, she or he prints the word on an index card or a piece of oaktag. These words become part of each child's "word bank."

The Third Step

A word bank is simply a collection of the words in a child's sight-word vocabulary. Each word that has been identified as a word known to the child is kept in his or her word bank. Askland (1973) suggests modifying the word-bank concept by including not only known words, but also a "Words I Am Learning" section. The words in this section may not have been included in experience stories, but are of great personal interest to a particular child. For example, one child may develop a sudden fascination for motorcycles and ask for word cards for *motorcycles, Honda,* and *bike,* even though no story has been written using these words. Another child may select *grandmother* and *visit* to reflect a unique event in his or her own life. The teacher can keep a tally on whether the individual words are truly being learned, by placing a checkmark on the back of a word card each time the word is correctly decoded. Then, after three or four checks, the word can be included in the regular section of the word bank.

Words that have been learned from the language-experience stories themselves can have numbers printed on the back of their cards corresponding to the number assigned to each story. For example, all of the word-bank cards that have been learned from the third story would have the number 3 on them. This enables a child who may have "forgotten" a previously learned word to return to his or her collection of stories, identify the appropriate story, and unlock the word with the assistance of the original story context.

Shoe boxes, file card boxes, folders, or envelopes may be used to hold the cards for word banks. Many teachers prefer to use fairly large word cards (about 3″ × 9″). These large word cards allow children to trace the letters with their fingers, thereby helping them attend to the distinctive features of the words. Small word cards, on the other hand, permit students to manipulate

Uses of Word Banks

the cards easily, as when they arrange the words in sentences as an independent learning activity.

Both Quandt (1973) and Veatch *et al.* (1973) suggest excellent follow-up activities that can be used with word cards found in word banks. Some of them are:

1. Classifying things that you can see.
2. Classifying things that you can hear.
3. Classifying things that you can eat or drink.
4. Classifying things that make you happy.
5. Classifying things that make you sad.
6. Using the word cards for making sentences.
7. Making a picture of the word.
8. Finding matching or similar words in books, magazines, or newspapers.
9. Making compound words.
10. Making riddles using the words.
11. Writing the words on the chalkboard.
12. Typing the words on a primary typewriter.
13. Using the words for an individualized spelling program.
14. Flashing the words to a partner.
15. Finding rhyming words in the bank.
16. Illustrating the words on the back of the word cards.
17. Acting out words.
18. Telling stories about favorite words.
19. Finding words that describe someone.
20. Writing words in sand or in salt.

Many activities can be designed around word banks. Most of these activities can be pursued individually by children as free-time choices, once classroom routines have been established.

THE LANGUAGE-EXPERIENCE CLASSROOM

The teacher becomes the director of learning in the language-experience approach (Matteoni, 1973; Shohen, 1973). Whereas teachers who use basal readers may feel that the essential skills of reading can be taught simply by following the commercially published material, teachers who use the language-experience approach do not have this security (be it real or imagined). Instead, unless they use some type of diagnostic testing, they must rely heavily on their own observations to determine skill needs. Furthermore, they must offer suggestions for writing, help students with spelling difficulties, organize independent activities for children, and evaluate each student's progress in reading as well as writing, usually without the guidance of a teacher manual (Allen, 1968). Clearly, this is a difficult and demanding job.

One way of making the teacher's job somewhat easier is to enlist the aid of parents or older-student volunteers. Volunteers can help students write their stories and books or can aid the children in word-bank activities. Care should be taken, however, that these helpers are thoroughly familiar with the philosophy and techniques of the language-experience approach. For example, they must understand that they are to write down exactly what the child says and not edit the child's writing. They must be careful to use manuscript writing and to give the child many opportunities to read the story aloud. The teacher will need to give volunteers specific tasks and explicit guidelines for carrying out these tasks.

The physical appearance of the language-experience classroom usually differs from that of the basal-program classroom. Science, math, or art areas are often found interspersed throughout the room. At these learning areas children learn to use reading in functional ways. Trade books as well as student-produced books abound so that the students can practice their reading skills with unfamiliar materials. A listening center or recording area may be set off to one side of the room. Materials for writing, such as chalk, felt-tipped pens, crayons, pencils, paper, and slates are available for student authors. Filmstrips or a picture file might be set up for the students to use as sources for story ideas. "Idea files," which stimulate written stories, and "story starters" (unfinished stories) are sometimes used. Spelling helps, such as lists of high-frequency words or picture dictionaries, are readily accessible. Frequently, the teacher will have labeled many of the objects around the room, such as *tables, chairs, desks, clock, door, windows, flag,* and *chalkboard,* so that student writers can use these labels as spelling aids.

Criscuolo (1976) describes what he terms "discovery spots," which can be set up in the language-experience classroom and which assist students in becoming independent readers. "Discovery spots" are creative enrichment projects designed to allow children to work independently or in small groups. "Discovery spots" can be formed from a variety of materials, including large envelopes, file folders, cartons, or boxes. Bulletin boards or counter top and table displays can also contain "discovery spots." Craft corners, magazines, suggestion boxes, a plant area with related books, a biographical picture area, an old typewriter, reference materials, and a story-shaping corner all have been effectively used in classrooms to foster interest in reading and writing (Criscuolo, 1976, p. 378).

SPECIAL USES OF THE LANGUAGE-EXPERIENCE APPROACH

The language-experience approach need not be used only as an approach for teaching first graders to read. Some children will be ready for this type of instruction in kindergarten. In addition, the language-experience approach may be especially beneficial for students who speak non-standard English or for whom English is a second language. Finally, the language-experience approach can be used at any elementary-grade level by teachers interested in integrating their reading and writing programs.

Language Experience in the Kindergarten

Challenged by the number of youngsters coming to school with a sight-reading vocabulary, many kindergarten teachers are turning to the language-experience approach to assist them in meeting the needs of these precocious young-sters. The kindergarten curriculum of ten years ago is no longer applicable for many of today's avid television viewers. A number of these students come to school with the readiness skills they need to ensure a successful beginning in reading.

Many kindergarten teachers are opposed to using basal readers with their students. Using the language-experience approach is often a very satisfactory alternative. There is no pressure on students when this approach is used. There are no books to be finished, no workbooks to complete, and no calls for work-sheets to be answered correctly. Students can feel confident and secure when reading their own sentences or stories. And there is seldom the pressure to compete against their peers. Children with extremely varied reading skills can be "successful" in reading because of the flexibility of the language-experience approach. Sandy, who is already beginning to read, can read the entire chart to the teacher. Anna can feel successful by reading just the one sentence she dictated herself. Eddie can be made to feel that he is doing a good job by finding two words in the story that he can read or three words that begin with the same letter. Each child can truly learn to read as much and as fast as she or he is able. Most important, those who are not ready to learn to read will not feel that they are failures at the age of five.

Black Dialect and Reading

Each region of the country has a unique dialect. You are probably familiar with regional dialects. A Midwesterner traveling through Rhode Island, for example, would soon learn that *cah* is simply another way to say *car*. *Soar* is not something you do in a sailplane, but what you do when you're cutting a piece of wood. Each geographic region of the United States has its own par-ticular language idiosyncrasies. But one dialect is no better than the others. These language variances should be thought of simply as being *different*, not deficient. This is true for ethnic dialects, such as black dialect, too. Unless black students have been totally deprived of language experiences, they too have acquired the syntactic forms of their language by the time they come to school (Saville, 1970). So although black dialect is different from the standard forms of English, it is not a deficient form of language, since it has its own fully formed phonological and grammatical systems.

It is important to remember that a child need not be black to speak black dialect. Any child, regardless of race, raised in a neighborhood where black dialect is spoken will more than likely speak some form of that dialect. Furthermore, not all blacks speak black English.

The most important instructional implication of dialectal differences is that a "mismatch" may exist between the child's language and the language of the printed text. This mismatch may be in any or all of the three language systems: phonology, syntax, or semantics. The greater the divergence between the language of the reading text and the student's language, the greater this "mismatch" will be. Unfortunately, "the black child is baffled by this con-fusing and arbitrary relationship between unfamiliar sounds and symbols" (Melmed, 1973).

Labov (1970) points out five major phonological differences between standard English and most varieties of black English:

		Text	Speech
1.	Vowel variations	pin	pen
		beer	bear
2.	r'lessness	tore	toe
		Paris	pass
3.	l'lessness	toll	toe
		tool	two
4.	Simplification of final consonant clusters	ghost	ghoss
		past	pass
5.	Weakening of final consonants	road	row
		seat	sea

As a result of these dialectal differences, a student may pronounce some words or phrases differently from the teacher. For example, when reading "The man tore past me on the road," a speaker of black dialect might actually say, "The man toe pass me on the row." However, if the words pronounced in the student's dialect are the words of the text, the child is successfully reading, and attempts to change the child's pronunciation should not be made under the guise of reading instruction.

More important problems arise when the grammatical patterns (syntax) of the reader and the text differ to any great extent. The reader relies heavily on language to help predict which words will be encountered as a sentence is read. If the syntax of the reader and the author are dissimilar, the predictability of the printed text will decrease, and a greater opportunity will exist for confusion or misconceptions than if the syntax of reader and writer matched (Goodman and Burke, 1972).

A teacher wishing to increase the correspondence between the language of the reader and the language on the printed page may consider three alternatives (Martin and Castanada, 1970). The first is to change the language of the child. Trying to change five or six years of preschool language development is almost impossible, however. (Have you ever tried to correct a person who says "ain't"?) Furthermore, "correcting" a child's language may lead to a negative self-concept. Another alternative is to change the reading material. One way this can be accomplished is by writing and publishing "dialect basal readers." But because so many different dialects are spoken in this country and because of the high cost of producing such a set of materials, this option is not very practical. A third alternative is not to rely on commercially prepared materials, but instead use the language of the child as a basis for instruction — the language-experience approach.

Many educators and linguists (Baratz, 1969; Cramer, 1971; Goodman, 1971) view the language-experience approach as the most valid alternative for teaching reading to children who speak black dialect. The language-experience approach has two important advantages over the other alternatives mentioned: It is inexpensive to implement, and it can strengthen the concept that the child's language is only different, not deficient.

Although it is generally accepted that speakers of black dialect will eventually need to learn to read standard dialect, there is little reason to ask young children to cope with unfamiliar syntactic structures during the early stages of reading (Stewart, 1969). Accordingly, teachers must be willing to accept and transcribe the dictated language of the speaker of black dialect. To edit these stories is to destroy the very advantage initially gained when choosing this approach.

Bilingual Readers

Students whose native language is not English may also experience difficulty when learning to read. The closer the sound-symbol correspondence between the two languages, the less trouble beginning readers will have with learning to decode (Modiano, 1973). If there is great divergence between the two languages, however, the child may be unable to recognize some of the spoken sounds of English. For example, in Spanish the sound heard at the beginning of *Jane* and *jump* is not used. The letter *j* in Spanish usually has the /h/ sound, as in *hot (La Jolla)*, or the /w/ sound, as in *Juanita* and *San Joaquin*. If there is significant mismatch between the sound system of English and that of the student's native language, reading instruction for this student should deemphasize phonic analysis and rely more on using the whole language of the child. Finocchiaro (1964) recommends using the language-experience approach to help overcome the mismatch between two different phonological systems.

The language-experience approach has often been quite successful (Garcia, 1974) for students for whom English is a second language. Steinberg (1976) helped non-English-speaking students write experience stories in a comic-book format. She found that she was able to successfully introduce reading through this modified language-experience approach; the students found the stories to be meaningful and enjoyable. Chapman (1977) found the language-experience approach valuable when dealing with syntactic differences between Spanish and English. Students were allowed to dictate stories in a combination of English and Spanish that reflected their current ability to use English. The assumption made was that as their ability to use English orally improved, their stories would more nearly resemble standard English. But in the meantime, the students would not be hampered by having to translate English syntax into Spanish syntax before they could understand what they had decoded.

Bilingual students need not find reading to be a frustrating experience if they are given reading material that is geared to their language patterns and experiences. The language-experience approach seems to be the most appropriate vehicle for ensuring their reading success.

Writing and Reading

An interesting, yet simple, way of interrelating the teaching of writing and reading is through the *Can't Stop Writing* program (Allington, 1975). In this program teachers set aside specified amounts of time each week just for writing. The students are allowed to write about any topic they choose. Quantity, rather than quality, of writing is emphasized during these sessions, and the children are encouraged to get their *ideas* down on paper without undue concern about perfectly accurate spelling or punctuation. Unknown spelling words are provided when needed, since the goal of the program is to practice written composition, not spelling. At the end of the period, papers are collected, and positive comments are supplied whenever warranted. Skill needs are also identified from these papers. These needs form the basis for instruction in writing techniques at a later time. Papers are not marked for errors; instead, the positive characteristics of writing are stressed.

Because of its flexible nature, the language-experience approach may be adapted in many different ways to meet the special needs of different students. Although the lack of a structured program may at times be viewed as a disadvantage, the unstructured nature of the language-experience approach is actually one of its greatest assets, because the program is so readily adaptable.

One potential weakness in relying exclusively on the language-experience approach to teach reading is the lack of a structured skill-development program. Using students' oral language as the basis for their reading instruction makes good sense. Yet we have seen competent teachers become unnerved and rattled because parents—and principals—have questioned whether students are learning the necessary reading skills. Even the strongest teacher is bound to crumble and discontinue this approach if badgered long enough. This is unfortunate. A skills-management system may be useful as a means of checking the skill-development progress of students as they dictate or write their own reading material. Then when parents inquire about their child's reading ability, the teacher will be able to offer some specific information of a concrete nature about skill development as well as overall reading progress.

APPLICATION: USING A SKILLS-MANAGEMENT SYSTEM WITH THE LANGUAGE-EXPERIENCE APPROACH

One way to work on skill needs while using the language-experience approach is to have the children construct stories that call for the use of specific skills. Let's set up a hypothetical situation: You are (at last!) a first-grade teacher and are using the language-experience approach. You have learned, through either the results of a test in your skills-management system or your own observation, that eight students in your classroom need help with learning contractions. You group these students for focused instruction on that skill while the other students are working independently. Before you actually take dictation for the story, you present a short "minilesson" on contractions to these eight students. You show them that a contraction is simply a shortened form of a word, and you list examples on the chalkboard for reference during the dictation of the story.

Next, you follow the normal steps for constructing the story. But instead of permitting the students to supply any type of sentence, you encourage them to think of sentences that make sense in the story and, whenever possible, also contain contractions. Naturally, you don't want the quality of the story to

Constructing Skill Stories

suffer at the expense of including a contraction in every sentence, but the children will likely be able to use contractions in very natural ways in the story. The story becomes the vehicle for learning the skills, and the rereading of the dictation reinforces the skills in a meaningful context. Thus you have the best of both worlds—instruction in skill development and stories made up of the children's own oral language.

One word of caution: Some skills lend themselves to this approach more readily than others do. For example, structural-analysis skills, such as the recognition of plural and possessive forms, can probably be taught in this manner more easily than many phonics skills. However, at times somewhat artificial stories using particular phonics elements can be constructed by presenting stimuli that incorporate those elements. For example, if a group of children need work on the /sh/-*sh* sound-letter correspondence, the teacher might show the children pictures of shoes, a shovel, a lamp shade, a window shade, and a shack. After discussing these objects and after having a short lesson on the /sh/-*sh* correspondence, the children could be asked to create a story that uses as many words with the /sh/ sound as possible.

After-the-Fact Instruction

A second way to work on skill instruction with the language-experience approach is to focus on specific skills after a story has been written. Again, in your hypothetical class, you have identified several students who need help in comprehension, specifically in reading for details at the literal level. Rather than conduct a mini–skill lesson before the story is written, in after-the-fact instruction you will eliminate this step, since the skill of reading for details is one that lends itself to being taught *after* the story has been written.

In this approach, after the story has been dictated and recorded, you reread it to the class, and some children volunteer to read selected sentences aloud. Then, after the oral rereading, skill instruction takes place as students are asked to find answers to detail questions at the literal level. The students verify their answers by finding the appropriate section(s) of the story and reading it orally. Students who have difficulty answering the questions are shown how to find the answers.

This approach, too, lends itself to some skills and not others. Regardless of what words are dictated for a story, you will always be able to teach sight vocabulary, initial and final consonants, some vowel patterns, main idea, and detail. Words for which other skills might be taught may not appear as spontaneously as those just identified. Nor will all stories lend themselves to lessons on sequence or inferences. With experience, however, you'll learn which skills need to be taught in a more "structured" lesson.

THINKING ABOUT THE LANGUAGE-EXPERIENCE APPROACH

We think that the language-experience approach has many advantages, especially for beginning readers or for students who have experienced failure when learning to read with another approach. Let's examine some of the reasons why we think the language-experience approach has much to offer. We will alert you to some of its shortcomings, too.

The language-experience approach, more than any other technique used to teach reading, requires the students to integrate the encoding skills of speaking and writing and the decoding skills of reading and listening. The students' thoughts can be expressed verbally, and this speech can be transcribed and read. Thus the material children are asked to read is a visual representation of their own speech.

Furthermore, reading skills are used to read fully formed language right from the start. Comprehension skills and decoding skills are applied in story contexts rather than only when completing worksheets or workbooks. Because instruction in and application of these skills take place in meaningful contexts, there is greater chance for transfer of learning to reading tasks outside of reading class.

Another major advantage of using the language-experience approach is high student involvement. The dictated stories are meaningful to the students because these stories are related to student experiences. In addition, the language of the students forms the text of the story, thereby ensuring a close match between speech and print. Both of these factors result in high student interest and in greater comprehension.

Contrary to the fears of some teachers, students who learn to read with the language-experience approach do not suffer from exposure to a restricted vocabulary. Packer (1970), for example, found that students taught with this approach learned to read many of the same words found in basal readers. Henderson (1972) found similar results. This is only to be expected, because function words (conjunctions, articles, prepositions, etc.) make up a large proportion of the words that appear in both children's oral language and printed material. This fact led Henderson (1972, p. 28) to conclude: "Thus it would appear that the natural frequency of their (function words) occurrence in the language suffices for their early acquisition and that unnatural schedules of reinforcement are not necessary to insure their selection."

Children taught with the language-experience do not suffer from inadequate sight vocabularies. Instead, with the exception of story-specific words found in basal readers, they basically learn the same words that their peers using the basal reader learn.

One of the major dangers in teaching reading with the language-experience approach is that the teaching of skills may be haphazard, since there is no identified sequence of skills to be followed. Unless the teacher keeps track of skill development, some skills may never be taught, and others may be taught over and over, needlessly. In addition, some students may need a structured approach to skill development. They benefit from focused skill-development lessons before being asked to apply the skill in context. These students need step-by-step directions indicating how skills can be applied.

There are also inherent dangers in using student-dictated stories. Although these stories may indeed foster high student involvement, students should learn that reading also includes such things as being able to locate information in reference materials and reading content-oriented texts. The language-experience approach, because it is primarily a program for beginning reading, does not provide instruction in these types of study skills. In addition, because the stories are so familiar to the young readers, some children may tend to memorize the stories rather than read them.

Another problem with this approach is that it requires a great deal of teacher time to implement correctly. Furthermore, the teacher must be confident that he or she has both the time and expertise to organize and manage a relatively unstructured program. The other demands placed on classroom teachers make it difficult to find the time for planning and implementing this approach properly.

SUMMARY: EXPANDING HORIZONS—THE LANGUAGE-EXPERIENCE APPROACH

In this chapter we have introduced the language-experience approach, which capitalizes on the language ability students possess. The language-experience approach may be used by itself, as a supplement to a basal reader program, or in conjunction with a skills-management system.

After reading this chapter, you should be familiar with three steps that can be used when teaching with the language-experience approach. As you gain confidence and experience, you may choose to make modifications in these steps to better suit the strengths and weaknesses of your students.

The classroom of a teacher who uses the language-experience approach may differ from one in which only the basal reader is used. We have given several examples of how learning activities and learning centers can be used in this type of classroom. We have also shown how the language-experience approach can be used to teach kindergarten students and students with nonstandard English dialects. Because using the language-experience approach reduces the chance of a mismatch between the language of the printed page and the reader's language, this approach has much to offer when teaching speakers of nonstandard English or bilingual students to read.

We have presented two plans that can be used to help integrate the teaching of specific reading skills with the language-experience approach. In the first method the teacher first focuses on specific skills and then integrates these skills with the dictated story. In the second approach the teacher focuses on specific skills that appear in a story after the story has been transcribed. Each of these two methods lends itself to instruction in specific types of skills.

Finally, we discussed several advantages and disadvantages of using this approach. We pointed out that the integration of reading skills, the high degree of student involvement, and the acquisition of a meaningful sight vocabulary are positive features of this approach. One major shortcoming of this approach, however, is that skill development may be haphazard. In addition, its unstructured nature fails to help those students who need direct, focused skill instruction. Integrating a skills-management system with the language-experience approach may help the teacher overcome this disadvantage.

We believe that the language-experience approach has much to offer those individuals who are willing to move beyond basal readers. That's why we have called this chapter "Expanding Horizons: The Language-Experience Approach."

1. Think of implementing the language-experience approach using a three-step process. Can you identify the specific procedures you might follow within each of the three major steps? List them in a simple outline form to help you remember them.

2. Describe how a skills-management system can be used with the language-experience approach. How might a skills-management system enhance your language-experience reading program? How might it be used to assist skill development in this program?

3. Are there any situations in which the language-experience approach would clearly be the most appropriate technique to use to teach reading? Are there situations in which this approach would *not* be appropriate? What criteria would you use for making these decisions? List them.

4. Explain the advantages and disadvantages of using this approach to teach reading. Are there any precautions you might take to overcome the disadvantages of this program? Describe them.

Allen, Roach Van. "How a Language-Experience Program Works," in Elaine Vilscek, ed., *A Decade of Innovations: Approaches to Beginning Reading* (Newark, Delaware: International Reading Association, 1968).

Allen, Roach Van, and Claryce Allen. *Language Experiences in Reading*, Level I, Teacher's resource book (Chicago: Encyclopaedia Britannica Press, 1970a).

_____. *Language Experiences in Reading*, Level II, Teacher's resource book (Chicago: Encyclopaedia Britannica Press, 1970b).

Allington, Richard. "Sustained Approaches to Reading and Writing," *Language Arts* **52**, 6 (1975): 813–815.

Askland, Linda C. "Conducting Individual Language Experience Stories," *Reading Teacher* **27**, 2 (1973): 167–170.

Baratz, Joan. "Teaching Reading in an Urban Negro School System," in Joan C. Baratz and Roger W. Shuy, eds., *Teaching Black Children to Read* (Washington, D.C.: Center for Applied Linguistics, 1969), pp. 92–116.

Chapman, Barbara H. "LEA Solves Syntax for the Spanish Speaking Child," *Reading Teacher* **31**, 2 (1977): 151–153.

Criscuolo, Nicholas P., "Mag Bags, Peg Sheds, Crafty Crannies, and Reading," *Reading Teacher* **29**, 4 (1976): 376–378.

Cramer, Ronald L. "Dialectology—A Case for Language Experience," *Reading Teacher* **25**, 1 (1971): 33–39.

Finocchiaro, Mary. *Teaching Children Foreign Languages* (New York: McGraw-Hill, 1964).

Garcia, Ricardo L. "Mexican Americans Learn Through Language Experience," *Reading Teacher* **28**, 3 (1974): 301–305.

Goodman, Kenneth S. "Children's Language and Experience: A Place to Begin," in Helen M. Smith, ed., *Coordinating Reading Instruction* (Glenview, Ill.: Scott, Foresman, 1971), pp. 46–52.

_____. "Psycholinguistic Universals in the Reading Process," in Frank Smith, ed., *Psycholinguistics and Reading* (New York: Holt, Rinehart, and Winston, 1973), pp. 21–27.

Goodman, Yetta M., and Carolyn L. Burke. *Reading Miscue Inventory* (New York: Macmillan, 1972).

Hall, MaryAnne. "Linguistically Speaking, Why Language Experience?" *Reading Teacher* 25, 4 (1972): 328–331.

Henderson, Edmund H. "Group Instruction in a Language-Experience Approach," *Reading Teacher* 26, 6 (1973): 589–597.

Henderson, Edmund H., Thomas H. Estes, and Susan Stonecash. "An Exploration Study of Word Acquisition among First-Graders at Midyear in a Language Experience Approach," *Journal of Reading Behavior* 4, 3 (Summer 1972): 21–31.

Labov, W. "Language Characteristics—Blacks," in T. D. Horn, ed., *Reading for the Disadvantaged: Problems of Linguistically Different Learners* (New York: Harcourt, Brace and World, 1970), pp. 139–157.

Martin, Clyde I., and Alberta M. Castaneda. "Nursery School and Kindergarten," in T. Horn, ed., *Reading for the Disadvantaged* (Newark, Delaware: International Reading Association, 1970), pp. 169–177.

Matteoni, Louise. "Developing Reading Ability through the Language Experience Approach," in Thomas C. Barrett and Dale D. Johnson, eds., *Views on Elementary Reading Instruction* (Newark, Delaware: International Reading Association, 1973), pp. 49–55.

Melmed, Paul Jay. "Black English Phonology: The Question of Reading Interference," in James L. Laffey and Roger Shuy, eds., *Language Differences: Do They Interfere?* (Newark, Delaware: International Reading Association, 1973), pp. 70–85.

Modiano, Nancy. "Juanita's Reading Problems: Foreign Language Interference and Reading Skill Acquisition," in James L. Laffey and Roger Shuy, eds., *Language Differences: Do They Interfere?* (Newark, Delaware: International Reading Association, 1973), pp. 29–39.

Packer, Athol B. "Ashton-Warner's Key Vocabulary for the Disadvantaged," *Reading Teacher* 23, 6 (1970): 559–564.

Quandt, Ivan. "Investing in Word Banks—a Practice for any Approach," *Reading Teacher* 27, 2 (1973): 171–173.

Ruddell, Robert. "Effect of the Similarity of Oral and Written Patterns of Language Structure in Reading Comprehension," *Elementary English* 42 (1965): 403–410.

Saville, Muriel R. "Language and the Disadvantaged," in T. Horn, ed., *Reading for the Disadvantaged* (Newark, Delaware: International Reading Association, 1970), pp. 115–134.

Shohen, Sam. "A Language Experience Approach to Reading Instruction," in Thomas C. Barrett and Dale D. Johnson, eds., *Views on Elementary Reading Instruction* (Newark, Delaware: International Reading Association, 1973), pp. 43–48.

Stauffer, Russell G. *The Language Experience Approach to the Teaching of Reading* (New York: Harper & Row, 1970).

Steinberg, Zina. "Batman Books: Homemade First Readers," *Reading Teacher* **29**, 7 (1976): 676–682.

Stewart, William A. "On the Use of Negro Dialect in the Teaching of Reading," in Joan C. Baratz and Roger W. Shuy, eds., *Teaching Black Children to Read* (Washington, D.C.: Center for Applied Linguistics, 1969), pp. 156–219.

Tathum, Susan. "Reading Comprehension of Materials Written with Selected Oral Language Patterns," Ph.D. diss., University of Wisconsin—Madison, 1968.

Thorn, Elizabeth. "Language Experience Approach to Reading," *Reading Teacher* **23**, 1 (1969): 3–8.

Veatch, Jeannette *et al. Key Words to Reading: The Language Experience Approach Begins* (Columbus, Ohio: Charles E. Merrill, 1973).

Chapter 11
Individualized
Reading
Instruction

After reading this chapter, you will be able to:

1. Define what is meant by the term "individualized reading instruction."
2. List several reasons why a need for this type of instruction exists.
3. Describe the procedures followed when implementing an individualized reading program.
4. Conduct teacher-pupil conferences.
5. Explain how to coordinate a skills-management system with an individualized reading program.
6. List the advantages and disadvantages of the individualized approach.

INDIVIDUALIZED READING INSTRUCTION IN PERSPECTIVE

We have already described two major approaches used to teach students to read in kindergarten or first grade: the basal-reader and language-experience approaches. Once students have begun to acquire a sight vocabulary and decoding skills, they may move into a program based more on free selection of reading materials. This type of program is called individualized, or personalized, reading. Individualized reading instruction is based on the premise that students' interests, abilities, and needs should largely dictate the material they read. This type of reading program rejects the notion that any single textbook is appropriate for a group of students.

A DEFINITION OF INDIVIDUALIZED READING INSTRUCTION

Individualized reading instruction is based on the beliefs that students can: (1) find their own reading materials; (2) select materials that are interesting to them and at an appropriate reading level; and (3) read these materials at a pace commensurate with their abilities. If a cross section of classrooms in which individualized reading instruction was used were examined, a number of elements common to these classrooms could be identified, even though the classrooms might be noticeably different.

1. Trade books (library books) would constitute the primary source of reading material. In addition, some students might be reading newspapers, magazines, and basal readers.
2. Children would spend a large portion of the "reading period" doing independent, silent reading in materials of their own choosing.
3. There would be some type of focused skill instruction. In some instances the teacher would supply needed skill instruction on an impromptu basis, whenever the needs of students dictated. In other instances there might be a more formal plan for supplying needed skill instruction, such as daily, 15-minute meetings of small skills groups.
4. Teachers would maintain some type of record-keeping system to keep track of the students' skill development, the number and types of books they had read, and other instructional data. In some instances students might be responsible for some of the record keeping, noting the number and type of books they had read and maintaining a list of unknown words that they had encountered in their reading.

An individualized reading program can take many forms.

5. Teacher-student conferences would be held frequently to assess and discuss each student's reading progress. Decoding, comprehension, and study skills would be frequently checked during these 10- to 15-minute meetings. Teachers might use this conference to encourage a student to read in other interest areas or to try more (or less) challenging books.

6. Small-group or whole-class sharing periods would be conducted to give students an opportunity to discuss the books they had read with other members of the class.

Now that you know what individualized reading instruction *is*, you should also know what it is *not*. First, it is not *individual* instruction. Individual instruction is one-to-one teaching—one teacher meeting with each student alone. We feel that it is unnecessary for the teacher to meet with every student individually. Whenever students demonstrate common needs, such as in the area of skill development, it only makes good sense to group the students together for instruction. By doing this, the teacher makes more efficient use of his or her time and energy. There may be instances, though, when one-to-one instruction is necessary in an individualized reading program, as with any reading program. A precocious first or second grader, for example, may be so advanced that he or she could benefit from a quick lesson on how to use the library and card catalog. Naturally, a good teacher would try to supply the needed instruction. On the other hand, one student may be having great difficulty learning a particular skill and may need individual tutoring temporarily. However, such one-to-one teaching situations would be an exception rather than common practice in an individualized reading program.

In addition, individualized reading programs should not be confused with recreational-reading programs. Recreational-reading programs are designed only to help students understand that reading can be an enjoyable experience (Dolch, 1962). These programs foster independent reading, but lack some of the essential features of an individualized reading program: a skills-instruction component, a plan for keeping records of students' progress, teacher-student conferences, and book-sharing sessions.

THE NEED FOR INDIVIDUALIZED READING INSTRUCTION

There is an obvious need for individualized reading instruction. If students are expected to transfer school learning outside of the confines of the elementary school classroom, their experiences should be structured in ways that make clear the relationship between classroom and nonclassroom learning. We question whether many students understand that basal-reader programs are intended to "liberate" them to read trade books. So often students perceive "reading" to be reading orally from basal readers, completing workbook pages, or handing in duplicated worksheets. Often these students fail to see reading as an enjoyable, leisure-time activity. Reading is perceived as what they do in school 8:30–10:00 A.M.

Because individualized reading instruction doesn't rely on basal-reader texts, students are not as likely to have misperceptions about what constitutes this thing called "reading." Reading can be done at any time, in any place and with a variety of materials, and (surprise, surprise!) can even take place in the absence of a teacher.

Range of Reading Abilities

Classroom teachers often discuss how difficult it is to meet the needs of all their students. First-grade teachers are concerned that each student experience success in the initial steps of learning to read. Sixth-grade teachers face a different problem; they must supply appropriate instruction to students of widely differing abilities. Individual differences *increase* as students pass from grade to grade. Consider a commonsense rule of thumb: By multiplying the chronological age of a child by two-thirds, one can estimate the range of reading abilities in an average classroom at that age level. This formula can be expressed as: $\frac{2}{3} \times$ chronological age $=$ reading range. If the average age in a class of first graders is assumed to be six years, the range of abilities in this class would amount to a four-year span, according to the formula. Some children might be reading at a second-grade level, whereas others might be nonreaders who will not begin to read for another year or two.

Sixth-grade teachers face an even wider range of abilities. If you take eleven years as the average age and apply the formula, the range of ability in this class can be predicted to be a little more than seven years. Some of the students might be reading at a second-grade level, whereas others might be reading at almost a tenth-grade level. The expected range of abilities in any one grade can be illustrated as in Fig. 11.1.

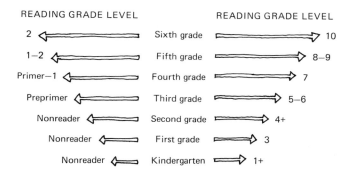

Fig. 11.1. Range of reading abilities in elementary-grade classroom.

Because of such wide ranges in reading abilities, if children are divided into only three or four reading groups, based on overall reading achievement level, some students are likely to be working with materials that are too difficult, and others will be reading materials that are not challenging enough. One technique for better meeting the needs of students is to replace the practice of achievement grouping with an individualized reading program.

Personalized Reading Instruction

A second reason for implementing individualized reading programs is that such programs place strong emphasis on the personal satisfactions that can be achieved through reading. Hunt (1967) contends that basal-reader programs are inclined to stress intensive analytical reading, which restricts the enjoyment that can be derived from reading. A program in which students are allowed to choose their own reading materials and are given ample time actually to *read* will help children learn to enjoy, rather than just to tolerate, reading.

GETTING READY

A casual observer of a well-functioning individualized reading program may assume that such a loosely organized program virtually "runs itself." Actually, because of the lack of structure, an individualized reading program may require a great deal of "behind-the-scenes" management, even before the program is implemented.

Knowing What You're Getting Into

Preparation for launching an individualized reading program involves two important steps. First, the teacher must be convinced that he or she is really committed to this kind of program. Second, the teacher must feel professionally ready to deal with an individualized program.

We would strongly urge teachers contemplating the use of an individualized program to be sure that they are willing to make the great commitment of time and energy necessary for the success of such a program. Because no manual exists to tell the teacher what to do and no prepackaged set of materials is available for children to work with, the *teacher* must prepare all of the instructional procedures and gather all of the reading matter and other instructional materials. Unless the teacher is willing to spend the needed time, the program may degenerate into an unstructured program of free reading in which either children teach themselves to read or no one does.

In addition to the commitment of time for preparing for instruction and for gathering materials, time must also be allotted for preparing children to work within the unstructured freedom of the program. We have found that it takes anywhere from nine to twelve weeks just to get intermediate-grade youngsters acquainted with the necessary routines and responsibilities. Younger students will probably need even more time.

The teacher must also feel confident about his or her own professional competence to teach reading with so little guidance from published materials. The teacher must be certain that he or she has a thorough grasp of the complexities of reading, of reading-skill development, and of techniques for improving reading abilities. If a teacher feels uncertain in any of these areas or does not have a clear picture of how an individualized program would work on a day-to-day basis, he or she might consult professional journals, such as *The Reading Teacher* or *Language Arts*, or reading-methods textbooks for further descriptions of how to make individualized reading successful. A series of visits to a nearby school in which individualized reading is used might be planned. An inservice program presented under the guidance of a local university professor, reading consultant, or language arts director might be organized. These kinds of outside guidance can help a teacher gain the confidence necessary for a successful reading program.

Preparing Parents and Students

The teacher is not the only person who needs to be prepared for an individualized reading program. The parents of the students and the students themselves need to have a clear understanding of the program and how it works.

Informing Parents

It is a good idea to "sell" the program to parents before actually beginning to implement it, since they may become concerned when their child doesn't have a basal-reader text. This can be accomplished in several ways. One technique is to explain the plan to parents individually during teacher-parent conferences. Because of the privacy of the conference, parents may feel free to ask questions, especially about their own child's ability to cope with this type of program.

Another way of informing parents is to explain the individualized reading program at a parent-teacher organization meeting. The principal and/or reading specialist might respond to questions about the overall organization and implications of the program. Then individual teachers might meet with the parents of children in their classes to answer specific questions.

A third way of informing parents about the program is to send a letter home with each child. In the letter the teacher should explain that there are many ways to teach reading and that he or she has chosen the individualized reading approach. A brief description of the approach should be given, including an emphasis that this approach fosters a love for reading by permitting students to read materials that they choose. There should also be some mention of how skill instruction will be provided.

The following is an adaptation of a letter a second-grade teacher sent home with her students. You may want to use it as a model for a letter of your own.

Dear Parents,

Reading is an important subject in the school curriculum, especially in the primary grades. Therefore, it is necessary that each child develop a permanent interest in and love of reading and master a variety of reading skills.

There are different methods of teaching reading, many of which group children according to their level of reading achievement.

One method of teaching reading *not* based on reading groups is the individualized reading approach. We have started this approach in our classroom this week. In this method each child reads at his or her own level from a book in which the child is interested. The child chooses a book, under my guidance, that he or she wants to read. After the child has read the book, we have an individual conference. At that conference comprehension is checked, and help may be given with skill instruction. In addition, tests are given to check the areas in which each child needs special help. Skills will be taught individually or in groups, depending on the results of these tests. Any grouping will be based on interests and needed skills. I will keep records of each child's progress and will take note of any problems that he or she may have in reading.

Children will have their own word lists taken from the books they select and read. Spelling will be integrated with all subjects of the curriculum. Words will be taught as they are used in writing, language, and other subjects.

This individualized reading program should enable your child to progress at his or her own rate, read material of personal interest, and develop independent study habits.

If you have any questions about this, please feel free to contact me.

Sincerely,

Barbara Patterson

Introducing Students to the Program

The students must have a thorough understanding of the program and the teacher's expectations in order for the program to succeed. First, the overall idea of the program—that library books will form the nucleus of the reading program—must be explained. The students should understand that there is no group competition in this type of approach. Instead, the challenge is for each student to become the best reader possible. Students must then be taught how books are arranged in the library. They must learn to select an appropriate book, how to keep records of their reading, what to do when they encounter unknown words, and what takes place during a teacher-pupil conference. Most important, they must learn to work independently, with a minimum of teacher direction.

Perhaps the most crucial portion of an individualized reading program is the silent, independent reading period. Hunt (1970) calls this USSR—Uninterrupted Sustained Silent Reading. Some children may have trouble reading quietly by themselves for any length of time. For that reason a teacher would be wise to introduce the students gradually to USSR, starting with a short independent reading period and then slowly lengthening it. In the primary grades USSR may last for only five or ten minutes; in the fifth and sixth grades it may continue for up to an hour. One suggested time schedule you might use as a guide is shown in Table 11.1. The schedule attempts to take into account the first grader's short attention span and the older child's ability to concentrate for relatively long periods of time.

TABLE 11.1
Suggested durations of silent reading in an individualized reading program

Grade level	First half of year	Last half of year
	Minutes per day	
First	5–10	10–15
Second	10–15	15–25
Third	10–15	15–30
Fourth	15–20	20–30
Fifth	15–20	20–40
Sixth	15–20	20–50

During this silent-reading period, it is important that students have an adequate amount of material to read. An easy 20- to 30-page joke book will probably be read by a fluent sixth-grade reader in just a few minutes. Each child should have something else to turn to once a book is finished. A cardinal rule of the uninterrupted sustained silent-reading period is that students must have an adequate supply of reading material at their fingertips. The students may need reminders at first about what to do when they finish reading early, but gradually they will learn to quietly choose another reading material.

Making the Transition

After the preparatory steps have been taken, the transition phase—moving from relying (in all likelihood) exclusively on the basal reader to a truly individualized reading program—may begin. This transition needs to be carefully planned and slowly implemented. If the children are moved too quickly into the routines and responsibilities of the program, both teacher and students may be needlessly frustrated.

It is important to establish everyday classroom routines, such as methods for selecting a book and for keeping records of materials read, before implementing an individualized reading program. Rather than starting an individualized program as soon as school begins, a teacher would be wise to hold off immediate implementation of the program. Basal readers could be used until the teacher gets to know the students and they know what to expect from the teacher. This may take several weeks. Once classroom routines are almost second nature to the students, the new approach may be introduced.

Not everyone needs to begin the program at the same time. In fact, it's wise not to! Often starting with just one group is a better method. Many teachers initiate individualized reading instruction with their better readers as a first step. These readers might first be permitted to read their basal readers at their own pace, which would require them to accept responsibility for their own work habits and behavior. After they were able to handle this freedom, the members of the group might be allowed to choose supplementary reading materials to read in conjunction with their basal readers. At this stage the choices might be limited to only certain supplementary materials that the teacher had selected.

If all goes well, the final step would be to allow members of the group to have an unlimited choice of reading material. Some individuals will probably choose to read basal readers, others will select trade books, while still others will choose magazines or newspapers.

If all students in a class were capable of handling an individualized reading program, an alternative plan for getting the program under way might be used. Rather than beginning the program with only one group of students, as just described, everyone in the classroom would start at the same time. To help make a whole-group plan manageable, the teacher might plan to use one day a week for individualized reading. The remaining four days would be spent using the basal-reader materials. As students became more independent and capable of working without the structure of the basal reader, two days a week could be spent in the individualized reading program. Eventually, three, four, or even five days per week could be devoted to the program.

These two plans represent only two of many ways by which this approach can be implemented. The ease in making the transition from the basal approach to the individualized reading approach will depend on many factors. The larger the sight vocabulary of the students and the more developed their reading skills, the easier the transition, because the students will be able to read more independently. Some of the students may have worked in an individualized program in previous classrooms. These students will pick up the necessary routines quickly. Students who are introduced to the program for the first time may need more time to "learn the ropes." Smaller classes are likely to be ready for an individualized reading program more quickly than classes in which there are 30 or more students. Students who come from homes in which books are valued may be ready for individualized reading before students coming from homes in which education and reading are not valued. In fact, some students (and occasionally whole classes) need so much structure in their school day that an individualized reading program is the *last* program that should be used.

MAKING THE PROGRAM WORK

In order to have a successful individualized reading program, a teacher needs to answer many questions, such as "How do I teach skills?"; "How do I assess students' abilities?"; "How do I manage the various facets of record keeping?"; and "What materials do I need to begin the program?" We have already talked about the general procedures to follow when making the transition from a basal-reader approach to an individualized program; more specific details of individualized reading instruction will now be given.

Skill Development

We have discussed the implications of teaching reading from a skill-development perspective many times already (see Chapters 3 and 4). A major shortcoming of individualized reading programs is that they are often really *recreational-* or *independent*-reading programs, because they fail to include a legitimate skill-development program as an integral part of their structure. Individualized reading programs must include provisions for instruction in skills. Otherwise, the skill development of the students will be haphazard at best.

Skills can be taught directly or indirectly. The advantage of teaching them directly is that the teacher can schedule periods throughout the week specifically for skill instruction and can thereby be assured of a systematic approach to skill development. Teaching skills indirectly has the advantage of permitting the teacher to conduct impromptu skill sessions—teaching as the need arises, usually on a one-to-one basis. Teaching a skill right when a child needs that skill can help the child understand the relationship between skill instruction and actually reading.

Naturally, skill instruction should be focused. Only students who need specific skills should receive instruction in them. But skills work should also be interesting. Many teachers and parents perceive skills work as boring. But it need not be. An imaginative teacher can find many exciting ways for children to learn and practice specific skills (see Chapters 6 and 7). In addition, many commercial resource books are available with ideas to put a little "pizzazz" into skill practice. *Spice* (Platts, Marguerite, and Shumaker, 1960), *Learning Activities for Reading* (Herr, 1970), *Reading Aids Through the Grades* (Russell and Karp, 1973), and *Reading Activities for Child Involvement* (Spache, 1976) are only a few. Textbook publishers can also supply additional reference material for teaching the skills.

The best way to ensure that students will remember a skill is to give them opportunities to *use* it. Teachers can help in this process by providing specific follow-up activities after a teacher-directed lesson. In this way the students can practice the skill fairly independently, but under some teacher guidance. Of course, the USSR procedure we have already described provides a natural place for students to apply the skills they have learned. Even if the materials are relatively easy, there will be ample opportunities for the student to practice reading and to use their skills (Fry, 1975).

In its broadest sense assessment involves the evaluation of the entire reading program. We deal in more depth with this topic in Chapter 12. Our purpose here is to examine some of the *specific* assessment procedures a classroom teacher may wish to employ when implementing an individualized reading program.

A variety of tests and other less formal assessment techniques can be used to determine if students are making satisfactory progress in their acquisition of reading skills. Criterion-referenced tests, such as those described in Chapter 4, may be especially useful for assessing mastery of specific skills. In addition, norm-referenced tests, which permit comparison of the performance of the students in a particular classroom with pupils across the country, may be given. (Norm-referenced and criterion-referenced tests are contrasted in Chapter 12.)

Other procedures for learning more about the students should be considered. Since an individualized reading program is based heavily on the reading interests of the students, some type of interest inventory may be appropriate. A simple inventory can be constructed with the help of the school or public librarian to find out what kinds of books the students like to read. The librarian may provide a list of suitable topics from which to choose. These topics should be listed on a duplicating master, with a check space next to each topic. The students are to check those topics about which they would like to read. Noting which topics are most popular will help the teacher select books likely to be of interest to the students.

After an individualized program has been in operation for a period of time, the teacher might begin to look for signs that the students are becoming more mature independent readers. For example, students might begin to spend more time on voluntary reading. They might be able to concentrate for increasing amounts of time during their reading and be less distracted by the commonplace noises and disturbances of a classroom. The students might begin to talk about books they had read and to encourage others to read the same books. An observant teacher will be able to identify many behaviors that indicate that students are developing the attitudes and skills necessary for successful reading.

Assessment of reading growth is not limited to the administration of formal norm-referenced reading tests. Criterion-referenced tests, interest inventories, and teacher observation may also be used, especially to assess an individualized reading program in which attitudes and interests in reading are emphasized.

Keeping an individualized reading program running smoothly day after day is very demanding. Obvious though it may be, the more thought and preparation that have gone into a program, the easier it will be to manage. To help you learn to be a better manager of an individualized reading program, we have subdivided the topic of management into three categories: general suggestions, record keeping, and independent activities.

General Suggestions An individualized program entails a great deal of free movement around the classroom. In addition, the students spend much time working independently. Unless a teacher has good rapport with his or her students, managing the day-to-day activities that are part of this type of program will be difficult. Management of student behavior can be accomplished in three ways (Dolch, 1961). The first way is through the use of teacher control; that is, students behave in a particular fashion because there is a felt teacher presence. This does not mean that students should fear the teacher's presence, but they should respect it. In fact, teacher control should continue to exist even when the teacher is not physically in the room.

Another way to improve student behavior is through interest control. Interest control does not imply regulation of the students' interests. Rather, it is a technique for enlisting student cooperation by allowing them to choose some of their in-school activities according to their own inclinations, rather than according to the dictates of the teacher. Since individualized reading programs are based on the reading interests of the students, interest control should be a powerful factor to assist in management of the program. When students are free to select their own reading materials, there may be a reduction in disruptive behavior because they feel they have some choice in their activities.

The final type of control is routine control. Choosing a book independently, scheduling a conference, and keeping oneself occupied productively are examples of classroom routines that should be learned by everyone in order to ensure that the program goes smoothly from day to day. Many children are unable to work easily in classrooms in which they must plan and carry out many of their own activities. The teacher can help these children to develop self-discipline and a sense of responsibility by providing structure through a loose framework of routines.

Another way to make an individualized reading program—or any reading program, for that matter—more manageable is to enlist the help of teacher aides or volunteers. We realize that it is difficult to pay for the services of these individuals with the tight budgets most school districts have; yet many parents or senior citizens are anxious to assist teachers in whatever ways they can. We urge you to explore the feasibility of securing this type of help.

Aides and volunteers can perform a host of tasks in the classroom. They can administer informal tests, duplicate worksheets, correct students' work, listen to children read, and take care of record-keeping chores. Furthermore, they can just "be there" whenever students need help.

Record Keeping Three kinds of records are needed in order to implement an individualized reading program fully. First, information should be available on each student's skill development. Second, there should be a record of both the amount and type of reading each student does. Finally, information describing the date and content of each teacher-student conference should be recorded.

To help keep track of each student's skill development, a checklist of skills may be kept in separate student folders. Such a checklist will allow the teacher to quickly determine the skill needs of students. In addition to a skill-development profile, a notebook should be maintained to record pertinent information about each teacher-pupil conference. The record should give each student's reading level, the dates of all conferences, the title and type of material that has been read, and other anecdotal information. (See Fig. 11.2 for an example of a conference record form.) Copies of this form can be duplicated and kept in a loose-leaf binder so that additional pages can be added whenever they are needed.

Student's name ___*Billy Adler*___

Date	Book title	Appx. level	Pages read	Comments
Feb. 18	Monkeys of South America	third grade	1-28	good compr. of details. needs work on -tion suffix
Feb. 21	Abraham Lincoln	fourth	all (207 pages!)	He loved it. Get more biographies for him
Mar. 2	The Case of the Missing Shark	fifth-sixth	1-15	Just too hard. Needs work on sequence.
Mar. 7	Famous Men and Women of the South	fourth	all (151 pp.)	Still trouble with -tion. Also needs review of oi/oy

Fig. 11.2. Teacher's reading-conference record.

Intermediate-grade teachers might require students to assume responsibility for some record keeping. By doing so, students are likely to become more responsible for their own learning. In addition, the teacher will be relieved of some of the record-keeping duties.

One type of record students could maintain is a listing of the books they have read (see Fig. 11.3). The author, number of pages read, and the time spent reading each book should be recorded. The students might also evaluate each book, keep a list of interesting or new words, and maintain a list of unknown words that can be brought to the next teacher-student conference. The unfamiliar words can be recorded on bookmarks duplicated on construction paper and kept by each student (see Fig. 11.4). The bookmark can also serve as a reminder to students that too many unknown words might mean that the reading material is too difficult.

Student's name _Billy Adler_

Book title	Author	No. of pages read	Date started	Date completed
Monkeys of South America	John Peebles	28	Feb. 11	Feb. 17
Abrah. Lincoln	Rogers	207	Feb. 16	Feb. 20
Case of Missing Shark	Akins	15	Feb. 23	Feb. 24
Famous Men and Women of the South	Carr	151	Feb. 24	Mar. 5

Fig. 11.3. Student reading record.

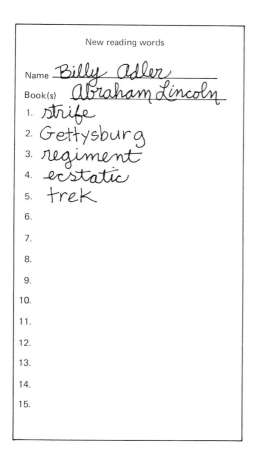

New reading words

Name *Billy Adler*

Book(s) *Abraham Lincoln*

1. *strife*
2. *Gettysburg*
3. *regiment*
4. *ecstatic*
5. *trek*
6.
7.
8.
9.
10.
11.
12.
13.
14.
15.

Fig. 11.4. A reading bookmark.

Some students may enjoy reading about a variety of topics. Others may read only one kind of story, such as mysteries or biographies, or only about a few topics. To help monitor the kinds of reading students are doing and to help the students monitor *themselves,* the teacher may have each child keep a reading wheel, such as the one shown in Fig. 11.5. Every time a student finishes a book, he or she should color a section of the "graph." A profile of the student's reading soon begins to appear. A student whose wheel indicates an excessive amount of reading in only one or two areas might be gently guided to read in other areas.

A reading wheel may be divided into fairly general categories, such as mysteries, science stories, animal stories, humor, and biographies. Such a broadly based wheel could be used by each member of the class. Another approach is to use more specialized categories, such as those shown in Fig. 11.5. If specialized categories are used, each student could design his or her own wheel, with the teacher serving as a guide to make sure that a wide variety of topics was included.

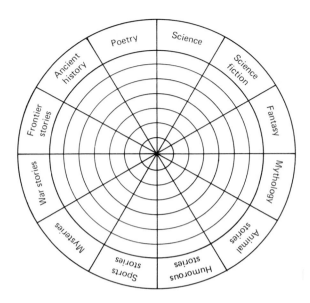

Fig. 11.5. A student reading wheel.

Independent Activities for Students

One of the most difficult, yet important, tasks when implementing an individualized reading program is keeping students profitably occupied while the teacher is working with individuals. There are many things pupils can do while the teacher is otherwise engaged.

INDEPENDENT READING

The most obvious activity is independent reading. There is no better way to become a good reader than to practice!

UPDATING RECORDS

Another activity that can be done independently is the updating of reading records. If students keep some personal records of their reading progress, such as the ones we have already described, they can check to see that information contained on the records is current and accurate.

WORKSHEETS

While the teacher is holding conferences with individual children, other students may work on worksheets that have been assigned for practice to reinforce a teacher-directed lesson. Such worksheets should not be arbitrarily assigned just to keep students busy. They should be carefully designed practice exercises for which the student can see the need.

SHARING READING EXPERIENCES

After a student has finished reading a book or other reading material, he or she may choose to write a report or complete a creative project as a means of telling the rest of the class about the book. Such activities can help students perceive reading as an enjoyable, exciting experience to share with others. However, if students are *required* to do some sort of report after every book, they will quickly learn that the fewer books they read, the fewer projects they'll have to do!

We have grouped activities for reporting about books into three categories, according to the modes of expression: oral expression, written expression, and artistic expression.

We think you will find these activities to be helpful for two reasons. First, they keep students engaged in activities that are related to the materials they have read; second, the products of the activities can serve as stimuli for encouraging other students to read additional books, magazines, or newspapers.

1. *Independent activities promoting oral expression*
   a) Dramatize a portion of the story.
   b) Give a presentation using audiovisual aids.
   c) Present an oral description of an interesting character in the book.
   d) Tell about the most humorous incident.
   e) Tell about the most exciting event.
   f) "Broadcast" a book review to a radio or television classroom audience.
   g) Role play a person in the story.
   h) Participate in a group discussion with others who have read the book.
   i) Assume the role of the author and discuss the book.

2. *Independent activities promoting written expression*
   a) Write an advertisement for the book.
   b) Prepare a monologue from the story.
   c) Write a different ending for the story.
   d) Write about the part liked best.
   e) Write about the happiest (saddest) part.
   f) Write a letter recommending the book to the class.
   g) Write a story of a similar personal experience.
   h) Write a poem about the story.
   i) Write a brief sketch about the author.
   j) Construct a true-false test about the book.
   k) Create a game using character descriptions.

3. *Independent activities promoting artistic expression*
   a) Construct a diorama for a favorite section of the story.
   b) Create an original book jacket.
   c) Make a project from a "How to . . ." book.
   d) Make a scrapbook about the subject.

e) Present a puppet show.

f) Construct a pictorial time line of the story.

g) Construct a clay, wood, soap, or plaster model depicting something in the story.

h) Paint a picture to illustrate the book.

i) Develop a flannelboard story.

j) Paint or draw a "TV picture" roll.

k) Create a mobile.

l) Make a map of an area discussed in the book.

m) Design and prepare a bulletin board illustrating the story.

n) Draw a cartoon of a humorous incident in the story.

LEARNING CENTERS   Another way of keeping students involved in independent activities that can be related to their reading is to establish learning centers around the room (Miller, 1971). After completing their assignments, students could be permitted to work at one of the centers. Miller suggests making arithmetic, art, communication, science, or book centers available and including the following materials (1971, pp. 749–751):

1. *Arithmetic center:* scales, buttons, number lines, flash cards, geometric shapes, abacus, graph paper, bottles of various sizes, play money, cuisinaire rods;

2. *Art center:* construction paper, crayons, scissors, paste, colored chalk, paints and brushes, beads;

3. *Communication center:* chalkboard, typewriter, tape recorder, paper and pencils, magic markers, magazines, flannelboard, picture file;

4. *Science center:* filmstrips, live animals, compasses, old clocks, aquarium, microscope, flower pots and seeds, rock collections, leaf collections;

5. *Book center:* library books, basal readers, supplementary readers, children's newspapers, children's magazines, paperback books, language-experience stories.*

Each center should include one or more activities designed to reinforce some particular learning or to help the students discover a specific concept. The activities should be written so that the students can complete them with a minimum of teacher guidance. Some of the activities may be just exploratory, and others may involve a final product, such as a finished worksheet, a piece of creative writing, or a complete puzzle. When at all possible, learning-center activities should be self-correcting so that the teacher does not have to be interrupted during conferences to check work done at the learning centers.

*Wilma Miller, "Organizing a First Grade Classroom for Individualized Reading Instruction," *Reading Teacher* (May 1971): 748–752, 761. Reprinted with permission of the International Reading Association.

In many classrooms there are students who have difficulty working independently. These children might be kept in a highly structured reading program, such as a basal-reader program, until they can develop the ability to work with less teacher guidance. To help them improve their independent work habits, the teacher might gradually give them more and more responsibilities. However, some students may never be able to work successfully in the free atmosphere of an individualized reading program.

One of the greatest problems in implementing an individualized reading program is locating and organizing an adequate supply of books and supplementary materials for students to read. Unless there is a sufficient number of books and other reading materials available, students will soon get bored or restless. If the reading matter is poorly organized, much time will be wasted finding something appropriate to read.

Library books are the nucleus of any individualized reading program. Although the minimum number of books needed before attempting to implement an individualized reading program varies with the individual class, between three and five books per student are generally recommended. Thus if there are 25 students in a classroom, students will need access to between 75 and 125 books.

Of course, the more books available to the students, the greater the chance of everyone's finding an interesting selection. Ideally, everyone—students and teachers alike—should have unlimited access to the school's library. Students should be free to use the library whenever there is a need. Going to the library once a week for 30 minutes *does not* foster a love of reading, nor does it increase the odds of a program's succeeding. If students are expected to read library books, they must have access to them!

Students who may not have acquired a substantial sight vocabulary can still be part of an individualized reading program. They can read picture books (with or without a text). Larrick (1976) has compiled a list of wordless picture books that may be of interest to children with limited reading ability (pp. 745–746):

Aliki. *Go Tell Aunt Rhody* (Macmillan, 1974).
Alexander, Martha. *Bobo's Dream* (Dial, 1970).
_____. *Out! Out! Out!* (Dial, 1968).
Ardizzone, Edward. *The Wrong Side of the Bed* (Doubleday, 1970).
Carle, Eric. *Do You Want to Be My Friend?* (Crowell, 1971).
_____. *I See a Song* (Crowell, 1973).
Carroll, Ruth. *What Whiskers Did* (Walck, 1965).
Charlip, Remy, and Jerry Joyner. *Thirteen* (Parents', 1975).
Goodall, John S. *Paddy's Evening Out* (Atheneum, 1973).
Hoban, Tana. *Count and See* (Macmillan, 1972).
_____. *Look Again!* (Macmillan, 1971).
_____. *Shapes and Things* (Macmillan, 1970).
Hutchins, Pat. *Changes, Changes* (Macmillan, 1970).

Structured Activities for Students

Reading Materials

Library Books

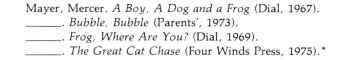

Mayer, Mercer. *A Boy, A Dog and a Frog* (Dial, 1967).
_____. *Bubble, Bubble* (Parents', 1973).
_____. *Frog, Where Are You?* (Dial, 1969).
_____. *The Great Cat Chase* (Four Winds Press, 1975).*

Another major problem in individualized reading programs is finding enough books that are high in interest, yet have a vocabulary that can be handled by poorer readers. Children with reading problems often have poor self-images. If materials are not available at both their reading and interest levels, poor readers are likely to lose even more self-confidence and become frustrated and embarrassed. If the available books are too difficult, these students won't read them because they *can't;* if the books are easy but "babyish," the poor readers *won't* read them, because they are embarrassed to be seen with the books.

It's imperative, then, that the teacher locate materials that will have student appeal. Zimet (1966), however, cautions that what adults think children like to read and what students actually select and enjoy may not be the same. For this reason, we reemphasize the importance of conducting an interest inventory with the students. Children's interests vary greatly. No theoretician can prescribe what any teacher should have available for a particular group of students to read just on the basis of age, sex, or socioeconomic background. Indeed, with more than 300 studies of children's reading interests reported (Zimet, 1966), no agreement has been reached over what students prefer to read. And as children mature, their interests become even broader and deeper. To gain an accurate picture of what a group of students likes to read about, we suggest a simple procedure—ask them!

Regardless of what topics are favored by a class, if the students are given an opportunity to select their own reading material, "reading" should take on a new, positive meaning. "Reading" no longer will be considered to be a subject, per se, but instead, will, ideally, become something that is done in order to learn about any topic of interest.

Supplementary Materials

In spite of their pleas, shouts, and tears, some teachers do not have unlimited access to a library or are given only a few dollars to spend on library books. We can suggest two options if these teachers still want to implement an individualized reading program. The first is to use basal readers exclusively for reading material. When you think about it, basal readers are really anthologies written at different grade levels. In most schools an energetic teacher will be able to collect a variety of different readers simply by searching closets and storerooms. Other teachers may also have extra copies of readers and will be only too glad to get rid of the books they are not using.

The next step should be to check the table of contents of each book to see the types of stories that are included. By categorizing each story under a topic,

*Nancy Larrick, "Wordless Picture Books and the Teaching of Reading," *Reading Teacher* (May 1976): 745–746. Reprinted with permission of the International Reading Association.

the teacher can compile a bibliography for the students to help them pick stories in which they are interested. The following categories may be useful:

1. History
2. Biography
3. Everyday life
4. Mystery, suspense, and adventure
5. Humor
6. Classics
7. Myths and fairy tales
8. Poetry
9. Hobbies
10. Sports
11. Science
12. Science fiction
13. Travel

The story title, name of the basal reader, and page numbers should be included in the bibliography. (See Table 11.2 for an abbreviated sample of such a bibliography.)

Title	Basal-reader source	Page number	
			TABLE 11.2
Marian Anderson	Launchings and Landings	394–395	**Sample basal-reader bibliography: history and people**
Garrett A. Morgan	Launchings and Landings	396–410	
The Ernie Davis Story	Open Highways	34–42	
Jefferson Davis and Operation Camel	Open Highways	89–103	
Robert Goddard, Rocketman	Seven Seas	247–255	
Master Builder: Frank Lloyd Wright	Seven Seas	294–300	

A second alternative for a teacher with limited library access and limited funds is to purchase a commercially prepared individualized reading program. Scholastic Book Services, among others, has such a program; the complete kit, *Individualized Reading from Scholastic* (1969), includes everything needed to implement the program: paperback books, conference records and forms, questions to ask about each story, and suggested follow-up activities students can do once they have finished reading their books. In mid-1978 the cost for a classroom set of materials was under $200.00. The primary shortcoming of such kits is that they include only a limited supply of books. However, for the teacher who has little money or an inaccessible school library, such kits can provide a suitable set of materials for individualized reading instruction.

Role of the Librarian
An enthusiastic school librarian can be an important asset to an individualized reading program. The librarian can help the teacher select appropriate books once the students have completed an interest inventory. He or she may help stir up student interest by introducing new acquisitions to the students and can provide instruction in how to use the library's resources. Finally, and most important, the librarian can help students find books that are appropriate in both content and reading level.

Some librarians may assign readability levels to many of the reading materials in the library. In some instances books may be categorized only as "easy" or "difficult." In other instances an actual grade-level designation may be assigned to each book. At least one library reference volume, the *Elementary School Library Collection* (1976), indicates the readability level of thousands of published children's books. However, because of the inherent inaccuracies of readability formulas and their failure to account for student motivation, readability assessments should be interpreted with caution. The child's interest in the book is more important than the exact level of the book.

TEACHER-STUDENT CONFERENCES
During the teacher-student conference the student has an opportunity to meet individually with the teacher for ten or fifteen minutes and to share what he or she has been reading. In this section we will point out some of the purposes of teacher-student conferences. Alternative methods for scheduling conferences with students will also be examined. Finally, we will provide some explicit directions on how to assess students' decoding, comprehension, and study-skills abilities during conferences.

Purposes for Conferences
The teacher-student conference is not just a time for listening to a student read orally. Conferences should serve a variety of purposes. Because the students in any classroom will have widely different needs, the teacher will have to adjust the purpose of each conference to match the particular abilities—and disabilities—of the student.

One of the primary objectives for meeting individually with pupils is to check informally their reading-skill development. This is done during a diagnostic conference. The teacher will want to determine whether a student can decode unknown words, utilize basic comprehension skills, and make use of elementary study skills. The diagnostic conference provides an excellent opportunity to see whether the student is applying the skills he or she has been taught.

Another type of meeting is the instructional conference, during which the student is given a short, highly focused, minilesson. In a sense the instructional conference is individualized teaching: The student has a known skill deficiency, and the teacher attempts to remedy it. Instructional conferences require that the teacher be able to improvise a lesson "at the drop of a hat."

A teacher-pupil conference can have important benefits for both teacher and student.

However, the wise teacher plans ahead for an instructional conference whenever possible so that appropriate follow-up worksheets, games, or activities will be immediately accessible if needed.

A third type of meeting, the motivational conference, can be used to build the child's confidence. During this meeting the teacher may check the student's reading record to see how many books he or she has read. A reassuring word given at this time about the number or choice of books being read may inspire the student to read even more. Because this type of conference is designed to encourage the student to keep moving ahead, the teacher should be alert for any situation that justifies a word of praise. Of course, there will be times when no word of praise is warranted! If, for example, a child has been bothering others during the silent-reading period or has not been reading independently, she or he needs motivation of a different sort. The motivational conference can be used for a private "pep talk" during which undesirable behaviors are discussed and discouraged.

A fourth purpose for scheduling a conference is to assist the student in selecting appropriate reading material. After consulting the student's completed interest inventory and spending some time talking with him or her, the teacher should be able to direct the child to additional reading materials. In some instances a student may be devoting too much time to reading about only one or two topics. During the conference the teacher may wish to encourage the student to read materials in other areas and may even provide some alternatives.

Scheduling Conferences

One of the authors can still remember his initial attempts at conducting teacher-student conferences. At the time, reading experts were suggesting that a conference last between three and five minutes. Yet five minutes hardly was enough time to accomplish what needed to be done. At first, he thought that there must be something wrong with the way he was conducting the conference. As he gained more experience, however, five minutes still seemed to pass too quickly. Finally he realized that if a conference is to have any substance, a *minimum* of ten minutes with the student is necessary. Frequently the conference needs to run up to 15 minutes in length. This experience has led us to recommend, therefore, that the teacher plan on scheduling at least ten minutes with each child, although occasionally less time may be needed.

There are numerous ways to schedule meetings with students. Whenever possible, the students should assume the responsibility for signing up for conferences. If a sign-up sheet like the one shown in Fig. 11.6 is posted, each student can choose to meet with the teacher at least once per week (assuming that no more than 30 students are in the class and that the teacher spends 90 minutes per day in conferences).

Occasionally there will be students who want to sign up for a conference every day. When this happens, other students don't get to see the teacher as much as they should because a few students monopolize the conference time. One way to eliminate this situation is to post a schedule of pupils and their designated conference times. The teacher may also just restrict each pupil to no more than two conferences a week.

A combination of the two plans already mentioned may be used. If time has been allocated for six teacher-pupil conferences each day, for example, the teacher might request meetings with three particular students and leave the three remaining blocks of time available for volunteers to sign up. This plan enables the teacher to meet with those individuals who seldom, if ever, volunteer to have conferences while at the same time making a provision for students who want conferences.

Application: Checking Decoding Skills

As we mentioned earlier, one of the most important kinds of teacher-student conferences is the diagnostic conference. During the diagnostic conference, the teacher can assess a student's ability to apply the various skills that have been

Time	Day	Name of student
9:00—9:15	Monday	*Lynn*
9:15—9:30	Monday	*Susan*
9:30—9:45	Monday	*Ricky*
9:45—10:00	Monday	*Bev*
10:00—10:15	Monday	*Sandy*
10:15—10:30	Monday	*Jeff*
9:00—9:15	Tuesday	*Jan*
9:15—9:30	Tuesday	
9:30—9:45	Tuesday	*Mark*
9:45—10:00	Tuesday	*Willie*
10:00—10:15	Tuesday	*K.K.*
10:15—10:30	Tuesday	*Juanita*
	etc.	

Fig. 11.6. Teacher-student conference sign-up sheet.

taught. If the teacher suspects (either after consulting the students' records or on the basis of personal informal evaluation) that a student may be weak in a particular skill, he or she may structure the conference ahead of time in order to focus on that skill.

A diagnostic conference may be used to check a student's decoding skills. During the individual conference, the teacher can listen privately to the oral reading of the student, making notes on both the quantity and quality of reading errors (miscues). (We discussed the analysis of oral-reading errors in Chapter 6.) These notes will help the teacher analyze the kinds of decoding problems the student may have.

In addition to listening to the child read orally, the teacher might ask some specific questions, like the ones listed below, to check further on a student's decoding ability.

1. How did you figure out this unfamiliar word?
2. When you come to a word you don't know, how do you figure it out?
3. If you were trying to teach your friends how to "unlock" this word, what would you tell them?
4. There are a number of ways you could have used to "unlock" this word. Can you tell me some of them?

General Strategy Questions

Specific Skill-Based Questions	1. How do you know this word isn't *bread*? (to check ability to use semantic, syntactic, and graphophonic cues)

Specific Skill-Based Questions

1. How do you know this word isn't *bread*? (to check ability to use semantic, syntactic, and graphophonic cues)
2. What sound does this (written) word begin with?
3. Divide this word that you missed into syllables. Now, what is the word?
4. You called this word *quiet*. Read the sentence again. Does *quiet* make sense? What would make sense? Why?

Application: Checking Comprehension Skills

Some students will have little difficulty in decoding, but may need to develop further specific comprehension skills. The teacher-student conference provides an excellent opportunity to informally assess acquisition of comprehension skills.

In Chapter 7 we suggested numerous activities that can be used to teach comprehension skills. We also discussed several techniques for evaluating comprehension. In this section we offer a list of questions that might be used during a teacher-student conference to assess a student's comprehension ability in three major areas: detail, sequence, and main idea. Of course, a teacher would not assess just these three comprehension skills during conferences. We have purposely limited the skills to three, however, in order to emphasize that at a *single* conference the teacher should strive to minimize the number of skills assessed. Assembling massive lists of comprehension questions in an effort to assess every "subskill" will result only in confusion. Two or three comprehension skills (at most) should be chosen, and the questions should focus on these skills in order to provide enough information for evaluation. Some suggested questions that might form the nucleus for an enlarged set of questions follow:

Detail

1. Describe your favorite person in the story.
2. Identify the characters (things) in this picture from the story.
3. Find the sentence that describes . . . .

Sequence

1. Describe what happened before this picture (event).
2. Describe what happened after this picture (event).
3. Briefly summarize the sequence of events that occurred in this story.
4. What was the first (or last) important event in this story?

Main Idea

1. Describe what this book was about in just one sentence.
2. What was the plot of this story?
3. How is this book's title related to the story?
4. Read this paragraph (page). What is it about?
5. What kind of book was this?
6. Describe what is happening in this picture.
7. Draw a picture of the main idea of this book.

Whereas decoding and comprehension skills are usually assessed and taught with regularity, study skills are often overlooked. Yet in an individualized reading program the ability of the student to apply study skills is crucial. The teacher-student conference provides an excellent opportunity for assessing a pupil's understanding of some of these skills. The following questions may be helpful for evaluating some of the more important study skills:

1. If you wanted to read a chapter about _____, what page would you turn to? (Table of contents)
2. If you wanted to learn about _____, what would be the quickest way to find the right page? (Index)
3. Read and explain this chart for me.
4. Read and explain this graph for me.
5. Read and explain this table for me.
6. How would you find another book on this topic? (Card catalog)
7. Can you find _____ on this map? How did you locate it?
8. How far is it between _____ and _____ on this map?

The teacher-student conference also permits the teacher to assess a student's attitudes toward both reading in general and what he or she has read. Typically, questions such as these might be asked:

1. Why did you choose this particular book?
2. Did you like this book? Why or why not?
3. What was the most interesting portion of the book? Why?
4. Who was your favorite character in the book? Why?
5. Did this book remind you of any others you have read? Why?
6. How did this story make you feel? Why?
7. Do you know any other children who might like this book? Who? Why?
8. Have you read any other books by this author?

A teacher may wish to develop a file box of questions that could be used during a diagnostic conference. Cards in this box would contain questions for assessing decoding, comprehension, and study skills, as well as attitudes about the material that was read. Then, during a conference, the teacher could simply skim the cards and choose the questions that were most appropriate for the particular situation.

One reason for the declining popularity of individualized reading instruction after the 1950s and 1960s was that teachers felt the need for a structured skill-development program. Unfortunately, few commercial skill-development programs were available from which to choose, nor had sets of criterion-referenced tests been developed to help teachers diagnose the reading needs of their students. As a result, most individualized reading programs were really recreational reading programs.

Today teachers have many more supplementary materials available with which to augment their individualized reading programs. In this section we will describe briefly how one kind of supplementary material, a skills-management system, might be used to help the teacher provide structured skill development for students in an individualized reading program. (Reread Chapter 4 if you need to review the organization and components of skills-management systems.)

Using a skills-management system with an individualized reading program is a relatively straightforward procedure. With the tests provided, students can be pretested to identify their specific strengths and weaknesses. Then, after the initial testing has been completed and student records brought up to date, skill groups can be formed for instructional purposes. After a period of two or three weeks—or whenever the teacher felt that the students were ready—posttests can be administered to determine whether students learned the skill(s). If they did, the students would be moved into groups for instruction in other needed skills. Students who had not mastered the skill yet might remain in the original skill group for additional instruction. An alternative procedure would be to move these students to another skill group and then return for instruction on the original skill at a later time.

Simply using a skills-management system in an individualized reading program will not ensure that the skills will be learned. After instruction, the teacher must provide opportunities for the students to apply the skill when reading independently. The only way to become a good reader is to practice. Skill instruction without large amounts of time devoted to independent reading will not produce good readers. Opportunities must be provided for both— skill instruction and free reading.

THINKING ABOUT INDIVIDUALIZED READING INSTRUCTION

As with each of the other major approaches we have presented, there are specific benefits and problems in taking an individualized approach to reading instruction. To help you better understand these strengths and limitations, we will discuss each of them briefly.

Benefits

The major advantage of the individualized reading approach is that it capitalizes on students' reading interests. Because individuals are free to choose material that appeals to them, they are likely to read for enjoyment rather than simply because the teacher has given them a book (usually a basal reader) and told them to read it. When students select their own books, reading usually takes on more meaning.

A second advantage is that students progress at their own rate. Some students will choose long, difficult books, whereas others will choose short, easy selections. So long as a child doesn't consistently pick materials that are too difficult, the length and difficulty levels of the books chosen are not very important. A great deal of reading in easy books may help a child feel better about reading than just a little reading in a few difficult books.

A third advantage, and one that is related to self-pacing, is that in an individualized reading program there is a decrease in student competition. If a student is working up to his or her ability, that student is making satisfactory progress, regardless of the grade level of the material. In addition, because two or more students will rarely be reading the same material at the same time, students will find it difficult to make comparisons with one another.

Children who participate in individualized reading programs are likely to develop more independence and to accept greater responsibility for their actions than are students in other programs. This fourth advantage is an important one for the teacher, because once students learn the necessary classroom routines, the teacher is able to devote increasing amounts of time to working with individuals or small groups of students.

A fifth advantage of this approach is that the teacher-student conferences promote a close relationship between the teacher and the students. The questions asked and the responses supplied by students are personalized and specifically related to what the student is reading. The conference, therefore, has a special appeal for students, because this is a time when all of the teacher's attention is focused on the pupil.

A final advantage of individualized reading is that a greater quantity of materials will most likely be read when children are free to select their own materials. Children who read extensively are likely to become better readers than are students who read fewer books. The process goes full circle: Children select books they enjoy, they read more, they enjoy reading, and then they select additional books they are interested in.

Problems

Even if you are convinced that an individualized reading program is a good program for you, you should be forewarned of potential disadvantages of this approach. By pointing these out to you now, we may enable you to take the necessary precautions to avoid some of them.

One disadvantage, at least at the beginning stage, is that a large quantity of reading materials must be available for students. Unless a good supply of materials is easily accessible, an individualized reading program is not likely to work. If the teacher has ready access to the school library, however, the problems will be fewer than if he or she must secure all of the reading material personally.

Another problem that might develop is that students may be unable to select material that is appropriate. If students continually choose material that is too difficult, they can become both frustrated and demoralized. To avoid this situation, the teacher should spend time introducing students gradually to the techniques for choosing material they can actually read. In addition, they should be given many opportunities to use these techniques under teacher guidance.

A third problem may be scheduling everything that needs to be done. Keeping up with skill groups, conferences, and record keeping will require the teacher to organize the program in such a way that little time is wasted. Keeping to the schedule can also be a problem. The teacher must be firm about interruptions of teacher-pupil conferences. Imagine the amount of rapport you will establish, as a beginning teacher, with George if Mary, Susan, Kurt, and

Konrad all come to ask you questions during George's ten-minute "individual" conference. Your timetable as well as your personal relationship with George will suffer.

The best advice that we can offer is to be thorough in your planning. Don't expect to have a smooth-running program if you have to stop and put out a "brush fire" every five or ten minutes.

Unless the teacher is skilled in assessing students' reading strengths and weaknesses and teaching to these weaknesses, the students may miss essential reading skills. One way to avoid this shortcoming and to keep track of skill development is to use a skills-management system with an individualized reading program. This will allow the teacher to monitor each pupil's skill development and to provide instruction where needed. An experienced reading teacher may not need a skills-management system to help with skill instruction. However, many teachers like to add to their subjective evaluations with more objective data. The criterion-referenced tests supplied with skills-management systems can help provide this information.

Another potential problem in using this approach is lack of group interaction. Unless special provisions are made, there is little interaction among students in an individualized program. Most students—and adults—like to feel part of a group at times. Students may dislike always having to read alone. To promote group interaction, the teacher might have students read stories along the same theme and then share their books with one another. In this way students can select their own books and yet meet in a group occasionally.

As we have implied, these five problems will trouble you only if you let them. By taking precautionary steps, you will be able to eliminate many of the problems and develop a program that both you and your students will find exciting.

SUMMARY

Individualized reading, as we have described it, is an approach to reading instruction that makes extensive use of library books, magazines, and newspapers for the students' reading material. Students select the material that they want to read, and each child reads at his or her own pace. Because individualized reading programs are based on the student's self-selection of materials, each student is given opportunities to read at a level commensurate with his or her ability. As a result of the self-selection and self-pacing features of the individualized approach, reading instruction becomes highly personalized.

Good individualized reading programs are the result of careful planning. If you select this approach, you will not have the helping hand of a basal reader's teacher manual to guide you through daily activities. Instead, you will be totally responsible for learning about the approach, for informing parents, and probably for leading your students through the transition from using basal readers to a completely individualized reading program.

In this chapter we have tried to provide practical suggestions on how to manage individualized reading instruction. Examples of the types of records the teacher—as well as the students—should keep were described. We also have discussed the materials needed for an effective program. Because a key part of an individualized reading program is the teacher-student conference, we have explained the reasons for holding conferences, shown how to schedule them, and provided some "starter" questions that can be used during conferences. Because one of the important potential problems in an individualized reading program is the lack of focused skill development, we have shown how a skills-management system might be used to supplement an individualized reading program. Finally, following the model established in the preceding two chapters, we have described what we feel are the benefits and problems of individualized reading instruction.

An individualized reading program can be exciting and rewarding. But because of its unstructured nature, it can be one of the most difficult kinds of reading programs to implement. Following the guidelines we have suggested in this chapter may enable you to develop an effective program of individualized reading.

1. Describe how an individualized reading program differs from an individual reading program. Can you identify some of the distinguishing characteristics of individualized reading programs?

2. Why is there a need for individualized reading instruction? Is such a program worth all the teacher time and the expense? Compare your response with others and see if they agree.

3. Skill development, assessment, management, and materials are all important facets to consider when developing your individualized reading program. Explain how these components are interrelated. Which do you think is of most concern to classroom teachers? Why?

4. In this chapter we identified four reasons for holding teacher-pupil conferences in an individualized reading program. Reread the section on teacher-student conferences if necessary. Then complete the chart below by identifying the four kinds of conferences and the purpose of each conference. In addition, for each type of conference list at least two possible questions or activities that would help the teacher and student fulfill the purpose of the conference.

Type of conference	Purpose	Sample questions or activities
1.		
2.		
3.		
4.		

5. Explain how a skills-management system can assist you in implementing an individualized reading program. What alternatives are available to you if a skills-management system is not used in your district or school?

6. If your principal asked you to defend your individualized reading program, how would you respond? What would you tell parents to convince them that this type of program is best for their child? What are the dangers in instituting a program such as this?

REFERENCES

Dolch, Edward W. "Individualized Reading vs. Group Reading," *Elementary English* 38, 8 (December 1961): 566–575.

———. "Individualized Reading vs. Group Reading," *Elementary English* 39, 1 (January 1962): 14–21, 32.

Elementary School Library Collection: A Guide to Books and Other Media: Phases 1-2-3, ed. Phyllis Van Orden, 10th ed. (New Brunswick, N.J.: Bro-Dart Foundation, 1976).

Fry, Edward. "The Readability Principle," *Language Arts* 52, 6 (September 1975): 847–851.

Herr, Selma. *Learning Activities for Reading*, 2d ed. (Dubuque, Iowa: William C. Brown, 1970).

Hunt, Lyman. "The Effect of Self-Selection, Interest, and Motivation upon Independent, Instructional, and Frustrational Levels," *Reading Teacher* 24, 2 (1970): 146–151, 158.

Hunt, Lyman C. "The Individualized Reading Program: A Perspective," in Lyman C. Hunt, ed., *The Individualized Reading Program: A Guide for Classroom Teaching* (Newark, Delaware: International Reading Association, 1967).

Individualized Reading from Scholastic (Englewood Cliffs, N.J.: Scholastic Book Services, 904 Sylvan Ave., 07632, 1969).

Larrick, Nancy. "Wordless Picture Books and the Teaching of Reading," *Reading Teacher* 29, 8 (May 1976): 743–746.

Miller, Wilma. "Organizing a First Grade Classroom for Individualized Reading Instruction," *Reading Teacher* 24, 8 (1971): 748–751, 761.

Platts, Mary E., Sr. Rose Marguerite, and Ester Shumaker. *Spice: Suggested Activities to Motivate the Teaching of the Language Arts* (Benton Harbor, Michigan: Educational Services, 1960).

Russell, David H., and Etta E. Karp. *Reading Aids Through the Grades* (New York: Teachers College Press, Columbia University, 1973).

Spache, Evelyn. *Reading Activities for Child Involvement*, 2d ed. (Boston: Allyn & Bacon, 1976).

Zimet, Sara F. "Children's Interest and Story Preferences: A Critical Review of the Literature," *Elementary School Journal* 67 (1966): 122–130.

Part V
The
Wholeschool
Reading
Program:
Evaluation and
Organization

By now you probably realize that teaching reading is not a simple matter of telling young children to "read what the words say." In Parts I–IV we described reading as a complicated process that can be taught systematically in spite of its complex nature. We told you what we think you should teach children about reading, and we identified the three most common approaches to providing such instruction. In Part V (Chapters 12–13) we suggest how you should go about evaluating your instruction. Good intentions are fine, but teachers need accurate feedback about the success of their efforts. We also present several grouping procedures and instructional techniques that may be used to help organize instruction effectively and that therefore will help you become a successful teacher of reading.

Chapter 12
Evaluating
for a Purpose

After reading this chapter, you will be able to:

1. Discuss the difference between *evaluation* and *testing.*

2. Analyze and discuss the evaluation process applied to reading in terms of *why* evaluation is needed, *what* ought to be evaluated, and *how* evaluation can be implemented.

3. Select and defend norm-referenced or criterion-referenced tests for specific, given purposes.

4. Compare and contrast objective measures and informal procedures in terms of strengths and weaknesses for evaluating reading performance.

5. Describe ways in which evaluation procedures can be used to demonstrate teacher accountability.

6. Describe ways in which evaluation data can be applied in specific teaching situations.

"Show me your reading tests," said a wise guru we once knew," and I will tell you your definition of reading."

After thinking about reading (see Chapter 2), one could probably come up with a reasonable definition of reading, but real beliefs and inclinations will always be reflected better by actions than by words. Teachers who are satisfied with tests that neglect important aspects of reading are likely not only to have an inadequate *operational* definition of reading, but also to be satisfied with a haphazard approach to teaching reading. Or, worse yet, teachers who are content to use standardized tests that have no particular relationship to the specific objectives of their reading program probably have no operational definition of reading at all! The guru was on the right track. But unfortunately he did not say whether he viewed *testing* and *evaluation* as synonymous.

Tests, as we will show, are only one aspect of a comprehensive program of evaluation. An inventive teacher might tolerate inadequate tests required by an unenlightened administration and still approach evaluation in ways that are consistent with a comprehensive view of the reading process. The guru should have said: "Show me what you look for as an end result of your teaching, and I will tell you your operational definition of reading." The end results of teaching are best assessed through comprehensive evaluation, not just testing.

Thinking about reading, then, is not an exercise you completed when you finished Chapter 2. Some of the most explicit thinking about reading that you will ever do will be needed as you contemplate approaches to its evaluation. Our main intent in this chapter is to help you to, first, see the general purpose of evaluation, and second seek important information through evaluation. We do not identify or review specific tests, except for purposes of illustration. Tests are best examined and selected *after* you know the specific objectives of your reading program. We tell you where to find the tests. Nor do we try to give you a capsule course on evaluation. We give a heavy topic a light touch and hope that it will at least get you started.

Mager, who did more than anyone else to bring objectives into the classroom, has lamented the fact that many teachers and administrators are seduced by broad generalizations (Mager, 1972). These people have not sufficiently or sensibly thought through their goals of instruction, yet they want to show that they are decent human beings, so they rely on "goals" such as: *All students will learn to comprehend better*. But what does that mean? What *is* comprehension? Learn *what*? Better than *what*—or *whom*? Such statements are not goals, and they have no place in evaluation efforts. Good evaluation demands careful definitions and concrete statements. And good teachers will care enough to see that their goals are worked out with care and precision. Teachers who take that approach have a basis for purposeful evaluation.

As you attempt to clarify your goals in your evaluation efforts, you will need to think about *why* evaluation is important in the first place, exactly *what* you should be attempting to evaluate, and *how* to proceed with the evaluation. In the sections that follow, we discuss these concerns in terms of the purpose (why) for evaluation, the content (what) of evaluation, and approaches to (how) evaluation. Keep in mind that the focus may be on either the individual reader or the reading program. Certain points are relevant to one focus but not the other, so try to keep the referent clear at all times.

THE NEED FOR CLEAR GOALS

In general, the purpose for evaluation is to get objective, reliable information as a basis for making sound decisions. We need such information in order to, first, gain confidence that what we *think* is happening when we teach reading *is in fact* happening and, second, understand what is happening sufficiently well to make improvements. Stated another way, there are *two* main purposes for evaluation: (1) to get objective, reliable information; and (2) to improve instruction by becoming accountable as teachers.

The Purpose for Evaluation

Ultimately, what teachers need to know about their teaching of reading is whether their students are learning to read. How can we *know* that our students are learning to read well?

Kerlinger (1964) has suggested four ways of *knowing:* blind faith, authority, personal perception, and controlled investigation.

Getting Information

1. *Blind faith* is the least objective of the four and the most given to emotional involvement. A blind-faith teacher *knows* that his or her students are reading well because he or she has good intentions and uses good materials and techniques.
2. Although *authority* is also subjective, it gains substance from the support of someone (or ones) who has the credentials for knowing. Thus a teacher *knows* that students are reading well when the reading consultant observes and pronounces them to be good readers.
3. *Personal perceptions* go beyond blind faith in that they are taken in through the senses and are shaped by previous experiences, beliefs and knowledge. As personal interpretations of reality, they can be as good as

all the knowledge and experience that is brought to bear, but they will always be colored by personal prejudices and biases. A teacher's estimate of a student's reading ability is, for example, almost certain to reflect that teacher's beliefs about the reading process and about appropriate reading behavior.

4. *Controlled investigation* goes the next step in getting at the facts by correcting for prejudices and biases while making full use of available knowledge and experience. The degree of certainty is strongest because controls, like explicitly stated objectives and reliable test items, are imposed to curb personal biases and inclinations.

Each of the above is an acceptable way of knowing for certain purposes, so each has its own function in evaluation. But in order to increase the *certainty* of our knowing, we must draw more heavily on experiences than on beliefs, and we must impose controls on personal biases. We evaluate in order to gain more confidence in what we *know*.

Becoming Accountable   In its most positive form accountability, as it relates to reading instruction, amounts to demonstrating that the best possible decisions are being made—in good faith—about children and the instruction they are given. Unfortunately, though, the notion of accountability in education has taken on negative connotations. This has happened mainly because some poor applications of the concept have demanded highly defined, standardized outcomes, e.g., "Every student will increase at least one grade level in reading ability during each school year." Such unreasonable demands under the name of accountability have caused teachers to be judged unfairly when some of their students fail, as often as not for reasons beyond the teachers' control. And because evaluation is often associated with the kind of accountability that is required to get federal money, or satisfy the board of education, or mollify the taxpayers, it shares the negative connotations.

Lessinger (1971) and others have argued that professionalism goes hand in hand with *accountability*, with clearcut proof of results. Yet such proof is seldom produced in education. More attention is paid to financing education than to demonstrating the *effects* or the *effectiveness* of education. How much it costs in dollars to *keep* a pupil in school for a year is known, but what it costs in resources to produce a year's growth in reading is not.

Viewed and applied positively, the concept of accountability promises much for the improvement of reading instruction. To be accountable is to be responsible for one's own actions. Teachers who accept responsibility for their instructional acts examine their successes and their failures in order to learn from them. They *evaluate* in order to make "professional" decisions. They are accountable to themselves, and in their accounting they continue to grow as teachers.

Content of Evaluation   Perhaps teachers have more difficulty with the *content* of evaluation than with the *purpose* for evaluation. That is, they find it harder to decide *what* to evaluate than *why* they should evaluate. The fact is that there are many aspects to evaluation, so the matter of deciding what to evaluate is largely one of picking the particular aspect to be dealt with at any given time. The following discussion of four types, or aspects, of evaluation offers some direction regarding the content—the *what*—of evaluation. The four types are borrowed from a model for evaluation—the CIPP model—devised by Stufflebeam *et al.* (1972). The model includes *context* evaluation, *input* evaluation, *process* evaluation, and *product* evaluation. See Worthen and Sanders (1973) if you would like to examine some other models for evaluation.

Context evaluation is the foundation for all evaluation efforts. Unlike the essential sequence for building a house, foundation first, the foundation provided by context evaluation can take shape only after some of the other aspects have been dealt with. As it relates to reading instruction, context evaluation involves a careful examination of the theoretical context from which instruction evolves. One employs context evaluation in pursuing such important activities as: (1) the analysis that precedes formulation of a philosophy of teaching reading and the broad goals to be sought, whether it be for a total reading program or for an individual teacher; (2) the identification and subsequent statement of specific objectives or standards consistent with the philosophy and goals—these statements set the criteria for determining whether the approach is working well; and (3) the identification of problems and unmet needs that can be the basis for efforts to improve both the overall program and the instruction offered to an individual learner.

Context Evaluation

The questions raised in context evaluation tend to be broad and program-oriented. These are some questions that you might examine in the process of context evaluation:

- How have we (i.e., the people involved in implementing the program) defined reading? Is it a clearly stated definition that is understood and accepted by everyone involved?

- Are our program objectives clearly stated in terms of student growth and development?

- How does our program accommodate individual differences, needs, and patterns of growth in children?

- Is the program we have defined compatible with the characteristics and needs of our particular student population?

- What are the unmet needs we must tackle in order to improve our reading program?

Note that the focus of context evaluation may be on the overall reading program, the instructional approach of an individual teacher dealing with individual learners, or anywhere in between. Note, too, that the issues can be resolved on the basis of blind faith or controlled investigation or any combination of the bases for *knowing* that were discussed earlier. The main point here is that context evaluation is a process for making decisions that in turn provide the basis for making decisions in all aspects of evaluation. The quality of the decisions that are made depend on the quality of the information considered.

Input Evaluation Through input evaluation one: (1) takes a look at the resources that are available; (2) attempts to determine what resources are needed to implement the *ideal* instructional program; and then (3) makes the compromises required by *reality*. The need for some degree of compromise is almost always present. Seldom are all of the resources needed to implement the ideal reading program either available or forthcoming. That is why the foundation of context evaluation must emerge rather than be set in place before anything else is done.

Input evaluation helps one take a realistic approach to not only program implementation, but also program planning. There is little sense in planning a program that requires four aides for every classroom and a million-dollar budget for supplementary materials when there will be no aides and a substantially smaller budget. Take a positive approach and find the best materials and other support available for the resources that can be identified.

The questions raised in input evaluation tend to be, like the ones in context evaluation, program-oriented. But the focus is restricted to examination of the resources required for effective instruction that is consistent with program goals. These are some examples:

- Are my instructional materials—whether these be "total packages" such as basal readers or collections of supplementary materials—consistent with our reading philosophy and program goals?
- Do I have ready access to materials with appropriate interest and readability levels for all of my students?
- Do I (the teacher) have access to resource persons (e.g., psychologist, reading specialist, librarian, evaluation specialist) who can help me solve problems that are either beyond my level of expertise or outside the scope of what I can do in the classroom?
- Do I have a record-keeping system that is comprehensive but efficient and that expedites communication among teachers?
- How much of my time am I able to spend in *eyeball-to-eyeball* teaching, whether it be an individual, a small group, or a class-size or larger group?

Process Evaluation Efforts to clarify goals come into the classroom through process evaluation, which amounts to looking carefully at what goes on when reading is actually taught. Context and input evaluation have mainly to do with program *planning*; process evaluation deals with program *implementation*. The main purposes of process evaluation are to: (1) monitor program implementation—that is, to examine the extent to which instructional practices reflect program goals; (2) detect flaws in the curriculum plan—that is, to find whether or where the program plan and the instructional practices are out of phase; and (3) guide day-to-day decision making by seeking balances between the plan and the practice. Process evaluation, then, is the scrupulous analysis that one does in order to be assured that carefully made plans are actually being implemented in day-to-day teaching.

In process evaluation the focus shifts from the program itself to the implementation of the program. The questions, then, tend to become more specific as they are directed to the actions of teachers and students. Some examples:

- How much time do I devote daily to reading instruction? How is that time distributed among students?

- Are my instructional activities consistent with those of other teachers who also serve the needs of children I serve? Why or why not?

- Are my students making the progress I have reason to expect? How do I know?

- Am I actually using the resources that are available and that I had planned to use? Do I need others?

- Do I have current records regarding each child's performance and preferences in reading? (Note that one of the questions related to input evaluation also had to do with record keeping. There, however, the question was simply whether a usable record-keeping system is available; here the question is whether the available system is in fact being used effectively. The difference in focus demonstrates the difference in focus between *input* and *process* evaluation.)

Most of us enjoy talking about our philosophies, goals, and materials, but we start to feel a chill when the focus of evaluation is on our day-to-day efforts to implement our programs. And that is precisely where the focus of process evaluation is. We can hide behind high-sounding phrases such as *personal prerogatives* and *sanctity of professional judgment*, but if we do, program planning is a sham, and program implementation is closed to improvement. Or, we can carry on like responsible, *accountable* professionals and benefit from the constructive self-criticism that comes with process evaluation.

Product Evaluation

Product evaluation deals with the *outcomes* of the program once it has been implemented. Through process evaluation teachers try to find out if they are actually implementing the program they planned. They find out whether goals and objectives are being met, whether the program is doing what it was designed to do. They find out if their students are learning to read in a way that is in line with the program's definition of reading.

Product evaluation should occur at the end of a program, e.g., completion of grade 12, to determine whether the individuals *and the group* were successful in meeting the program goals. But it must also occur at checkpoints all along the way—e.g., after a lesson has been completed, after a unit of instruction, at the end of an activity or an objective-based sequence of lessons—to provide continual feedback on the success of the instructional efforts.

Because the focus is on *outcomes*, the questions raised in product evalu-ation deal explicitly with students' performance. The questions must, of course, be formulated in view of the program objectives. Here are some examples:

- Are the students learning to read according to the definition and goals set by the program?
- Do the students value reading as a leisure-time as well as a school-time activity? Do they read a variety of materials?
- Do the students read well enough, and persistently enough, to pursue both their in-school and out-of-school interests and goals?
- In terms of student performance, am I meeting my day-to-day instruc-tional objectives? On the same basis, is each of my students meeting his or her instructional objectives?

A Multifaceted Process The main point for you to understand is that evaluation is a multifaceted pro-cess, not simply a matter of giving tests and writing down scores or awarding grades. If you have a broad conception of evaluation, you are likely to look critically not only at what happens when children take tests, but also at what you are doing and how effective it is. The CIPP model, with its four aspects, provides such a broad conception of evaluation. If you pay attention to each aspect as you plan and implement your teaching, you are almost certain to become a more thoughtful and, as a consequence, a more effective teacher.

Approaches to Evaluation Once the purpose for and the direction of evaluation are set, the question is *how* to proceed with evaluation in reading. Clearly, the *how* will depend very much on the type of evaluation. The instruments and procedures for context and input evaluation will differ from those used for process or product evalua-tion. And the *how* will be directed by the *why*—the program goals and objec-tives. We cannot offer a few pat statements to see you through the *how* of evaluation, but by limiting the discussion that follows, perhaps we can help you get sufficient focus to begin.

The discussion is limited mainly to *process evaluation*, with a bit of over-lap into *product evaluation*. Such evaluation is most relevant to day-to-day teaching, so it deserves a teacher's continued attention. Furthermore, because *tests* are the most commonly used instruments for process-product evaluation, the discussion is limited mainly to consideration of the types of tests available for different purposes. Remember, though, that testing is only one aspect of a broader evaluation process and that ultimately, the tests you select must be consistent with decisions based on the broader view. With the discussion limited mainly to the testing aspect of evaluation, we consider, first, the matter of quality control and then the range of options available.

Quality Control Tests, particularly paper-and-pencil tests, have a certain mystique about them for many teachers and administrators. Such tests are tangible and seemingly "objective," and many bear the names of recognized authority figures; hence the inclination to accept them without raising any serious questions about how good or how appropriate they are. But the fact is that tests are an adequate basis for *knowing* only if they are carefully chosen and properly used. Tests, like every other aspect of an overall evaluation effort, need to be subject to quality control. Stufflebeam (1974) suggests three aspects of quality control: technical adequacy, usefulness, and cost/effectiveness. We will try to briefly characterize each kind of quality control, but we acknowledge that adequate coverage of the related issues would require an entire text or course.

The *technical adequacy* of an evaluation effort can be judged largely on the basis of its objectivity, reliability, validity, and credibility. A test achieves *objectivity* when its format and content are such that the data obtained are uncolored by the views of the test maker. Thus an "objective" test of, say, decoding ability would sample a child's ability to pronounce words without bias as to the particular skills applied to accomplish the task. A test that is *reliable* yields results that are (1) internally consistent, i.e., all of the items contribute to the issue being assessed, and (2) reproducible, i.e., the results, given similar conditions, would be identical at another time. A reliable test, then, gives you an uncluttered look and assurance that what you see today you will see tomorrow. A *valid* test does in fact measure what its makers claim it measures. The most blatant example of tests that are not valid are the ostensible intelligence tests that in fact measure reading ability. And, finally, a test has *credibility* when the results it yields are believable in view of other information the teacher has. A test fails in credibility when a child who "passed" the test is unable to perform more naturalistic classroom tasks.

You should expect some help in judging the technical adequacy of tests from the technical manuals that accompany them. An adequate manual addresses the matters of reliability and validity, and it may even give you some basis for assessing the objectivity of the test. But you need to use your own common sense in examining credibility. Unless you are able to believe what you get when the results are in, a test is not worth giving, no matter what other criteria it meets.

Too often the technical adequacy of tests gets all the attention, and there is no real consideration given to their *usefulness*. Yet the utility of data gathered through testing is probably the ultimate consideration in quality control. Utility can be judged by answering two questions: "Who cares?" and "What difference does it make?" If in the process of choosing a test, the answers to both of those questions are not completely clear, then there is probably good reason to choose no test at all.

Cost/effectiveness is closely related to utility in the application of quality control. If data are not used, then the cost is too high no matter how much or how little it happens to be. But aside from that, with limited resources one must decide whether the data to be got are worth the price in terms of both time and money. Some teachers and administrators appear to be totally dedicated to a standardized testing program that has little impact on either instructional improvement or program planning. The cost is high in terms of time and dollars, and the yield is virtually nonexistent. The cost/effectiveness ratio is very poor. A classroom testing program with emphasis on day-to-day diagnosis and implications for instruction would probably be much more cost-effective in terms of impact on reading improvement.

Quality control, then, amounts to consideration of the integrity and the utility of a particular approach to evaluation, *testing* in the present discussion. In the classroom the *how* of evaluation can realistically be approached by identifying tests that meet quality-control considerations. At the same time, consideration must be given to the options available for testing.

Options Available

Bloom, Hastings, and Madaus (1971) have made a useful distinction between *formative* and *summative* evaluation. Formative evaluation occurs during the process of planning, development, and implementation; summative evaluation is mainly *outcome evaluation* for the purpose of accountability. As we suggested earlier, teachers' day-to-day decisions will be influenced more heavily by formative than by summative evaluation. Yet the instruments of summative evaluation—most prominently, standardized achievement tests—are often viewed as the "testing program." Informal assessment techniques, diagnostic tests, observations, most criterion-referenced measures—the instruments of formative evaluation—are in fact the essence of the testing program insofar as impact on instruction is concerned. In the classroom, then, the *how* of evaluation proceeds best when the concerns of formative evaluation are emphasized. Those concerns are discussed in detail in the next section of this chapter.

WHAT YOU SEEK IS WHAT YOU GET

Comedian Flip Wilson's best character is curvaceous, seductive Geraldine, who delights in telling her admirers, "What you see is what you get!" Although getting what one sees may be a lot, in evaluation that simply is not adequate. In evaluation, *what you SEEK is what you get.*

Wiener and Cromer (1967) made that point in a now-classic article. To oversimplify, they say that the assumptions with which one approaches the diagnosis of reading difficulties will shape not only the findings as to the cause for the problem, but also the procedures used to remedy the problem. In short, you get what you look for in evaluation. What you need to do, then, is to collect the information that will be most useful to you in planning and implementing instruction.

Ten Brink (1974, p. 134) offers four rules of thumb or guidelines for collecting and/or selecting information. An adaptation follows:

- If the judgments and decisions to be made are important and if more accurate information can be obtained with relative ease, gather new information.
- If any new information is unlikely to be more accurate than what is available, use what you have.
- If it is relatively easy to obtain new information, do it.

- If more accurate information is needed but lack of time or money precludes getting it, use what you have with caution. Supplement the available information wherever possible, and seek confirmation—or lack of it—that the information is/was correct.

What the four points amount to is an application of the kind of common sense we talked about in Chapter 2. Seek the information you need; get the best information available with the resources at hand; and check to see whether what you are getting is in line with what you had.

To repeat a basic theme of this chapter, the aspect of evaluation that will have the most explicit impact on your day-to-day teaching is a combination of *process* and *product* evaluation, with emphasis on the formative processes. And, again, what this amounts to is *testing*—or, more properly, *assessment*—insofar as day-to-day evaluation is concerned. We have discussed many of the instruments and procedures used in assessment in earlier chapters that deal with the specifics of *teaching* reading. That is by design, because teaching and evaluation ought almost always to be considered together. Yet it may be instructive to review the main approaches—standardized tests, informal procedures, criterion-referenced measures—to show how each can contribute to your store of information as you seek what you need.

Most standardized tests are *norm-referenced*. That is, a given individual's performance is examined in relation to the performance of other individuals. Keep the following points in mind when you select a standardized test.

Standardized Tests— Select One

1. *Define your purpose for testing.* Standardized tests may be given for any number of reasons—to compare class achievement with local or national norms, to determine the current achievement status of classes or individuals in order to learn whether corrective or remedial steps should be taken, to screen in order to determine the need for further testing, or to evaluate the program. With the purpose for testing clearly in mind, you can decide whether a *survey test* or an *analytical test* would best suit the purpose. Generally, survey tests are group tests designed to do what the term implies: to survey the overall performance of individuals or groups in order to see how well group or individual scores compared with the scores of others at the same age or grade level. Analytical tests may be either group or individual tests. They are like criterion-referenced tests in that they are designed to break total reading performance into specific strengths and weaknesses. They are different from criterion-referenced tests in that group norms, not objectives, set the standards for comparison. Group tests have the obvious advantage of testing more pupils in less time than individual tests, but individual tests are likely to provide much more information regarding the idiosyncrasies of an individual's performance.

2. *Locate suitable tests.* From among the many tests currently available, several will typically appear to be appropriate for the purpose identified.

Probably the most useful single source of assistance in locating and sorting out suitable tests is the *Seventh Mental Measurements Yearbook* (Buros, 1972). (Previous editions were published in 1938, 1940, 1949, 1953, 1959, and 1965.) Available tests in education and psychology are listed and described in the yearbook. Brief descriptions of cost, coverage, and source, as well as one or more critical reviews, are included for each test.

3. *Consider quality control.* The tests that appear to meet the requirements of a given situation need to be subjected to quality control, as discussed earlier. For an extended discussion of things to consider in selecting tests, consult *Standards for Educational and Psychological Tests and Manuals*, available from the American Psychological Association, 1200 Seventeenth Street, N.W., Washington, D.C. 20036. But remember that the best way to become completely familiar with a test in order to make judgments about it is to take it yourself and to administer it to a few children. In that way you can get a good notion of what the test is really like and whether it is appropriate for your purposes.

Standardized tests share certain limitations that must be considered even after the "best available" have been identified. The more salient limitations follow:

1. The very fact that a test is "standardized" in terms of administration and scoring may make it inappropriate for use with certain groups or individuals. The test may be too difficult or too easy; items may be meaningless or placed at inappropriate levels; directions may be incomprehensible.

2. Group administration may work to the disadvantage of certain individuals. The group situation combined with standardized conditions may invalidate the test in some instances. For example, a child who fails to understand one or two words in a set of directions may be unable to respond to all of the items, some of which she or he may or may not have known.

3. The test maker's quest for brevity, which unfortunately but pragmatically enhances the salability of tests in some circles, may result in unrealistic time limits and unfortunate choices between depth and breadth in sampling. As a result, the test scores of children who work very slowly but accurately are likely to be meaningless, and/or the sampling of behavior is likely to be superficial or constricted.

4. The format of the test may restrict the type of items used. A machine-scorable format, for example, virtually demands some form of multiple-choice items. Certain behaviors are not adequately sampled with multiple-choice items.

5. Tests at upper grade levels assume ability at lower levels. Thus a pupil may be able to score at a certain base level by simply signing his or her name to the test booklet. Furthermore, it is generally acknowledged that

standardized tests tend to yield overestimates of a year or more of children's instructional reading levels.

Taken together, standardized tests comprise an important aspect of *formal* evaluation. The good ones meet rigorous quality control criteria, and they offer you a chance to take a controlled look at children's performance, particularly as compared to the performance of specified others. So long as their limitations are fully appreciated, standardized tests can be a valuable source of information.

In the process of assessing the impact of your teaching, you will often find it necessary to seek information that is not available from existing tests or to supplement information from them. When this is so, it is up to you to devise your own informal assessment procedures. Since in many instances you will want to determine whether particular students know how to handle a particular task, the assessment, though informal, is likely to be objective-based. The following sequence can serve as a guide to the effective use of informal assessment. First, decide exactly what information is desired and what this means in terms of observable behavior. Next, devise new or adapt existing test items, materials, or situations to sample the behavior to be evaluated (or, if an appropriate one is available, simply use an existing test). Third, keep a record of the behavior evoked in the test situation. Fourth, analyze the information obtained; and finally, make a judgment as to how the information fits the total picture and how well it fills the gap for which it was intended.

Informal Procedures— Devise Your Own

Examples of some of the most useful and most used informal devices for gathering information follow.

1. *Informal observation.* The most naturalistic informal procedure for gathering information is *informal observation* of the pupil. This technique is often overlooked, but it is one that alert, skillful teachers use effectively for a number of purposes—systematically observing children's overall performance, learning about their interests and attitudes, finding out about their approaches to problem solving and to study situations, and detecting physical problems and limitations. Observing with a purpose can provide real insight into the problems a child is encountering when, for example, she or he attempts to tackle story problems in arithmetic or to attack new words.

2. *Anecdotal records.* In its simplest form, an anecdotal record can consist of a manila folder in which children's work samples and observations are kept in chronological order. The primary purpose for such a record is to help keep in mind the developing characteristics of a child. If there are no readily available checkpoints, gradual but steady improvement may be seen as lack of improvement. Obviously, the record loses its value if it is simply cluttered with an occasional drawing and general statements like, "Clyde appears to be doing better." Entries must describe or reflect real behaviors, and they must be dated.

Informal observation can give the teacher important information about a child.

3. *Informal tests.* Many of the books, workbooks, and periodicals designed for school use include informal, nonstandardized tests that can be used for quick checks of pupils' comprehension, writing ability, grasp of arithmetic concepts, and the like. You can construct similar informal tests to check on pupils' grasp of just-presented material and get samplings of various kinds of behavior.

4. *Checklists.* In this general category are included such things as interest and personality inventories; questionnaires of work habits, interests, activities, playmates; and lists of specific skills that can be used to check a pupil's mastery in certain areas. Such lists can provide practical means for systematizing observations.

5. *Informal reading inventories.* Informal reading inventories can be used to observe a pupil's oral and silent reading at several difficulty levels. An inventory consists of sample passages from the various grade levels of a basal reader series plus comprehension questions. Four levels of reading ability are

typically identified: (a) independent level—the level at which the pupil can read independently with at least 99 percent accuracy in word recognition and 90 percent or better comprehension; (b) instructional level—the level at which the pupil can read with some help from the teacher (at least 95 percent accuracy in word recognition and 70 percent or better comprehension); (c) frustration level—the level at which the pupil can no longer function effectively; and (d) listening capacity level—the highest level at which the pupil can comprehend at least 75 percent of material that is read to him or her. In addition, the child's decoding errors can be analyzed to gain insights into the source of the errors. Procedures for using informal reading inventories to assess decoding and comprehension are described in Chapters 6 and 7. You may also wish to read Johnson and Kress (1965) for a how-to-do-it treatment of informal reading inventories.

You should feel free to adapt these informal procedures to increase their applicability in given situations. Note that all of the informal procedures discussed lend themselves very well to objective-based assessment. Once criterion behaviors have been identified, they can be sampled with paper-and-pencil tests or through informal procedures.

Criterion-referenced measures relate test performance to absolute standards, usually stated in terms of behavioral objectives, rather than to the performance of other students. Such measures are most useful for assessing pupils' performance related to the objectives you have set. Some of the salient contrasts between norm-referenced (standardized) tests and criterion-referenced measures follow:

Criterion-Referenced Measures—Use Your Objectives

1. Standardized tests have little overlap with the objectives of instruction at any given time and place. The overlap for criterion-referenced measures is absolute, for the objectives of instruction *are* the referents (see Chapter 2).

2. Norm-referenced tests are not very useful as aids in planning instruction, because of the low overlap just mentioned. Criterion-referenced measures can be used directly to assess the strengths and weaknesses of individuals with regard to instructional objectives and to plan appropriate instruction.

3. Again because of their nonspecificity, norm-referenced tests often require skills or aptitudes that may be influenced only to a limited extent by experiences in the classroom. This is not so for criterion-referenced measures, because the referent for each test is also the referent for instruction.

4. Standardized tests do not indicate the extent to which individuals or groups have mastered any spectrum of instructional objectives. Again, there is no such problem with criterion-referenced measures, because taken together, they focus on the spectrum of instructional objectives in a given situation.

The main advantage of criterion-referenced measures is that they get directly at the performance of individuals with regard to specified instructional objectives. But the advantage can also be the chief disadvantage, because the measures can be no better than the objectives they were written for. Poorly conceived or badly stated objectives must always give rise to inadequate or inappropriate criterion-referenced measures.

Examples of criterion-referenced tests are given in Chapters 6 and 7. Be aware, though, that criterion-referenced assessment may take a variety of forms, ranging from paper-and-pencil tests to objective-based observation of performance or work samples. Your objective *sets* the criterion, and the criterion-referenced measure *samples* the behavior.

Assessing Attitudes— Proceed with Caution

Readers' attitudes toward reading and the reading process *can* affect not only their immediate comprehension of a printed passage, but also their overall development of functional reading ability and inclination to read. Attitudes *are* important, and teachers ought to pay attention to their students' attitudes toward reading and what shapes them. Yet the fact is that more often than not, attempts to assess attitudes are very badly done. What you are likely to see is a few items like this:

Reading is one of my favorite things.

strongly agree   agree   uncertain   disagree   strongly disagree

and a claim that somehow the items amount to a scale that measures an individual's attitude toward reading. But of course such a scale can have no more credibility than a six-item multiple-choice test that claims to measure reading ability.

Attitudes are elusive. They tend to have little substance, and more often than not an "attitude" is simply a label that is attached to a behavior that has been observed with some consistency. If, for example, a student consistently chooses to read sports stories, one might be inclined to infer that the student has a positive attitude toward sports and sports stories. But the interpretation could be completely erroneous. Closer investigation might reveal that the student reads sports stories only because of peer or parental pressures or because sports stories are the ones she or he *dislikes* least.

The main points here are that observations and inferences about attitudes must be made with caution and that attitude surveys are likely to be as fallacious as observations. Students may check their likes and dislikes or state their preferences with more attention to pleasing—or to displeasing—the teacher than to what they really believe or value. So if you elect to use an attitude inventory, be certain that the instrument is sufficiently well constructed to be reliable and that the items are sufficiently unambiguous to have validity. Perhaps the best way to assess a student's attitudes toward reading is to nurture an empathic relationship with the student. A trusting, open relationship will make for an open expression of likes, dislikes, and preferences.

If you would like to examine some existing attitude inventories, look at the work of Dulin and Chester (1974), Estes (1971), and Kennedy and Halinski (1974).

If you do everything we have suggested to evaluate the teaching/learning that goes on in your school and in your classroom, you will accumulate a substantial amount of data. More often than not, the *accumulation* of the data seems to have been the goal, and the process stops after scores have been recorded and reports have been filed. The product, then, represents nothing more than a waste of time and effort; more important, because there is no apparent payoff from much effort, everyone involved begins to be frustrated by and alienated from the whole evaluation process. Talk to a dozen teachers, and one of the main frustrations that most of them will tell you about is their resentment that the time required for evaluation/assessment/testing is stolen from the time available for instruction. So long as *any* evaluation effort is seen as something apart from the instructional program, that frustration and resentment will continue.

But the fact is that evaluation *for a purpose* is a part of the instructional process. Test scores are not to be filed; they are to be used to plan programs, focus instruction, and influence policy. The identification of instructional objectives is not merely a committee activity and the basis for a committee report; it is a basic process that sets direction and provides a basis for continuous planning and evaluation. Evaluation provides a basis for improving instruction.

Evaluation theorists talk about the *ownership* of data. Their point is that data that are not owned are not used. Owned data were gathered for a purpose, and they are used with a purpose. The problem is that too often, evaluation is merely a process of pleasing others. The solution lies in getting yourself involved in the evaluation process. When you cannot see a purpose, say so. But when you can see a purpose, be certain that you make use of the available data. And do not hesitate to become involved in efforts to demonstrate the outcomes of instruction (e.g., see Reynolds [1971] for perspective on performance contracting) or to examine the performance of teachers (e.g., see McNeil and Wanat [1972] for two views regarding performance tests for teachers). *Ownership* of data and of the evaluation process itself requires not only an intellectual involvement, but also a personal involvement in the process.

When one of the authors was taking a course in experimental psychology, an admonition that often appeared on the chalkboard was: Live with Your Data. The message was that once we had collected data, it was ours forever, whether it supported our biases and hypotheses or not. We could, of course, question the data, and we could gather other data under other conditions. But all the data we had were there to be considered—whether we liked it or not.

The admonition is equally valid when it comes to dealing with evaluation results. Living with your data amounts to accepting evaluation results for the

IT'S WHAT YOU DO WITH WHAT YOU'VE GOT

Live with Your Data

reality they represent and to seeking interpretations that make sense. The points that follow will be helpful as you seek to analyze and interpret—to *live* with—your data.

1. Analyze information as soon after it is gathered as possible. To delay the analysis is to risk forgetting insights that were gained in the gathering or risk having the information go stale because children change so rapidly.

2. Save samples of students' work so comparisons can be made over time. Look for patterns of behavior that may emerge; look for contradictions; be prepared for setbacks as well as for progress.

3. Take care not to jump to quick conclusions. Test out tentative conclusions by considering all of the data and other possible interpretations. Share your insights with others. Be prepared to modify or even to reject a tentative conclusion.

4. Seek and analyze *all* the relevant information. If, for example, a student seems to comprehend adequately when reading orally but not when reading silently, find out what makes the difference. Do not just conclude that there is a "comprehension problem." Or, at the program level, if decoding test scores are going up, but comprehension test scores are coming down, find out why. Do not simply conclude that a new instructional program is required. Gather additional information if necessary.

5. Remember that analysis of information must be continual. No program is static; no student is unchanging. Living with your data involves seeking new information that reflects changes that are occurring constantly.

Application: Use Your Data Gathering and analyzing information amounts to nothing unless and until there is impact on what you do. To suggest that we can tell you—in the absence of any specifics—how to make the best use of your data would be unrealistic. But we can suggest some areas of concern where data can be brought to bear with reasonable expectation of a positive impact.

1. *Focusing instruction.* Children who are learning to read, particularly poor readers, have so much to learn that one might be inclined to begin almost anywhere. But the fact is that *everybody* is *somewhere*, and you can use your data to find out where that is for individual students.

2. *Establishing instructional sequences.* This concern is closely related to the preceding one, but it also involves the teacher's conception of reading. One must decide, ultimately, not only where a student is in terms of instructional needs, but also what comes next in the sequence. Data from all of the aspects of evaluation that we have discussed can be brought to bear here.

3. *Utilizing varied instructional strategies.* Some children respond better to certain teaching strategies than to others. Data derived from process evaluation can help you to decide *what* works best with *whom*.

4. *Utilizing varied materials.* Adequate reading instruction makes use of recreational and functional as well as "instructional" materials. Your data can help you to decide *when* a particular type of material can be used to the best advantage because it will help you to understand the preferences as well as the needs of your students.

5. *Ensuring the transfer of skills.* Teachers who teach skills explicitly and systematically worry about the application of those skills. Part of the problem lies in the fact that a skill must be acquired—*mastered*, if you will—before it can be reliably applied. Data from objective-based, criterion-referenced tests can help you to decide when an individual is *ready* to apply a given skill.

6. *Stimulating interest in reading.* Almost everyone likes to do what she or he can do successfully. Combine assurances of success with an ability to cater to personal interests and you can be virtually certain of students who are interested in reading. Your data give you the basis for directing students' reading with confidence.

7. *Building a positive self-concept as a reader.* Success also contributes to a positive view of oneself as a reader. The better you understand your students—which is to say, the more reliable data you have—the better you will be able to contribute to their success by combining all of the concerns we have just discussed.

REVIEW QUESTIONS

1. How does the specific term "testing" relate to the more general term "evaluation"? In thinking about your answer, consider ways in which "testing" alone neglects important aspects of an adequate evaluation program.

2. Review the section in the chapter headed "The Purpose for Evaluation." Basing your answer on that discussion, can you give two or three good reasons *why* evaluation is important to teachers? Do you think that teachers ought to be accountable for their teaching? If so, to whom?

    a) Now review the section headed "Content of Evaluation." Can you, in your own words, show how the *what* of evaluation, as described by the four types in the CIPP Model, address legitimate concerns of teachers? That is, can you show how *context, input, product,* and *process* evaluation add up to a means for increasing the effectiveness of reading instruction?

    b) Finally, review the section headed "Approaches to Evaluation." Are you inclined to agree with us that *process* and *product* evaluation are most relevant to teachers' day-to-day *teaching*? If so, can you reconcile this with the *four* aspects of the CIPP Model? Do you agree with us that the *how* of evaluation boils down to *testing* for classroom teachers? Do you need to qualify your agreement or disagreement?

3. In general terms, when would you use *norm-referenced*, and when would you use *criterion-referenced* tests? Go back to the chapters on decoding,

comprehension, and study skills and identify two or three specific objectives related to each area. Then decide whether a norm-referenced or a criterion-referenced test would be most appropriate for assessing performance related to each objective. What are the important considerations in making such decisions?

4. What are some of the main advantages of informal assessment procedures? What are the limitations? Can you think of situations in which informal procedures could profitably be used to supplement the findings from formal standardized tests?

5. If we would tell you that we prefer criterion-referenced tests related to specific subskills, what would you infer about *our* definition of reading? If we said that we feel it essential to supplement skill-related tests with informal reading inventories and general comprehension tests, how would you modify your inferences about our definition of reading? Which do you think ought to come first for a beginning teacher of reading: a collection of tests or a personal definition of reading? Can teachers whose personal definitions of reading differ work effectively together in the same reading program? What compromises, if any, would be needed?

REFERENCES   Bloom, Benjamin S., J. T. Hastings, and G. F. Madaus. *Handbook on Formative and Summative Evaluation of Student Learning* (New York: McGraw-Hill, 1971).

Buros, O. K., ed. *The Seventh Mental Measurements Yearbook* (Highland Park, N.J.: Gryphon Press, 1972).

Dulin, Kenneth L., and Robert D. Chester. "A Validated Study of the Estes Attitude Scales," *Journal of Reading* 18 (1974): 56–59.

Estes, Thomas H. "A Scale to Measure Attitude Toward Reading," *Journal of Reading* 1 (1971): 135–138.

Johnson, Marjorie S., and Roy A. Kress. "Procedures for Individual Inventory," in *Informal Reading Inventories*, Reading Aids Series (Newark, Delaware: International Reading Association, 1965), pp. 15–22.

Kennedy, L. D., and R. S. Halinski. "Measuring Attitudes: An Extra Dimension," *Journal of Reading* 18 (1974): 518–522.

Kerlinger, Fred N. *Foundations of Behavioral Research* (New York: Holt, Rinehart and Winston, 1964).

Lessinger, L. M. "Robbing Dr. Peter to "Pay Paul": Accounting for Our Stewardship in Education," *Educational Technology* 11 (1971): 11–14.

Mager, Robert F. *Goal Analysis* (Belmont, Calif.: Fearon, 1972).

McNeil, J. D., and Stanley F. Wanat. "Performance Tests: Assessing Teachers of Reading," *Reading Teacher* 25 (1972): 622–633.

Reynolds, J. D. "Performance Contracting . . . Proceed with Caution," *English Journal* 60 (1971): 102–106.

Stufflebeam, Daniel L. *Meta-Evaluation: Paper #3*, Occasional Paper Series (Evaluation Center, College of Education, Western Michigan University, 1974).

Stufflebeam, Daniel L. *et al. Educational Evaluation and Decision-Making in Education* (Itasca, Ill.: Peacock, 1972).

Ten Brink, T. D. *Evaluation: A Practical Guide to Teachers* (New York: McGraw-Hill, 1974).

Wiener, Morton, and Ward Cromer. "Reading and Reading Difficulty: A Conceptual Analysis," *Harvard Education Review* 37 (1967): 620–643.

Worthen, B. R., and J. R. Sanders. *Educational Evaluation: Theory and Practice* (Worthington, Ohio: Charles A. Jones, 1973).

Chapter 13
Organizing
and Managing
Instruction

OBJECTIVES FOR THE CHAPTER

After reading this chapter, you will be able to:

1. Describe seven different types of grouping techniques that can be used to organize instruction.
2. List the benefits and limitations of each of the grouping plans.
3. Describe how to organize your instructional materials for teaching reading.
4. Explain how the principles of reinforcement can be used in teaching reading.
5. Explain how the principles of transfer affect the acquisition of reading skills.
6. Evaluate your preparedness for teaching reading.

This chapter is designed to help you organize a classroom for reading instruction. We will describe seven different grouping plans that can be used to organize reading groups. As you think about how you will teach reading, you may choose to use one or more of these plans in your classroom. We will tell you about each plan and alert you to the benefits and limitations of each. We will also offer some advice on what you can do to make effective use of the books, workbooks, worksheets, and instructional games available to you as you teach.

We feel that you should also be familiar with two important sets of learning principles directly related to reading instruction: reinforcement and transfer. A skill-centered approach to reading instruction allows many opportunities to apply these learning principles, and several suggestions for implementing these principles will be offered for your consideration. The final section of this chapter is a checklist that should help you take stock of yourself before organizing your own reading program. For a beginning teacher, this checklist can provide direction for making the transition from college student to elementary school teacher.

SELECTING AN ORGANIZATIONAL PLAN

Good teachers have a sincere desire to individualize instruction for their students. Professors of education and educational psychology have long admonished preservice and in-service teachers to "meet the needs" of their children and to individualize instruction so that learning may be an enjoyable, rewarding experience. Unfortunately, by now the desire to individualize instruction has become so great that organizational schemes and instructional techniques are often adopted without much scrutiny or careful preparation. Moreover, the labels used to identify these organizational patterns and techniques are confusing and open to misinterpretation. Imagine the confusion that prevails when terms such as *responsive environment, integrated day, vertical grouping, open planning, open classroom, Joplin plan, nongradedness,* and *achievement grouping* are thrown loosely about. No wonder that even experienced teachers are befuddled by the profusion of plans for organizing children for instruction.

One way for beginning teachers to learn more about the different ways to organize for instruction might be to have experienced teachers describe their organizational plans. But simply asking teachers to describe what is done in their classrooms is not an effective way to determine what takes place during instructional sessions. Sipay (1968) found that what teachers say they do and what they actually do may differ. Furthermore, good teachers adapt instructional programs to coincide with their personal abilities, philosophy, and teaching style, borrowing features from one program and combining them with features from other programs. As a result, identifying the salient characteristics of specific plans in practice is difficult because the programs do not exist in their "pure" form. In addition, a single plan is rarely used exclusively. Instead, teachers in a school are likely to use a combination of plans. Hence, trying to identify the actual grouping procedures employed in teaching reading may be a frustrating task.

Nevertheless, as a beginning teacher you will need to decide on a plan to use when teaching reading. In reality, the plan you finally adopt may not resemble others used in your school or even any of the ones we are about to describe. Yet you will use *some* type of grouping plan. To help decide which plan, or combination of plans, is best for you will probably take time and involve trial and error. We believe that organizational patterns used for teaching reading should be based on the students' needs and teacher competencies rather than on administrative convenience. We want to stress that you should carefully consider your particular strengths and weaknesses and then match an appropriate organizational pattern to your own abilities. If you are well organized and systematic, for example, you might be able to handle a less structured organizational plan; if you have difficulty establishing routine schedules for yourself, you might be wiser to use a more structured plan. Ideally, the organizational plan you choose should complement your abilities.

Although almost countless variations in grouping plans are actually used, we have identified seven plans that seem to include unique features for organizing classrooms:

POPULAR GROUPING PLANS

1. Skill grouping
2. Interest grouping
3. Departmental grouping
4. Joplin plan
5. Achievement grouping
6. Nongraded grouping
7. Open classroom

Other plans have been devised and could also be included in this list. Tinker and McCullough (1975) and Southgate (1973), for example, list additional plans that could be described, but we feel that these others are simply variations of the seven we have identified. The point is, grouping can be done in an infinite number of ways. An enterprising teacher, for example, might simultaneously use skill grouping, interest grouping, achievement grouping, and open-classroom grouping. However, in order to differentiate among the essential characteristics of each plan, we have chosen to present them separately. As you read about these seven plans, keep in mind that you may choose to integrate two or more of the plans in your classroom.

Skill Grouping   It should be clear by this time that we tend to favor skill grouping. Skill groups, or special-needs groups, as Durkin (1974) calls them, are relatively easy to form with the aid of a skills-management system. The teacher simply examines each child's skill profile to determine who needs instruction directed toward which specific skills. Then students can be placed in temporary skill groups for instruction. Instruction continues until the students have mastered the skill being taught. Individual students may leave the group early if they learn the skill before the majority of the group members do.

Skill groups can be formed without using a skills-management system, as long as the teacher has specific instructional objectives in mind. Grouping will then be based on teacher observation and informal assessment instead of criterion-referenced test performance, however.

Ruddell (1974) states that decoding, study skills, comprehension, oral-language development, and oral reading can all form the broad basis for skill instruction. Within these more general areas, groups based on a need for specific skills should be identified. For example, when dealing with decoding skills, the class might be divided into groups that could benefit from instruction in sight vocabulary, initial and final consonant sounds, and consonant digraphs. When this level of specificity is attained, there is a greater chance that all students will be receiving individualized instruction in skills in which they are deficient.

Once children have been placed in skill groups, it is difficult to say how long they need to remain there for instruction. The complexity of the skill being taught, the amount of instructional time given during the week, and the quality of instruction all need to be considered when planning the weekly teaching schedule. Whereas a simple visual-discrimination skill may be learned in a week, or even in a day or two, learning to discriminate auditorally between two or three short vowel sounds may take much more time. However, as a guideline to assist in planning, a good rule of thumb is to schedule roughly two hours of skill instruction per week, per child, per skill, if instruction on skills is to be effective.

Benefits   There are several important benefits to be derived from working with children in skill groups. First, students receive instruction only in areas in which they have a demonstrated weakness. Thus students who already know a skill aren't forced to join a group for additional instruction. This eliminates much of the boredom that often accompanies daily instruction. A second benefit is that groups are created and disbanded at relatively frequent intervals, thus reducing the danger of a child's being assigned to one instructional group for the

Placing children in small groups can facilitate skills instruction.

entire year regardless of any change in reading skills. Furthermore, since children with different overall abilities work side by side with one another and in ever changing groups, there is little danger that any student will be considered a member of the "top" or "bottom" group. A final benefit of skill grouping is the positive effect it can have on the attitudes of students. When instruction is specific, many students can be taught in the classroom instead of "down the hall" in the reading specialist's room. This can do much to eliminate the negative self-concept some students develop and can do much to foster better acceptance by their classroom peers (Stevens, 1971).

Limitations

Despite the many positive points to be made for organizing students into skill groups, there are also some limitations. The limitation most often mentioned by classroom teachers is the amount of testing required. Before children can be placed in groups for skill instruction, they need to be pretested on those skills. And once pretesting has been concluded, plans must be made for assessing students' skill development after instruction has been completed. Teachers often complain that they never have time to teach; all they do is test. However, we would counter that argument by pointing out that *unless* the testing is done, teachers may be wasting even more of their instructional time by providing skill instruction based on the old "by-guess-and-by-gosh" method: *"Gosh*, the manual says to teach short *a*, so I *guess* I'll teach it to all of the middle group."

A second limitation is the need for up-to-date and accurate records of each child's skill development (see Chapter 4). However, choosing a record-keeping system is only a start. Time must be spent each week in keeping records current. Fortunately, a growing number of school systems have paid aides or volunteers to help teachers with these kinds of clerical tasks.

Application Because we feel that skill grouping is one of the most important organizational plans, we are going to illustrate how this plan might be implemented in a hypothetical classroom, under the direction of Ms. Marvel. As a first step (way back in September), Ms. Marvel should have identified the skills she hopes to teach during the year and chosen either prescriptive or descriptive objectives for each of the skills (see Chapter 2). Next, Ms. Marvel would administer the appropriate skill pretests to the class. Let's assume that she has just completed this. In recording the students' test results, she has noticed that several of the students need additional help with consonant digraphs. Being a conscientious teacher, Ms. Marvel decides to group these children temporarily for daily instruction on consonant digraphs. Ms. Marvel plans several kinds of instructional activities for working with these children during the next week. She will use some chalkboard activities with the students, as well as worksheets and games. She also is careful to make specific plans for giving the children opportunities to use the skill while reading prose material, such as library books.

Now let's move ahead to the end of the week. After several days of instruction, Ms. Marvel has a *general* idea of how well the students have learned and applied the skill. She feels that most of the students have learned the skill. Simply through her own observation, Ms. Marvel is certain that Tammy, Jill, Paul, and David have mastered consonant digraphs. However, she is not sure about Barbara, Annie, and Manuel. For these three children Ms. Marvel decides to use a more formal, pencil-and-paper test to check for mastery. To her delight, she finds that all of the children except Barbara have learned the skill. For Barbara, Ms. Marvel plans some additional skill work, using some of the same instructional materials and techniques from the earlier lessons, but also adding some new instructional procedures. She plans to give Barbara three more days of individual help on that skill. If, at the end of that time, Barbara still has not learned the consonant digraphs, Ms. Marvel intends to stop work temporarily on that skill and begin with other skills. Perhaps Barbara will be able to learn that skill more easily at a later time.

We have described Ms. Marvel's plans for only one skill group. In most classrooms, of course, the teacher will need to teach more than one skill group at a time. We have found that about 40 percent of the teachers using this method of grouping have been able to teach two or more groups at the same time, with one group working with the teacher and the others working independently.

To be able to keep more than group actively involved in meaningful activities requires a great deal of organizational ability. A beginning teacher may need to work with only two or three skill groups at first, until he or she feels comfortable with working with more groups. If only two or three skill groups are identified, the children who do not need to work in these groups must have other worthwhile tasks to do. They may read library books or their basal readers at this time. They may practice penmanship, write creative stories, or listen to taped books. Many language arts activities may be completed by these children while the teacher is working with a skill group. Of course, planning for these activities is more work for the already overburdened teacher. However, to require these children to participate in skill groups for which they have no need is indefensible.

Interest Grouping

Interest grouping, as the name implies, involves bringing students together to share ideas and to learn about similar topics. Interest groups can be formed to read about animals, biographies, or any other topic in which students have shown interest. The groups remain together for a relatively short time, say, two to four weeks, reading about their topic, sharing what they have learned, and perhaps preparing a final project. The teacher's most important tasks during this period are to help the students find materials and to give additional guidance when necessary. An adequate selection of books at various reading levels concerning the chosen topics must be readily available so that the students may select the book(s) they want to read and then share their stories with other members of the group.

Some primary-grade youngsters are unable to work independently. They may be immature or lack the necessary reference skills needed to do much of their own library research. Older students are usually able to work more independently in interest groups. They may use the library to search for answers to specific questions they have raised during earlier group meetings. These students, because they are able to gather information through independent research, may need to meet on a formal basis only once a week to compare notes and discuss their findings. Between these formal group meetings, though, the teacher should check each student's progress individually.

Benefits

Interest grouping has some of the same advantages of skill grouping. For example, there is frequent regrouping of students. Hence a child is less likely to be labeled as a good or poor reader, since students of varying abilities usually comprise each group. Another beneficial feature of this plan is that children have selected topics that they are interested in and therefore *want* to be in a particular group. Since membership in a group is on a voluntary basis, student interest is high, and pupils are usually excited about their chosen topics. There are likely to be fewer behavior problems when all learners are working on a topic of their choice. As a result, the teacher can devote more energy to guiding learning instead of controlling disruptive behavior. A final advantage of this plan is that reading instruction can be integrated with other subject-matter areas such as science and social studies. We have found most elementary school students to be extremely interested in science topics. It makes good sense, then, to capitalize on this interest and let science class be another vehicle for teaching reading skills.

Limitations Unless some type of structure within which students must operate is provided, interest grouping can get out of hand. To simply allow every child to pursue interests at will is to invite chaos. The easiest way to group children according to interest is to limit their choices. They might be asked to choose to be in one of three or four groups. Some children may choose to read about animals, others may prefer mystery stories, and still others may read autobiographies. Presenting the children with a limited number of alternatives still gives the children some freedom of choice of a topic, but the range of topics has been limited to provide some overall structure. The key is to select topics so that all children will be interested in at least one of the choices.

Another limitation of this approach is that the teacher must have a good command of the subject matter if he or she plans to interrelate reading instruction with other academic areas. This calls for a knowledgeable, creative, and highly organized teacher. A person who possesses these characteristics and can teach without having commercially prepared lesson plans at hand may find interest grouping a valuable organizational alternative. However, a person who relies heavily on detailed instructions from a basal-reader teacher manual or other published material should implement this plan cautiously.

Application Interest groups can be formed for any number of reasons. One of the authors has used interest grouping at the intermediate grades to conduct panel discussions and debates. In one instance a classroom was divided into two groups, and each group did the necessary library research to learn about the advantages and disadvantages of a socialistic state versus a democratic form of government. After each interest group completed its preparation, a very effective debate was staged. By recording the event on audio tape, it was possible to replay the debate and objectively evaluate which group's presentation had been more convincing. Through the use of interest groups, the students were able to see the relationships among reading, reference skills, and social studies.

Another effective use of interest groups was found in a fifth-grade class in which the teacher used an integrated reading-science approach. Students were free to choose and study an array of topics and to work in small groups to seek answers to their formally prepared questions. Topics ranged from "How to set up your own aquarium" to "How babies are born." Once the members of each group had studied their topic in sufficient detail, they were asked to present their information via lectures, skits, or discussions to the other members of the class.

Note that in both of these examples the teachers used a concluding activity or project to end the unit of study. In one case, a debate was staged. In the other, presentations were made. Requiring some tangible evidence of the group's efforts will do much to foster goal orientation and will help keep the group on track.

If interest grouping is successful, it will create a heavy demand for library books on many topics. The classroom teacher and the librarian must work

Interest groups can be used to integrate a variety of skills and subject-matter areas.

together to make sure that there is an abundance of appropriate books of varying readability levels for all topics. Finding an adequate number of easy-to-read books for less able readers may be particularly difficult. But without a large selection of reading material available, grouping by interest simply will not work.

For subject-matter grouping, different academic subjects are taught by different teachers. Under this plan, two teachers may agree to concentrate their teaching on specific subjects; children move from teacher to teacher. In other instances four or more teachers may choose to teach only one or two subjects each during the day. Each teacher may teach the same subject to several different classes.

 Subject-matter grouping is more common at the middle school and high school levels than at the elementary grades. A more prevalent grouping pattern at the elementary school level is for two teachers to share a joint responsibility for curricular subjects. Generally, one teacher assumes the responsibility for teaching mathematics and science; the second teacher gives instruction in language arts and social studies.

Subject-Matter Grouping

Benefits   There are three main advantages in using the subject-matter grouping plan. The first is that the teacher is able to develop a greater personal understanding of the subjects he or she teaches. Because fewer subjects are taught, each teacher can "specialize" in one or two areas rather than try to be knowledgeable in four or five subjects.

A second advantage of grouping by subject matter is that of cooperative planning. When several teachers plan lessons together, they have an opportunity to exchange information and teaching ideas. Co-workers may be able to suggest or even share alternative materials or activities. In addition, teachers may coordinate goals and topics in order to reinforce what the children are taught in other subject areas.

A third benefit of this plan is that each teacher will be able to bring his or her own subject-matter strengths as well as personal strengths to more than one group of students. In subject-matter grouping the students can be exposed to each teacher's "best" subject(s). If you accept the idea that we teach best in areas we enjoy, high-quality teaching should be a hallmark of this approach.

Limitations   The advantages of this approach seem to be outweighed by the disadvantages. Often subject matter, rather than the students' needs, becomes the most important facet in this plan. Elementary schools become miniature high schools, and student needs and abilities become secondary to the subject-matter content. Poorer readers are often overlooked and fail to receive the type of instruction they need while teachers inadvertently favor the more capable students.

A second disadvantage of this plan is that massive amounts of time need to be spent coordinating the teaching efforts of the staff. Although cooperative planning has many benefits, in some situations so much planning time is needed to integrate the teaching efforts of the staff that another grouping plan might have been just as effective and would have required less planning time. Teachers do not always have the luxury of joint planning sessions during the school day. Although planning can take place after children go home for the day, most teachers simply lack enough energy to spend the amount of time necessary to truly coordinate their teaching efforts this late in the day.

Joplin Plan   The Joplin plan, which originated in Joplin, Missouri (Ruddell, 1974, pp. 555), is a type of cross-class and cross-grade grouping. In this plan children from two or more classrooms are divided into groups on the basis of reading-ability level, and during a mutually agreeable time they move between classrooms for reading instruction. For example, third-, fourth-, and fifth-grade teachers (one teacher at each grade) might agree to exchange students during their 8:30–10:00 A.M. reading period. To understand how the Joplin plan might work, examine the abbreviated class lists in Tables 13.1 and 13.2.

Benefits   In our opinion there is only one apparent advantage in using this plan. The Joplin plan allows the range of *general* reading ability in each classroom to be reduced. For example, if the fifth-grade teacher worked only with the children originally assigned to that room, he or she would need to have four reading

Third grade		Fourth grade		Fifth grade	
Student	*Reading level*	*Student*	*Reading level*	*Student*	*Reading level*
Adam	2.8	Anna	4.3	Bart	3.5
Blair	3.9	Cerise	5.9	Donna	6.0
Charlie	4.2	David	2.9	Esther	6.3
Hannah	2.6	Ella	3.4	Fran	5.2
Isaac	5.3	Nathan	3.6	George	5.4
Joanna	4.1	Ozzie	4.1	Pete	4.8
Maria	3.5	Rebecca	4.5	Rusty	5.1
Pauline	3.0	Robert	4.7	Steve	6.4
Preston	3.8	Tom	5.1	Tina	4.3
Willie	2.6	Zak	4.4	Yolanda	4.8

TABLE 13.1
Grade-level room assignments

Mr. Wonderful's room

High second/Low third grade		Middle/High third grade	
Student	*Reading level*	*Student*	*Reading level*
Adam	2.8	Blair	3.9
Hannah	2.6	Maria	3.5
Pauline	3.0	Preston	3.8
Willie	2.6	Ella	3.4
David	2.9	Nathan	3.6
		Bart	3.5

Ms. Motherly's room

Low fourth grade		Middle/High fourth grade	
Student	*Reading level*	*Student*	*Reading level*
Charlie	4.2	Rebecca	4.5
Joanna	4.1	Robert	4.7
Anna	4.3	Zak	4.4
Ozzie	4.1	Pete	4.8
Tina	4.3	Yolanda	4.8

Ms. Charming's room

Fifth grade		Sixth grade	
Student	*Reading level*	*Student*	*Reading level*
Isaac	5.3	Cerise	5.9
Tom	5.1	Donna	6.0
Fran	5.2	Esther	6.3
George	5.4	Steve	6.4
Rusty	5.1		

TABLE 13.2
Reading-class assignments

groups: a third-grade group for Bart; a fourth-grade group for Pete, Tina, and Yolanda; a fifth-grade group for Fran, George, and Rusty; and a sixth-grade group for Donna, Esther, and Steve. Similarly, the third-grade teacher would need a second-grade group (Adam, Hannah, and Willie), a third-grade group (Blair, Maria, Pauline, and Preston), a fourth-grade group (Charlie), and a fifth-grade group (Isaac). If the third-grade teacher felt unable to work with so many groups, Charlie and Isaac might be placed in the third-grade group and as a result asked to do assignments that were much too easy for them. In the fifth grade Bart might be forced to work with fourth- or fifth-grade materials. Using the Joplin plan to organize students into roughly homogeneous groups can help to ensure that students can be placed in reading groups that are appropriate to their achievement level and that teacher do not have to teach a large number of reading groups.

Limitations   We feel there are severe limitations with this plan. First, although students who participate in such a plan may be homogeneously grouped on the basis of general reading ability, their specific skill-development abilities may vary widely (Oliver, 1970). Thus when the skill-development profiles of students in any one group are examined, the group no longer is homogeneous. In fact, differences in the skill needs within any one group, based on overall reading ability, are likely to be as great as the differences *between* groups.

Second, there is the danger that once students are placed in a group, they will remain there for the duration of the school year. It is easy to become complacent once students have been placed at what seems to be their appropriate reading levels. Because students progress at various rates, however, the teacher needs to be constantly aware of changes in students' reading ability. Unless frequent adjustments are made in reading groups, there is the danger that some students will be misplaced.

A third limitation of this plan is that reading instruction tends to become separated from other classroom activities. "Reading" becomes a subject that is taught apart from the content areas instead of being taught as a part of those subjects. In addition, the "homeroom teacher" may lose sight of the reading development of his or her own students.

A final danger is stressed by Durkin (1974). She believes that this type of grouping may result in whole-class instruction, which eventually may lead to the students' disinterest in learning to read. This can easily happen if teachers fail to provide for the specific needs of students within each reading group. Simply because all of the students are reading at the same general level does not justify giving them all the same type of instruction. Yet this sometimes occurs. When it does, students are likely to become "turned off" to reading.

Achievement Grouping   In achievement grouping students are ordinarily grouped on the basis of the results of an informal reading inventory or their scores on standardized reading-achievement measures. Achievement grouping is perhaps the most common form of grouping used to teach reading. It is an *intraclass* grouping method and usually results in three reading groups per classroom. Experienced teachers sometimes refer to this plan as a "three-ring circus" because it is necessary to keep two groups occupied with independent activities while the teacher works with the other group. In reality a teacher may need to have more than three reading groups in a single classroom if all students are to receive instruction at their appropriate reading levels. As a rule of thumb, a greater range of reading abilities should be expected in the higher grades than in the lower ones. The range of abilities in first grade may span only two or three years, whereas there may be a seven- or eight-year range of ability at the sixth-grade level. The teacher must meet the reading needs of as many of these students as possible. As you can imagine, this is no small task.

Benefits

Achievement grouping has benefits for both the teacher and the students. Because students have been placed in reading groups on the basis of their overall reading achievement, they are more likely to receive instruction at the appropriate level than are students who are instructed as a whole-class unit. When compared to another alternative—completely individualized instruction— achievement grouping provides needed interaction among students that should help foster a concept of reading as a communication process and as a pleasureable experience.

Achievement grouping is an aid to the teacher because it provides a reasonably sound basis for dividing children into a manageable number of instructional groups. The teacher has the satisfaction of knowing that she or he will be able to differentiate instruction to some degree but without meeting with each student individually.

Limitations

One of the shortcomings of this plan, as with the Joplin plan, is that students are often grouped for instruction on the basis of their general reading achievement scores rather than their specific skill-development needs. In addition, when groups are not flexible and are achievement-based, the children in the lowest reading group often become stigmatized as the "dumbies" simply because they are always grouped together for instruction.

Another limitation of this plan is that there is seldom mobility among reading groups (Oliver, 1970). As a result, if a student is accidentally misplaced in a group, there may be a self-fulfilling prophecy effect. That is, more able students who have been inappropriately placed in a group of less able students may soon think of themselves as being poorer readers than they actually are. Another undesirable outcome can occur if less able students are grouped with more proficient readers. The poorer readers may soon consider themselves to be failures even though they may be working up to their capability.

Nongraded Grouping

The nongraded organizational pattern is generally found in the primary grades. Once a group of children is assigned to a teacher or group of teachers, they remain with the same instructor(s) for three or more years. Grouping for instruction in all subjects, including reading, is based on achievement, not on "grade level" or age. As a result, it is not unusual to find six-, seven-, and eight-year-olds working side by side in reading groups or in other classroom activities. Because of the lack of emphasis on grade level, children in this plan may progress at a rate commensurate with their individual abilities, without fear of failing.

Benefits The nongraded organizational plan has received much favorable publicity and is widely acclaimed as one of the more successful grouping plans. Two major advantages can be derived from this plan. First, it appears to enhance school achievement (Brody, 1970; Hillson *et al.*, 1964; and Martin and Pavan, 1976). This may be the result of teachers being able to work closely with students for more than one year. Many teachers in traditionally organized schools complain that by the time they really know their students, the children pass on to another teacher. In a nongraded unit, once teachers have had an opportunity to learn their students' individual needs, they are able to supply focused instruction for these students for two or three years.

A second benefit of this plan, when it is properly implemented, is the positive effect it has on students' self-concepts. Because students are taught according to their needs, they can clearly see that teachers are attempting to help them as individuals, not as members of an undifferentiated group. When this type of relationship exists, students will probably be motivated to do their best. Furthermore, because of individually focused instruction, the children should be able to have many successful experiences.

Hillson *et al.* (1964) point out several reasons why this plan has been successful. First, teachers usually volunteer to work with the plan. Hence, such teachers are likely to be willing to work hard to make the plan successful. Second, extensive in-service education has usually been conducted for teachers who want to teach in a nongraded setting. Third, there has usually been strong administrative support for this plan, and special materials have been purchased to help teachers individualize instruction. Finally, parents of children who will be enrolled in nongraded schools have often received a special orientation to the plan and hence may be more interested in the success of their children than parents of students enrolled in schools that did not use this plan.

Limitations As with all plans, the nongraded plan has also been criticized. Brody (1970), for instance, stated that there is little academic enrichment when this plan is implemented. Martin and Pavan (1976, p. 311) agree: "While it may be that some nongraded programs have progressed to providing experiences appropriate to each child's present level of development, potential, interest, etc., most of them have so far achieved individualization in only one respect: Pupils proceed through the same materials in pretty much the same way, but they do so at their own rate."*

Another limitation of this plan is that often the concept of nongradedness breaks down, and students are in actuality placed in grades once again. Thus a student may be promoted to the next nongraded room simply because he or

*Lyn S. Martin and Barbara N. Pavan, "Current Research on Open Space, Nongrading, Vertical Grouping, and Team Teaching," *Phi Delta Kappan* (Jan. 1976): 311. Used with permission.

she has completed the appropriate number of years' attendance in a previous nongraded room. When this happens, social promotion becomes the sole criterion for advancing students.

The concept of the open classroom is one of the most misunderstood in education. To some, "open" classroom refers to the architectural arrangements found within a school building. Such classrooms might be better termed "open space" classrooms. Open classrooms, or open education as some have labeled it, should be the term to describe a philosophy of education. Rogers (1976) and Weiner (1974) have listed some of the characteristics of open classrooms. They include such practices as using a great many manipulative materials, providing an abundance of books, and establishing a variety of interest centers. The open-classroom organization permits free movement within the room, as children move from activity to activity and teachers encourage a nonauthoritarian atmosphere. Furthermore, multiage and multigrade grouping usually exist. Ideally, the teacher serves as a facilitator of learning rather than as a dispenser of knowledge.

"Open classroom" refers more to a philosophy of education than to a physical arrangement within the classroom.

Many teachers continue to use the basal reader in this organizational plan. Both Rogers and Weiner found that between 50 and 75 percent of the teachers using this plan relied on the basal-reader program and its components to help them teach reading. Over 60 percent of the teachers that Rogers questioned used short-term skill grouping, too.

Benefits There are at least four benefits to be derived from using this plan. First, communication among teachers and between students and teachers seems to be enhanced. This may be due to the informal atmosphere of the classroom.

Second, the students in this plan seem to have more positive attitudes toward school and better self-concepts than do students who are grouped in some of the other organizational plans. (Similar positive effects were also found in the nongraded classroom.) These attitudes and self-concepts are probably directly related to the teachers' efforts to individualize instruction.

Third, because teachers often attempt to correlate subject-matter content with reading instruction, learning takes on a more functional, or "real world," note. Children are more inclined to search out answers and read because they are genuinely interested in a topic, not because it's "reading class."

A final positive feature of this plan is that there is an improvement in the cooperative working atmosphere existing among students. Since small-group projects are often an integral part of this plan, students learn to work closely with one another. Teachers may ask each group to provide some type of tangible evidence of its effort. Such requirements force students to pull together and work toward a common goal.

Limitations There are also disadvantages in using this plan. Because of the unstructured daily schedule, some teachers are reluctant to give direct instruction in subject-matter areas. Children who aren't motivated or are withdrawn may not get the focused instruction they need.

Second, some teachers do not have the organizational capability to operate effectively in an open classroom. As a result, instructional efforts may lack the focus that many students need. Or, teachers may teach only their favorite subjects and overlook the other necessary subject areas.

A third danger of this plan is that teachers may emphasize the affective aspects of the curriculum at the expense of the cognitive areas. School, in other words, may turn into a place to "have a good time" rather than a place to learn. Unfortunately, some teachers view basic skills instruction and affective education as being mutually exclusive.

Grouping Plans in Perspective Now that we have explained some of the grouping plans that are available to choose from, you should be aware of a few additional points to help you put grouping into its proper perspective. First, grouping patterns in reading have been in existence for more than half a century (Smith, 1965). During that period a number of organizational plans have been proposed, most of them without a research-supported base. Harris (1976) contends that nongraded schools, subject-matter grouping, and open schools have been instituted primarily due to bandwagon effects. We agree and suggest a reason why this is so. With only slightly over 20 percent of the teacher-training institutions in the country requiring more than a three-semester credit hour course in reading (Morrison and Austin, 1976), teachers do not have enough time to study the issues involved with grouping in sufficient detail. And, in their desire to better meet the needs of their students, they are quick to adopt plans that promise to make their teaching increasingly effective, but that are not really suited to the personalities of the teachers involved or to the needs of the students.

Two more important points concerning grouping need emphasis. First, no one research study ever *proves* that one organizational pattern is superior to another. A plan may work well with one set of teachers and students and not another. A number of well-designed and well-executed studies need to be examined to determine if trends *across* studies are evident. Second, and very important, a grouping plan is simply an organizational plan and has only a minor direct effect on efforts to improve the reading ability of students. The success of any grouping plan depends more on the quality of the teacher than on the organizational plan per se.

Choosing a grouping plan that is suited to the characteristics of both the teacher and the students is an important first step toward effective instruction. Once the students have been grouped, teachers need to turn their attention to techniques for enhancing instruction through daily lessons. In this section we have chosen to emphasize three important matters that lead to effective instruction: choice and organization of instructional materials, application of the principles of reinforcement theory, and provision for aiding students in transferring what they learn in directed lessons to less structured situations.

TECHNIQUES FOR IMPROVING INSTRUCTION

Any experienced classroom teacher will agree that it is important to keep instructional materials organized so that the materials are available when needed. Most teachers would also agree that *they* and what they do with the materials are more important than the materials themselves. There is less agreement about what should guide the choice of materials for individual students.

Choosing, Organizing, and Using Materials

A teacher who has decided to use a skills-management approach like those described in Chapter 4 will be well on the way toward getting the available instructional materials keyed to the objectives of his or her program. However, since new materials become available almost daily, the teacher must continually update instructional materials and match them to program objectives. Furthermore, organizing such a multitude of materials so that they are easily accessible is a very time-consuming enterprise. Sometimes schools have instructional materials centers staffed by individuals who can classify and house many of these materials in a central location. A checkout system may be established whereby a teacher uses materials for a period of time and then returns them to the central depository. Reading specialists can also assume the responsibility for coordinating use of instructional materials. We feel that it is

Organizing Instructional Materials

economically unrealistic for each teacher in a building to have a duplicate set of materials. Instead, a more financially responsible plan is to have fewer sets of materials kept in a central location. If these materials are organized by skills, each teacher can quickly choose the material appropriate for teaching a particular skill.

Using Your Materials   Sometimes teachers and administrators become quite concerned about the quantity of instructional materials needed to do an adequate job. School boards often proudly cite high dollar costs per pupil as proof that the children are receiving a good education. However, the concern should not be with the *quantity* of instructional materials, but with the *quality* of the instruction that makes use of those materials.

Educators often naively rely on "good materials" to ensure effective instruction. Unfortunately, a rating of "good" may be based solely on the publisher's advertising claims. Fewer than ten percent of the over 10,000 separate games, books, and audiovisual-material available to assist the teacher of reading have been field-tested (Maxwell, 1972). This means that most of the educational products available to teach reading were never tried out, and as a consequence their usefulness has never been demonstrated.

But the more basic problem is that the materials themselves are less important than the ways in which they are used. Sipay (1968), for example, found that when the same instructional materials and approaches were used by different teachers, there was a great difference in the manner in which the materials were used. No matter what publishers *say* about using materials, teachers will use them as they see fit! And some teachers will use them more effectively than others.

In another effort to determine how teachers use instructional materials, Morrison (1968) studied the use of hardware and software materials in elementary school classrooms. She visited 81 classrooms in 33 inner-city, mid-city, and suburban schools. She categorized each teacher's classroom according to the activities being conducted, the type of instructional materials being used, the teacher's teaching styles and pupil responses, and the affective climate of the classroom. Morrison suggested that classroom teachers may be categorized into three groups: (1) those who use the same reading or subject-area text with all pupils; (2) those who use multilevel texts in reading groups or ability-subject grouping; and (3) those who use supplementary and/or individualized reading materials. In classrooms in which teachers used the same text for all students, there was significantly less class participation, assistance to pupils, and mobility within the room. Teachers in the multitext group gave significantly more assistance to pupils, allowed more mobility within the classroom, used significantly more instructional materials, had more positive verbal statements, and used significantly fewer punitive behaviors. Teachers in the supplementary reading materials group were similar to the multitext group in that their students had significantly more positive physical behaviors, more positive pupil covert actions, and fewer negative covert behaviors.

The point we are trying to make is that it is not the quality, or quantity of materials per se that will make an effective teacher. Rather, it is how the materials are used. Teachers who individualize their instruction with appropriate group or individual materials enjoy classrooms that have a positive, healthy learning climate. Teachers who do not provide for individual differences, on the other hand, have classrooms in which students are disruptive and demonstrate unacceptable school behavior. No "magic" material can substitute for the magic of a concerned teacher who instructs children as individuals.

Learning Modalities

The choice of a specific instructional material to teach a particular skill may be based on many different criteria. With the recent interest in the field of learning disabilities, some teachers have been led to believe that instructional materials should be matched to a child's dominant learning channel. Advocates of this modality concept suggest that some children are visual learners, some are auditory learners, and still others rely on a kinesthetic approach to learning. Children who learn best through a visual mode, the proponents contend, should be taught to read through a sight-word approach. Auditory learners would make the best progress if taught with a phonics approach. According to the theory, children who learned best through the kinesthetic approach should receive instruction that emphasizes the tracing or copying of words.

Several studies (Cooper, 1972; Robinson, 1972; Bateman, 1968; Vandever and Neville, 1974) have tried to determine whether it is worthwhile to teach to a child's dominant learning modality. These investigators and others found little evidence to support this practice. As a result, in spite of much attention to the question of learning modalities in both professional literature and the popular press, we believe that the time spent categorizing instructional materials according to learning modalities is largely wasted, since there appears to be no demonstrated payoff.

Reinforcement and Reading Acquisition

The principles and techniques of reinforcement of learning should be considered whenever planning for instruction. Reinforcement techniques can be used to help children become better readers and to help teaching to be more rewarding for both the teachers and the pupils.

In its simplest form, reinforcement can be considered to be a method for rewarding and thereby encouraging a desired behavior. Whenever a student exhibits a desirable action, a teacher may choose to reinforce the behavior in some manner. Often, a gold star or a word of praise can serve as a form of reinforcement. The purpose for administering the "reinforcer" is to increase the probability of the response occurring again (Restle, 1975). According to Gargiulo (1971, p. 21): "The whole process of teaching beginning readers is based on a continuous or partial reinforcement schedule* used by the teacher to keep the child going, to keep him motivated, and to make him feel good that he is learning."

---

*A continuous-reinforcement schedule rewards the child for every occurrence of the desired behavior. A partial-reinforcement schedule rewards the child for only a portion of the desired behaviors.

Reinforcement can take many forms. The very act of learning to read, for example, may be pleasurable and therefore reinforcing in itself. An "A" or a smiling face on a worksheet are other meaningful forms of reinforcement to most students. Receiving encouraging words from the teacher or perhaps the praise of a fellow student also is important to most children and hence reinforcing. (Of course, peers can also reward one another for behavior the teacher does not want reinforced, such as making "smart" remarks or falling off a chair.) Verbal reinforcement can come from parents, teachers, volunteer aides, or any person whose opinion is important to the child. A supportive word from such individuals goes a long way toward making a reader feel good.

Nonverbal behavior can also be reinforcing. A warm, friendly smile when a student finally succeeds in unlocking a multisyllabic word will encourage her or him to try again the next time a similarly long word is encountered. Children may be reinforced for quick mastery of a skill by being permitted to leave a skill group early.

Gibson and Levin (1975) contend that there is a natural, or intrinsic, reward in learning to read. The young child who has just learned that the four squiggly lines on the red octagon on the street corner say *STOP* has certainly made an important discovery—important enough to tell anyone and everyone he or she sees. In this case the child has received no external reward, but yet there is good reason to suspect that he or she has found the decoding experience to be highly satisfying and hence rewarding. Beginning readers learning to "break the code" will almost immediately discover that a few decoding skills will allow them to unlock many new words. These skills permit the young readers to venture into an entirely new learning experience that will strengthen their self-concepts and therefore be intrinsically rewarding (Robeck and Wilson, 1974).

All teachers should structure their lessons and other classroom activities to ensure that every child has many successful experiences. Instruction that focuses on specific skills can help each child be successful by avoiding learning tasks for which that child is not yet ready. A note of caution needs to be interjected regarding the use of reinforcement in reading situations, however. Not all reading behavior is immediately observable and hence may not be readily reinforceable (Gibson and Levin, 1975). A child who independently deduces that the phonogram *at* is able to help in decoding not only *mat* and *fat*, but a host of additional words as well (e.g., *rat, bat, sat, hat, cat, pat,* and *vat*) may not immediately demonstrate overt behaviors which can be reinforced by the teacher. The teacher may be unaware of this newly learned ability for some time before the student finally utilizes the skill under direct observation. Furthermore, teachers should be aware that they may be reinforcing "hidden" behaviors unknowingly. If the teacher praises a child for a right answer obtained (unbeknownst to the trusting teacher!) by looking at a neighbor's paper, the child may be encouraged to use this method of getting the right answer another time.

An elaborate plan for reinforcing behavior in the classroom need not be drawn up. Instead, the teacher should try to find out through informal observation when students need reinforcement and what kinds of reinforcement each child responds to. Some students may respond favorably to a sticker on a paper on which they get 16 out of the 20 words correct. Other students may respond positively to other, less tangible kinds of reinforcement, such as an arm around the shoulder or a pat on the back.

Regardless of which type of reinforcement is used, teachers should keep in mind that all students (indeed, all human beings) need *positive* reinforcement. They need successful experiences. Whenever students fail to succeed, they are in essence being punished (Staats, 1971); they are receiving *negative* reinforcement. Sometimes simply "correcting" a child's reading can have a negative effect on the student. Smith (1971, pp. 66–67) warns us: "A child negatively reinforced for making a mistake in speech or reading, even though he is in effect only testing a potential rule, is a little less likely to risk testing a new rule in the future. Willingness to risk errors, to test hypotheses is . . . one of the most critical aspects of learning to read."*

Reinforcement is a powerful tool for helping children learn to read. Used intelligently, reinforcement can help make a classroom an exciting place in which the joy of learning and of succeeding is part of *every* child's day.

Transfer of Reading Skills

The act of applying a skill from one situation to another is called transfer. One of the major shortcomings of instruction is failure to provide instruction that will result in children being able to apply skills to different contexts. Transfer has failed to occur, for example, when students learn a skill so that they are able to perform satisfactorily on a worksheet, but are unable to apply the skill when it is encountered in a story. Similarly, no transfer has taken place when students recognize the new words that are introduced in the first step of the Directed Reading Activity, but fail to recognize them when they appear later in the story.

The principles of transfer are relatively complex and beyond the scope of this text. The most important principle, however, is easily understood: Transfer will not occur unless the teacher has provided amply opportunity for practice. The teacher *must* give the students a chance to apply a skill in varied contexts, not just in certain limited settings during "reading class."

APPLICATION: A CHECKLIST FOR SELF-IMPROVEMENT

Several models for organizing instruction have been presented in this chapter. In addition, several principles from psychology have been discussed in order to show their application to reading instruction. We now offer a self-checklist that you can use as a beginning teacher, to help you judge whether you have organized your program for effective reading instruction. The list is lengthy, and anyone who wants to modify or shorten it should feel free to do so. If you use this list as a beginning teacher, you may not be able to check the "Yes" column for all of the questions right away. However, the checklist can serve as a guide to help you identify those areas of your program that still need strengthening.

*From *Understanding Reading: A Psycholinguistic Analysis of Reading and Learning to Read* by Frank Smith. Copyright © 1971 by Holt, Rinehart and Winston, Inc. Reprinted by permission of Holt, Rinehart and Winston.

Checklist for Organizing and Managing Reading Instruction

Personal Factors   *Yes*   *No*

____ ____ 1. Have I established goals or objectives for the year?

____ ____ 2. Have I made arrangements to be evaluated by others?

____ ____ 3. Do I have a personal definition of reading?

____ ____ 4. Am I aware of current ideas, techniques, and materials in the field of reading?

____ ____ 5. Am I familiar with what other teachers in my building are doing in reading instruction?

____ ____ 6. Do I know the support personnel who are available to assist me (e.g., school psychologist, school guidance counselor, reading specialist, speech therapist)?

____ ____ 7. Have I inquired into the opportunities for personal professional advancement (e.g., college and university courses, in-service training, reading conferences)?

Skills and Objectives   *Yes*   *No*

____ ____ 1. Have I identified the specific skills I want to teach?

____ ____ 2. Am I familiar with the skills and objectives in the reading program I have chosen?

____ ____ 3. Do the skills and objectives take into account the varying levels of ability in my classroom?

____ ____ 4. Could I defend my objectives as important for the teaching of reading?

____ ____ 5. Are my objectives realistic and attainable?

____ ____ 6. Do my classroom skills and objectives fit in well with the skills and objectives of the school and school system?

____ ____ 7. Are both prescriptive and descriptive objectives included in my program?

____ ____ 8. Are students aware of the program objectives?

Record Keeping   *Yes*   *No*

____ ____ 1. Do my records reflect what each student has been taught, what each student has learned, and what each student needs to learn?

Yes No

_____ _____ 2. Does my record keeping reflect subjective data as well as objective data?

_____ _____ 3. Have I recorded information about my students' reading interests?

_____ _____ 4. Do students keep records of books read?

_____ _____ 5. Does the school administrator understand my record-keeping system and is he or she kept abreast of student progress?

_____ _____ 6. Are my records in a form that will be understandable by next year's teachers?

Yes No

Instructional Materials

_____ _____ 1. Do I select instructional materials in line with my program objectives?

_____ _____ 2. Do I preview my materials so that I know how they best may be used?

_____ _____ 3. Do I have an inventory system to keep track of what materials I have on hand?

_____ _____ 4. Have I made provisions for the easy retrieval of materials?

_____ _____ 5. Have I developed a system whereby I keep a record of areas in which I have found materials to be lacking, thereby allowing me to quickly and easily order materials for the following year?

_____ _____ 6. Have my materials been chosen to reflect not only *learning* of skills, but also *application* of skills?

_____ _____ 7. Do I have an adequate supply of instructional materials to cover the reading range in my classroom?

_____ _____ 8. Do I have sufficient quantity of trade books to cover a wide range of interests and reading levels?

_____ _____ 9. Do I have an adequate supply of reference materials such as maps, globes, etc.?

_____ _____ 10. Do I have a supply of educational games to supplement my skill-development instruction and enrichment?

_____ _____ 11. Do I have an appropriate and sufficient supply of film-strips, film, and other audiovisual materials to supplement my instruction?

Classroom Organization	Yes	No	
	____	____	1. Have I thought about specific seating arrangements that may be used?
	____	____	2. Have I considered various types of grouping practices and chosen the one that is best suited for my classroom?
	____	____	3. Have I set up designated times for skill instruction?
	____	____	4. Have I set aside time for independent, silent reading?
	____	____	5. Have I made arrangements to interrelate reading instruction with the content areas of math, social studies, science, etc.?
	____	____	6. Have I made provisions for experiences that will expand the student's listening and speaking vocabularies?
	____	____	7. Have I thought about what specific duties will be assigned to parent volunteers, aides, student teachers, etc.?

Assessment	Yes	No	
	____	____	1. Do I know what assessment instruments are available?
	____	____	2. Are the assessment procedures I use in line with my objectives?
	____	____	3. Have the evaluation instruments I've chosen been normed on students similar to mine?
	____	____	4. Are the tests I've chosen to administer straightforwardly interpreted?
	____	____	5. Are alternative forms of the tests to be used for pre- and postassessment available?
	____	____	6. Is there an adequate supply of tests available?
	____	____	7. Do I know who will score the tests and record the test results?
	____	____	8. Have I established an assessment schedule so I know when to administer tests?
	____	____	9. Am I thoroughly familiar with the test administrator's manuals for the tests I propose to use so that I can give the tests efficiently?
	____	____	10. Have the children received an explanation of why certain tests will be administered?
	____	____	11. Will I confirm the results of any tests through my own observation?

Yes   No

____ ____ 12. Will I use work samples as a portion of my assessment program?

____ ____ 13. Have I thought how test results will be logically and clearly reported to parents?

____ ____ 14. Is my classroom testing program in line with the evaluation program of the entire school and school system?

SUMMARY

In this chapter we have discussed some techniques that should help you become more effective in your efforts to teach reading. One way to make teaching more effective is through appropriate classroom organization of reading groups. We have presented seven different plans that might be used, either singly or in combination. We have emphasized the importance of organizing and using instructional materials intelligently and have shown how the principles of reinforcement theory and of transfer can lead to more successful daily instruction. As a final step to prepare you to move from simply reading about reading instruction to actually teaching reading, we have provided a checklist to guide you in planning a classroom reading program.

Organizing and managing a reading program is a very complex task. No one method is best for everyone. We hope that this chapter will have made you aware of some of the reasons for the complexity and will have provided you with some guidelines for developing and implementing your own reading program.

REVIEW QUESTIONS

1. Identify and describe the seven different grouping techniques presented in this chapter. Can you list the benefits and limitations of each plan? Which plan do you think would work best for you? Why?

2. Imagine that you and another teacher have decided to group your two classes of third-grade children together for skills instruction. The children will be divided temporarily into six skills groups. Each of you will teach three groups. Describe how the two of you might organize your instructional materials from the two classrooms efficiently so that each of you has ready access to the materials you need. How would you organize these materials physically? What kind of a checkout system would you use? Would you develop a filing system? How would new materials or instructional ideas be integrated into your system?

3. Reinforcement can be a powerful technique available to teachers of reading. Can you describe what is meant by this term? Discuss how reinforcement theory can help children become better readers. Then list five ways in which you would positively reinforce a child who had just completed reading a difficult book. Compare your list with a friend. Do each of you think that the other's reinforcement techniques would be truly rewarding for a child? (Better yet—ask a child!!)

4. Review the importance of transfer when learning to read. Then for each skill listed below, design an activity for providing transfer to "real" reading after instruction has been given in the skill:

    a) identifying the main idea of a paragraph

    b) using the *ch* digraph to help decode unknown words

    c) utilizing the key of a map

    In your opinion, what are the major reasons transfer sometimes doesn't occur? How might these problems be overcome?

5. In this chapter we provided you with an extensive checklist to help you evaluate your preparedness for teaching reading. Briefly describe the major areas you need to be aware of. Identify any additional areas we have overlooked that you feel should be considered. Finally, ask yourself if you have the basic knowledge needed for teaching reading. If not, in what areas do you need additional work? How do you propose to meet these needs?

REFERENCES   Bateman, Barbara. "The Efficacy of an Auditory and a Visual Method of First Grade Reading Instruction with Auditory and Visual Learners," in Helen K. Smith, ed., *Perception and Reading* (Newark, Delaware: International Reading Association, 1968).

Brody, Ernest B. "Achievement of First- and Second-Year Pupils in Grades and Nongrades Classrooms," *Elementary School Journal* **70** (1970): 391–394.

Cooper, J. David. "Learning Modalities and Reading," in L. A. Harris and C. B. Smith, eds., *Individualizing Reading Instruction: A Reader* (New York: Holt, Rinehart and Winston, 1972).

Durkin, Dolores. *Teaching Them to Read* (Boston: Allyn and Bacon, 1974).

Gargiulo, Raymond J. "Applying Learning Theory to the Reading Process," *Reading Teacher* **25**, 1 (1971): 20–23.

Gibson, Eleanor J., and Harry Levin. *The Psychology of Reading* (Cambridge, Mass.: MIT Press, 1975).

Harris, Albert J. "Practical Applications of Reading Research," *Reading Teacher* **29**, 6 (1976): 559–565.

Hillson, Maurie, *et al.*, "A Controlled Experiment Evaluating the Effects of a Nongraded Organization on Pupil Achievement," *Journal of Educational Research* **56**, 10 (1964): 548–550.

Kirk, Samuel A., and James J. McCarthy. *Illinois Test of Psycholinguistic Abilities* (Urbana, Ill.: University Press, 1961).

Martin, Lyn S., and Barbara N. Pavan. "Current Research on Open Space, Nongrading, Vertical Grouping, and Team Teaching," *Phi Delta Kappan* (1976): 310–315.

Maxwell, M. J. "Results of the Survey of the Literature on Methods and Materials in Reading," in F. P. Greene, ed., *Investigations Relating to Mature Reading: Twenty-first Yearbook of the National Reading Conference* 1972, pp. 203–211.

Mills, Robert. *Mills Learning Methods Test* (Ft. Lauderdale, Fla.: Mills Center, 1954).

Morrison, Coleman, and Mary C. Austin. "The Torch Lighters Revisited—a Preliminary Report," *Reading Teacher* **29**, 7 (1976): 647–652.

Morrison, Virginia B. "Teacher-Pupil Interaction in Three Types of Elementary Classroom Reading Situations," *Reading Teacher* **22**, 3 (1968): 271–275.

Oliver, M. E. "Organizing for Reading Instruction," *Elementary School Journal* **71**, (1970): 97–104.

Restle, Frank. *Learning: Animal Behavior and Human Cognition* (New York: McGraw-Hill, 1975).

Robeck, Mildred C., and John A. R. Wilson. *Psychology of Reading: Foundations of Instruction* (New York: Wiley, 1974).

Robinson, Helen M. "Visual and Auditory Modalities Related to Methods for Beginning Reading," *Reading Research Quarterly* **8**, 1 (Fall 1972): 7–39.

Rogers, Janette S. "Reading Practices in Open Education," *Reading Teacher* **29**, 6 (1976): 548–554.

Ruddell, Robert B. *Reading-Language Instruction: Innovative Practices* (Englewood Cliffs, N.J.: Prentice-Hall, 1974).

Sipay, Edward R. "Interpreting the USOE Cooperative Reading Studies," *Reading Teacher* **22**, 1 (1968): 10–16, 35.

Smith, Frank. *Understanding Reading* (New York: Holt, Rinehart and Winston, 1971).

Smith, Nila Banton. *American Reading Instruction* (Newark, Delaware: International Reading Association, 1965).

Southgate, Vera. "The Language Arts in Informal British Primary Schools," *Reading Teacher* **26**, 4 (1973): 367–373.

Staats, Arthur W. *Child Learning, Intelligence, and Personality* (New York: Harper & Row, 1971).

Stevens, Dean O. "Reading Difficulty and Classroom Acceptance," *Reading Teacher* **25**, 1 (1971): 52–55.

Tinker, Miles A., and Constance M. McCullough. *Teaching Elementary Reading*, 4th ed. (Englewood Cliffs, N.J.: Prentice-Hall, 1975).

Vandever, Thomas R., and Donald D. Neville. "Modality Aptitude and Word Recognition," *Journal of Reading Behavior* **6**, 2 (1974): 195–210.

Weiner, Roberta. "A Look at Reading Practices in the Open Classroom," *Reading Teacher* **27**, 5 (1974): 438–442.

Index

Labor, W., 269
Language-experience approach,
    258–277
  advantages and disadvantages of,
    273–274
Larrick, N., 297–298
Learning, modalities of, 353
Learning centers, 251, 296
Letter names, knowledge of, 109
Levin, H., 354
Listening comprehension, 161–162
Lundsteen, S., 26

Maps, 210–212
Martin, L., 348
Mastery of skills, 55–56
Mental age and reading readiness,
    80
Miller, W., 296
Minority representation, 231, 234
Morrison, C., 226, 236, 351
Morrison, V., 352

Nature/nurture controversy, 76–79
Niles, O., 35
Norm-referenced tests, 58, 181,
    323–325
Note-taking, 216–218

Objectives, 34–49, 327
  advantages and disadvantages of,
    34–35, 41–42
  kinds, 37–41
  levels of, 35–37
Oral-language development, 82–83
Oral reading, analysis of, 139–141
Otto, W., 38, 63, 84, 132–133
Outlining, 215–216

Pavan, B., 348
Phonics, 113–130
  activities, 125–130
  consonants, 118–121, 125–127
  guidelines for teaching, 115–118
  methods for teaching, 124–125
  syllabication, 123–124, 129–130
  utility of, 114–115

vowels, 121–123, 127–129
Phonograms, 124–125
Prescriptive reading inventory, 66,
    68–69
Pronunciation guides, 207
Psycholinguistics, 19, 24–27,
    106–108

Questions, importance of, 164–165

Rate, 202
Readability, 194–201
Readiness, 76–101
  for comprehension, 160–164
  definition, 83
  factors affecting, 79–83
  prereading skills, 109–111
  programs, 94–98
  workbooks, 91–94
Record-keeping systems, 58–61
  in individualized reading,
    290–293
Retelling, 183–184
Reinforcement, 353–355
Robinson, F., 204
Rude, R., 54, 83, 89–90

Samuels, S. J., 15–17, 19–20, 54–55,
    109, 149
Scanning, 202–203
Self-monitoring, 108
Semantics, 19, 25, 106–107
Sex as a factor in reading readiness,
    80–81
Sight words, 131–136
  activities for teaching, 134–136
  guidelines for teaching, 134
Skill assessment, 56–58
Skill sequences, 55
Skills-management systems, 52–73
  with basal-reading programs,
    249–252
  characteristics of, 54–61
  with individualized reading
    programs, 305–306